For Sophia and Nicholas

Realistic Decision Theory

Realistic Decision Theory

Rules for Nonideal Agents in Nonideal Circumstances

Paul Weirich

OXFORD
UNIVERSITY PRESS

2004

OXFORD
UNIVERSITY PRESS

Oxford   New York
Auckland   Bangkok   Buenos Aires   Cape Town   Chennai
Dar es Salaam   Delhi   Hong Kong   Istanbul   Karachi   Kolkata
Kuala Lumpur   Madrid   Melbourne   Mexico City   Mumbai   Nairobi
São Paulo   Shanghai   Taipei   Tokyo   Toronto

Library of Congress Cataloging-in-Publication Data

Weirich, Paul, 1946–
Realistic decision theory : rules for nonideal agents in nonideal circumstances / Paul Weirich
   p. cm.
Includes bibliographical references and index.
ISBN 0-19-517125-X
1. Decision making. I. Title.

HD30.23.W446 2004
003'.56 — dc22   2003060369

9 8 7 6 5 4 3 2 1
Printed in the United States of America
on acid-free paper

Preface

Theories of all sorts appeal to idealizations. Idealizations simplify theory construction by tabling intractable problems. They introduce assumptions that prevent the problems from arising. Normative decision theory, which describes rational decision making, invokes idealizations to put aside problems arising from our cognitive limits and mistakes framing our decision problems. As decision theory matures, it pays more attention to its idealizations and works to remove them. Its ultimate goal is a general theory that evaluates and provides direction for our decisions, decisions made by nonideal agents in nonideal circumstances.

This book treats decision theory's idealizations systematically. It focuses on the evolution of one decision principle as idealizations supporting it are removed. The principle says to maximize informed utility: among your options, adopt one with maximum utility given all relevant information. Lack of information impedes compliance with this principle. A companion principle allowing for uncertainty says to maximize expected utility: among your options, adopt one with maximum expected utility. The step from the original principle to its companion, with the move from full to actual information, illustrates the type of revision of decision principles that takes place as I roll back idealizations. Chapters 2 and 3 discuss the revision process more fully. Later chapters revise the original decision principle further as they remove other standard idealizations concerning agents and their decision problems. Chapters 6 and 7 explore a new and important topic: the way an agent's mistakes before or after a decision problem influence standards of rationality for the problem's resolution.

The writing style aims for precision and thoroughness to satisfy theorists attending to detail but also aims for accessibility to interested students unacquainted with decision theory. The reader does not need prior training in decision theory; principles are explained when introduced; understanding technical sections requires only high school algebra. Chapter 5, which treats higher-order probabilities, may be skipped without loss of continuity. Material for the specialist is confined to appendixes. A glossary at the book's end lists definitions, distinctions, and principles for handy reference.

My interest in idealizations for decision principles began with my dissertation, *Probability and Utility for Decision Theory* (Weirich 1977). My advisor, Tyler Burge, and another of my teachers, Warren Quinn, encouraged me to investigate idealizations further, and over the years I wrote several articles on them and their removal. Some sections of this book are offshoots (as acknowledgments throughout the text indicate), but this book aims for organization and scope greater than those articles provide. It complements *Decision Space* (Weirich 2001a), which presents decision rules for ideal cases. The two works were originally written together and would have stayed together had they not grown beyond the limits of a single volume.

I benefited from the perceptive suggestions of anonymous referees. Portions of chapters 6 and 7 were presented at the University of Oklahoma, the Bled Conference on Rationality in Bled, Slovenia, and the LOFT 5 Conference in Turin, Italy. I am grateful to the audiences for valuable comments. I thank Brad Armendt, Robert Audi, Avrom Faderman, William Harper, Ned McClennen, Adam Morton, Wlodek Rabinowicz, Reed Richter, Brian Skyrms, and Peter Vallentyne for illuminating conversation and correspondence. Howard Sobel's comments on preliminary versions of some sections and Ellery Eells's comments on the entire first draft prompted many improvements. I have profited enormously from their insights. The University of Missouri–Columbia Research Council and University of Missouri Research Board generously supported preparation of the final draft. My editor, Peter Ohlin, his associates Julia Balestracci, Judith Hoover (copyeditor), and Rebecca Johns-Danes, and other Oxford University Press staff provided expert assistance at every step.

Contents

Realistic Decision Theory

Realistic Standards
for Decisions

When traveling on an airplane, have you ever discovered that the passenger next to you paid a fare lower than yours? How can you get the best deal possible on plane tickets? A traveler has many options. Besides buying directly from an airline, she may buy through a travel agent or buy online. Fares depend on days and times of travel, the number of connections, the period between initial and return flights, and the date of purchase. Tickets with restrictions cost less than tickets without restrictions. The restrictions impose penalties for changing travel dates, but insurance covering those penalties is available. The number and complexity of options make it difficult to find the best option. Besides assembling all options, one must rank them. How should one compare, for instance, the convenience of a nonstop flight with the lower price of a flight involving connections? Adding time pressure from daily life, the possibility that desirable flights will sell out, and anxiety about safety, the best deal seems an unattainable goal. Surely, a person may decide rationally without securing it.

The familiar decision principle to select the best of your options expresses an ideal. People have many excuses for falling short of that ideal. Compliance with the principle is advanced as a necessary condition of rationality only for ideal agents in ideal circumstances. What standards of rationality must ordinary people in ordinary circumstances meet to be rational? I seek completely realistic standards for decisions, standards that people have no good excuse for failing to meet. This book moves toward that goal by removing some, although not all, idealizations.

Decision theory has already made progress of the type I envisage. Suppose that an agent is making a decision but is uncertain of the best option, that is, the optimal option, the one superior in light of all the facts. Her uncertainty hinders application of the principle to select the best option, to optimize. It provides an excuse for failing to comply. Taken as the expression of a necessary condition of rationality, the principle of optimization assumes knowledge of the best option. An agent without that knowledge must make do with information in hand. To formulate a standard that accommodates ignorance of the best option, decision theorists introduce *utility*. An option's utility for an agent is an assessment of the option's effectiveness in promoting the agent's goals according to the agent's beliefs. An agent may know each option's utility and so know which option's utility is greatest without knowing which option is best. A familiar decision principle more realistic than optimization recommends selection of an option of maximum utility. Uncertainty about the best option does not hinder application of this principle. Properly circumscribed, it expresses a necessary condition of rationality for agents possibly uncertain of the best option.

Moving from optimization to utility maximization is a big step toward realistic standards for decisions. The move accommodates common uncertainties. However, the principle of utility maximization still relies heavily on idealizations concerning agents and their circumstances. My project is to remove some of those idealizations and reformulate the principle of utility maximization to make it a more realistic standard for decisions. I extend its range from ideal cases to various nonideal cases and so generalize the principle.

Before removing idealizations, I carefully present the principle to be generalized. The initial principle must be accurate if its generalization is to be accurate, too. The first step is orientation. This chapter locates utility maximization within the broad field of decision theory and compares my project concerning that principle with similar projects. It also previews idealizations to be removed.

1.1. Decision Theory and Its Schools

Decision theory is multidisciplinary and has diverse objectives. My project falls within normative decision theory. It treats rational decision making and related matters. Furthermore, my approach to rational decision making is philosophical. It lacks the empirical objectives of the behavioral sciences, such as economics, which also study rational decision making. The behavioral sciences construct accounts of rational decision making to serve as approximate accounts of actual decision making, whereas my approach does not adopt that empirical purpose.

I take normative decision theory, which for brevity I often call decision theory tout court, to treat practical reasoning and therefore to be a branch of logic, broadly construed. Its roots go back to Aristotle's study of practical syllogisms. Its principal innovation is the introduction of degrees of belief and degrees of desire to replace beliefs and desires in traditional treatments of practical reasoning.[1] Because decision theory explicates rationality in terms of degrees of belief and desire, it belongs to the internalist school of practical reasoning. It attends to reasons for an agent's decision that concern the agent's mental state and so are within the agent and accessible to her in normal circumstances. It generally puts aside distinctions between a decision's being rational and its being reasonable or justified. Also, it generally makes no distinction between a decision's being rational and its being not irrational. It presumes that a decision is either rational or irrational and does not introduce grades of rationality for a decision, although, of course, it recognizes that some departures from rationality are more grave than others and so influence more heavily an assessment of an agent's overall rationality.

Rationality provides norms for an agent, in particular, norms promoting the agent's good. Its norms do not extend to the agent's treatment of others. That extension is the job of morality, normativity's other main engine. The relationship between rationality and morality is a rich topic of perennial interest, studied, for example, by Aristotle and Kant. I do not investigate it but assume the distinctness of rationality and morality. Many cases demonstrate their distinctness. For instance, a morally blameless agent may irrationally paint himself into a corner. Also, the basic grounds of rational acts are self-regarding, whereas the basic grounds of moral acts include reasons that are other-regarding. Rationality, although it requires sensible goals as well as sensible means to goals, makes demands different from morality's demands. Even if it demands morality, it demands other things, too, such as getting your sums right.

Being rational is roughly being sensible or reasonable. It is not being self-interested or successful. I offer no precise, philosophical definition of rationality but give it a brief introduction to ward off misunderstanding. Rationality is a theoretical concept filled out and "implicitly defined" by principles of rationality such as *modus ponens* for inferences and transitivity for preferences. The principle that "ought" implies "can" governs rationality as well as morality. It is always possible to choose rationally. Standards of rationality adjust to circumstances so that rationality given the circumstances is possible (see section 7.2).

To call someone irrational, or not rational, is to blame him. Because excuses are exemptions from blame, excused irrationality does not arise. Apparently excused irrationality is really an excused failing to meet a goal of rationality such as utility maximization. For instance, an agent may have a justified belief that he is maximizing utility when in fact he is not. The belief may excuse his failure to maximize. Then he is rational, not excusedly irrational. Similarly, someone taking pain medication under doctor's orders may be excused for lapses in utility maximization. This failing need not constitute irrationality. Rationality makes allowances for obstacles to goals of rationality. When pain medication excuses falling short, the shortfall is not irrational.

I assume a shared concept of rationality that forms the basis for studies of rationality. Decision theorists share that concept despite disagreements about principles of rationality, just as ethical theorists share the same concept of morality despite disagreements about principles of morality. Beneath diversity on the surface, unity exists. That is to the good. Conceptual unity promotes theoretical system and structure. Decision theory prospers from having its roots in a single concept of rationality.

Studies of rationality arise in many fields. Different fields may seem to view it differently. However, their results are variations on the same theme. Evaluations of rationality diverge chiefly because they differ according to topic, scope, and assumptions. An evaluation's topic may be an agent's goals, beliefs, or decisions. It may be his attitudes and actions in certain areas. Economic rationality, for instance, is just rationality in economic matters. It is not a distinct type of rationality. Also, an evaluation's scope may be narrow or broad. An evaluation of an agent's choice, for instance, may take for granted the agent's goals and examine only the agent's pursuit of those goals. It may attend to the choice's instrumental rationality and so may not be completely comprehensive. Instrumental rationality is just partial rationality, however, not an independent type of rationality. Finally, an act's evaluation may make assumptions about the agent and her circumstances. It may assume, for instance, adequate time for deliberation. A standard of rationality is sensitive to an agent's abilities and circumstances, so assumptions about them are critical. A standard of bounded rationality does not introduce a new concept of rationality but rather applies the usual concept in cases where idealizing assumptions are relaxed and agents face obstacles such as a shortage of time for reaching a decision.

Because some fields treating rationality seek a precise definition of rationality, it is tempting to define a type of rationality that conforms to the principles of rationality the field accepts. Bayesian statisticians may define a type of rationality, Bayesian rationality, that conforms exactly to Bayesian principles of probability. The definition is merely a technical convenience. Bayesian principles do not introduce a novel type of rationality. They just advance rules for rational probability assignments. Bayesian rationality is not rationality at all unless those principles are accurate. Bayesians and non-Bayesians debate the ramifications of the same concept of rationality.

I do not argue that people should achieve the widespread goal of being rational. I just describe and explain rationality, extending traditional lines of thought. Arguments appeal to judgments about particular cases and general principles and aim for a reflective equilibrium, as in other normative fields, such as ethics and epistemology.

My school of decision theory, although philosophical, is allied with economics and statistics. It includes among its prominent contributors Jeffrey, Ramsey, Savage, and von Neumann and Morgenstern. Utility maximization is its main principle, and it takes utility for an agent broadly so that utility registers all that an agent cares about, not just self-interest. For example, an altruist may want to reduce world hunger. Then famine relief generates utility for him even if his contributions reduce his own welfare.[2]

Because my school evaluates a decision in terms of possible outcomes, sometimes taken broadly as possible worlds, it is consequentialist. Because causal, not evidential, consequences matter to rational choice, it favors causal decision theory as expounded, for example, by Gibbard and Harper (1978), not evidential decision theory as expounded, for example, by Jeffrey (1983). Causal decision theory attends to the good an act produces rather than the good it merely portends. Section 7.3 explains the significance of this distinction.

My branch of consequentialism focuses on acts open at a time. Another branch focuses on acts open during a period of time, including forming dispositions, resolutions, and plans and then acting in accordance with them. Gauthier (1986: chap. 6) and McClennen (1990: chap. 1), for instance, promote checks on utility maximization among acts open at a time. They claim that certain types of restraint over a period have benefits justifying the decisions they yield. Bratman (1987: chap. 2) holds that commitment to plans over a period may be rational even if not justified by utility maximization among acts open at a time. Their arguments notwithstanding, chapter 2 favors utility maximization among momentary acts over utility maximization among extended acts. It maintains that taking a momentary act's consequences broadly swallows up the reasons for maximization among extended acts. For example, planning makes good future acts more likely, and sticking to plans reduces deliberation costs. These good consequences of adopting a plan and following it accrue to that procedure's steps.

Some schools of decision theory evaluate a decision without much attention to its consequences. One school, promoted by Anderson (1993: chap. 2), takes a rational choice to be an expression of rational values. Another school emphasizes procedural standards of rationality. Adherents assess a decision according to the procedure that produced it rather than according to a comparison of its consequences with the consequences of other possible decisions. In general, the school takes a rational decision to be a reasoned decision, one generated by the faculty of reason as opposed to the passions, for instance. Simon (1982: vol. 2, 424–43), Sen (1977: 342–44), and Suppes (1984: 187–203) adopt varieties of this view.

My response to these nonconsequentialist schools has three parts. First, I acknowledge a role for procedural standards of rationality, especially in the formation of basic goals, but do not rely on such standards exclusively. Second, I carefully defend substantive, consequentialist standards of rationality, such as utility maximization. I acknowledge that an insistence on utility maximization assumes idealizations that are not always stated explicitly. I also explain that I do not propose utility maximization as a decision procedure. I do not claim that an agent ought to calculate and compare options' utilities before reaching every decision. That proposal is fraught with problems, as Mongin (2000: 95–104) observes; the decision procedure's costs are prohibitive. I advance utility maximization as a standard of evaluation. The standard applies to a decision made spontaneously, and an outside observer may apply it to a decision already made. Third, I modify the standard of utility maximization to make it less reliant on idealizations and more easily attained. The difficulty of meeting this consequentialist standard often motivates the search for alternative standards. So, greater realism makes the standard more attractive.

Some theorists adopt a deontological approach to rational decision making. They characterize a rational decision in terms of its own features rather than its comparison with other options. Their school generally says that a decision is rational provided it does not select a prohibited act. Gert (1998: 39, 83–84) lists acts prohibited, including, for example, self-infliction of gratuitous pain. A deontologist usually objects that utility maximization is a merely instrumental standard of rationality, insufficiently tethered to rational values. Even when an agent's goals are misguided, it mistakenly counts her decision as rational just in case it serves her goals.

Chapter 2 defends consequentialism by highlighting the advantages of evaluating options by comparing them with their rivals. It also sidesteps criticisms of instrumentalist views of rationality. It modestly claims that some, not all, standards of rationality are instrumental. It admits that utility maximization, construed in a purely instrumental way, is not sufficient for a rational decision. Such utility maximization may yield an irrational decision if it proceeds from an irrational utility assignment. Chapter 2 acknowledges the deontologist's points about rational values and adjusts its consequentialist standard of evaluation to accommodate them.

It formulates a standard of utility maximization using a characterization of utility and a set of idealizations that together ensure the rationality of a utility-maximizing decision. Later, chapter 6 rolls back idealizations about rational values and more thoroughly discusses comprehensive assessment of a decision's rationality.

In my consequentialist school theorists differ about the mental states that degrees of belief and desire represent. Some say that degrees of belief and desire collectively represent preferences among acts. Taken by itself, a single degree of belief or desire represents nothing. An agent's degree of desire to perform an act, for instance, does not represent a strength of desire to perform the act. A rational agent decides *as if* she selects an act she desires to perform at least as much as any other act. But in reality, only preferences back her choice. Nonrelational quantitative strengths of desire are fictions.[3] This position takes a metaphysical stand similar to the relativist's stand on the nature of time. According to that view, time represents relations among events and not a feature of a single event. Independently existing moments of absolute time are fictions, it maintains.

My version of decision theory takes degrees of belief and desire to represent individually attitudes toward propositions. It takes the attitude a single degree of desire represents to be real, not just a convenient fiction. As chapter 2 claims, degrees of desire have an inferential, but not a definitional, connection to preferences and choices. Their reality is independent of other phenomena. Thus, in another, secondary sense, the theory I present is realistic.

My realism about mental states extends to preference, too. In rational agents choices are evidence of preferences, but preferences direct choices, contrary to the revealed preference theory of, for instance, Binmore (1994: 27). Preferences are parts of causal networks and not mere representations of choices. *Pace* behaviorists and operationists, preference is not defined by choice. Indeed, contemporary psychology recognizes causes of choice besides preference and effects of preference besides choice, as Colman (2003: n. 6) observes. An agent may, for example, choose contrary to preference. Although I prefer not to eat a second piece of chocolate, I may do so out of weakness of will. Psychological realism about mental states urges decision theory to accommodate cases in which agents fail to maximize utility. Chapter 6 treats such cases.

1.2. Making Decision Theory More Practical

Many decision theorists note that optimization and utility maximization are often unrealistic goals. They adopt various strategies for making decision theory more practical. Let me review these strategies and explain my approach.

Some theorists, for the sake of practicality, propose replacements for standard decision principles. To obtain replacement principles, they may forgo generality and focus on a particular type of decision. For example, those working on portfolio theory often construct principles accommodating only common desiderata for investments. A typical proposal reviews possible investments for which one knows the average or mean rate of return and also the amount of risk. It rates each investment according to the investment's mean-return minus a proportion of the investment's risk. Then it recommends selecting an investment with the highest mean-risk rating. Such proposals bypass difficulties facing general decision principles covering all domains.

Simon (1955, 1959, 1982) boldly advances a general rule to replace optimization. He advises an agent to set a level of aspiration by which to assess options. An option counts as satisfactory if and only if it reaches that aspiration level. Then, Simon (1982: vol. 2, 250–51) urges the agent to begin a search for options and to observe this principle:

> *Principle to satisfice.* Adopt the first satisfactory option discovered.

He calls following this advice "satisficing" and says that it accommodates a person's "bounded rationality." To illustrate, a chess player who satisfices makes the first satisfactory move she finds instead of searching at length for the optimal move.

The principle to satisfice is programmatic. It leaves open the setting of aspiration levels, methods of searching for options, and selection of a satisfactory option when several are discovered simultaneously. Articulating the principle to handle these matters is a topic of current research.[4] Section 8.2 uses a special version of it.

Theorists inspired by cognitive psychology sometimes try to extract principles of rationality from folk methods of making decisions. Those methods often deviate from utility maximization in systematic ways. Kahneman and Tversky (1979: 286–88), for instance, find that people decide differently depending on whether, when evaluating a decision's possible outcomes, they adopt a baseline with respect to which its possible outcomes are gains or adopt a higher baseline with respect to which its possible outcomes are losses. According to utility theory, an option's utility-rank is not affected by the baseline of comparison, and some theorists view such departures from utility maximization as irrational. However, other theorists contend that those departures follow alternative decision principles that are reasonable because simple and effective in routine cases. Gigerenzer (2000: vii), for instance, asserts that people employ adaptive thinking; they cope rationally with specific environments, especially ones similar to the environments in which humans evolved. For instance, in decision problems where multiple reasons support conflicting options, they simplify by ignoring all but the most important reason for each option. The shortcut works well in most everyday decision problems (125). This approach to practicality looks for heuristics, rules of thumb, and maxims that approximate optimization in standard decision problems. It promotes them because with modest effort, they usually yield sensible decisions. It claims that they are smart decision methods even though they provide only rough-and-ready guidelines rather than precise standards.

Instead of replacing maximization principles with rules targeting specific types of decisions, or procedural rules, or rules of thumb, another approach to practicality, exemplified by Raiffa (1968), applies maximization principles to the process of reaching a decision. To reach a decision, an agent may gather more information, calculate, and reflect. These steps have costs, however, and an agent has limited resources for reaching a decision. A rational agent reaches a decision in a utility-maximizing way. To be justified, information gathering and deliberation must improve the final decision, and the value of improvements must compensate for their costs. If additional information is unlikely to alter a preliminary, tentative decision, then even though it will strengthen the final decision's grounding, collecting it may be an unjustified effort. Because maximization principles apply to the decision process as well as its result, they justify practical economies in deliberation and choice.

Of course, attention to decision costs requires effort, too. So Raiffa (1968: ix–x) advances his method of thoroughgoing maximization only for important decisions in which people sensibly make a large investment. As a result, his method of handling human limits is not completely general. Its advantage is precision. It treats with exactness the problem of tidying up messy, realistic decision problems. It is precise about human limits, just as probability theory is precise about uncertainty. Its articulateness has advantages that rules of thumb lack. The principles it advances are practical but also explain the nature of rational decision making in ways that imprecise rules of thumb cannot match.

Raiffa's maximization principles have the practical orientation of Simon's principles of bounded rationality. In fact, Simon (1982: vol. 2, 435) considers them a version of his theory of bounded rationality; he regards forms of maximizing that take human limits into account as forms of satisficing. However, Raiffa's approach locates the relevant bounds in decision makers and decision problems rather than in rationality and its principles. It does not revise basic principles of rationality but applies them with more sensitivity and comprehensiveness. That makes his approach distinctive.

In decision theory, traditional philosophical methods suggest searching for explanatory conditions necessary and sufficient for a decision's rationality. Such conditions take into account the difficulty of the decision problem, the resources for solving it, the circumstances in which it must be solved, and the decision maker's limits. For instance, the standards for a favorably positioned decision maker are stiffer than the standards for a decision maker operating under duress. One expects philosophical investigation to yield standards of rationality that people often meet. In fact, philosophers outside decision theory commonly propose such standards of rationality. For example, epistemologists such as Foley (1993) propose attainable standards for rational belief.

My approach to decision theory adopts traditional philosophical objectives. I aim for precise, explanatory principles, rather than rules of thumb. In addition, I seek general principles that formulate necessary and sufficient conditions for rational decision making. That is my ultimate objective, although this book advances primarily necessary conditions of rationality and does not attain complete generality. Among authors reviewed, I follow most closely Raiffa but focus on standards of evaluation for decisions rather than decision procedures and propose standards of evaluation applicable to decisions regardless of their importance.

1.3. Steps toward Realism

Traditional decision principles such as optimization make many idealizations. For a taste of their role, consider the decision problem at the chapter's start: purchasing a plane ticket. An idealization for optimization assumes knowledge of all options and their outcomes. The traveler knows whether flights depart and arrive on time. Another idealization assumes a ranking of options. Perhaps a cheap, long flight ranks higher than an expensive, short flight. A third idealization assumes that the traveler identifies options at the top of the ranking. No cognitive blind spot or time pressure prevents their emergence. A fourth idealization assumes that the traveler has no flaw that excuses failing to optimize. For example, she has enough resolve to rise for an early-morning flight if it is optimal. Given all the idealizations, the traveler, if rational, adopts the best option, say, an inexpensive flight with just one layover. The mind-boggling demands of optimization are satisfiable given the principle's strong idealizations.

Later chapters remove idealizations for decision principles and then adjust the principles to achieve greater generality. My main targets are idealizations concerning agents' mental states, their access to their mental states, their success in meeting goals of rationality, and the tractability of their decision problems.

According to a common idealization for utility maximization, given incomplete information, agents have accessible probability and utility assignments for all possible outcomes of every option. For example, an agent considering a gamble that pays $2 if heads turns up on a coin toss may assign probability 0.5 to getting heads. Using a gain of $1 as a unit for a utility scale, he may assign utility 2 to gaining $2. In compact notion, the assignments are $P(\text{heads}) = 0.5$ and $U(\$2) = 2$. According to the idealization, such probability and utility assignments extend to all possible outcomes of his options and so may direct his decision.

Familiar cases of incomparable outcomes conflict with the assumption of complete probability and utility assignments. An agent may be unable to compare, much less compare quantitatively, going to a concert with having dinner, or contributing to the arts with contributing to relief of world hunger. Even if a comparison of two outcomes is implicit in his other preferences, he may be unable to discover it. Chapters 4 and 5 modify maximization principles to dispense with the idealization of complete, accessible probability and utility assignments. They advance principles using estimates of probabilities and utilities and also quantitative extensions of probability and utility judgments.

I also remove the idealization that agents are fully rational. I treat, for example, cases in which agents enter decision problems having made mistakes, a possibility section 1.1's realism about mental states recognizes. Perhaps they have irrational beliefs or fail to update their preferences in light of new experiences. Then standards of rationality for their decisions may adjust for their mistakes. If agents have beliefs, desires, and preferences without their standard manifestations in behavior, the departure from the norm may be a mistake or a rational adjustment to a mistake.

Suppose an agent falsely believes that she has a desire on balance to become a doctor. Perhaps she has that belief because throughout her youth her parents expressed their expectation that she maintain the family tradition of careers in medicine. An aversion to disappointing her parents pushes her toward medicine, although she thinks that she finds being a physician independently attractive. Contrary to her beliefs, she does not want to be a physician, all things considered. She has a passion for creative writing but deceives herself about its intensity to reconcile her beliefs about it with her career plans. She finds herself absorbed for hours in poetry and daydreams about a life in literature but chides herself for wasting time she could spend preparing for the MCAT. Psychotherapy would reveal that her true goal is to be a poet, but she does not have a therapist. When deciding whether to enter medical school, is it rational for her follow her true goal or her mistaken beliefs about her goal? Is it irrational for her to act contrary to desire but in accord with belief about desire? Section 6.4 argues that the answers depend, in part, on whether her false belief about her desires is irrational.

The irrationality of a desire can certainly excuse a failure to satisfy it. Imagine that, stumbling through a room in the dark, I stub my toe. Out of anger, I want to smash the furniture around me. In fact, smashing the furniture is more appealing than anything else I might do at the moment. My anger is irrational, so the act it urges is irrational, too. I might know this without having the power to quiet my emotion and its demands. Because my desires are irrational, it is not rational for me to adopt the course of action I most want to follow. Standards of rationality for my decisions make adjustments for the irrationality of my desires.

Values may also conflict with desires, even rational desires. Suppose that an agent meandering through the buffet at a banquet notices a shortage of desserts. All things considered, he would rather take the last slice of apple pie for himself than leave it for someone else. His self-interested desire is not irrational. Nonetheless, the interests of others nag him, and he forgoes the pie. Introspecting, he finds his preference for taking the pie has not changed. It is still what he most wants to do, although he cannot bring himself to do it. He finds his will out of alignment with his preference. In this case, the diner acts contrary to his preference but in accord with his values. How should we evaluate him? He mistakenly maintains his self-interested preference despite his reflections prior to his choice. Is his decision irrational? Do values he acknowledges excuse his failure to maximize utility? A standard of rationality appropriate for his decision considers his failure to update his preferences so that they conform with his values. Then it tells us whether deciding altruistically is a way of rationally compensating for his error in preference. The answer depends on the evaluation's scope, as section 6.4 explains.[5]

Chapters 6 and 7 present a method of handling decision problems that arise in a context of mistakes. The method relies on a distinction between comprehensive and noncomprehensive standards of rationality. It observes that not all standards evaluate a decision with respect to every relevant factor. Some standards take for granted certain features of the decision's context, including mistakes. They noncomprehensively evaluate a decision for a type of conditional rationality. Some decisions are rational when taking for granted mistakes already made but are not rational if those mistakes are not taken for granted. They are conditionally rational, but are not rational nonconditionally. My method of handling decisions made by errant agents identifies mistakes that drive a wedge between a decision's rationality and its conditional rationality. These are the mistakes for which standards of comprehensive rationality adjust. Chapters 6 and 7 describe the adjustments. They explain how standards of rationality accommodate certain mistakes.

I also rescind the idealization that decision problems have options that maximize utility in the ordinary way. Some decision problems have options with utilities higher and higher without end. Other decision problems have options whose utilities are unstable; for some option, the option's utility changes under the assumption that the option is adopted. Such decision problems arise in games of strategy, for instance. When no option has stable maximum utility, the principle of utility maximization needs adjustment. Chapter 8 presents a new, more general principle agreeing with utility maximization in routine cases but able to handle problem cases also. Chapter 9 applies the new principle to game theory, building on Weirich (1998, 1999). It shows that in noncooperative games, the new principle resolves issues concerning the existence and realization of equilibrium outcomes. Unlike Skyrms (1990a), it does not invoke the cognitive limits of agents, and, unlike Bacharach (1999), it does not invoke principles of collective rationality. Instead, it shows how strategic reasoning affects generalized utility maximization. Its methods extend to the ideal agents of classical game theory and employ only rules of individualistic reasoning.

1.4. Procedures for Theory Generalization

This book introduces decision principles more general and practical than the traditional principle of utility maximization. As a foundation, chapter 2 formulates a precise and accurate version of that principle. It explicitly lists the principle's idealizations.

To generalize chapter 2's version of utility maximization, I remove idealizations and make adjustments for their absence. To ground my procedure, chapter 3 advances an account of idealizations and their function in theory formation. It distinguishes idealizations from other assumptions and classifies idealizations according to role. I use my account of idealizations to evaluate from a theoretical standpoint various common assumptions in decision theory and game theory, for example, assumptions about the dispositions and knowledge of agents in games of strategy. I show that certain idealizations are especially fruitful theoretically because they yield principles expressing goals of rationality. Under the idealizations, compliance with the principles is necessary for rationality, but even when the idealizations are not met, compliance with each principle is a goal of rationality and rational agents must have good excuses for failures to comply. To achieve additional generality, one may devise ways of accommodating excuses for falling short of the goals and then use those accommodations to dispense with the idealizations. The principles lend themselves to further generalization because it requires only accommodating excuses for falling short of the goals the principles express. Although accommodating those excuses may be challenging, the principles provide valuable direction for future research in realistic decision theory.

Chapters 4 through 9 undertake the book's main enterprise. They remove idealizations and generalize utility maximization for their absence. As explained, they dispense with some common idealizations about agents and their decision problems. Chapters 4 and 5 remove idealizations about agents' psychological resources and abilities. Chapters 6 and 7 remove the idealization that agents are error-free. Chapters 8 and 9 remove the idealization that options' utility comparisons have a stable top, and, in particular, treat games of strategy in which utility comparisons are unstable.[6]

These chapters work independently. A typical chapter removes just one standard idealization and retains others. None removes all targeted idealizations simultaneously. I take small, regulated steps and do not leap to full generality. This procedure highlights and explains each adjustment my decision principles make in response to problems that realism creates. The concluding chapter combines all adjustments and states the general decision principle they yield. It summarizes the book's progress toward a realistic decision theory and suggests directions for future research.

My proposals do not remove all idealizations. They assume that agents are well positioned to meet the principles advanced. Despite residual reliance on idealizations, my revised principles of decision and utility analysis move closer to a thoroughly realistic decision theory. Although I do not reach decision and utility principles for completely realistic decision problems, I take significant steps in that direction. The progress makes my theory a practical guide to decisions and sets the stage for further advances.

Optimizing and Its Offspring

L eibniz's (1969: 682–83) famous argument for time's relativity imagines God's creation of the universe. If time is absolute, it exists independently of the universe. So God might create the universe at various times. Being perfect, God must create the universe at the time best for creation. All times are equally good, however. No time is the best for creation. Because God cannot act without reason, he cannot create the universe at any time. But creation is a fact, so time is not absolute. It was created along with the universe and depends on the universe's existence. It is relative to the rest of creation.

According to Leibniz, reason demands that God act in the best way possible. I take Leibniz's principle of optimal action as the starting point for my account of rationality but, unlike Leibniz, allow for tiebreaking where reason creates ties. Obviously, the principle's high standard governs only ideal agents in ideal circumstances. Ordinary people generally do not know which acts are best. They violate the principle because of excusable ignorance.

My account of rationality first formulates principles for ideal cases and then adjusts the principles as it removes idealizations. This chapter starts with the principle of optimization for perfect, fully informed agents and then considers imperfect, incompletely informed agents, making adjustments that are already part of the canon. This procedure highlights and explains realistic features of traditional decision theory concerning options and their evaluation. The chapter ends with two principles. The first concerns decisions and says to maximize utility. The second concerns utility and says that in cases with uncertainty about options' outcomes, an option's utility equals its expected utility. Although these principles rely on idealizations, they make progress toward realism by accommodating imperfect agents and incomplete information. Later chapters make further advances.

The two principles that form my base—the principle of utility maximization and the expected utility principle—are the nucleus of decision theory. Theorists expound them in a variety of ways. This chapter formulates them to promote realism but also aims for simplicity where attainable without sacrificing precision.

Refinements facilitating later generalization—for decision costs, mistakes, and the like—receive attention. But other refinements are relegated to appendix A because my generalization techniques are largely independent of the initial versions of the principles.

2.1. Optimizing

Optimizing is performing the best of available acts, or, more precisely, an act at least as good as every other available act. Thus, an agent may optimize even though several acts are best acts. It suffices to perform one of the best acts. Any will do. If all times are equally good for creation, God optimizes by creating the universe at any time.

> *Optimization*. Among the acts you can perform at a time, perform one that is at least as good as any other.

The principle to optimize is fairly clear, but making it precise requires answering some questions. Among which acts does it prescribe optimization? How are those acts compared? What is the principle's force? What idealizations does it presume?

2.1.1. *Acts*

Let me start with the metaphysical status of acts. Different realizations of the proposition that I close the door have different consequences.[1] In some realizations, the door closes with a bang; in other realizations, it closes silently. The principle of optimization, being a principle of rationality, should discriminate between different concrete acts represented by the same proposition. So I take acts as concrete particulars, not abstract propositions representing concrete particulars. However, when a proposition specifies all the relevant features of a concrete act it represents, it may substitute for the act. If how I close the door does not matter, then the proposition that I close the door is an adequate representation of one of my concrete acts. Also, if it matters whether I close the door loudly or quietly, but given that I close the door I close it quietly, then the proposition that I close the door is again an adequate representation of one of my concrete acts. The adequacy of an act's propositional representation depends on how the proposition would be realized if it were realized. When a proposition is an adequate representation, its realization is determinate in every way that matters.[2]

I take the principle of optimization to express a standard of evaluation for acts. It applies to an act issuing from an action problem's resolution. An action problem specifies possible acts and is resolved by realizing one. The possible acts are ones the agent can realize. They are available to him. Although it is logically possible for George Bush to consult Julius Caesar, this act is not available to him and does not figure in any of his action problems. Because most possible acts are not realized, most remain merely possible acts. For brevity, I often call them acts nonetheless.

Often, textbook examples of optimization specify action problems without characterizing generally the action problems optimization targets. Crafting a precise principle of optimization, however, requires characterizing those problems. The principle of optimization cannot be applied to all sets of possible acts without inconsistency. A possible act optimal in one set need not be optimal in another set. The other set may not even contain it.

The principle of optimization evaluates an act for rationality. Rationality holds an agent responsible for acts in his direct control and holds him responsible for other acts only if circumstances warrant the extension. Some of an agent's acts are not billed to his account because he does not have direct control over them. For example, rationality may excuse an agent for an act not optimal in the set of all possible acts if others participate in its realization. Suppose a voter along with others elects an inferior candidate. The voter participates in the electorate's act even if he does not vote with the majority. His lack of control over that act excuses him, however. Similarly, a pitcher's losing a baseball game and a lawyer's losing a case may be excused because of the influence of teammates and clients on those acts.

I apply the principle of optimization to an agent's basic acts only. These are acts in the agent's direct control, for example, raising an arm. Many of an agent's acts are not in his direct control. To break bread, one needs bread. To buy bread, one needs a baker. In routine cases, the principle of optimization may apply to nonbasic acts without trouble, but for general reliability I apply it to basic acts only. Applying optimization to basic acts tables the task of characterizing more inclusively the acts for which rationality holds an agent responsible. That characterization is controversial. It must address thorny issues concerning foreseen but unintended consequences, for instance. Extending the principle of optimization beyond basic acts is not necessary for my purposes. Section 2.1.3's version of the principle allows extensions, and, as section A.1 argues, that version is consistent with any accurate extension.

The basic acts of humans, in contrast with the basic acts of God, are just momentary acts, that is, acts at a moment. Longer acts are not in a human agent's direct control because they require at least continuing to live. If optimization is to be a necessary condition of an agent's rationality in an action problem, the agent must have direct control over the possible acts composing the problem. Restricting optimization to momentary acts promotes realism in applications of the principle to humans. Given the restriction, the principle does not need the idealization that an agent have God-like direct control over extended acts. An agent has the power to comply with the restricted principle. She does not need help from nature or other agents. Given full information, rationality assigns her full responsibility for compliance.

As I apply the principle of optimization, optimization is relative to a time. To optimize at a time is to perform one of the best acts available at the time. Relativization to a time identifies precisely a set of acts, the acts available at the time. The acts available at a time are the acts that the agent can perform at the time.

Given prior events, what an agent can do at a time is settled by the laws of nature. For each metaphysically possible act, the laws of nature determine whether the agent can perform it at the time. The way the laws of nature tell us what an agent can do is vague. I do not try to dispel the vagueness; too many philosophical questions arise. I assume only that the vagueness is resolvable. Given a resolution, it is determinate whether a possible act is one the agent can perform and hence sensible to ask whether an act she can perform is at least as good as all others she can perform. I proceed as if the vagueness were resolved, but do not presume any particular resolution.

What type of act may an agent perform at a moment? The acts may be physical or mental. Opening the window is a physical act. However, being intentional, it has a mental component. All the physical acts I consider are intentional and have a mental component. I put aside unintentional acts such as perspiring, because, as noted, rationality attends to acts under an agent's control. Some acts, such as doing a sum in one's head, are mental. Decisions are mental acts of special interest, and section 2.2 examines them.

A wide variety of acts, such as swimming the English Channel, take more than a moment to complete. An agent performs them moment by moment by persevering in their performance. An agent cannot perform such acts at a time. She can only begin them or persevere. How does the principle of optimization address such acts? It does not compare the extended acts to alternative extended acts. Instead, it recommends an extended act only if each step in its execution is an optimal momentary act. Swimming the English Channel is recommended only if starting, continuing moment by moment, and finishing are all optimal. Section A.1 defends this evaluation of extended acts.

2.1.2. *Evaluation of Acts*

The principle of optimization presumes that each act receives an evaluation. The evaluation has five important features. First, the evaluation attaches directly to a proposition representing the act. The proposition specifies the act as fully as matters.[3] Second, the evaluation is subjective. It depends on the agent's desires and aversions. A best act is therefore subjectively best. Third, the evaluation is informed. It uses full information about the desires and aversions that would be realized if the act were performed. Fourth, the evaluation is quantitative. It generates the act's desirability, a quantity increased by realization of desires and decreased by realization of aversions. Fifth, the evaluation is comprehensive. It evaluates an act by evaluating the act's *outcome*, taken as the possible world that would be realized if the act were realized. The foregoing points provide a quick introduction of the evaluation of acts. Let me elaborate the points about desirabilities and outcomes, starting with outcomes.[4]

Taking an act's outcome as the world it yields, not just the causal consequences of the act and not just the temporal aftermath of the act, is a technical convenience. Evaluation of an act's world makes moot the division of events into causal consequences and other events and makes moot the time of complex acts (acts that may be evaluated as part of the evaluation of momentary acts contributing to them). It is theoretically simpler to evaluate an act's world, which does not require controversial causal and temporal distinctions, than to evaluate an act's causal consequences or temporal aftermath.[5]

To make a *possible world* a proposition and so an object of desirability, I take it as a maximal consistent proposition. A proposition is maximal if and only if for every proposition p it entails p or p's negation. It is consistent if and only if it does not entail a contradiction. When taken as an act's outcome, a possible world may be trimmed of matters to which the agent is indifferent. They do not affect its evaluation. Accordingly, I generally consider only trimmed possible worlds, which may be represented by sets of untrimmed possible worlds.[6]

An act is evaluated by the desirability of its outcome. I assume that an agent attaches a *degree of desire* to each act's outcome, which yields the act's desirability. This assumption is an idealization chapter 4 removes. To clarify the idealization, let me introduce degrees of desire. A degree of desire that an outcome obtain represents an attitude to the outcome all things considered and may therefore direct action. Degrees of desire are positive for outcomes the agent desires, negative for outcomes to which the agent is averse, and zero for outcomes that are matters of indifference. So typically, the degree of desire attached to an outcome involving only pleasure is positive, and negative if the outcome involves only pain. Although I adopt indifference as a zero point for degrees of desire and take them to form a ratio scale, I need only an interval scale with an arbitrary zero point.[7] Degrees of desire may extend beyond acts and their outcomes to arbitrary propositions, all but impossible propositions for which degrees of desire are undefined, as Jeffrey (1983: 78) observes. A degree of desire, strictly speaking, attaches to a proposition's realization, but for convenience may be attached directly to the proposition.

A desire's degree indicates its strength's quantitative comparison to the strength of a unit desire, the desire for the realization of some conventionally designated proposition. For example, on a scale with a desire for a dollar gain as unit, an agent's degree of desire for a \$2 gain may be two units because of that desire's comparison with the unit desire. I do not define an agent's degrees of desire in terms of his preferences among gambles. A desire's strength does not depend on a function from objects of desire to numbers representing preferences among objects of desire. The comparisons to a unit that generate strengths of desire entail preferences with respect to the proposition establishing the unit, but not preferences with respect to other propositions. Degrees of desire need not represent preferences. The preferences of a fully rational person in ideal conditions conform to strengths of desire, but the preferences of an irrational person may not. Strengths of desires, which are transitive, may coexist with irrational preferences that are not transitive.[8]

Although an act's evaluation is circumspect, an irrational agent may assign different desirabilities to an act and its outcome, the act's world. If an agent is rational and ideal, her assignment of desirabilities to propositions follows certain principles of utility, in particular, the principle that an act's utility equals its outcome's utility. In cases where desirabilities follow the utility principles, they are called utilities. Because this chapter treats rational ideal agents, I often conflate the distinction between desirabilities and utilities and henceforth generally talk about utilities of acts and outcomes.

The structure of rational degrees of desire in ideal conditions provides a good way of characterizing degrees of desire. Their structure as elaborated by various principles of utility, such as the expected utility principle (section 2.4), identifies them. However, I take their structure only to characterize them and not to define them. To give the principle of optimization normative force, I take utility as a primitive theoretical entity. More precisely, I take interval comparisons of utility as primitive. I do not define utility as a quantity maximized by rational action. That would make the principle of optimization hold by stipulation and surrender its normative force. Also, forgoing a definition in terms of preferences allows for cases where utility comparisons explain preferences. Utilities do not explain preferences in every case. Some preferences arise without the formation of corresponding quantitative attitudes. Still, in some cases, quantitative attitudes generate preferences. Taking utilities as primitive accommodates this generative power.[9]

My view of utility, which section 4.2 and appendix A elaborate, is common. Economic textbooks describe utility as satisfaction, meaning not a feeling of satisfaction but realization of basic desires. I depart from only the operationist and behaviorist schools that take utility to be defined in terms of choice or preference. This departure adds psychological realism, as section 1.1 notes, and subtracts nothing essential. In particular, representation theorems showing how to obtain utility assignments from preferences may be retained as inferential rather than definitional tools.

My methodology acknowledges the meaningfulness of primitive theoretical terms. As Weirich (2001a: chap. 1) explains, it accepts theoretical terms introduced by theories using them. I take utility as meaningful without operational definition. Trimming away operationist accounts of meaning leaves decision theory in good health and robust enough to give life to the concept of utility. Utility has a long history in economic and moral theories. Its history serves as its introduction. Although not every principle of utility ever proposed is correct, the general field of utility theory adequately presents utility.

2.1.3. *Utility Maximization*

Utility, because it arises from desire, all things considered, depends on information. Under the idealization of full information, the principle of optimization may be restated as a principle of utility maximization:

> Among the acts you can perform at a time, perform one whose utility is at least as great as any other's utility.

Under the idealization, following the principle displayed amounts to maximizing informed utility, that is, optimizing. Full information makes acts' comparisons according to utility agree with their comparisons according to subjective betterness. I use this principle of maximization in place of the original principle of optimization because the principle of maximization generalizes to nonideal cases in which agents are not fully informed more easily than the original principle of optimization does.

To illustrate the principle of utility maximization, suppose that creation is better than noncreation and God is about to create the world. He can create various possible worlds. Each world has an intrinsic value, the sum of all the basic goods and bads it contains. That intrinsic value is the world's utility for God. If God maximizes utility, he creates a best of all possible worlds.

The principle to maximize utility makes some assumptions. Suppose, for example, that creation of a world includes creation of values. As a result, one world is best according to the values it establishes, whereas another world is best according to the values it establishes. Perhaps the first yields hedonistic values and maximizes pleasures, whereas the second yields epistemic values and maximizes knowledge. The basis of comparison of worlds is then unstable. To table such problems, the principle to maximize utility assumes a stable basis of comparison of acts. It also assumes that each act has a utility and that an act of maximum utility exists. If there were acts of greater and greater utility without end, no act would have maximum utility. It would be impossible to comply with the principle.

I take the principle of utility maximization to express a standard of rationality. This means that compliance with it is a necessary condition of rational action. Taken this way, the principle assumes an agent ideal in several respects. The idealizations remove excuses that we humans have for failing to maximize utility. An ideal agent knows the acts available, knows their utilities, and can compare their utilities. In other words, she can knowingly comply with the principle. Moreover, she can do this instantaneously and without cost. Thinking takes no time and is effortless; the agent is cognitively unlimited. In addition, the agent is fully rational, except possibly in her current action problem. Thus, her act need not compensate for errors before or after it. I allow for her act's being irrational because otherwise, its evaluation would assume its rationality. I want to explain an act's rationality in terms of utility maximization and so do not want utility maximization to presume rational action. Finally, the idealizations put aside conflict between goals of rationality. I assume that no goal of rationality conflicts with the goal of utility maximization; each goal's attainment is compatible with utility maximization. In every way, the agent's situation and abilities are perfect for utility maximization. In these circumstances, a failure to maximize utility is irrational.

Given my idealizations, I take utility maximization as necessary for an agent's acting rationally, but not necessary for an act's rationality. The principle of utility maximization requires performing an act whose utility is maximal, but does not discourage performing an act of nonmaximum utility. Such an act may be entailed by an act of maximum utility. For instance, it may turn out that buying a red hat maximizes utility, whereas buying a hat does not. Then, an agent complies with the principle by buying a red hat even if thereby she performs the nonmaximal act of buying a hat. The nonmaximal act may be rational in virtue of being part of a rational act's realization. Section 2.2 returns to this issue.

Is utility maximization sufficient for an agent's acting rationally? No, an agent who maximizes utility may fall seriously short of other standards of rational action. For instance, an agent's utility assignment may be mistaken. Then, he may act irrationally even though he maximizes utility. However, the agents this chapter treats are fully rational except possibly in their present acts, and their situations are ideal so that other goals of rationality do not conflict with utility maximization. Given my idealizations, utility maximization is sufficient for an agent's acting rationally. The idealizations rule out every way that maximizing utility might fail to be rational.

Besides taking utility maximization as a standard of rationality, I also take it as a goal of rationality (one of several possibly conflicting goals of rationality). This means that rational but nonideal agents aspire to comply with the principle, even though, on many occasions, they have good excuses for failing to comply. Because compliance is a goal of rationality, rational nonideal agents are motivated to deliberate about the utilities of available acts. They are motivated to put themselves in a position to comply with the principle of utility maximization. How they fare influences a comprehensive evaluation of their decisions.[10]

2.2. Optimal Decisions

Section 2.1.3 assumes that agents are ideal in various ways. They are *perfect* agents, whose desires control action directly. Because they are perfect agents, they can maximize utility spontaneously. They have no need for deliberation and decision. One way of adding realism is to allow for the value of deliberation and decision. This section treats imperfect agents for whom it is useful to deliberate, to compare acts' utilities and the like. I imagine that it is also useful for them to make decisions, to form intentions to act in certain ways. These mental acts help them perform rational nonmental acts. For example, deciding on an extended act may make more attractive that act's first step by affecting the context in which it is performed. The decision promises to make it part of a coordinated series of acts, not just an isolated act. The decision may make it the first step of a walk to the store, say, and not just a step through the doorway. The value the step gains from being part of a projected walk makes it and the walk more likely to occur.

Although this section dispenses with the idealization that agents are perfect, it retains other idealizations, in particular, the idealization that agents are cognitively unlimited so that they can deliberate and make decisions instantaneously and effortlessly. The agents I consider sometimes benefit from deliberation and decision, but they do not always benefit. Sometimes they are well advised to act spontaneously. The goal of deliberation and decision is to guide action, to facilitate the performance of maximizing acts, to achieve them or make them more likely. Sometimes deliberation and decision do not help, and rationality does not require them. Clearly, rationality does not require deciding before acting in every case because a decision is a mental act and the requirement would demand an infinite regress of decisions, an unending series of preliminary decisions. One may act without a decision to act; in particular, one may decide without a decision to decide.

Let me formulate a decision principle for this section's slightly more realistic agents. It supplements section 2.1.3's principle of utility maximization among acts and is the principle that other steps toward realism generalize. It applies to decision problems, situations where it is rational for an agent to decide among possible acts. Decision problems are special action problems to which the utility maximization principle applies. The *options* in a decision problem at a time are possible decisions at the time. They are momentary mental acts, included in the general category of acts available at the time. Although a decision occurs at a moment, a decision's content may concern an act to be performed over an extended period of time, an act of any duration, including an act whose execution is uncertain. For example, one may decide to drive home without knowing that the car has enough gas. A reasonable decision's content is typically a proposition that expresses an act by the agent because other decisions are inefficacious. Almost every possible decision has content. There is just one exception: when an agent acts without deciding, I say that she adopts the *null decision*, a decision without content. The null decision is the default resolution of a decision problem.

My principle for decision problems is to adopt a decision that has maximum utility. Following the format of my maximization principle for action, I state the principle this way:

> *Utility maximization.* Among the decisions you can make at a time, make one whose utility is at least as great as any other's utility.

This decision principle advances a standard for the evaluation of decisions, not a standard for the evaluation of decision procedures. An agent need not apply the rule to make a rational decision. Rather, given my idealizations, an agent's decision is rational only if it maximizes utility.

A decision procedure is an extended act. It culminates in a decision, a momentary act. It may involve preliminaries such as gathering information and deliberating. Some preliminaries may involve secondary decisions, say, about collection of information. Other preliminaries may involve acts not issuing from any decision at all. An agent may spontaneously begin deliberation.

Sometimes the best way to reach an objective is not to aim for it directly. If one wants to keep a topic out of mind, it is best not to aim for that objective directly but rather to think about other topics. If one wants to relax or fall asleep, it may be best not to concentrate on those objectives but to let one's mind drift. Butler (1950: 49–65) claims that to attain happiness, it is best to aim for something more concrete, perhaps, more time with friends and family. Gigerenzer (personal communication, June 28, 2002) observes that to catch a ball by being at the place where it falls when it falls, it is best not to aim directly at the objective by calculating where the ball will land and then running to that spot. The calculation is very hard and the time available very short; it is better to run toward the ball, keeping constant the angle of sight to the ball. This heuristic works. He concludes that maximizing utility is a bad strategy. I conclude that sometimes an agent maximizes utility by aiming at something else.

Such issues concern utility maximization taken as a decision procedure. They are especially complex when agents and circumstances are not ideal. To simplify, I advance utility maximization as a standard of evaluation. Even for heuristics such as Gigerenzer's, utility maximization is the measure of success. Of course, an agent should take appropriate steps for meeting the standard as closely as warranted, but I do not specify those steps and the decision procedures they form. My objective is to formulate accurate standards of evaluation. I leave open the problem of formulating accurate decision procedures and make only occasional comments about them.[11]

Following tradition, I state the principle of utility maximization using the imperative mood or infinitive construction. I often speak of the rule to maximize utility instead of the generalization that in ideal circumstances a rational decision maximizes utility. Stating the principle as a rule indicates that it is a goal of rationality for nonideal cases, not just a necessary condition of rationality in ideal cases. Given the idealizations, the rule implies the generalization, but it also expresses a goal of rationality that motivates even when the idealizations are not met and the generalization does not apply. For example, even if, because of time pressure, an agent does not meet the idealizations for the rule, utility maximization still serves as a guide to a rational decision. Approximating it may justify an act that falls short. Appropriate pursuit of a goal of rationality is mandatory even if in nonideal circumstances meeting the goal is not mandatory. Although a goal of rationality is neither a standard of evaluation nor a decision procedure, it influences rational decision procedures and so matters in a comprehensive assessment of a decision's rationality.

I adopt the principle of utility maximization restricted to acts of a certain type, namely, decisions. The principle evaluates a decision at a moment with respect to other possible decisions at the moment. The principle is realistic about the acts in a human's direct control. For a human, direct control covers decisions at a moment but generally does not go much further. Executing a decision takes time and so is beyond the agent's direct control. Decision theory traditionally evaluates decisions at a moment to put aside issues about the extent of an agent's control and responsibility. An agent's decisions are clearly in his direct control. Extending the standard to other acts requires caution. Applying the standard to, say, all acts at a moment, including spontaneous acts, which are not the product of a decision, raises the standard beyond the capabilities of imperfect agents, who are imperfectly directed by their minds, in particular, by their desires on balance. Section A.1.2 elaborates these points.[12]

Although decisions have propositional content, the set of possible decisions generally does not include a possible decision for each proposition. Possible decisions must meet certain psychological restrictions. Even an ideal agent may be limited to thoughts in her mother tongue and so limited to decisions with content expressible in that language. Furthermore, one may conflate distinctions between propositions whose realizations differ only in matters irrelevant to the decision maker. Agents typically have only a finite number of basic goals, and so their basic goals typically distinguish only a finite number of worlds. I generally assume that there are only a finite number of worlds trimmed of irrelevant matters and correspondingly only a finite number of propositions representing relevant possible decisions.

The principle of utility maximization presumes that an agent assigns a utility to every possible decision, but not to every proposition. A decision's utility is its outcome's utility. Worlds besides outcomes need not receive utility assignments. Given full information, agents know whether a nonmental act chosen will be executed. If it will, it and the choice have the same outcome (even if their causal consequences differ) and so have the same utility. Nonetheless, maximization among decisions at a time and among acts at a time differ subtly.

One difference concerns standards for an option's rationality. Must an option realized be maximizing to be rational? As in the case of the red hat, a maximizing act may entail some nonmaximizing act, so maximization is not necessary for an act's rationality. Entailment by a rational act may suffice for the rationality of some nonmaximizing act. But in a decision problem, decisions are individuated by content, and just one decision is made. Even if its content entails nonmaximizing acts, they are not the content of the decision made. Because a unique decision is realized, one need not worry about a maximizing decision's entailing a non-maximizing decision. So I take maximization as necessary for a rational decision given my idealizations.

Another difference concerns the resolutions of action and decision problems. I take the resolution of an action problem to be a momentary act and use maximization to evaluate momentary acts only. This raises issues about the accommodation of extended acts. On the other hand, the resolution of a decision problem is a decision, a momentary mental act. There are no analogous issues about the accommodation of extended mental acts. All decisions are momentary acts. Even if a decision's content concerns an extended act, say, a multistage strategy whose execution takes place over a period of time, the decision itself is a momentary mental act. Hence, maximization among decisions skirts issues about the accommodation of extended acts. They arise only indirectly in evaluations of decisions about extended acts. Thus, the case for the decision principle is simpler than the case for the action principle.

Finally, the decision principle is easier to generalize for nonideal cases than is the action principle. As the next section shows, adding realism by providing for uncertainty generates a strong reason to switch attention from the maximization principle for action to the maximization principle for decision. The principle to maximize utility among decisions is the mainstay of the decision theory chapters 4–9 generalize.

2.3. Pursuit of Optimization Given Uncertainty

This section removes the idealization of full information. First, it removes that idealization for utility maximization among acts in general. Then, it shows that without full information, utility maximization works best applied to decisions, which the previous section concluded on independent grounds.

Suppose that an agent is certain of his psychological state but uncertain of the external world. Because not fully informed, he is uncertain of the outcome of acts he can perform. How should he pursue the goal of optimization? Rationality still urges maximizing utility, but given uncertainty, an act's utility is an estimate of the utility of the act's outcome, the act's world. This section explains in a preliminary way the form of estimation it involves. Section 2.4 completes the picture.

Given uncertainty, an act's utility may not be the utility of the act's world. An agent may not know the world his act produces. It might, for all he knows, produce any of many worlds. Hence, an act's utility is an estimate of the utility of the act's world. Because utility adjusts to uncertainty, the principle of utility maximization has the same formulation with and without the idealization of full information. Without full information, the ground of utility changes, however. It includes beliefs along with desires.

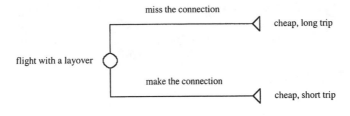

FIGURE 2.1. Possible outcomes.

In the example concerning purchase of a plane ticket, removing the idealization that the traveler knows the outcome of each possible purchase makes it sensible to evaluate purchases using utilities of their possible outcomes. The estimated utility for a flight with a layover factors in uncertainty about missing the connection. Following figure 2.1, the estimated utility calculates the probability-weighted average of the utilities of the possible outcomes. If the utility of the cheap, short trip is 10 and the utility of the cheap, long trip is 6, then if the probability of missing the connection is 0.5, the probability-weighted average is 8.

If the traveler fails to make the optimal purchase, her ignorance of it may be a good excuse. Her making a purchase of maximum utility may be enough to make her act rational. In one sense, it is what she has most reason to do. It is most sensible given her limited information.

Besides complicating the interpretation of utilities, lack of information affects the acts among which an agent should maximize utility. Section 2.1.3 instructs a fully informed agent to maximize utility among available acts. But if an agent is not fully informed, he may be uncertain of the acts he can perform. Can he jump across that creek? If he tries, will he make it? Even if, unknown to him, he can jump across and this act maximizes utility among available acts, caution may advise not making the attempt. Because an agent's uncertainty about his abilities may provide an excuse for failing to maximize among available acts, I apply the principle of maximization only to acts the agent is certain he can perform—more precisely, acts over which he is certain he has direct control.

Despite ignorance about the external world, some acts remain matters of certainty. Mental acts are still matters of certainty, given my idealizations about agents. In particular, decisions are still matters of certainty. A possible decision is certain to be realized if adopted because it is a mental act wholly within the agent's power. An agent is certain that he can make any of the possible decisions available even if he is not certain that he can execute it. He is certain that he can decide to jump across that creek even if he is not certain that he can jump across it.

Section 2.2 applied the maximization principle to decisions rather than acts to accommodate the value of deliberation and decision for imperfect agents. Lack of full information provides another reason to apply the principle to decisions. Uncertainty motivates the move from action problems to decision problems and from action principles to decision principles. Taking an agent's options to be decisions the agent can make ensures that the effect of uncertainty is limited to uncertainty about options' worlds, not their realizations. It lets uncertainty influence options' utilities but makes their realizations a matter of certainty. If rational, an ideal agent considers and evaluates all possible decisions and realizes one of maximum utility. She knows she can carry out this task. She can knowingly comply with the principle. The move to decisions makes knowing compliance possible.

Except for full information, this section's principle to maximize utility among decisions assumes all the idealizations behind section 2.2's decision principle. Even though an option's realization may provide new information, it assumes that the agent's basic goals and her utility assignment are constant across suppositions of options. Also, because her information as well as her basic goals may affect her utility assignment, it assumes that she anticipates information bearing on options' utilities to be stable during the transition from deliberation to any decision. This ensures that all options are evaluated with respect to the same utility function and that the basis of comparison of options is stable. Given the idealizations, the principle to maximize utility among possible decisions is a standard of rationality. For ideal agents in ideal situations, except for uncertainty, compliance is a necessary condition of rationality. Furthermore, although in ordinary life a decision's rationality requires more than utility maximization, given the idealizations, utility maximization is sufficient.

Just as the maximization principle for informed agents expresses a goal of rationality, the maximization principle for agents with uncertainty expresses a goal of rationality. Rational but nonideal agents aspire to comply insofar as reasonable given other goals. However, the principle for informed agents expresses a more basic goal of rationality. It says to maximize informed utility, not just utility. These goals differ because utility is sensitive to information. The priority of the goal of maximizing informed utility explains why a rational but unsuccessful decision evokes rational regret. Also, because maximizing informed utility is the more basic goal, rational agents are motivated to acquire information about options' outcomes. They are not content to maximize utility, calculating utility with respect to their incomplete information. They want additional relevant information so that maximizing utility given their information is more likely to maximize informed utility. Gathering relevant information increases the chance of maximizing informed utility, the ultimate objective (see section A.7).[13]

Because of information's utility, strategic acts and other acts conditional on future events have an advantage. Strategic acts take advantage of future information. They are not just extended acts, sequences of momentary acts, but rather extended acts with future stages responding to future information. Given uncertainty, strategies dependent on future contingencies may have higher utilities than their nonconditional counterparts because the strategies respond to new information. For example, an agent may expect to do better by taking his umbrella tomorrow if and only if it rains tomorrow than by packing his umbrella tonight without regard for tomorrow's weather. This advantage of strategic action redounds upon decisions to adopt strategies. Deciding on a strategy may have greater utility than deciding on any nonconditional act extracted from the strategy.

2.4. Expected Utility Analysis

Given uncertainty, an option's utility is an estimate of the utility of the world the option would yield if it were realized. How should one estimate the utility of an option's world given uncertainty? The previous section presented an example of the estimation procedure. This section states it in a simple, general way. Appendix A adds refinements.

According to a common view, an option's utility is the option's *expected utility*. This is a weighted average of the utilities of the option's possible outcomes, taken as possible worlds where the option is realized. The weights are the outcomes' probabilities given the option's realization. For example, suppose an airline is deciding whether to add another flight to its schedule. The relevant possible outcomes are monetary. Take them to be gains or losses in whole dollars and take their utilities to equal the amounts of money gained or lost. The probabilities of the outcomes rest on the airline's statistical data about the habits of airline passengers. For each outcome, multiply its probability and utility. Then add the products to obtain the option's expected utility. Only a finite number of products are nonnegligible.[14] Their sum is the option's utility.

To state the general formula, I use P for probability, U for utility, o for an option, w for a world, and standard notation for sums. $\sum_i P(w_i$ given $o)U(w_i)$ with i ranging from 1 to n stands for $P(w_1$ given $o)U(w_1) + P(w_2$ given $o)U(w_2) + \cdots + P(w_n$ given $o)U(w_n)$. Adopting these conventions, an expected utility analysis advances this identity.

$$U(o) = \sum_i P(w_i \text{ given } o)U(w_i), \text{ where } w_i \text{ ranges over worlds that might be } o\text{'s world.}$$

The summation assumes, as in section 2.2, a finite number of trimmed worlds.

The probabilities used to compute expected utilities are subjective. They are rational *degrees of belief*. I take degrees of belief as primitive theoretical quantities that help explain betting behavior and other behavior in the face of uncertainty.[15] The literature on behavior given uncertainty is vast and forms an ample rough introduction of the concept of degree of belief.

For ideal agents, rational degrees of belief satisfy the basic structural laws of probability.[16] They may fail to satisfy the existence laws, however. For instance, an agent may assign a probability to p and to q but not to their conjunction. Because rational degrees of belief satisfy the structural laws of probability, they are called *probabilities*. Sometimes, for convenience, irrational degrees of belief are also called probabilities even though they do not satisfy the structural laws of probability.

An agent's probability assignment depends on the agent's information. The probability an airline assigns to a new flight's success depends on its information about the volume of air traffic, the number of competing flights, and so on. As its information changes, the probability it assigns changes. When it computes expected utilities to make a decision that maximizes utility, it should use current information.

Probabilities may arise independently of preferences among gambles. They may come from knowledge of physical probabilities, as in games of chance, or from statistical data, as in predictions of election results. The probability of heads on a coin toss and the probability that Bush will be reelected, for example, need not originate in preferences among gambles. They are not defined in terms of such preferences, although they are inferable from them. Section 4.2 elaborates this interpretation of probability.[17]

Sobel (1994) calls the foregoing form of expected utility analysis world Bayesianism. It computes expected utilities from the utilities of fine-grained outcomes — possible worlds. Using these maximally specific outcomes ensures that an option's expected utility overlooks no consideration relevant to an option's evaluation. Alternative forms of expected utility analysis simplify this basic form by using utilities of outcomes less fine-grained than worlds. The utilities of the coarse-grained outcomes are probability-weighted averages of the utilities of worlds. The main idea is to divide possible worlds into groups and evaluate them collectively rather than one by one. Instead of considering each possible amount of money won or lost by a new flight, an airline may consider ranges of amounts. It may, for instance, consider just whether a new flight will gain, lose, or break even. The probabilities of these eventualities are sums of probabilities of their various realizations, and their utilities are probability-weighted averages of those realizations. However, the coarse-grained forms of expected utility analysis must be designed carefully to avoid oversimplification.[18]

Often, the division of an option's possible outcomes into groups of worlds invokes possible *states*. These are features of possible worlds, perhaps worlds more fine-grained than the ones representing outcomes, and are represented by propositions. The states must be mutually exclusive and jointly exhaustive a priori and, to generate a helpful form of analysis, must express salient features of possible worlds, features affecting outcomes. For example, if an airline has a competitor, the outcome of adding a flight may be sharply influenced by whether its competitor responds by dropping a flight so that the new flight does not have to share the market. The competitor's dropping a flight is a possible state. Then, instead of using the probabilities and utilities of outcomes, the calculation of an option's expected utility may use the probabilities of states given the option and the utilities of the option given states. The probability of a state given the option equals the probability of a group of possible outcomes, and the utility of the option given the state equals the utility of that group of possible outcomes.[19]

Suppose that options do not influence states. In my example about the airline, one may imagine that the competitor's decision about cancellation of its flight depends on federal regulations rather than competition. Then, instead of using the state's probability given the option, one may use the state's nonconditional probability. They are equal by hypothesis. This simplifies expected utility analysis of an option's utility.

$U(o) = \sum_i P(s_i) U(o \text{ given } s_i)$, where s_i ranges over the members of a partition of states.

This form of expected utility analysis is the most common form. The partition of possible states generates an option's possible outcomes, which may be coarsely individuated. An option's expected utility is a probability-weighted average of the utilities of its possible outcomes. The option's expected utility is its utility given uncertainty.

If options may influence states, an analysis of an option's utility must use probabilities of states that reflect the option's influence on the states. Expected utility analysis generalized to accommodate that influence has this form, the one to which other sections refer:

Expected Utility. $U(o) = \sum_i P(s_i \text{ given } o)U(o \text{ given } s_i)$.

The probability of a state given an option responds to the option's influence on the state. Section A.6 refines the formula to handle subtle points about suppositions of options and states.

An expected utility analysis of an option's utility presumes section 2.3's idealizations about agents and their situations. Although agents may be uninformed about the external world, they are informed about a priori matters and their own psychological states. Also, the input probabilities and utilities are rational. Nothing stands in the way of an agent's assigning utilities to options that agree with the options' expected utilities. In particular, an agent's utility assignments to options given states cohere so that an option's expected utility has the same value whatever partition of states is used to compute it. Given these idealizations, a rational agent assigns a utility to an option that conforms with the analysis. Section A.3 supports this claim.

Strictly speaking, expected utility analysis sets a standard of rationality for desirabilities. When degrees of belief and desire satisfy basic laws, I call an option's expected desirability its expected utility. I do not assume that the degree of desire for an option is a rational degree of desire, or a utility properly so called. It meets a rationality constraint if it equals the option's expected desirability. For convenience, however, I sometimes call mistaken degrees of desire utilities. For instance, when I consider whether expected utility analysis is correct, I ask whether rationality requires that *utilities* conform to the analysis. This is intended only as a brief way of asking whether rationality requires that *degrees of desire* conform to the analysis given that conditions are ideal. If expected utility analysis is correct, utilities conform necessarily.

Because an option's utility equals its expected utility, the rule to maximize utility generates a companion decision rule to maximize expected utility. This offspring has the idealizations of its parent. It assumes that conditions are perfect for utility maximization. In addition, it presumes that expected utilities exist and hence that an agent has quantitative probability and utility assignments for at least one way of calculating each option's expected utility.

The expected utility principle joins the principle of utility maximization to form the core of the decision theory I generalize. These principles accommodate uncertainty but still rely on many idealizations about agents and their decision problems. The idealizations for them are strong but necessary to remove excuses for noncompliance. Presentations of decision theory often do not state the idealizations but assume them implicitly nonetheless. Chapter 3 presents a general account of idealizations and then reviews and classifies the idealizations for utility maximization and expected utility analysis.

Idealizations

Normative decision theory formulates principles for rational decision making. A basic principle is to choose what you prefer. What could be more sensible? If you have a choice between soup and salad and you prefer soup, pick soup. Even this simple principle has exceptions, however. If you are not aware of all your options, you may rationally pick one although you prefer another. To reduce complications, decision theorists rely on idealizations about agents and their situations. For instance, they often assume that agents know all their options.

This chapter offers a general account of the nature and purpose of idealizations. It distinguishes idealizations from restrictions and explains the role of idealizations in theory construction. It applies the account of idealizations to decision theory and classifies idealizations within decision theory according to their roles. Finally, it applies the account of idealizations to the assumptions behind my principles of utility maximization and expected utility analysis. It establishes that my theory's assumptions about agents and their situations are genuine idealizations, not just convenient restrictions. Having an account of idealizations organizes later chapters' plans to remove idealizations and reformulate decision and utility principles to make them more realistic.[1]

What is the point of presenting a theory of idealizations and classifying decision theory's assumptions? Why not just state decision theory's idealizations, relax them, and adjust decision principles for their absence? Decision theory aims to explain the rationality of decisions, not just identify rational decisions. The explanatory force of a decision principle depends on the roles of its assumptions. How its assumptions make the principle accurate affects its success at explanation. Moreover, because decision theory is incomplete, an account of its assumptions' roles guides its growth. The account indicates the most profitable ways of extending and enriching the theory.

3.1. A Theory of Idealizations

Chapter 2's decision rules and principles of utility analysis rely heavily on idealizations. The idealizations are standard but strong. The rules and principles are theoretically attractive despite their strong idealizations. They succeed because their idealizations meet certain explanatory criteria. This section presents those criteria.

3.1.1. *The Explanatory Role of Idealizations*

Idealizations are common in all disciplines. They are simplifying assumptions that facilitate theory construction. For example, in physics, a theory of motion may use the idealization that air resistance is absent. A principle governing free fall formulated under that idealization is simpler than it would be if it had to account for air resistance. Putting air resistance aside allows the principle to concentrate on the influence of gravity. The idealization focuses attention on that factor's affect on unsupported objects.

In general, idealizations aid partial explanations of phenomena by putting aside some explanatory factors to highlight others. These partial explanations are not just explanation sketches or incomplete explanations, with vague claims and missing components. They are precise and complete accounts of some factors affecting a phenomenon.

In decision theory, idealizations isolate factors regulating decisions and utility assignments to show the affect of those factors. They sacrifice generality to display in detail the workings of certain critical considerations. They explain, for example, how probabilities and utilities govern decisions, other considerations aside. By simplifying, they facilitate precision.

My way of characterizing an idealization highlights its function in explanations. Besides being a simplifying assumption, it must fulfill a certain explanatory role. To prepare for a specification of that role, I present some basic points about the context in which idealizations occur.

A theory treats a phenomenon such as motion, the pressure of gases, or rationality. It seeks an explanation of the phenomenon it treats and advances principles governing that phenomenon. An idealization is an assumption of a principle. Typically, the assumption establishes a boundary condition for the principle. The theory advances the principle only for cases where the assumption holds. Although the assumption does not hold generally, the principle, if successful, holds generally in the sense that its claims about the phenomenon are correct in all cases meeting that assumption and any other assumptions the principle employs.

Sometimes no actual cases satisfy an idealization. The idealization then restricts a principle to counterfactual cases. The principle may be useful nonetheless because an explanatory theory must cover counterfactual cases as well as actual cases. In the early stages of a theory's development, its principles may address counterfactual cases more easily than actual cases. A principle of free fall, for example, may at first precisely address only cases in which the force of gravity is constant. Later, it may precisely address more realistic cases in which the force of gravity increases slightly as a body falls closer to the earth's surface.

Some theorists may count as an idealization a false assumption nearly enough true in some cases that a principle advanced under it is approximately true in those cases. For example, a theory of motion may assume the absence of air resistance in actual cases despite its presence and obtain a principle of falling bodies approximately right nonetheless. I put aside this usage of the term idealization. I focus on theories that aim for precision, for example, a theory of motion that prefers a principle concerning bodies falling in a vacuum to a principle that addresses the ordinary cases of free fall but just ignores air resistance. I take an idealization as a restriction on a precise principle rather than as a claim of a theory aiming for approximate truth. Being an assumption of a principle, an idealization need not be true for the principle to be true. In contrast, a claim that a theory assumes must be true if the theory is to be true and usually must be approximately true if the theory is to be approximately true.

A theory to which an idealized principle belongs does not claim that the principle's idealizing assumption is true. It does not use the assumption as a premiss in an argument for a conclusion advanced as true. For example, the idealization removing air resistance introduces a fiction. A principle of free fall reliant on that idealization describes how a body would fall if air resistance were absent. Because air resistance as a matter of fact slows free fall, the principle does not describe how a body actually falls. An idealization's purpose is the truth of a principle employing it, not the truth of a conclusion derivable from it. Adding a boundary condition to restrict a principle's application may change the principle's truth value. In contrast, adding a premiss to an argument does not change its conclusion's truth value.

My characterization of an idealization applies only to an assumption that restricts an explanatory principle. It takes account of the principle to which the assumption belongs and the phenomenon the principle treats.

> An assumption of an explanatory principle concerning a phenomenon is an *idealization* if and only if it identifies and controls for a factor in the phenomenon's explanation.

If the principle using the idealization is true, it yields a partial explanation of the phenomenon. It describes the way the factors not controlled for affect the phenomenon.

To illustrate this characterization of idealizations, consider free fall again. Air resistance is one factor affecting free fall. To control for that factor, a principle of free fall may assume that it is absent. The force of gravity is another factor affecting free fall. A way of controlling for its variability is to hold it constant. So another idealization for a principle of free fall may assume that the force of gravity is constant. Under these idealizations about air resistance and gravity, a classic principle for brief periods of free fall asserts that $s = gt^2/2$, where s stands for space traversed or distance traveled during free fall, t stands for the time of free fall, and g is a constant giving acceleration due to the force of gravity.

Next, consider the pressure of a gas in a container. It is affected by the volume of the container. One may control for that factor's variability by keeping it constant. Under the idealization of constant volume, the pressure of the gas follows the law $P = kT$, where P stands for pressure, T stands for temperature, and k is a constant characteristic of the gas.

Finally, consider a normative theory, in particular, Rawls's (1971) theory of justice. It recognizes that obstacles to moral goals influence the justice of social practices (3–6, 248). In a belligerent society with a custom of killing prisoners of war, a just reform may call for enslaving them instead. That may be the biggest step possible toward moral goals, although it still falls short of the goal of liberty. Rawls's theory advances its two principles of justice, the principle of liberty and the difference principle, for a well-ordered society in which obstacles to liberty and equity are absent. It controls for those hindrances by assuming their absence. The assumption of a well-ordered society is an idealization of its principles of justice.

The purposes of idealizations and the principles that contain them elucidate the features of idealizations. The principles aim at explanation, and the idealizations control for explanatory factors. If all goes well, an idealization is part of an accurate principle contributing to the explanation of the phenomenon it treats. The principle describes the role of explanatory factors for which the idealization does not control. It yields a partial explanation of the phenomenon. Moreover, the principle, although restricted by the idealization, follows the contours of the general principle governing the phenomenon. Later, the idealization may be rescinded and the principle generalized to yield a more complete explanation of the phenomenon, one covering the explanatory factors that the principle originally covered and, in addition, the factor for which the idealization controlled. An idealization is a temporary assumption to be removed when the principle employing it is generalized. When a principle containing an idealization succeeds, it may be generalized without radical revision. For example, take the law of pressure for a gas of constant volume, $P = kT$. It gives a partial explanation of pressure in terms of temperature. Removing the idealization of constant volume leads to the more general law, $P = kVT$. Using idealizations aids theory construction by generating explanatory principles more readily generalized than those involving other restrictions.

Of course, an idealization may figure in an explanatory principle that fails to reach its aims. First, the principle may be false. Then, although the idealization controls for an explanatory factor, the principle does not yield a partial explanation of the phenomenon it treats. Second, the principle may be true but not explain. The factors it considers may be correlated with but not explain the phenomenon it treats. Then, despite appropriate idealizations, it does not yield a partial explanation. Third, it may yield a successful explanatory principle, but one that does not generalize without radical revision. Then, the principle falls short of its theoretical objective.

According to my characterization of idealizations, an assumption is an idealization only if the principle to which the assumption belongs aims at explanation. Consider, for instance, the principle that all ravens are black. Take it to treat the color of birds and to restrict itself by assumption to birds that are ravens. It is an empirical generalization that does not aim at explanation. It describes but does not explain the color of birds. Consequently, its assumption has no explanatory function and so is not an idealization.

Not every assumption of a principle attempting to explain some phenomenon qualifies as an idealization, even if the assumption contributes to the principle's truth and so does not restrict the principle unnecessarily. Some assumptions do not control for an explanatory factor. Consider the generalization that all mammals except platypuses bear live young. Take the generalization as a principle attempting to explain in part what it is for an animal to be a mammal, and take the generalization to make the assumption that the animals considered are not platypuses. This assumption puts aside an exception to the generalization. It does not control for a factor in an explanation of an animal's classification as a mammal. The factor put aside, being a platypus, is not part of the explanation of an animal's being a mammal. Although a platypus is a mammal, its being a platypus does not help explain why it is a mammal. An explanation appeals to traits common to all species of mammals. I do not count as an idealization an assumption that does not control for an explanatory factor. I call such an assumption a *restriction* and sometimes, for contrast with an idealization, a *mere restriction*. It restricts a principle, as an idealization does, but does not have an idealization's function in explanations.

For another example of a simplifying assumption that fails to be an idealization, consider a rule of inference in sentence logic. Sentence logic advances *modus ponens*, for instance, under the restriction that sentences are composed exclusively of sentence letters, sentential connectives, and parentheses. Predicate logic generalizes *modus ponens* for sentences composed using in addition quantifiers, variables, constants, and predicate letters. Sentence logic's restriction of *modus ponens* to simple sentences is not an idealization. It does not control for a factor in the explanation of valid inferences. It is a mere restriction.

Also, a principle's assumption may fail to be an idealization, although it controls for an explanatory factor, because it fails to identify the explanatory factor for which it controls. For example, consider the principle that every coin in my pocket is silver in color. Take this principle to treat the color of coins and to limit itself by assumption to coins in my pocket now. The assumption in effect restricts the principle to dimes because I have only dimes in my pocket. Moreover, a coin's being a dime figures in an explanation of its metallic composition and so its color. But the assumption does not identify the explanatory factor for which it controls, namely, being a dime. Hence, it does not qualify as an idealization. My characterization of idealizations rules out cases in which an assumption accidentally controls for an explanatory factor. I call such an assumption, too, a mere restriction.

I do not require that an idealization explicitly identify the explanatory factor for which it controls. It need only implicitly identify that factor. For example, a law about the pressure of a gas may specify that the gas is in a rigid container. Although the law does not explicitly say that the gas's volume is constant, it implicitly indicates this constraint. Hence, its assumption counts as an idealization.

The identification of explanatory factors raises subtle issues. For instance, a pair of extensionally equivalent properties may not both be explanatory factors even though one is. For instance, having a heart and having a kidney are extensionally equivalent in normal animals, but only the first property explains blood circulation. For the most part, I put aside such issues. My main points do not depend on them.

Idealizations have explanatory virtues that restrictions lack, but to classify an assumption for a principle as a restriction rather than as an idealization is not to disparage it. Although it may serve merely to put aside recalcitrant cases rather than to advance partial explanations, it may yield a useful generalization. It is not necessarily an ad hoc assumption. In fact, an assumption of a principle is less likely to be ad hoc than an assumption of a theory. Consider, for instance, the phlogiston theory of combustion. It assumes that phlogiston has negative weight to square its principle that a burning object emits phlogiston with the object's weight gain. The theory introduces that insufficiently supported assumption in a desperate attempt to reconcile itself with observation. Hence, the assumption is ad hoc. An assumption of a principle, unlike an assumption of a theory, cannot be ad hoc in this way. It does not advance a claim and so does not advance an insufficiently supported, ad hoc claim.

Applications of my distinction between idealizations and restrictions may be controversial for a number of reasons. Let me draw attention to a few. First, a principle may not clearly indicate its assumptions and the phenomenon it tries to explain. Their specification may be a matter of interpretation. Consequently, the principle's idealizations may also depend on its interpretation.

Second, even if a principle's topic and assumptions are clear, an assumption's classification as an idealization or a restriction may be in doubt because it depends on the sometimes difficult distinction between explanatory and nonexplanatory factors. Whether explanatory factors must be causal factors is unsettled, for instance. Also, whether chopping and mixing explanatory factors yields explanatory factors is a matter of debate. Perhaps explanatory factors are individuated only by carving at nature's joints. Sharpening the distinction between idealizations and restrictions by elaborating the distinction between explanatory and nonexplanatory factors demands a theory of explanation beyond my project's scope. So I must tolerate the potential for disagreement about the classification of factors and ensuing disagreement about the classification of assumptions.

Third, whether a factor is genuinely explanatory depends on the way the world works. Our ignorance of the world may prevent certainty that a factor is explanatory. Consider, for instance, cases involving the explanation of a decision's rationality. That a decision is made on a Friday may seem explanatorily irrelevant but may be relevant if Friday is payday. Also, that a decision's possible outcomes are described as losses with respect to a certain reference point rather than described equivalently as gains with respect to a lower reference point may seem explanatorily irrelevant but may be relevant if framing effects are part of rational decision heuristics.

For reasons such as these, claims that assumptions are idealizations or just restrictions may be disputable. Nonetheless, the distinction between idealizations and restrictions is serviceable because in many interesting cases an assumption's classification is clear.

Does the foregoing account of idealizations apply to normative decision theory as well as science? Explanations in science are often causal, whereas explanations in normative decision theory are generally justificatory and perhaps not causal. I formulate my account of idealizations in terms of explanatory rather than causal factors to facilitate the transition from science to normative decision theory. As science does, normative decision theory aims at explanation and uses idealizations to control for explanatory factors. For example, normative decision theory uses idealizations about information to control for it in the explanation of a decision's rationality. The explanatory role of idealizations carries over from the sciences to normative decision theory.[2]

3.1.2. *Idealizations in Decision Theory*

To apply my account of idealizations to decision theory, this section considers some assumptions of common decision and utility principles. It considers how to classify those assumptions and divides assumptions qualifying as idealizations according to their theoretical roles to enrich the scheme of classification for assumptions. Later, section 3.2 surveys assumptions of my decision and utility principles and classifies them according to this scheme.

The distinction between idealizations and restrictions applies to assumptions of principles of rationality. Take the familiar principle to maximize utility. It explains the rationality of decisions given certain assumptions. It has an explanatory function. Which of its assumptions are idealizations? To set the stage for an answer, consider the structure of an explanation of the rationality of an agent's decision. A general explanation assigns a role to utility maximization but also takes account of the agent's circumstances. Suppose she is rushed by the press of events. Then she may be excused for failing to maximize utility. To control for such excuses, the principle of utility maximization typically assumes that circumstances are perfect for utility maximization, in particular, the agent has time to identify an option of maximum utility. Because that assumption controls for an explanatory factor, it is an idealization. The assumption controls for an explanatory factor not by keeping it constant but by eliminating it. The phenomenon to be explained, rationality, and the factor to be controlled, excuses for falling short of the standard of utility maximization, are not quantitative. So the general principle governing rational decisions does not have the algebraic form of a law of motion. Still, it is possible using idealizations to obtain a principle that controls for explanatory factors.

In contrast, consider the assumption that if an agent prefers an option a to an option c, then for some option b she prefers a to b and b to c. The principle to maximize utility may make this continuity assumption to ensure that options' utilities are measurable using only the options' preference ranking. The assumption does not control for a factor explaining the rationality of decisions. It is just a restriction for principles of rational decision making. Similarly, the assumption that an agent has only a finite number of options is a restriction. It does not identify a factor that explains the rationality of a decision. It just removes certain problem cases, such as those in which an agent's options are better and better without end and no option has maximum utility.

Principles of decision and utility analysis should avoid mere restrictions. If they do, they have greater generality and explanatory power, even if they are idealized rather than completely general and yield partial rather than complete explanations. For example, my principle of expected utility analysis (section 2.4) applies wherever the quantitative input for it exists. The principle's generality enhances its explanatory power. It would less effectively explain the rationality of utility assignments if it included restrictions seeking only to put aside recalcitrant cases.

Besides distinguishing idealizations and restrictions, I also distinguish types of idealization. One method of division appeals to the type of principle an idealization serves. Idealizations may be normative, psychological, or mathematical, for instance, depending on the type of principle for which they are introduced.

Because my topic is normative decision theory, I formulate normative principles and employ normative idealizations for them. Justifying a decision is the same as explaining its rationality.[3] So normative decision theory has an explanatory function. Normative explanation of a decision's rationality differs from psychological explanation of a decision's occurrence, however, so a normative idealization differs from a psychological idealization. For instance, assuming the absence of distractions puts aside a factor in psychological explanations of decisions, but not a factor in normative explanations, because a rational agent overcomes distractions, at least minor ones. Although the absence of distractions is a psychological idealization, it is not a normative idealization. Similarly, the assumption that utility is bounded puts aside factors in the mathematical analysis of utility and so is a mathematical idealization, but it is not a normative idealization. A normative idealization puts aside factors in the justification of decisions, factors in the explanation of their rationality.[4]

Idealizations for my normative principles fall into two broad categories. Take idealizations for my decision principles. All control for factors affecting the rationality of decisions and so factors affecting the explanation of the rationality of decisions, that is, their justification. Some, in particular, control for obstacles to the attainment of goals of rationality, obstacles that may excuse shortcomings. A rational agent aspires to remove these obstacles and facilitate her path to goals of rationality. Some idealizations for principles of utility analysis similarly remove obstacles to goals of rationality. I call idealizations that remove obstacles to goals of rationality *aspirational* idealizations. Other idealizations I call *justificational* idealizations, or, for contrast with aspirational idealizations, *merely justificational* idealizations.

For example, an obstacle to the goal of maximizing utility is ignorance of options of maximum utility. A rational agent strives to prevent or overcome that ignorance. The idealization that the agent knows the options of maximum utility is therefore an aspirational idealization. In contrast, imprecise beliefs and desires do not create an obstacle to goals of rationality. Imprecision is not an obstacle to the goal of maximizing utility, for example, because that goal applies only if desires concerning options are quantitatively precise. An agent without quantitative beliefs and desires may be perfectly able to reach the appropriate goal, which section 4.4 states. A rational agent, therefore, need not strive to eliminate imprecision. In fact, imprecision may be warranted given the agent's limited evidence and experience. Hence, the idealization that beliefs and desires are quantitative is only a justificational idealization.

Although not every justificational idealization is an aspirational idealization, every aspirational idealization is a justificational idealization. Idealizing away ignorance, for instance, removes an obstacle to the goal of maximizing informed utility and also puts aside justificatory factors, such as probabilities, arising in decisions under uncertainty. Also, an idealization may be aspirational with respect to one goal but not another if it puts aside an obstacle to the first goal but not the second. The idealization of full information, for instance, is aspirational with respect to the goal of maximizing informed utility but not with respect to the goal of maximizing expected utility. Incomplete information is no obstacle to the second goal.

```
                    assumption
                   /      \
        restriction      idealization
                        /      \
                  normative      nonnormative (psychological or mathematical, say)
                  /      \
        justificational      aspirational (with respect to a goal of rationality)
```

FIGURE 3.1. Types of assumption for a principle of decision or utility.

The distinction between idealizations and restrictions is important because it guides theory construction. Reliance on idealizations creates a framework that identifies factors affecting the rationality of decisions and utility assignments. Such a framework sets the stage for future removal of idealizations and generalization of principles without radical revision. The distinction between aspirational and justificational idealizations also guides theory construction. Goals of rationality are the main components of justifications of decisions. Furthermore, goals of rationality direct preparations for decisions, including the production of computer software and other decision-making aids. A normative decision theory should pay special attention to goals of rationality, and use of aspirational idealizations promotes their study.

Figure 3.1 summarizes my scheme of classification for assumptions of principles of decision theory. Because normative principles are my topic, I attend principally to the distinction between restrictions and idealizations and the distinction between justificational and aspirational idealizations.

3.1.3. *Objectives of Idealizations in Decision Theory*

Idealizations promote partial explanations. While fulfilling this function they may also serve other objectives. This section reviews their objectives in decision theory.

Besides assisting partial explanations of rational decisions, idealizations in normative decision theory also serve two ancillary purposes. The first is practical. Because idealizations yield partial explanations, they yield partial understanding. This partial understanding has practical value. It reduces the scope of factors not understood and gives a decision maker his bearings. A decision maker gains by understanding some if not all factors behind a decision's rationality. Chapter 2's principles for decisions and utility assignments, for instance, offer practical guidance in decision problems despite their idealizations. The second ancillary purpose is theoretical. An idealized theory builds a framework for a more general theory. Later, one may rescind some idealizations while retaining the framework of the original theory and thus transform its partial explanations into more complete explanations of rational decision making. Chapter 2 illustrates the process. It removes the idealization of full information and generalizes the principle of utility maximization to accommodate uncertainty.

Let me explore these ancillary theoretical and practical purposes a bit further. The decision and utility principles my idealizations support are important for theory building because, although limited in scope, they treat their topics with precision. My idealizations make this precision possible. Other approaches to decision theory, especially in practically oriented disciplines such as management science, compromise exactness for the sake of principles that are readily applicable to realistic decision problems. These other approaches are useful and intellectually stimulating, but my objective here is theory construction. It is often better from a theoretical point of view to obtain a principle that is exactly right in idealized cases than to obtain a principle that is approximately right in realistic cases. The theoretician's goal is explanation and understanding, not practicality. Explanation and understanding thrive on precision. Approximate principles for realistic cases are often deficient in explanatory power unless derived from exact principles for ideal cases, which transfer explanatory power to them. For instance, a decision rule for a firm may instruct it to maximize profit. This rule is a simplification of the rule to maximize utility and is approximately right if utility for the firm is nearly the same as profit. However, it may go wrong in cases where the firm's objectives include risk avoidance and public service. Consequently, it does not fully explain a firm's decisions.

Although decision principles based on idealizations have mainly a theoretical function, they have practical uses, too. Precise, idealized principles may govern some, if not all, aspects of a realistic decision problem. Their precision may be helpful despite being circumscribed. To see how, consider an example outside decision theory. In classical logic, the law of excluded middle presumes an ideal setting in which every sentence has a complete interpretation and hence a truth value. The law is part of a theory of truth for the ideal case. In realistic cases in which sentences are only partially interpreted and perhaps without a truth value, it still has a role to play in a theory of truth. Although partial interpretation complicates the theory of truth, the law still treats some matters precisely. Consider the sentence "Socrates is bald." Because the predicate is vague, the sentence may be indeterminate. Then, neither it nor its negation is true. Nonetheless, their disjunction is true. Their disjunction is true given any way of settling the vagueness. This approach, which the theory of supervaluations advances, generalizes the law for realistic cases. The law survives despite the complications that partial interpretations cause for a theory of truth. Despite vagueness, it treats some truths with precision. In the same way, exact decision principles employing idealizations may treat some matters with precision even in cases where the idealizations behind them do not hold.

Also, knowledge of rational decisions in ideal cases guides decision making in realistic cases, especially ones that approximate ideal cases. For example, the idealization that probabilities and utilities are available in decision problems is unrealistic. Still, a decision theory for quantitative cases has value in realistic decision problems. It provides instructive examples of rational decision making that may guide problem solving. Despite recourse to idealizations, my theory places certain constraints on decisions in realistic cases and provides a useful framework for deliberations.[5]

3.1.4. *Aspirational Idealizations and Goals of Rationality*

In decision theory, aspirational idealizations remove obstacles to goals of rationality. An idealization's classification as an aspirational idealization thus depends on the nature and variety of goals of rationality for decisions and utility assignments. To aid classification of idealizations as aspirational or justificational, this section reviews familiar goals of rationality and their relationships to aspirational idealizations.

Principles of rational decision making reliant on aspirational idealizations do not regulate ordinary decisions. For ordinary people in ordinary conditions, satisfaction of the principles is not a requirement but a goal of rationality, that is, an achievement to which rational people aspire. A fully rational agent has a desire to attain the goal. The desire may compete with other desires and be overridden by them. Also, the desire may be conditional if the goal is restricted. Nonetheless, it is independent of information and in that sense has a universal grounding.

Rationality requires that agents work toward compliance with the decision rule to maximize utility. The required work depends on the agent's circumstances. It need not generate intentions to comply. It may instead generate character traits that promote compliance. Movement toward compliance with the decision rule, for instance, may involve decision preparation rather than intentions to comply, because the latter may create obstructions to compliance. For instance, forming and maintaining intentions to comply may use up cognitive resources needed to comply. One may work toward compliance with the decision rule without in each instance aiming to comply.

My principles of rationality are formulated to be explanatory, to be part of an explanatory theory. They are designed to serve as generalizations explaining the rationality of particular desires and decisions. For example, in a case where option o alone has maximum utility, I advance the principle to adopt an option of maximum utility rather than a principle to adopt option o. The latter principle does not explain the rationality of adopting option o. Because of their role in explanation, my principles are identified intensionally and are not the same as other principles that are extensionally equivalent.[6]

As does the goal to maximize expected utility, the goal to maximize utility allows for cases where uncertainty is an obstacle to attaining the goal to maximize informed utility. According to expected utility analysis (section 2.4), for rational ideal agents an option's expected utility equals its utility. The goals of maximizing utility and expected utility are therefore equivalent for rational ideal agents. Nonetheless, the two goals are distinguishable in such agents. The goal to maximize expected utility explicitly accommodates ignorance about options' outcomes. Because goals are individuated according to the intentions they generate, not just the behavior they generate, the two goals are distinct in virtue of their different psychological effects.

To show that an idealization is aspirational, the basic procedure is to identify an obstacle and goal such that the idealization removes the obstacle to the goal. However, because an aspirational idealization removes an obstacle to a goal, its realization is also a goal. So a secondary method of verifying that an idealization is aspirational is to establish that its realization is a goal. In addition, one may confirm that compliance with the principle is a goal when the idealization is removed, provided that the principle's other assumptions are met. Compliance should be a goal despite the idealization's absence because, if the idealization is aspirational, realizing it is a goal and because given the idealization, rationality requires compliance with the principle.

Let me clarify the last means of checking that an idealization is aspirational. Given my stipulations, a principle of rationality for an aspirationally ideal case expresses a goal of rationality for all cases. If there are no obstacles to meeting the goal, it must be met to achieve rationality. If there are obstacles, it still serves as a goal, although there may be excuses for failing to meet it. Compliance with a rule that binds an agent given aspirationally ideal conditions is itself a goal of rationality even when conditions are not ideal. For instance, the rule to maximize utility binds an agent in aspirationally ideal conditions, including awareness of all logical and mathematical truths. But even when a decision maker fails to know all logical and mathematical truths, she is rationally obligated to aim at utility maximization.

This connection between goals and principles of rationality for aspirationally ideal cases need not hold between goals and principles of rationality for cases meeting mere restrictions or justificational idealizations. For instance, consider maximization of expected utility. The common restriction that states are independent of options may not yield a decision rule with which rationality promotes compliance even in cases where states are not independent of options. Thus, a way to test whether a condition on a principle of rationality is an aspirational idealization is to consider whether compliance with the principle is a goal of rationality when the condition is removed. If it is not, then the condition is not an aspirational idealization.

Applying the test reliably requires attention to certain details. First, the principle using the idealization must identify basic explanatory factors. Factors extensionally equivalent are not sufficient. For example, a decision principle for cases with complete information may instruct an agent not to search for relevant information. Following this advice is not a goal of rationality for cases with incomplete information; in them, additional relevant information is desirable. The test goes awry because in ideal cases, not searching for information is just a consequence of meeting the basic requirement to maximize informed utility. Maximizing informed utility is the requirement that becomes a goal for nonideal cases. If a decision principle is to express a goal when an idealization is rescinded, its formulation must be apt for nonideal cases and so must identify basic reasons for a decision's rationality. A suitable explanatory principle identifies factors that generate desires for ends and so basic reasons independent of the agent's information, although it may be restricted and identify explanatory factors generating conditional desires for ends. For reliability, the test presumes a principle working with basic, but not necessarily general, explanatory factors.

Second, the test relies on a necessary condition for being an aspirational idealization and so yields only a means of disqualifying idealizations as aspirational. An idealization may pass the test without being aspirational. For instance, having quantitative beliefs and desires is merely a justificational idealization. Nonetheless, if a principle advanced under that idealization is general, say, the principle to be rational, then the principle may express a goal of rationality when the idealization is rescinded. The justificational idealization passes the test because the principle does not depend on the idealization.

Third, the goal obtained for cases not meeting the idealization still relies on the principle's other assumptions. It may be restricted by them. Take, for instance, the idealization of a priori knowledge for the principle to maximize utility. It passes the test, although in cases where agents lack a priori knowledge the goal of maximizing utility is subject to the principle's assumption that agents have quantitative beliefs and desires. It is a restricted goal.

The test displays a virtue of reliance on aspirational idealizations. The principles they yield furnish goals that guide the construction of principles for cases in which the idealizations are rescinded. This feature of aspirational idealizations is a reason for favoring them. Using them to formulate decision and utility principles facilitates future generalization of those principles.

An idealization may be aspirational in virtue of removing an obstacle to any type of goal of rationality. When identifying aspirational idealizations, it helps to keep in mind the variety of such goals. The remainder of this section classifies familiar goals of rationality.

Some goals of rationality take account of personal ends. This makes them subjective in the sense of having subjective input. Other goals of rationality also take account of personal information. This also makes them subjective in the same sense. The goal to maximize informed utility is subjective because informed utility depends on personal ends. The goal to maximize utility, that is, utility in light of current, perhaps incomplete information, is doubly subjective because utility depends on personal information as well as personal ends.

Some goals of rationality for decisions are goals of success, for example, the goal to choose an option whose outcome has maximum informed utility. Other goals of rationality for decisions are cognitive, for example, the goal to choose an option that has maximum expected utility. Its aim is support of an agent's decision by his beliefs and desires. The goals of rationality for decisions form an explanatory hierarchy. The success goals are primary, and the cognitive goals are secondary. The primary goals explain the secondary goals. The secondary goals come into play when obstacles threaten the primary goals. The secondary goals indicate how to pursue the primary goals in the face of obstacles. Uncertainty about options' outcomes is an obstacle to attaining the primary goal of maximizing informed utility, and the secondary goal of maximizing expected utility articulates a reasonable way of pursuing the primary goal given this obstacle. In conditions ideal for attainment of the primary goal, meeting the secondary goal ensures meeting the primary goal; that is, given full information maximizing expected utility entails maximizing informed utility.

Independent formulation of idealizations and rules is not necessary for justificational idealizations. However, an aspirational idealization should have a formulation independent of rules of rationality. This is necessary to make the rules express goals of rationality. Suppose, for instance, one says that maximizing expected utility is a rule of rationality and then also says that according to an aspirational idealization for the rule, an agent is perfectly able to maximize expected utility. Now, a rational agent complies with every rule of rationality when conditions are ideal for complying with it. So even if a rational agent complies with the expected utility rule under that idealization, one is not entitled to conclude that compliance with the rule is a goal of rationality, a goal for rational agents even when the idealization is not met. To make rational agents' compliance with the rule under an aspirational idealization indicate that the rule expresses a goal of rationality, the aspirational idealization should be stated in terms of cognitive resources and abilities, such as knowledge of a priori truths. These resources and abilities have a formulation independent of the rule's formulation even if the idealization's content is informed by knowledge of the maximization rule and the principle of expected utility analysis.

I also distinguish overall goals of rational decision making and subgoals that supplement each other and may conflict with each other. A subgoal of rational decision making is to gather relevant information before deciding. Another subgoal is to minimize the costs of making a decision. These subgoals generally conflict. The overall goal adjudicates conflicts between the subgoals and advances a reasonable compromise among them. The formulation of the overall goal of rationality is an immense project. It has to accommodate every principle of rationality. I leave its formulation open and examine only subgoals of rationality, such as utility maximization. Meeting this goal is at most a necessary condition for a rational decision (although, given the idealization that all other goals are satisfied, meeting this goal becomes a sufficient condition for a rational decision).

Finally, I distinguish general goals of rationality from goals of rationality for restricted cases. For instance, maximizing utility among options is a goal of rationality in cases where some option's utility is maximal. In other words, it is a goal for cases in which it is realizable. Some decision problems lack an option that maximizes utility among options, for example, the decision problem to pick an income under $100,000, in Savage (1972: 18). So maximizing utility is not a general goal of rationality for decisions. It is a restricted goal as well as a subgoal. Chapter 8 formulates a general goal, self-support, that subsumes the restricted goal of utility maximization. It is a subgoal subordinate to the overall goal of rationality.

An aspirational idealization for a decision rule or utility principle may remove an obstacle to a primary or a secondary goal, an overall goal or a subgoal, or a general or a restricted goal. An assumption may therefore be an aspirational idealization for a subgoal, but not for an overall goal. I therefore classify aspirational idealizations according to the type of goal to which they remove an obstacle. Typically, decision theorists advance aspirational idealizations for secondary goals given uncertainty about options' outcomes and for goals restricted to cases where utility maximization is feasible. Chapter 2's aspirational idealizations, for example, knowledge of a priori truths, fall into this category.

Figure 3.2 displays the division of goals of rationality according to type. It reviews the categories discussed and shows their relationships.

To compare goals mentioned, Table 3.1 classifies them according to type. For brevity, it treats only subjective goals for decisions. In the table, an x after a goal and under a type indicates that the goal is that type of goal, and a blank space indicates that it is not that type.

This completes my account of idealizations in decision theory. The chapter's appendix uses it to address controversial idealizations that some decision theorists advance. The next section applies it to the idealizations I adopt for my decision and utility principles.

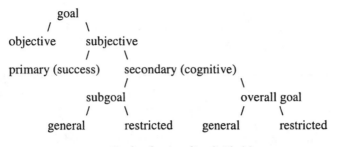

FIGURE 3.2. Goals of rationality divided by type.

3.2. Idealizations for My Decision Theory

Chapter 2 stated the idealizations behind its decision and utility principles. This section organizes those idealizations and classifies them according to the taxonomy that section 3.1.2 presented. It shows that they are genuine idealizations, not just restrictions, and that most are aspirational idealizations, not merely justificational idealizations.

Chapter 2's principles make two large idealizations. Both are standard idealizations in decision theory, although they are generally in the background. The large idealizations assume (1) rational ideal agents and (2) ideal decision situations. I examine each of these large idealizations in turn.

According to the idealization about agents, they have no cognitive limitations. They know all logical, mathematical, and other a priori truths. They know their own minds perfectly and never wonder about their beliefs and desires. They consider all their options. They think instantaneously and without effort. These idealizations about cognitive powers are genuine idealizations because an agent's abilities explain rationality's demands on her. They count as aspirational idealizations, because they remove obstacles to the attainment of goals of rationality, such as the goal of maximizing utility.

For simplicity, the idealization about knowledge is stated more strongly than necessary. It may say instead that agents know all a priori truths useful to them for making decisions that meet the goals of rationality given uncertainty about

TABLE 3.1. Classification of subjective goals for decisions

	Primary	*General*	*Overall*
Maximum utility			
Maximum expected utility			
Maximum informed utility	x		
Relevant information			
Minimal decision costs		x	
Rationality		x	x
Self-support		x	

a posteriori matters. This weakening allays doubts about the idealization's realizability. Some may suspect that the conceptual prerequisites of a priori omniscience are unsatisfiable, access to concepts being limited even for cognitively unlimited agents.

Also, although I assume that thought is instantaneous, I separate the time of deliberation and the time of decision so that it does not follow that an agent knows her decision as she deliberates. The temporal separation is not necessary to keep apart the reasons for deliberation and decision. Even if the times of deliberation and decision are merged, the processes of deliberation and decision differ in the inferences grounding them. Comparisons of options' utilities made in deliberations rest on beliefs and basic desires. Decisions rest on comparisons of options' utilities. Knowledge of the decision reached need not be a premise in the inferential process yielding comparisons of options' utilities.

Because I am interested in applying both decision rules and principles of utility analysis to decision problems, idealizations for my decision theory include idealizations for both the rules and the principles. I must distinguish between idealizations for decision rules and idealizations for utility principles when classifying an assumption as an idealization or a restriction. For example, the decision rule to maximize utility is advanced with respect to the idealization that an agent consider all options. This idealization is not also an idealization for an analysis of an option's utility. If imposed on utility analysis, it is a restriction.

The large idealization about agents also includes the agents' rationality. Their rationality's scope depends on whether the context is a decision rule or principle of utility analysis. Each context presumes no mistake in the other's area. A mistake might require compensatory departures from the rule or principle. Each states rationality's requirement in one area given rationality in the other area. When evaluating a principle of utility analysis, I assume that an agent has rational goals and beliefs and never makes irrational decisions. When evaluating a decision rule, I assume that an agent follows all rules of rationality for beliefs and desires and decides rationally except perhaps in the current case. Moreover, for both the principle and the rule, I assume that an agent knows about her rationality. The objective is to ensure that the principle or rule has rational input and that its output is used rationally so that it does not have to adjust for background irrationality. An ideal agent who complies with it, assuming its correctness, is then fully rational.[7]

Take the principle of expected utility analysis (section 2.4). For this principle, I assume that agents are fully rational concerning degrees of belief and desire for states and outcomes. Also, I assume that agents are fully rational in using degrees of desire for options to reach decisions. In other words, I assume that agents are fully rational except perhaps in their degrees of desire for options. Then I argue that to be rational given the idealizations, a degree of desire for an option must equal the options' expected desirability. I verify this by considering whether the equality produces rational decisions. On the other hand, when arguing for the decision principle to maximize expected utility, I assume fully rational input including desirabilities of options that conform to expected desirabilities, but do not assume decisions in conformity with expected desirabilities of options. To avoid begging crucial questions, the idealization of rational input varies in content as I shuttle between the expected utility decision principle and the expected utility analysis of an option's utility.

When later chapters review idealizations, they generally do not separate idealizations for decision rules and idealizations for utility principles. Usually, nothing important depends on their separation. However, the distinction is important occasionally. As part of its idealizations, chapter 2's theory supposes that in a decision problem, some option maximizes expected utility in a stable way. The idealization is not advanced for the expected utility analysis of an option's utility. Rather, it is advanced for the decision rule to maximize expected utility. The distinction between decision rules and principles of utility analysis, and the idealizations for each, enables chapter 8 to remove idealizations for the decision rule and modify it, while retaining the utility principle and idealizations for it.

When I assume that agents are rational and therefore inerrant about certain matters, I do not assume that they are infallible about those matters. For example, as an idealization for a utility principle, I assume that agents decide rationally. According to this idealization, it is possible for them to decide irrationally, although, in fact, they never do. The fallibility of agents allows me to define an option's utility given an assumption that some irrational decision is made. Although the assumption may be counterfactual, utilities with respect to such counterfactual assumptions are sometimes crucial for the justification of a decision.[8]

To illustrate the role of the idealization of rationality, suppose that a maximizing decision now would be followed by a nonmaximizing decision later. Then a rational decision now, by way of compensation for later errors, may forgo maximization among decisions possible now. This case involves an agent not rational to the extent required. An ideal agent fully rational, except perhaps in the current decision, maximizes at every past and future stage of her life. So my idealization about agents puts aside such cases. (Chapters 6 and 7 rescind the idealization and treat those cases.)

As another illustration of the idealization's role, recall that degrees of belief and desire ought to satisfy an expected desirability principle. However, if they do not satisfy other basic laws of probability and utility, satisfaction of the expected desirability principle may generate conflicts between principles of rationality. For instance, if degrees of belief are superadditive, it may turn out that the expected degree of desire for a gamble is greater than the degree of desire for the best prize the gamble offers. Then, if the expected degree of desire for the gamble is the degree of desire for the gamble, as the expected desirability principle requires, and the agent has to choose between the gamble and the best prize, a conflict arises between the decision principle to maximize expected desirability and the decision principle to avoid an option that is desirability-dominated by another option. The idealization that agents are fully rational before and after their decision problems eliminates conflict between principles of rationality and so puts aside excuses for violating those principles.

The idealization of rationality is a genuine idealization because compensation for mistakes is a justificatory factor for decisions and utility assignments. Also, the idealization is an aspirational idealization. Evidently, not being fully rational is an obstacle to attaining goals of rationality, and rational agents aspire to be fully rational. Moreover, rational agents aspire to conform to standards not compromised by compensation for error. For example, whatever the resolution of mistake-engendered conflicts between principles of rationality—even if it is rational to violate the expected desirability principle in some conflicts—the expected desirability principle still expresses a goal of rationality for degrees of desire. Rational agents must make reasonable efforts to overcome obstacles to compliance with the principle, and ideal agents in ideal circumstances must comply to be rational.

Finally, the large idealization about agents includes some justificational idealizations that are not also aspirational idealizations. Consequently, the whole large idealization counts as a justificational idealization. One component justificational idealization is that agents have stable basic goals. Their basic goals are constant across suppositions that arise in utility analysis. This is a justificational idealization because it puts aside factors affecting utility assignments when, for instance, given some option, basic goals would change. It is not an aspirational idealization, however, because its realization is not a goal of rationality.

Another justificational idealization is the existence of the probabilities and utilities needed for decision rules, in particular, the rule to maximize expected utility. This idealization does not assume that probability and utility assignments have universal scope. It assumes the existence only of probabilities and utilities required for application of decision theory to the decision problem at hand. In general, I formulate decision rules to impose minimal existence requirements on probabilities and utilities, and I keep the existence assumption for the rules at a minimum.[9]

My existence assumption is a justificational idealization, not an aspirational idealization, because goals of rationality for decision are fully attainable in the absence of probabilities and utilities. The goals applicable to nonquantitative cases are just more complex because they are responsive to more factors. In particular, imprecision complicates decision goals in nonquantitative cases. Section 4.4 advances a decision principle for such cases and, in showing how to accommodate imprecision, also demonstrates that imprecision is a factor in the explanation of rational decisions and therefore that the assumption of quantitative beliefs and desires, which implicitly identifies this factor, is a genuine idealization.

According to my large idealization about decision situations, there are no conflicts among the various subgoals for rational decisions, and there are no obstacles to meeting those subgoals and the overall goal except, perhaps, uncertainty about options' outcomes. Moreover, maximization of utility is feasible, and utility comparisons of options are independent of information provided by options.

The assumption about conflict among subgoals is a justificational idealization with respect to the overall goal of rationality because the resolution of such conflict shapes the overall goal for decisions. The idealization is not an aspirational idealization with respect to the overall goal because the overall goal addresses such conflict. However, it is an aspirational idealization with respect to the subgoal of utility maximization because conflicting subgoals of rationality are obstacles to its attainment.

The assumptions about utility are also justificational idealizations. They put aside factors that justify departures from utility maximization. They are not aspirational idealizations with respect to the general goal of rationality because utility maximization among options is not a general goal of rationality. Occasionally, no option maximizes utility in the appropriate way. In some cases, such as the case of picking your income, no option has maximum utility. In other cases, the grounds of utility calculations shift with the decision reached so that no option maximizes utility in a stable way. An option that has maximum utility with respect to information during deliberations, if selected, brings new, anticipated information with respect to which it no longer has maximum utility. The general goal of rationality addresses these cases despite their complexity. So the assumptions about utility are aspirational idealizations only with respect to the restricted goal of utility maximization. They eliminate obstacles to reaching this restricted goal of rationality.

To eliminate uncertainty about realization of options adopted, one may add the idealization that options are certain to be realized if chosen. This idealization about the realization of options counts as a justificational idealization. It puts aside a special type of uncertainty that may justify departures from my decision rule. It is not an aspirational idealization because conformity to that rule is not a goal of rationality when that uncertainty is present. The idealization is unnecessary, however, because other idealizations handle the problem it addresses. Because I take options as decisions and assume agents are ideal, options are certain to be realized if adopted. Also, under my idealizations, deliberation is instantaneous. So no agent is uncertain that she can realize an option because she may, for instance, die before deliberation is over. Moreover, strictly speaking, the expected utility decision rule does not require that an agent be certain that she can realize each option. It suffices if she is certain for each option that she will realize it *if* she decides in an appropriate way. This conditional certainty is all the rule requires, and it can obtain even if deliberation and reaching a decision take time. An agent may be certain that if she decides in such and such a way she will realize such and such an option, even if she is not certain she will live long enough to be able to decide in that way.

Taking the viewpoint of the overall goal of rationality and allowing for the assumption that the realization of a chosen option is certain, the entire large idealization about decision situations counts as a justificational idealization because it has components that are not aspirational.

Table 3.2 summarizes the classification of a representative sample of my idealizations for chapter 2's decision principles. The classification of my idealizations for that chapter's utility principles is similar. The table classifies idealizations as aspirational with respect to goals for cases with uncertainty about options' outcomes. Idealizations not classified as aspirational are merely justificational. In the table, an x after an idealization and under a type of idealization indicates that the idealization is that type of idealization, and a blank space indicates that it is not that type. Keeping track of a principle's idealizations and their classification aids theory construction. It points the way to new, more general principles.

TABLE 3.2. Classification of my idealizations for decision principles

	Justificational	Aspirational
Rational ideal agents	x	
Ideal decision situations	x	
Rational agents		x
A priori knowledge		x
Knowledge of beliefs and desires		x
No cognitive limits		x
No prior or subsequent mistakes		x
Quantitative beliefs and desires	x	
Stable basic intrinsic attitudes	x	
Options of maximum utility	x	
No conflicts among subgoals	x	

Although idealizations in decision theory are acceptable, one ultimately wants a decision theory without idealizations. The ultimate objective is a general theory of rational decision making that applies directly to human decisions and so dispenses with idealizations. One way to make progress toward such a theory is to begin with an idealized theory and then remove idealizations one by one, making adjustments to the idealized theory as idealizations are removed. I have already started the process. Section 2.1 advanced a theory for fully informed perfect agents, and the rest of chapter 2 adjusted the theory to accommodate uncertainty and imperfect agents. It required utility to equal expected utility and then introduced the decision principle to maximize expected utility. Chapters 4 through 9 remove additional idealizations. They formulate subsidiary goals for pursuit of the goal of maximizing expected utility when certain obstacles, such as cognitive limitations, stand in the way of expected utility maximization. These goals are expressed in revised principles for decisions and utility assignments.

Removing idealizations increases generality. Does it always increase realism, too? Can decision theory gain generality without gaining realism? Imagine a decision principle that assumes that agents know everything, and a generalization of it that assumes only that they know everything relevant to their decision problems. The gain in generality does not enhance realism. How do my generalizations promote realism?

Generality may promote realism in many ways. It may extend classification of real decisions as rational or irrational. For example, generalizing decision principles to cover nonquantitative cases does this. Even if, contrary to common opinion, nonquantitative cases are rare (so treating such cases does not offer practicality), extending coverage to any real cases adds realism.

Steps toward realism need not involve extended classification of real cases. A generalization for nonquantitative cases, for example, may retain unmet idealizations, such as unlimited cognitive power. Nonetheless, the generalization moves closer to real cases and yields better approximative treatment of them. Also, a principle's dispensing with an idealization may permit new helpful idealizations, as dispensing with certain limits on quantities permits new idealizations offering mathematical tractability. In addition, a principle gains realism by increasing coverage of epistemically possible cases even if in fact they do not arise. Just as a realistic security system guards against epistemically possible threats that may not actually arise, a realistic decision theory covers epistemically possible cases that may not actually arise.

The most important way to promote realism is to enrich explanations of real cases. Generality helps here. Principles do not offer complete explanations unless they are general. For example, a fully explanatory theory of free fall covers the fall of a one-ton diamond even if no such object exists. It covers cases in which magnetic forces halt a meteor's fall even if that never happens. A complete explanation of real cases such as an apple's falling from a tree uses principles that cover nonexistent objects and nonoccuring forces. Even if a principle already covers all real cases despite controlling for some explanatory factor, generalizing the principle by removing control for that factor adds realism to the explanation of those cases.

Consider the principle to maximize utility. Besides classifying decisions according to rationality, it explains the rationality of decisions. Because the principle relies on idealizations, its explanations are incomplete: it does not treat explanatory factors for which its idealizations control. A full explanation of a decision's rationality uses principles that handle all possible cases and explanatory factors. Moreover, for normative explanation, the relevant type of possibility is metaphysical, not just physical. The generalizations that chapters 4–9 make promote realism by moving closer to real cases but especially by enriching normative explanations of real cases.

3.A. Appendix: Debates about Idealizations

The literature on idealizations in decision theory displays a diversity of opinion about the general role of idealizations and the propriety of particular idealizations. This appendix surveys some prominent positions and uses my account of idealizations to respond. It replies to criticisms of decision theory's standard idealizations and evaluates some controversial idealizations.

3.A.1. *Views about Idealizations*

Some theorists deny the value of standard idealizations for decision theory. They say that rationality for ideal agents in ideal situations does not illuminate rationality for humans. For instance, Foley (1993: 158–62) repudiates the common idealization that agents are "perfect calculators." He observes that a person's degree of rationality is not the degree to which she approximates the standards of rationality for ideal agents. A person may be fully rational despite falling short of those standards. This observation is accurate, but justifications for idealizations may appeal to roles besides the measurement of rationality. Section 3.1's justification appeals to the role of idealizations in explanation. A standard of rationality for ideal agents may illuminate factors explaining the rationality of decisions even if the standard is too lofty to measure rationality in humans. For instance, options' utilities clearly are part of the explanation of a rational decision even if maximizing utility is often beyond human capabilities.

Plantinga (1993b: 142–44) criticizes the claim that because ideally rational agents satisfy the rules of Bayesian probability and decision theory, the school to which my rules belong, humans should aspire to comply with those rules. He concedes that in certain simple cases, conformity to probability laws is an ideal appropriate for humans (1993a: viii, 174–75). However, he says that because of human limits and fallibilities, it does not make sense for humans to try to comply with those laws generally. Plantinga's practical advice is sound, but it does not show that compliance with standard probability and decision rules is not an ideal of rationality. Of course, rather than attempt compliance with those rules, it may be better to invest one's time and effort in other, more easily attained goals. A person need not put attainment of ideals of rationality first among her goals. These ideals are just some goals among many that a rational person has. Other goals may compete with and take precedence over them. A rational person seeks to attain them, other things being equal, or in the absence of reasons to the contrary. More precisely, a rational person tries to attain those standards insofar as it is reasonable.

Moreover, even if the principles to which idealizations lead do not express goals of rationality for humans, the idealizations may be theoretically fruitful. The principles they yield may offer partial explanations of rational decision making. Not all idealizations are aspirational and generate principles expressing goals of rationality. Some are merely justificational and control for an explanatory factor. For instance, the idealization that beliefs and desires are quantitative controls for imprecision in belief and desire. It is not expected to yield a goal for agents without quantitative beliefs and desires.

This way of explaining the relevance for humans of standards of rationality for ideal agents appeals to principles of rationality. It says be rational in the pursuit of goals of rationality. The explanation is not viciously circular, however, because rationality is a primitive concept, not a concept defined in terms of goals of rationality. One may use rational pursuit of goals to explain the force of standards of rationality for ideal agents. Rationality furnishes both goals and ways of pursuing goals. The methods of pursuing its goals are the same as the methods of pursuing other goals. Although principles for rational pursuit of goals supplement my account of goals of rationality, an understanding of the goals does not require a formulation of those principles.

Some theorists defend the usefulness of idealized theories of rationality. M. Kaplan (1996: 36) says that his version of Bayesian probability theory presents a regulative ideal. By this, he means that violations of the theory's precepts open one's degrees of belief, or assignments of confidence, to legitimate criticism, even if compliance is not necessary for rationality. Sufficient freedom from legitimate criticism is required for warranted and cogent assignments of confidence (38, 186). Moreover, humans are rationally required to make a reasonable effort to comply with the theory's precepts, even though total compliance is beyond our capabilities (189). A reasonable effort to comply may, for instance, require the cultivation of new intellectual habits (190).

My standards for decisions and utility assignments, if resting on aspirational idealizations only, express regulative ideals in approximately this sense. Rational agents aspire to comply. Violations are mistakes, even if excused. My account of the standards accords with Kaplan's. I elaborate his account by explaining why the standards impose necessary conditions of rationality under my idealizations and by formulating reasonable ways of seeking compliance with those standards when circumstances are nonideal. For instance, I argue for maximizing utility in ideal conditions and show how to pursue that standard in nonideal conditions.

Levi (1997) propounds the usefulness of an idealized theory of rational full belief, a theory analogous in important respects to a Bayesian idealized theory of rational degrees of belief. Full belief, in contrast with partial belief, is certainty or maximum degree of belief. Logic sets standards of rationality for full belief. Levi explains those standards in terms of intellectual commitments:

> We are committed at . . . time *t* to have full beliefs that are logically consistent and to fully believe all the logical consequences of what we fully believe at that time. We no doubt fail to fulfill this commitment and, indeed, cannot do so in forming our doxastic dispositions and in manifesting them linguistically and in our other behavior. We are, nonetheless, committed to doing so in the sense that we are obliged to fulfill the commitment insofar as we are able to do so when the demand arises and, in addition, have an obligation to improve our capacities by training, therapy or the use of prosthetic devices provided that the opportunity is available and the costs are not prohibitive. (41)

Are we committed in this sense to complying with common principles of decision and utility, at least ones resting only on aspirational idealizations? The term commitment applies only metaphorically because we realize our inability to comply fully with those principles. But, yes, we do have obligations to make reasonable efforts to comply with the principles. This chapter explains the origin of those obligations, and subsequent chapters describe their demands when circumstances are nonideal. They proceed along the path Levi marks.

Two immediate points about the obligations are in order. First, an obligation to comply with a decision or utility principle is a requirement of rationality, not an overall obligation. It may be understood as a conditional obligation, an obligation conditional on having rationality as a goal. Even if rationality is an intrinsic good so that it is a mistake not to have rationality as a goal, it is not a moral mistake, and thus the conditional obligation generates no moral and absolute obligation to make reasonable efforts to comply with the principle. Second, the obligation is prima facie and defeasible. Compliance with the principle is a goal of rationality, and the goal generates a prima facie obligation to make reasonable efforts to comply, that is, an obligation to comply, other things being equal. Goals of rationality for ideal agents in ideal circumstances may conflict in nonideal cases. Then it is impossible to meet all the prima facie obligations they generate. Later chapters provide methods of resolving conflicts among the prima facie obligations. They explain how one goal may override another so that the prima facie obligation it generates gains the upper hand.

3.A.2. *Controversial Idealizations*

Although decision theorists recognize the need for idealizations, disagreements arise about the acceptability of certain assumptions advanced as idealizations. My account of idealizations clarifies the status of some controversial assumptions. This section investigates a sample of familiar assumptions to illustrate the type of clarification my account provides. Section 9.A examines in detail Skyrms's (1990a) assumptions concerning principles of strategy for agents with limited cognitive ability.

Jeffrey (1983: 80) uses standard conditional probabilities to define expected desirability or utility. Then, to avoid division by zero when computing the expected utility of a decision's rivals, he assumes that the probability of adopting an option is less than 1 (84–85). For, if an agent is certain he will adopt an option o, so that the probability of any other option o' is zero, then for any state s the ratio $P(s \& o')/P(o')$, that is, the conditional probability $P(s/o')$, is undefined and the expected utility of o' is undefined as well. The assumption that options have probabilities between zero and 1 is cumbersome in an agent's postdecision evaluation of his choice because typically he is certain of the option adopted. Even in deliberations prior to a decision, where options of practical interest have nonzero probabilities, the assumption is unappealing from a theoretical viewpoint. One would like to use the expected utilities of undesirable options to explain why they are not contenders. But if an option is not a contender, it lacks an expected utility. Jeffrey's assumption puts aside a technical problem, but does not put aside a justificatory factor. The assumption is therefore a restriction, not an idealization.

To handle cases where options causally influence states, some theorists impose requirements on the states used in an expected utility analysis of an option's utility. Skyrms (1980a: sec. IIC) requires the states to be causal hypotheses about the consequences of options, and Lewis (1981) requires the states to be dependency hypotheses about the consequences of options. Lewis shows that expected utility analyses honoring these requirements are equivalent to Gibbard and Harper's (1978) analyses using probabilities of counterfactual conditionals: the analyses yield the same rankings of options. Despite their ability to rank options correctly, analyses with these requirements on states are deficient from a theoretical point of view. They make expected utility analysis less general. Also, the requirements are inexplicable given section A.3's pros and cons justification of expected utility analysis. They are restrictions, not idealizations.

Next, take the cognitive ideal of knowing that one will make a rational decision. To defend definitions of expected utility in terms of standard conditional probabilities, Eells (1982: 214) assumes that decision makers meet this cognitive ideal. The assumption affects the computation of expected utilities so defined. In the context of standard assumptions about agents, it screens off information otherwise carried by an agent's choice. The agent knows that his choice provides no evidence he does not have independently of his choice—even if he has not worked out the ramifications of his evidence and the choice it supports.

Horwich (1987: 185–88) criticizes Eells's assumption about agents. Suppose that an agent knows his beliefs and desires, and knows his acts depend only on his beliefs and desires, so that acts and states are probabilistically independent. Then, if there is just one rational decision, Eells's assumption that an agent knows that he will make a rational decision entails his foreknowledge of his decision. Horwich thinks this consequence makes Eells's assumption an inappropriate idealization, because if an agent knows which act he will perform, deliberation is pointless.

Eells's assumption does not actually make deliberation pointless. An agent may deliberate using knowledge that he will make a rational decision to reach a rational decision. It is not circular, for instance, to use the rationality of eventual degrees of desire for options to support the rationality of forming those degrees of desire in certain ways. Deliberation is not pointless if an agent's foreknowledge of his decision comes as the culmination of deliberation, having the rationality of his decision as a starting point. Still, one wonders whether Eells's assumption is an appropriate idealization. Although it merely presumes attainment of a cognitive ideal, it may seem inappropriate as an idealization because it seems to distort deliberations: it puts information about the outcome of deliberations into the input for deliberations.

How does my account of idealizations classify Eells's assumption? First, it asks whether the assumption removes a factor in the justification of decisions. The assumption does this. It puts aside a justificatory factor, the uncertainty that one will make a rational choice. Hence, Eells's assumption qualifies as a justificational idealization. Next, my account of idealizations asks whether his assumption removes an obstacle to meeting a goal of rationality. By putting aside some uncertainty, the assumption does this, too, and so qualifies as an aspirational idealization. The supplementary tests for an aspirational idealization are also positive. The assumption's realization is a goal of rationality. It is a goal of rationality to decide rationally and a goal of rationality to possess information relevant to a decision's outcome, which, as Eells points, out may include information that one will decide rationally. So it is a goal of rationality to know with certainty that one decides rationally. Also, although the standard of rationality for cases where the assumption holds is a matter of controversy, its correct formulation, whatever it is, plausibly expresses a goal of rationality for other cases.

Being an aspirational idealization is relative to a goal of rationality. So, for a decisive classification of Eells's assumption, one should apply the basic criterion for aspirational idealizations. One should identify a goal and an obstacle to the goal such that the idealization removes the obstacle. These steps can be carried out, too. Eells's assumption is an aspirational idealization with respect to the goal of maximizing informed utility. It removes a type of uncertainty that may thwart that goal. Furthermore, an accurate decision principle stated under Eells's assumption expresses a restricted goal, a goal given the principle's other assumptions and given uncertainty, except possibly about one's making a rational decision. This goal imagines an agent who has uncertainty but may have certainty about one subject. Eells's assumption provides certainty about that subject. It removes an obstacle to the restricted goal. Given the goal's restrictions, agents uncertain of making a rational decision should strive to reach that goal. They should strive to reach the decision that would be required if they were certain they would decide in a rational way.

Eells's assumption is an aspirational idealization relative to each of the two goals mentioned. In contrast, Eells's assumption is not an aspirational idealization relative to the goal of maximizing utility. The assumption does not remove an obstacle to that goal. An agent may meet the goal despite being uncertain of making a rational decision. The goal is more general than the restricted goal that Eells's principle expresses.

Although Eells's assumption is a fruitful idealization, it still must be removed to achieve a general decision theory, one that identifies rational decisions even in cases where an agent will make an irrational decision. My decision theory dispenses with Eells's assumption. I take an ideal agent to be in a fully rational state of mind at the time of decision so that the input for decision rules is rational. But I regard an ideal agent as possibly without knowledge that he will make a rational choice. The theory I construct under my weaker idealizations makes progress toward a general theory.

As another example of the way my account of idealizations resolves controversies about the appropriateness of certain assumptions, consider standard assumptions for games of strategy. It is often assumed that the agents in such games are rational and have *common knowledge* of their rationality: each knows that all are rational, knows that each knows that all are rational, and so on. This assumption does not entail that an agent necessarily makes a rational choice. An agent is still capable of irrational choice. Although she makes a rational choice, in some counterfactual situations she makes an irrational choice (assuming not all options are rational). So the assumption provides for strategic reasoning about the possibility of irrational choices. But the assumption does have as a consequence Eells's assumption that an agent knows he will make a rational choice. Like Eells's assumption, the assumption of common knowledge is appropriate as a justificational idealization because it puts aside a justificatory factor, an uncertainty about the agents in the game. It is also an aspirational idealization relative to the goal of maximizing informed utility.

Another common assumption for games of strategy is that agents know the agents' choices. The assumption of common knowledge undergirds this assumption in certain types of games. The assumption of knowledge of agents' choices plainly puts aside uncertainty about agents' behavior. It is a justificational idealization and also an aspirational idealization relative to the goal of maximizing informed utility. But if taken with common knowledge of the agents' rationality, it is appropriate only if it specifies that the agents infer their own choices from information supplied by other idealizations and do not know them directly. Normative game theory seeks to explain the rationality of certain choices, and this requires explaining an agent's knowledge of his rational choices. To be explanatory, knowledge of rational choices cannot be used in deliberations yielding those choices. Deliberation should yield by inference the choices an agent may make if rational. Knowledge of rational choices should not be part of the input for deliberations yielding an agent's rational choices. Idealizations cannot give an agent direct knowledge of his rational choices without defeating theoretical objectives. Some idealizations, when used together, must be adjusted for each other if they are to serve their explanatory functions.

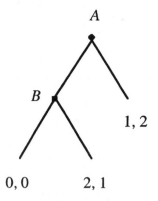

FIGURE 3.3. Backward induction.

As a final example, consider assumptions made for backward induction in game theory, a topic of, for example, Bicchieri (1989), Sobel (1994: chap. 16; 2000), and Rabinowicz (1998). These assumptions are advanced for backward induction in games such as the Centipede Game and repeated Prisoner's Dilemmas and not for general principles of rational decision. So I ask whether they are idealizations or restrictions for backward induction.

To illustrate backward induction, consider the two-stage game depicted in figure 3.3. Agent A moves left or right. Then Agent B moves left or right. The outcomes at the ends of branches list, first, the payoff for Agent A and then the payoff for Agent B. Agent A reasons that if she goes left, Agent B will go right because then he receives 1 rather than 0. She concludes that if she goes left, she will receive 2. Hence, she goes left rather than right to receive 2 rather than 1. Backward induction moves from the end of a game to its start computing the choices of agents. The example assumes that the agents are rational and maximize payoffs.

To apply backward induction, Sobel (1994: chap. 16) adopts the assumption that agents are resiliently rational so that if, contrary to fact, they were irrational, they would continue to be convinced of their rationality in the future. In each round of an extended game it is as if agents perceive anew their own rationality and the rationality of others, and the perception swamps any contrary evidence from past behavior. Alternatively, it is as if they have no memory of past behavior. Rabinowicz (1998: 97) objects that Sobel's assumption is unwarranted because it puts aside learning from experience. Indeed, the assumption is not an aspirational idealization because it is not a goal of rationality to prevent learning from experience or to achieve behavior that is rational given the irrelevance of experience. The lessons of experience are not obstacles to any goal of rationality. On the other hand, in multistage games, experience in a game's past stages is a justificatory factor for a decision in a current stage. So Sobel's assumption, which puts that experience aside, qualifies as a justificational idealization.

Realism about Agents:
Resources

To move toward realism, I dispense with some idealizations about the psychology of agents. This chapter removes the idealization that agents make the quantitative probability and utility assignments required for expected utility analysis. The next chapter removes the idealization that agents have total, unhindered access to their probability and utility assignments. These chapters extend my theory to cases where the quantities used to compute expected utilities do not exist or are not known. They introduce estimates to substitute for missing quantities and explain how maximization principles treat the cost of discovering quantities that exist but are unknown.

My idealizations about agents concern their rationality and cognitive resources. This chapter retains the idealization that agents are fully rational. Its goal is to remove some idealizations about their cognitive resources. The idealizations removed concern the psychological input for decision rules, not an agent's cognitive ability to process it. When I remove the idealizations, new obstacles thwart expected utility maximization. How should an agent pursue the primary goal of making an optimal decision given these additional obstacles? Specifying the appropriate method of pursuit expresses a new, secondary decision goal, a goal subordinate to the goal of optimization in the way that maximizing expected utility is subordinate to optimization. Just as, given uncertainty and section 3.2's idealizations, maximizing expected utility is the best way to pursue the goal of optimization, given the additional obstacles and this chapter's weaker idealizations a new decision method is the best way to pursue that goal. Following the new method is a secondary goal more realistic than maximizing expected utility given the additional obstacles.

4.1. Revised Idealizations and Goals

This chapter continues to suppose that an agent knows all a priori truths, such as the principles of utility analysis and the logical and mathematical truths involved in their application. It also continues to suppose that an agent can effortlessly conduct utility analyses. It studies impediments to utility analysis that arise for a computationally adept agent equipped with a priori knowledge, in particular, impediments that arise if the probabilities and utilities grounding utility analysis are not available. They may be unavailable either because they do not exist—the nonquantitative case—or because cognitive limitations prevent or inhibit access to them—the case of restricted access. The next chapter treats the case of restricted access. This chapter treats the nonquantitative case. It rescinds my idealization about the existence of the quantitative probabilities and utilities necessary for utility analysis. It considers cases where some options lack utilities and asks which options are rational then.

In cases with missing quantities, classificatory and comparative probability and utility judgments may direct decisions, for example, judgments that some event is probable, judgments that some event is more probable than another event, and judgments that some outcome is more utile than another outcome. Because the relevant types of probability and utility are subjective, involving belief and desire, these are not judgments that something is the case, but rather classificatory and comparative assessments. For example, a judgment that one outcome is more utile than another outcome is just a preference for the first outcome. The classificatory and comparative probability and utility judgments form the classificatory and comparative counterparts of quantitative probability and utility assessments, and do not constitute judgments about those quantitative assessments, which may not exist.

In nonquantitative cases the principle to maximize utility may not apply because options' utilities may not exist. The absence of crucial probabilities and utilities may prevent computing them according to principles of expected utility analysis. However, in such cases, the principle to optimize may still apply. It requires only comparison of options, not a quantitative utility assignment for each option. To extend its scope to cases where some comparisons are missing, one may formulate it this way: realize an option such that no option is better. Then, despite uncompared options, compliance is possible as long as some option is not definitely inferior to any option. Furthermore, to allow for uncertainty, the principle may shift from betterness to preference. It may say the following:

Realize an option such that no option is preferred.

This version of the principle expresses a goal of rationality for decisions facing uncertainty and imprecision. I say that the goal is to pick a *top option*. Picking a top option is a way of pursuing optimization, which is defined in terms of subjective betterness, or fully informed preference. It is a secondary goal for pursuit of the primary goal of optimization, picking a best or unbested option. When there is no danger of confusion, however, I conflate the distinction between primary and secondary goals and, for brevity, call the goal of picking a top option the goal of optimization.

This chapter's task is akin to the discovery of principles of utility analysis. It seeks principles of preference that flesh out the decision rule to pick a top option, just as principles of utility analysis flesh out the decision rule to maximize utility. Rather than separate the decision rule of optimization and the principles of preference, however, section 4.4 restates the decision rule of optimization in a way that incorporates the principles of preference. The decision rule to maximize expected utility makes a similar move. It restates the rule to maximize utility in a way that incorporates expected utility analysis of options' utilities.

Other theorists advance the optimization rule just presented and section 4.4's restatement of it. This chapter strengthens the case for both versions of the optimization rule. Section 4.4's argument for the rule's restatement simultaneously supports the principles of preference it incorporates and the basic optimization rule it elaborates.

4.2. Probability and Utility

Expected utility analyses furnish ways of computing options' utilities. But agents often lack the requisite probabilities and utilities. They often have not made the necessary quantitative probability and utility assignments. For instance, an agent deciding about having a picnic may not assign a precise probability to good weather, or a precise utility to having a successful picnic. Then he may not be able to apply expected utility analysis to compute the utility of going on a picnic. The problem is to specify rational decisions in such cases. Chapter 2 treated cases where information is rich enough to generate quantitative probability and utility assignments. This chapter treats cases where information is less rich.[1]

To begin, I clarify my interpretation of probability and utility, enriching chapter 2's account. I establish that quantitative probability and utility assignments are possible; some mental states do indeed generate them, *pace* theorists such as Pollock (1986: 100–102). Nonquantitative cases arise when the grounds of quantitative probability and utility assignments are absent. This happens commonly, but not inevitably. A clear view of the possibility of quantitative cases and the origin of nonquantitative cases suggests suitable principles for nonquantitative cases.

The mental states that probabilities and utilities represent, although primitive theoretical entities, are not basic psychological states like qualia. They are not sensations and feelings, *pace* Cohen (1992: 4, 115), who holds that beliefs and degrees of belief are cognitive feelings. They have a functional role that connects them to choice. Although I do not define probabilities and utilities in terms of choices, one may infer probabilities and utilities from choices, using a representation theorem such as Savage's (1972: chap. 3). Let me explain their midlevel psychological status.

Some theorists, for example, Russell (1938: secs. 155–58) and Kripke (1980: 54–56, 75–76), take empirical quantities, such as lengths, to express basic intrinsic quantitative empirical properties called *magnitudes*. Magnitudes are properties that are quantitative independently of their possessor's relation to anything else. They are not relational properties. Other theorists, such as Krantz, Luce, Suppes, and Tversky (1971: chap. 1), take every empirical quantity to express a position in an empirical relational structure. As operationalists do, they claim that empirical quantities express empirical relations, not empirical magnitudes. Hence, attaching a length to a single object in isolation from other objects is not meaningful. An object does not possess length independently of its relation to other objects. The object's length only encodes information about the object's empirical relations to other objects, for example, the information that it is longer than some objects, shorter than others, and just as long as still other objects.[2]

My interpretation of probabilities and utilities falls between the two views just sketched. Unlike operationalists, I sanction quantities that do not express empirical relations. I recognize both quantities that express empirical relations and quantities that express basic intrinsic quantitative empirical properties. But I do not take probabilities and utilities as quantities of either type. They fall into a third category.

To introduce the third type of quantity, let me start with an example. When a pollster asks a respondent to rate a political candidate on a scale from 1 to 10, representing worst to best, and the respondent assigns the candidate an 8, the rating expresses an intrinsic property of the respondent's attitude toward the candidate even if his attitude is not quantitative in a basic intrinsic way. The rating expresses a summary of the respondent's attitude toward the candidate in the way an average expresses a summary of a set of numbers. The property of the attitude expressed is not a basic intrinsic quantitative property because, as a set's average derives from other properties of the set, it derives from other properties of the respondent's attitude. But it is an intrinsic quantitative property because, as a set's average does not derive from relations of the set to other sets, it does not derive from relations of the respondent's attitude to his other attitudes. The rating, of course, implies attitudinal comparisons of the candidate with other candidates also rated. But the rating may be independent of such comparisons. The respondent may rate just a single candidate. Moreover, if he rates more than one candidate, it may be that his ratings explain the attitudinal comparisons they imply rather than that the comparisons explain his ratings.

Following Jeffrey (1992: 29), I take probabilities and utilities to express properties of mental states that are not necessarily basic intrinsic quantitative properties. Probabilities and utilities are quantities in a scheme of representation for mental states but do not necessarily have analogs in the mental states represented. A quantitative probability, for instance, may represent a belief state that is not quantitative in a basic intrinsic way. It has a role similar to a numerical grade's role in the representation of an essay's quality. A numerical grade represents an essay's quality even though the essay has no basic intrinsic quantitative property that the grade expresses. Numerical representation of properties that are not quantitative in a basic intrinsic way is possible because representation need not be analog; it need not work by exemplification.[3]

I take probabilities and utilities to numerically represent belief and desire states that are intrinsically quantitative, but not necessarily quantitative in a basic intrinsic way. Consider, for instance, an agent who believes that a ball is drawn from one of eleven urns randomly selected and that the proportion of red balls in the urns is, respectively, 0%, 10%, . . . , and 100%. For him, the probability of a red ball is 0.5. But this does not entail that he have a belief state with the basic intrinsic property of being of degree 0.5. An analog representation of his belief state may not be a single degree of belief, but rather figure 4.1's probability distribution function over degrees of belief. The distribution function assigns probabilities (which sum

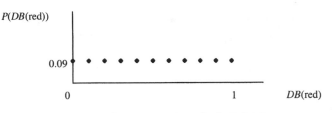

FIGURE 4.1. A representation of a belief state.

to 1) to degrees of belief that the ball is red. For example, $P(DB(red) = 0.5)$ equals 0.09. That probability represents the strength of an inclination to form that degree of belief. That red's probability is 0.5 then represents the agent's belief state in summary fashion. It does not express a basic intrinsic quantitative feature of his belief state. The representation of the belief state by a probability distribution function does not imply that the probability of a red ball is indeterminate, but rather that the belief state expressed by the probability is not quantitative in a basic intrinsic way.

Taking probabilities as intrinsically quantitative, but not necessarily quantitative in a basic intrinsic way, allows for the possibility that different belief states have the same probability representation. For instance, the probability of red is also 0.5 in a case where the agent knows that the draw comes from the urn containing 50% red balls. Hence, in my view, probabilities are undiscriminating representations of belief states.

Does the lack of discrimination confound my decision rules? No, the difference between the belief states represented by a probability assignment of 0.5 is noticed by my principles of utility analysis. It influences utilities even if it does not influence probabilities. In my example, the utility of a dollar gamble that red is drawn after random selection of an urn may be less than the utility of a dollar gamble that red is drawn from the urn with 50% red balls, even though the probability of red is the same in each case. For a typical agent, the first gamble is riskier and has possible outcomes of lower utility despite having identical possible monetary payoffs. The difference in belief states thus affects decisions through attitudes toward risk rather than through probabilities.[4]

To make the same point more graphically, consider the two belief states figure 4.2 depicts. The same probability 0.5 represents both belief states. Given risk neutrality, the difference in belief states does not matter for decisions. Given aversion to risk, it affects the utility assignment for outcomes. The point representation is therefore adequate for the probability's role in expected and intrinsic utility analyses. According to my view, a probability is a belief state's best representation for decision purposes. Probabilities depict the essences of belief states for decision principles and ignore other features of belief states.

A utility assignment may likewise represent in summary fashion a desire state that is divided among several basically intrinsic quantitative states. Such a divided state is a source of risk, and hence the utility of a possible outcome of an option, if it summarizes such a divided state, is lower than it would be without the division,

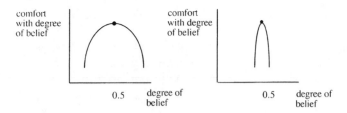

FIGURE 4.2. Belief states conflated by probability.

assuming an aversion to risk. A utility assignment in such circumstances represents an equilibrium between the elements of the divided desire state and the reduction in their intensity that their multiplicity causes.

The foregoing interpretation of probabilities and utilities is incomplete. I have not specified the properties that probabilities and utilities express. I have not said when belief and desire states lack quantitative representations and when they have more than one quantitative representation. A genuinely indeterminate probability occurs when a belief state has no unique best representation—when there is none or several. But I do not say when this happens. I issue only a promissory note, hoping to honor it on another occasion. For now, I make do with my partial interpretation of probabilities and utilities. What is crucial for the task at hand is, first, that probabilities and utilities imply intrinsic properties of mental states, not just relational structures, which is why they can explain the relational structures, and, second, that they do not imply basic intrinsic quantitative properties of mental states, which is why their existence is more realistic than some theorists allow. For convenience, I continue to call probabilities and utilities degrees of belief and desire, respectively, as in chapter 2, but they may be summaries of complex mental states rather than simple, precise mental states.

My interpretation of probabilities and utilities makes them more realistic than some interpretations do, but does not by any means ensure that the probabilities and utilities needed to compute options' utilities exist in every decision problem. In many cases, an agent's belief and desire states do not have unique quantitative representations. In these nonquantitative cases, utility analysis does not apply directly, and realism requires an extension of my decision theory. The next section explores nonquantitative cases, and the following section extends my decision theory to them.

4.3. Indeterminate Probabilities and Utilities

An agent's utility assignment to an option is the agent's degree of desire to realize the option all things considered. It depends on the agent's information and, more directly, his probability assignment to the option's possible outcomes. Expected utility analysis explains this dependency. According to it, an option's utility takes an option as a means to its possible outcomes. The utility indicates an *extrinsic desire*, a desire concerning a means. In contrast, an agent's desire for a maximally specific outcome, a possible world, is independent of information. It is a desire concerning an end, an *intrinsic desire*.

Following tradition, a world's utility may be analyzed in terms of the basic intrinsic desires and aversions it realizes. Section A.2 presents this method of analysis, which I call *intrinsic utility analysis*. It introduces *intrinsic utility*, which rests on intrinsic attitudes and which equals ordinary, extrinsic utility when both are applied to a world. Basic intrinsic utilities, together with appropriate probabilities, may be used to compute an option's utility. The method of computation, which section A.5 presents, I also call intrinsic utility analysis.

In brief, there are many ways of analyzing an option's utility. Besides expected utility analysis and intrinsic utility analysis, temporal utility analysis is also traditional. Broome (1991: chap. 2) presents it. He argues for a way of dividing an option's utility according to the temporal intervals during which the option produces gains or losses. Moreover, each form of utility analysis may be applied in many ways. Expected utility analysis, for example, may be applied with respect to any partition of states. Consequently, if an option's utility is indeterminate, no valid form of utility analysis generates the option's utility. An indeterminate utility resists computation according to any method of applying any form of utility analysis.

A decision problem pressures an agent to form probability and utility judgments yielding a preference ranking of options. However, a rational agent does not complete relevant probability and utility judgments in the absence of psychological grounding just to have them on hand for decision purposes. Rational judgments rest on the agent's cognitive or conative features. For instance, suppose that an agent has not made a preference comparison of two options, that is, either formed a preference or become indifferent. She need not proceed to make a preference comparison of them just to complete her preference ordering of options. All her preference comparisons must rest on her conative features (in the case of basic intrinsic preference comparisons, appropriate conative experiences) so that the comparisons reflect something deeper than themselves and are genuine. If nothing conative settles a preference comparison, an agent should suspend judgment.

There are two reasons for this stand. First, completion of relevant probability and utility judgments is not necessary for a decision. A decision among options need not be based on a preference ordering of the options. Even if some preference comparisons are suspended, an agent can still make a rational decision among the options. A decision is an opportunity to satisfy one's preferences, and if one's preferences dictate a certain choice, one ought to make it. But a rational decision need not satisfy preferences: one may not have made any preference comparisons concerning the options. Second, completing the preference ordering of options before reaching a decision carries a commitment in future decisions. If one completes the preference ordering, then future decisions must also honor that preference ordering (unless it changes in a grounded way). Such commitment is an unnecessary burden if the completion of the preference ordering is not justified by one's conative features. It is better to make the current decision without tying one's hands with respect to future decisions.[5]

Under this chapter's idealizations, agents have perfect minds. For cognitively perfect agents, thinking is instantaneous and cost-free. Hence, in a decision problem, where an agent is motivated to make probability and utility assignments that will assist his decision through the formation of preferences among options, the absence of the probabilities and utilities needed for utility analysis's application signals some impediment to their formation.

For probability assignments, shortage of information is an impediment. An agent's information about relevant possible states of the world may be too incomplete to serve as the basis for probability assignments. In fact, her information may be so incomplete that rationality requires suspension of probability assignments. Probabilities are degrees of belief, and the standards for them stem from the standards for belief. Because two primary cognitive goals for belief are truth and error avoidance, a secondary cognitive goal for degree of belief is an evidential foundation. When information is incomplete, this cognitive goal may require suspension of judgment, that is, no assignment of probability. For instance, a person's information about the weather may be so deficient that it would be irrational for her to assign a precise probability to rain tomorrow.

Utility assignments face two impediments. First, the incompleteness of an agent's information may block utility assignments. For instance, an agent may not assign a utility to winning a lottery because he does not know the prize. Because an agent lacks information about an option's outcome given some state, he may be unable to determine the degree to which his basic intrinsic desires would be satisfied if he were to realize the option and the state obtains. Thus, he may be unable to assign a precise utility for the option-state pair.

Rationality may even require suspension of utility assignments. Suspension may be required because information is insufficient for assigning probabilities to an option's possible outcomes and so insufficient for a quantitative estimate of its outcome's utility. If an agent has no reason for assigning a utility to an option in the absence of detailed information about the option's possible outcomes and he lacks that information, it is clearly irrational for him arbitrarily to assign a utility to the option. Nonbasic utility assignments require reasons.

Second, the absence of intrinsic utility assignments to an option's possible outcomes may block the option's utility assignment. The possible outcomes' intrinsic utilities may be absent, for example, because the outcomes are incomparable. Perhaps the agent finds culinary and musical pleasures too dissimilar to compare. Despite practical incentives to make comparisons, he cannot. Then he cannot quantitatively assess an option that offers chances for both.[6]

The intrinsic utility assignments may also be absent because the agent lacks experience necessary for assessing the possible outcomes. As Plato (1973: 306–9) observes in *The Republic* when discussing the lives of fortune, fame, and wisdom, a rational person hesitates to form preferences concerning things about which he lacks experience. What holds for preferences holds double for quantitative utility assignments. It would be difficult, even for a perfect mind, to sensibly assign intrinsic utilities to states of affairs in the absence of relevant experience. For instance, it would be difficult to assign intrinsic utility to tasting pineapple in ignorance of its taste, or to assign intrinsic utilities to eating items on the menu in an Ethiopian restaurant, even given their full descriptions, in the absence of experience with Ethiopian cuisine. Similarly, it would be difficult to assign intrinsic utility to the pleasure of visiting France if one has had no experience with that country. Understanding of a proposition may be independent of such firsthand experience, but the experience may be needed to entertain a proposition in the vivid way required for its intrinsic utility assessment. Intrinsic utility assesses only logical consequences, but its limited scope and its freedom from empirical information are no help if logical consequences are not entertained vividly.[7]

It may even be irrational for an agent to assign an intrinsic utility to a proposition in the absence of relevant experience. The argument is more complex than the argument for suspension of probability or (extrinsic) utility assignments. Intrinsic utility assignments do not need reasons (although in some cases there may be reasons). Rationality is permissive with respect to intrinsic utility, or degree of intrinsic desire. Rationality does not require all intrinsic desires to be founded in experience, as it requires all beliefs to be founded in evidence. There are no general cognitive goals for intrinsic desire analogous to truth for belief. The main reason is that, whereas any belief can be mistaken, most intrinsic desires cannot be mistaken. The only exceptions are intrinsic desires that disagree with intrinsic values, but these exceptions are limited. Every plausible theory of intrinsic value leaves intrinsic desire plenty of freedom. Intrinsic desires that result from exercising this freedom cannot be mistaken. So there is no general requirement that experience furnish reasons for intrinsic desires.

Although intrinsic desires need not rest on reasons drawn from experience, there are constraints concerning experience on the formation of intrinsic desires. Suppose a person intrinsically prefers the taste of pineapple to the taste of coconut even though he has tasted neither fruit, or even received the testimony of those who have tasted them or other secondary evidence about the fruits' tastes. Then his preference is irrational. It is irrational even though there is no requirement that his experience provide reasons for the preference. His preference is irrational simply because he ought not to form a preference in the absence of experiences making the objects of his preference vivid. Suspension of intrinsic desire is required if the agent does not know enough about the subject to ground an intrinsic desire. Before judging something on its intrinsic merits, one ought to understand it and in some cases understand it vividly. Even though rationality does not require that experience provide reasons for intrinsic preferences, it does require that experience precede some intrinsic preferences. It imposes a similar requirement for intrinsic utility assignments, too. Thus, in some cases, an agent may be required to suspend an intrinsic utility assignment, just as he may be required to suspend a probability assignment or (extrinsic) utility assignment.

Some decision theorists hold that in an ideal case where a fully rational agent has unlimited cognitive power and can think without cost, probabilities and utilities will be formed. The absence of probabilities and utilities in real-life cases, they claim, is a result of not thinking hard enough. Suppose, for instance, that an agent's comparative probability judgments are complete. Those judgments entail quantitative probability judgments in accordance with standard representation theorems, as in Savage (1972: chap. 3). To illustrate, imagine that a picnicker compares the probability of rain to the probability of outcomes of gambling devices. Also imagine that rain is more probable than drawing a heart and less probable than drawing another suit. As the probability of rain is more and more circumscribed by similar comparisons, its value becomes settled, perhaps as a limit of a sequence of intervals confining it more and more narrowly.

Resnik (1987: 24) holds that a complete preference ranking of gambles is a goal of rationality, one met by rational ideal agents in ideal circumstances. As noted, such a complete preference ranking circumscribes quantitative probability and utility judgments so that if an agent makes a probability or utility assignment at all, she must assign a particular value. Then, in a decision problem where quantitative assignments are useful, they are made with the prescribed value, given my ideal-izations. Assuming the cognitive goal Resnik advances and the additional goal of having quantitative probability and utility assignments, and assuming that no standard of rationality prohibits the formation of quantitative probability and utility assignments, a rational ideal agent in ideal circumstances has complete probability and utility assignments.[8]

This case for quantitative probability and utility assignments is not compel-ling, however. Even in ideal cases comparative judgments may be incomplete, and then quantitative probabilities and utilities may be indeterminate. In some ideal cases not all propositions are compared with respect to probability or utility. For instance, consider the propositions that it will rain in Chicago tomorrow and that interest rates will rise sometime next year. A reasonable agent may fail to rank these propositions according to probability. In general, there may be propositions p and q such that it is not the case that p is more probable than q, it is not the case that p is less probable than q, and it is not the case that p is just as probable as q. Similarly, a preference ranking of gambles may be incomplete. Even if agents are forced to choose between gambles, their choices need not reveal preferences. A complete preference ranking of gambles is not a goal of rationality. Rationality is content with incomplete preference rankings when information is short. In fact, rationality may prohibit preference formation in the face of an information shortage. Just as one should suspend belief when information is insufficient to justify a belief, one should suspend the formation of preferences when information is insufficient to justify them. In that case, probabilities and utilities may be indeterminate. Without the requisite preferences, the representation theorems are of no avail. Without information, cognitive power cannot generate well-founded probability and utility assignments.[9]

To summarize, the rule to maximize expected utility is inapplicable when options lack expected utilities because subjective probabilities of states and utilities of outcomes are not quantitative. Similarly, the rule to maximize utility cannot be applied when options lack utilities. Probabilities may be indeterminate when there is insufficient information for a quantitative assignment. Utilities may be indeter-minate when there is insufficient information for requisite probability assignments, when there is insufficient experience for requisite intrinsic utility assignments, or when those assignments' objects are incomparable. Quantitative probabilities and utilities may be nonexistent even though decision problems exert practical pres-sures to form them. Rationality may prohibit their formation despite those practical pressures. The result may be an incomplete preference ordering of options that leaves the set of top options indeterminate.[10]

4.4. Quantizations' Reply to Indeterminacy

I have reviewed the reasons why the probabilities and utilities needed to apply utility analysis may be missing. Next, I consider what remains to serve as the basis of a decision in the absence of those probabilities and utilities. One may at first say that an agent should simply use whatever probability and utility judgments she has made. A decision need not rest on a complete preference ordering of options. Even if current probability and utility judgments are insufficient for constructing a preference ordering of options, decision making may proceed. Simply pick an option such that none is preferred. In an extreme case without any preferences between options, any option will do.

This response ignores the role of preference formation prior to decision. Latent preferences ought to be given a chance to emerge before a decision is reached. A decision ought to be responsive to latent preferences between options, as well as patent preferences, in cases where thinking is instantaneous and cost-free. An agent may have failed to reach some relevant probability and utility judgments prior to her current decision problem simply because her attention has never before been directed to their topics. If thinking is instantaneous and cost-free, then before deciding, even if quantitative judgments are inappropriate, an agent should as far as warranted form relevant classificatory and comparative probability and utility judgments.

How does an agent follow this advice? Two cases arise. First, suppose that probability and utility judgments already made, together with rules of rationality, imply additional relevant judgments. If so, then the agent makes those judgments. For instance, some preferences and the rule of transitivity may imply an additional relevant preference. Then the agent forms that preference. Second, suppose that if the agent reflected in an appropriate way, she would make additional relevant probability and utility judgments. If so, then the agent reflects and makes those judgments. For instance, it may be that if the agent were to consider two options in a vivid and thoughtful way, then she would form a basic intrinsic preference for the first option. In this case, the agent reflects and forms the preference. These new judgments cohere with earlier probability and utility judgments because by assumption the agent is fully rational except possibly in her decision. For the same reason, the new judgments do not infringe on any requirement to suspend judgment.

Standards of rationality for probability and utility judgments constrain the additional judgments. Although I do not specify these standards fully, because my primary topic is decision and only secondarily probability and utility, I nonetheless point out that they go beyond the probability calculus, expected and intrinsic utility analyses, and their implications. For example, various substantive and procedural rules constrain intrinsic desires. Few substantive rules are noncontroversial, but one traditional rule prohibits an intrinsic desire for pain and another requires an intrinsic desire for happiness.[11] One plausible procedural rule, discussed earlier, requires that intrinsic desires be formed in vivid awareness of their objects.[12]

Also, noncontroversial substantive rules constrain the formation of beliefs given one's information. Quantitative beliefs are governed not only by the coherence requirements of the probability calculus, but also by content-sensitive regulations such as Lewis's Principal Principle (1986b: 86–87), which demands that the subjective probability of an event equal its objective probability if known. When these substantive rules leave some slack, is the agent free to pick it up according to his cognitive tastes, or should he suspend judgment? I do not take a stand on subjectivism concerning probability but claim only, as earlier, that on some occasions the scantiness of one's information requires suspension of judgment. I do not also assert, against subjectivism, that one is never free to exercise cognitive tastes in probability judgments. However, granting that one is free to pick up slack left by substantive rules according to one's cognitive tastes, then some procedural rules apply. For example, one should have relevant information vividly in mind and reflect on it before exercising one's cognitive tastes.

Suppose, then, that an agent's decision problem has focused her attention on relevant options, states, and outcomes. After extending relevant probability and utility judgments as far as warranted, she still does not have a preference ordering of her options.[13] Probability and utility assignments for options' possible outcomes do not yield utility judgments about options that in turn yield a ranking of options. Preference comparisons of options are incomplete and insufficient for ascertaining that all and only certain options are at least as good as all other options. What options are rational?

An option is rational just in case it is sufficiently supported by reasons. Being sufficiently supported is being at least as choiceworthy as other options. I seek a criterion that does not identify just one option that is at least as choiceworthy as others but rather identifies the set of options that are each at least as choiceworthy as others. To obtain a criterion, I have to explore the reasons for and against choices and see how far they go beyond the reasons for preferences among options.

Are there reasons for choices that are not reasons for preferences among options? An agent chooses an option to resolve a decision problem. The need to resolve the problem furnishes a reason for a choice that need not also be a reason for preferences among options, because making a choice does not demand a preference ranking of options. However, the need to resolve the decision problem is the only reason for a choice that is independent of reasons for preferences. All other reasons discriminate among options and so are grounds for preferences. What about reasons against choices? Are there any such reasons that are not reasons for preferences among options? None appears. A reason against an option is a reason for an alternative and so a reason for a preference. These observations prompt classifying as rational any option that reasons for preference rankings do not condemn. Every such option responds to all reasons for choices and contravenes no reason against choices.

To make the standard precise, I adopt a test that identifies the options that reasons for preference rankings let pass: embeddability in a quantitative model of belief and desire. This standard appeals to certain quantitative extensions of the agent's belief and desire states, including intrinsic desire states, or, assuming rationality, extensions of his probability and utility judgments, including intrinsic utility judgments. The extensions are quantitative probability and utility assignments to relevant options, states, outcomes, and objects of basic intrinsic attitudes.

They are compatible with the agent's established probability and utility judgments and comply with all probability and utility principles. Following Jeffrey (1983: chap. 6), I call these probability and utility assignments *quantizations* of the agent's probability and utility judgments.

A quantization of an agent's probability and utility judgments is a representation of the agent's beliefs and desires by means of probability and utility functions. A quantization agrees with current probability and utility judgments and makes them precise in ways that conform with probability and utility principles. For example, suppose an agent judges that rain tomorrow is more probable than heads on a coin toss, that is, has a probability greater than 0.5. Then, according to one quantization of this judgment, $P(\text{rain}) = 0.8$ and according to another, $P(\text{rain}) = 0.6$. The probability and utility judgments generating the set of quantizations are also the judgments every quantization entails.

Assuming that an agent's probability and utility judgments have been extended as far as warranted, his decision is rational if and only if it maximizes utility under a quantization of those judgments, as Good (1952: 114) contends. The following decision rule expresses this view:

> *Quantization.* Choose an option that maximizes utility under some quantization of your probability and utility judgments.

Another formulation of the rule is: Choose an option at the top of the preference ranking of options according to some quantization of your probability and utility judgments. This rule may be divided into the rule to choose a top option, one such that none is preferred, and also the principle that preferences among options should agree with an ordering of options established by some quantization of your probability and utility judgments. Appeal to quantizations just makes explicit the implications of utility analysis for preferences among options.

The quantization rule is a generalization of the rule to maximize utility for nonideal cases in which quantitative probabilities and utilities do not exist. It does not require probability and utility judgments with any particular structure or degree of precision. It works even given only trivial probability and utility judgments. In conditions ideal except for uncertainty and imprecision, an agent's decision is rational if and only if it complies with the rule. Maximizing utility under a quantization is both necessary and sufficient for rationality. In contrast, maximizing utility is sufficient for rationality, but necessary only if all options have utilities.

To illustrate the rule, suppose that in my meteorological example the agent's probability and utility judgments extend as far as warranted, and yet his judgment about rain is still only that its probability is greater than 0.5. Should he pay $0.70 for a gamble that pays $1.00 if it rains tomorrow and nothing otherwise? Given that the only relevant consequences are monetary and an amount of money equals its utility, betting maximizes utility with respect to the quantization in which $P(\text{rain}) = 0.8$. Not betting maximizes utility with respect to the quantization in which $P(\text{rain}) = 0.6$. Both decisions are rational according to my decision rule.

Other familiar decision rules are similar to my quantization rule. According to one, an agent is told to assign probabilities and utilities to relevant option-state pairs as best he can, compute options' expected utilities with respect to his assignments, and identify options with maximum expected utility so computed. Afterward, he is told to assign a range of acceptable values for the probabilities and utilities of the option-state pairs. Then he is asked to consider whether the options of maximum expected utility change as the probabilities and utilities vary over their range of values. Those considerations, in common terminology employed, for example, by Behn and Vaupel (1982: 111–16), constitute a *sensitivity analysis*. The last step is to use the sensitivity analysis to reach a decision. According to one version of the last step, if some options have maximum expected utility with respect to all acceptable probability and utility values, the agent should select one of them. Otherwise, he is left to his own devices. According to another version of the last step, the agent should adopt an option that has maximum expected utility at some point during sensitivity analysis, that is, for some acceptable probability and utility values. There will always be an option meeting this condition. This version says that any option meeting the condition will do, even if the option does not have maximum expected utility throughout sensitivity analysis, whereas some alternative option does. My quantization rule agrees with the second version of the last step. It requires only maximizing utility with respect to some quantization of probability and utility judgments.

The quantization rule articulates my claim that utility analysis is a guide to decision. It expresses the view that even in nonquantitative cases where utility analysis does not yield a preference ranking of options, it directs decisions. Even in nonquantitative cases decisions must maximize utility under some quantization that complies with utility analysis. Moreover, this is the only restriction on decisions in the nonquantitative case. Utility analysis is not only a guide, it is the only guide. There is nothing else to go by. Compliance with the quantization rule is necessary and sufficient for a rational decision.

The short argument for my decision rule is that utility maximization under a quantization takes into account all the reasons for preferences among options, and reasons for preferences among options take into account all the reasons against choices. More precisely, there is no reason against choosing an option that is not a reason to prefer an alternative (although there are some reasons for choosing an option—say, to break a tie—that are not reasons for preferring it to an alternative). Choices not eliminated by quantizations are therefore rational. When the reasons for preferences among options are insufficient for a complete preference ranking of options, any choice that does not contravene those reasons for preferences is rational.

To elaborate this argument, let me review the four main factors on which it relies. First, note that a quantitative representation of probability and utility judgments is strictly richer than a classificatory or comparative representation. Everything that can be represented by classificatory or comparative means can be represented by quantitative means. Every quantization of probability and utility judgments therefore completely represents those judgments. Because, by assumption, these judgments extend as far as warranted, they comprise every reason that bears on the preference ranking of options. Because their quantization complies with methods of utility analysis that neither omit nor double-count considerations, it also attends to all reasons for preferences among options. Utilities of options under a quantization therefore register all reasons that bear on the options' preference ranking.

Second, I treat only cognitively unlimited agents in fully rational states of mind. The idealization to such agents eliminates excuses for failure to comply with my decision rule and guarantees that the structure of probability and utility judgments after maximum warranted extension does indeed reflect every reason bearing on the preference ranking of options.

Third, a maximal warranted extension of probability and utility judgments reduces a decision problem to the problem of making a decision justified by those judgments. Besides including new probability and utility judgments, the extended judgments include any modifications of former probability and utility judgments needed to accommodate the new judgments. The extended judgments embody all the reasons for preferences among options. Using them simplifies the task of formulating a standard for decision.

Fourth, idealizations about decision circumstances avert special problems independent of uncertainty and imprecision. They guarantee the existence of an option that maximizes utility under a quantization and the stability of a preference ranking of options under a quantization.

Appealing to these four factors, there is a straightforward argument for the necessity of utility maximization under a quantization. A quantization of probability and utility judgments does not reverse any judgments but only makes them more precise. So if a decision is inferior under every quantization of probability and utility judgments, it is inferior given those judgments. A decision must maximize utility under some quantization of probability and utility judgments to cohere with those judgments. In other words, to decide in accordance with the probability and utility judgments, one must decide in a way that maximizes utility under some quantization of those judgments. Thus, if an option is inferior throughout sensitivity analysis, it is irrational even though no alternative option maximizes expected utility throughout sensitivity analysis.

There is also a straightforward argument for the sufficiency of utility maximization under a quantization. Only reasons for preferences among options constrain rational choice. But a quantization of probability and utility judgments, after maximum warranted extension, represents all the agent's reasons for preferences among options. My idealizations preclude reasons for preferences ignored by quantizations of probability and utility judgments. The judgments of ideal agents do not need correction for errors, for instance. Hence, insofar as a choice is undetermined by quantizations, it is arbitrary. Therefore, all options that maximize utility with respect to a quantization are rational.

Consider the demand that an option maximize expected utility throughout sensitivity analysis. This contrasts with my view that maximization at one point suffices. Suppose that some option does maximize expected utility throughout sensitivity analysis. A second option that maximizes at just one point ties the first option at that point and loses to it at every other point. The first option may seem to be a better choice than the second. But the one point at which the options tie is a quantization that expresses all reasons for preferences between the options. If the options tie with respect to those reasons, then the second is at least as choiceworthy as the first.

Suppose, for instance, that a risk-neutral agent is asked to bet at even odds that it will rain. His only judgment about rain rates it no more probable than heads on a coin toss. That is, $P(\text{rain}) \leq 0.5$. Given standard simplifying assumptions about desires for amounts of money, accepting the bet maximizes expected utility only on the quantization according to which $P(\text{rain}) = 0.5$. Declining the bet maximizes expected utility on every quantization. Still, accepting is a rational option because the quantization on which it maximizes expected utility represents all the reasons bearing on a preference between accepting and declining. Any reason to prefer declining is a reason to judge that $P(\text{rain}) < 0.5$. Because that probability judgment is not made, even after reflection, there is no reason to prefer declining. Accepting is permissible.

Any factor that effects an option's choiceworthiness also effects its utility according to all quantizations. Is the quantization rule inviolable and trivial because quantizations are so comprehensive? No, an agent may choose contrary to the quantization rule no matter how comprehensive quantizations are. The quantization rule accommodates an agent's judgments but still directs him.

My case for the quantization rule brings out the importance of clarity about the reasons for indeterminate probabilities and utilities. If they were indeterminate simply because all mental states are nonquantitative, then the set of quantizations would not delimit the grounds for preferences among options. In fact, appeal to quantizations would seem a metaphysical fantasy. Because indeterminacy actually arises from insufficient grounds for quantitative judgments of the sort section 4.2 describes, quantizations do delimit the grounds for preferences among options. This makes them a sound foundation for decisions.

4.5. Objections to Reliance on Quantizations

My decision principle for nonquantitative cases, where relevant probabilities and utilities are missing, embodies two ideas. The first is that even if probabilities and utilities do not exist, there are ranges of admissible values for probabilities and utilities. These are their ranges of values under quantizations of probability and utility judgments. The second idea is that quantitative utility analysis is the one and only guide to decisions even when beliefs and desires are nonquantitative. Decisions ought to maximize utility under some quantization of belief and desire that conforms to the principles of utility analysis. The psychological thesis about decision resources and the normative thesis about decision standards are both controversial. This section replies to objections.

4.5.1. *Indeterminacy's Limits*

The quantization principle assumes that probabilities and utilities have ranges of admissible values. Do these ranges exist? One objection says they do not. The ranges of admissible values for probabilities and utilities may be indeterminate as well as the values themselves. There may be no determinate set of probability and utility functions compatible with current probability and utility judgments. For example, consider someone deciding about having a picnic. He may not have a probability assignment for rain. I say that he should decide in a way that maximizes utility under a quantization of his probability judgments about rain. That is, he should decide so that he maximizes expected utility under some admissible probability assignment for rain. But there may be no determinate set of admissible values for the probability of rain. The admissible values may seem to form some interval about 0.5, and probabilities less than 0.25 and more than 0.75 may be clearly ruled out, but the exact lower and upper bounds of the interval of admissible values may be indeterminate. Just as the picnicker has no determinate probability assignment for rain, he has no determinate probability interval, say, [0.25, 0.75], for rain. Shifting from points to intervals just compounds the problem of indeterminacy because specifying an interval requires two numbers, not just one. In general, the admissible probability values may be as indeterminate as the probability of rain itself. Quantizations make no progress with the problem of indeterminacy.

Let me examine this objection more closely. The claim that the set of admissible probability and utility values is indeterminate may mean two things. It may mean that the set does not exist because of suspension of judgment, just as the probability and utility values do not exist because of suspension of judgment. Or it may mean that the set is ill-defined because of vagueness concerning the probability and utility judgments that the set is supposed to represent. The response to the objection depends on the source of the alleged indeterminacy.

First, suppose the source is understood to be suspension of judgment. Then the objection is just mistaken. The alleged indeterminacy does not exist. Although quantitative judgments about probability and utility may be suspended and so indeterminate, whatever classificatory and comparative judgments are made will delineate a set of admissible probability and utility assignments. If the picnicker suspends quantitative belief about rain, he may nonetheless judge that rain is at least as probable as drawing a heart and no more probable than drawing another suit, that is, $0.25 \leq P(\text{rain}) \leq 0.75$. If this is the only relevant probability judgment, then the set of probability assignments meeting the constraint forms the set of admissible probability assignments. If he does not judge that the probability of rain is greater than 0.25, then that number is definitely in the interval of admissible probability values. Quantizations represent judgments made and only these. They ignore suspended judgments. The difference between suspended and unsuspended judgments determines the set of quantizations. If indeterminacy is understood to arise from suspension of judgment, the set of quantizations is not indeterminate.

Next, suppose that the source of the alleged indeterminacy is understood to be vagueness concerning the classification of mental states. Then the objection to the quantization principle is not serious. Standard methods for dealing with vagueness are a sufficient remedy. The relevant vagueness is in the system used to classify mental states, not in the mental states themselves. One may eliminate it by making the system of classification precise. Once this is done, it is a determinate matter whether according to a person's probability judgments the probability of rain is 0.5. Likewise, it is a determinate matter whether according to those judgments rain is more probable than drawing a heart. The set of admissible probability values is determinate.

How should one resolve the vagueness surrounding classification of probability and utility judgments? I do not advance an answer. Although an account of vagueness would significantly contribute to a realistic decision theory, I leave its formulation for other studies. I concentrate on the progress that a theory of rationality can make without it. In the example about the picnicker, if what counts as a probability judgment is vague, then upper and lower bounds on the admissible probability values of rain are a vague matter. According to my theory, the rationality of his decision is then also a vague matter. Whether his decision is rational or not depends, in borderline cases, on the resolution of the vagueness concerning his probability and utility judgments. In claiming that his decision is rational if and only if it maximizes utility under a quantization of his probability and utility judgments, I claim that the vagueness surrounding his probability and utility judgments is matched by a vagueness surrounding his decision's rationality. Clearing up one clears up the other. The classification of probability and utility judgments and the evaluation of decisions hang together. The quantization principle stands despite a certain vagueness about its application.

For example, suppose that the picnicker's mental state is not definitely one in which the probability of rain is greater than or equal to 0.25. Then the vagueness infects the application of my decision principle as well. Given one way of resolving the problem of classification, it may yield one verdict about his decision, and, given another way of resolving the problem, it may yield another verdict. The principle stands, however. Although the principle's application depends on a resolution of vagueness about the classification of mental states, it does not presume any particular resolution. It survives under any resolution of the vagueness.

4.5.2. *Liberality and Strictness*

The second idea embodied in my decision principle for the nonquantitative case, normative reliance on quantizations of probability and utility judgments, is sometimes rejected as being too liberal. The objection claims that not all quantizations are equally good. Consequently, the decision principle of utility maximization under some quantization licenses irrational decisions that maximize under inferior quantizations. For example, if the admissible values for the probability of rain form the interval [0.4, 0.9], then although betting against rain is optimal under a quantization in which $P(\text{rain}) = 0.4$, the bet seems unjustified. The value 0.4, although admissible, is not representative of the whole interval of admissible values.

My reply uses section 4.4's points about applications of sensitivity analysis. The quantization principle takes into account all the reasons relevant to a preference ranking of options. It applies only after probability and utility judgments are extended as far as warranted. If there is a reason for not betting against rain, then after the agent's probability and utility judgments are extended, he will prefer not to make such a bet. Consequently, any quantization of his probability and utility judgments will make $P(\text{rain}) > 0.5$, given standard simplifying assumptions about the utilities of bets' outcomes. However, if the interval of admissible probability values after extension of judgments is [0.4, 0.9], then betting against rain is reasonable. In particular, the nonrepresentativeness of the value 0.4 for the probability of rain is no reason to reject the bet. All quantizations are equally good because each represents all the agent's probability and utility judgments.

Cases of incomparable options generate another objection to the quantization rule's liberality. Consider a decision problem involving two incomparable options. The agent does not compare the options, and so quantizations favoring each arise. Each option is rational according to the quantization rule. The objection claims that this assessment is incorrect. It claims that neither option is rational.

This objection assumes that the options are neither quantitatively nor qualitatively comparable. Hence, every quantization of their utilities is admissible by my standards because none is contrary to a preference ranking of the options. Each option therefore maximizes utility under some quantization. To make the objection forceful, suppose that the options' incomparability cannot be remedied by more information, experience, imagination, reflection, and the like. It does not involve an incomparability of two untasted flavors of ice cream but, say, an incomparability of two possible careers, one in medicine and the other in music. It rests on the agent's considered judgment that no grounds are adequate for comparing the two options. Each quantization flouts this judgment by implying a comparison. Consequently, making the decision the quantization recommends prompts regret and perhaps even anguish.[14]

In response to the objection, I acknowledge that every quantization has implications contrary to the agent's judgment of incomparability. Still, no quantization is contrary to a preference between the options. Under my idealizations, only preferences affect a decision's rationality. The agent has no reason against any option a quantization recommends, and so the option is rational. As far as rational decision goes, incomparability is just another obstacle to quantitative utility assignments to options. It does not affect the case for the quantization rule. The regret and anguish occasioned by a decision involving incomparable options may arise from many sources, not necessarily the decision's failure to meet standards of rationality. These emotions may arise from having forgone an attractive opportunity, not having the consolation of a decision resting on a preference, frustration with unproductive attempts to form a preference, and the like.

On my view, every decision problem meeting this chapter's idealizations has a rational resolution. That is, some option is rational. In a decision problem with two incomparable options at least one option is rational. Because preference favors neither, both are rational. The quantization rule accommodates this liberal standard of rationality.[15]

Another common objection to the second, normative part of my proposal is that it is too demanding; it should not insist that decisions maximize utility under a quantization. According to the objection, it is inappropriate to apply standards for the quantitative case to the nonquantitative case. Quantifying probability and utility judgments eliminates reasons for decisions that are crucial in the nonquantitative case. In nonquantitative cases, quantizations of probability and utility judgments do not represent all reasons for preferences among options. They suppress important urn 1, 50–50   urn 2, mystery

FIGURE 4.3. Ellsberg's paradox.

considerations, the objection claims. For example, they misrepresent preferences among options.

Take this version of Ellsberg's paradox (1961). Imagine two urns, one with 50 red balls and 50 black balls, the other with 100 red and black balls in an unknown proportion (see figure 4.3). The agent prefers a gamble that pays $100 if a red ball is drawn from the 50–50 urn to a gamble that pays $100 if a red ball is drawn from the mystery urn. She also prefers a gamble that pays $100 if a black ball is drawn from the 50–50 urn to a gamble that pays $100 if a black ball is drawn from the mystery urn. The preferences are rational, but no quantization allows both preferences. To conform to the preferences, a quantization must yield the inequalities $P(R_1)U(\$100) > P(R_2)U(\$100)$ and $P(B_1)U(\$100) > P(B_2)U(\$100)$. But to conform to the probability laws, the quantization must also yield the equality $P(R_1) + P(B_1) = P(R_2) + P(B_2)$. No quantization satisfies all the constraints. So every quantization rejects some preference. Quantizations that ignore preferences, however, are not a good basis for decisions. The quantization principle therefore seems unreliable.

According to the objection, quantizations are unreliable because indeterminate probabilities and utilities generate risks that affect preferences. Gambling with the mystery urn is riskier than gambling with the 50–50 urn. The added risks disappear when a quantization is adopted. Risks stemming from the nonquantitative character of probability judgments are inevitably lost in quantitative representations of those judgments. Their disappearance forces changes in preferences. The distortion discredits decision rules using quantizations. Utility maximization under a quantization cannot be a standard of rationality for decisions in nonquantitative cases.

This objection makes two mistakes. First, it assumes that risk is a legitimate concern but nonetheless does not include risk in a gamble's outcome. It takes outcomes narrowly so that they include only factors such as monetary gains that can be produced with various probabilities by various acts. Expected utility analysis (section 2.4) takes outcomes broadly, so risk is included in the outcome of a risky option. Because of risk, the outcomes of bets involving the mystery urn are less attractive than their counterparts involving the 50–50 urn, as Weirich (1986a) explains. Consequently, the agent's preferences maximize utility under a quantization whereby the probability of black is the same from each urn and, similarly, the probability of red is the same from each urn. Quantizations represent both preferences in Ellsberg's paradox. Decisions in accord with the agent's preferences satisfy the quantization principle.[16]

Second, the objection claims that risks generated by indeterminate probabilities and utilities disappear under quantizations. This claim misunderstands quantizations. A quantization is a numerical representation of actual judgments. It does not represent hypothetical judgments that would hold if the quantization were actualized. In a nonquantitative case, a quantization represents actual nonquantitative judgments. It does not present the probability and utility assignments that an agent would make if he were to make his judgments quantitative. The utility it assigns to an option need not be the utility of the option in any quantitative case. Options' utilities under a quantization are numerical representations of the content of nonquantitative judgments. In the example of the urns, if some quantization were actualized, then, of course, the risks stemming from the absence of quantitative probabilities would disappear. Consequently, the outcomes of bets involving the urns would change, and so preferences concerning the bets might change. The original preferences might not maximize utility under the hypothetical utility assignment for option-state pairs. Nonetheless, the original preferences may maximize utility under a quantization of the agent's original judgments. The factors such as risk that would disappear if a quantization were actualized are unaffected by the quantization itself. To be faithful, a quantization has to represent the effect of all relevant factors on probability and utility judgments. It represents their actual effect, not the effect they would have if the quantization were actualized. Despite the disappearance of relevant factors given a quantization's hypothetical realization, a quantization still represents their actual effect on probability and utility judgments. A quantization registers the effects of risk by taking outcomes as they are. It attaches determinate probabilities to outcomes that include risks arising from indeterminate probabilities. It is not a representation of any quantitative case. Quantizations regulate rational choices not because they represent possible quantitative refinements of actual judgments but because they represent actual judgments.[17]

Once one corrects the objection's two mistakes, it loses its punch. The quantization principle does not suppress reasons for choice that arise from indeterminacy. It respects them by taking outcomes broadly and by taking quantizations realistically.[18]

The general worry behind the objection involving Ellsberg's paradox is that quantizations misrepresent probability and utility judgments. They represent them as precise even when they are imprecise. No single quantization represents the imprecision of the judgments.

This worry assumes a view of representation different from mine. As I use the term represent, quantitative probability and utility functions may represent imprecise probability and utility judgments, just as a black-and-white photo may represent a colored object. A representation does not attribute each of its features to the object it represents. By convention, quantizations represent probability and utility judgments for decision purposes. They are adequate representations if they represent everything relevant to the rationality of decisions made using the quantization rule. By convention, a precise quantization may represent imprecise probability and utility judgments without representing them as precise. A quantization according to which $P(\text{rain}) = 0.4$ represents probability judgments about rain only as grounding a quantization with that probability assignment.

As mentioned, quantizations do not ignore the effect of imprecision on rational decision making. The imprecision affects a quantization's assignment of utilities to options' outcomes. Imprecision in probability judgments may influence utility assignments because a quantization is a pair consisting of a probability function and a utility function, not just a precisification of probability judgments.

The claim that each quantization is equally good for making a decision according to the principle to maximize utility is analogous to the claim that each scale for length is equally good for comparing the lengths of objects. Just as an assignment of length in meters represents the same features of objects as an assignment of length in feet, different quantizations represent the same reasons bearing on choiceworthiness. Moreover, just as an assignment of length in meters represents everything bearing on length comparisons, a quantization represents everything bearing on a rational decision.

4.5.3. Coherence among Decisions

Another objection to my decision principle for the nonquantitative case claims that the principle is incoherent when applied to multiple simultaneous decisions. A set of simultaneous choices might each maximize utility under some quantization of probabilities and utilities although the combination of choices does not maximize utility under any single quantization. My principle yields the result that each choice is rational taken by itself, but also the result that the combination of choices, taken as a single decision to realize the object of each choice, is irrational.

This objection treats simultaneous decisions. How do they arise within my theory? Because the options in a decision problem are possible decisions, only one of which is realized, multiple simultaneous decisions are resolutions of contemporaneous but distinct decision problems. For example, suppose that in one decision problem a and b are the contents of possible decisions. In another simultaneous decision problem c and d are the contents of possible decisions. Also suppose that the resolution of the first problem is a choice that a and the resolution of the second problem is a choice that c. Then the resolution of the combined decision problems is a combination choice, the decision that a and c.

Section 2.2 treats simultaneous decisions problems as a single decision problem whose resolution is a combined choice. However, when the component choices have distinct topics, say, distinct bets, it is natural to treat the components as resolutions of distinct decision problems. Strictly speaking, my decision principle applies only to the combination choice, but for the sake of argument, this section grants its application to the component choices, too.

Here, then, is an example of the incoherence the objection imagines. Suppose that the admissible values for the probability of rain form the interval $[0.25, 0.75]$. According to the quantization rule, given standard simplifying assumptions about desires for amounts of money, it is rational to pay $0.60 for a lottery ticket that pays $1.00 if it rains and nothing otherwise, because this maximizes utility under a quantization that assigns 0.6 as the probability of rain. Also, it is rational to pay $0.60 for a lottery ticket that pays $1.00 if it does not rain and nothing otherwise, because this maximizes utility under a quantization that assigns 0.4 as the probability of rain.

But it is irrational to buy both tickets at those prices, because under no quantization does the combination of decisions maximize utility; the combination yields a loss of $0.20 no matter whether it rains or not. So, if the two tickets are offered in distinct simultaneous decision problems, my decision rule says it is rational to bet on rain in the first problem and to bet against rain in the second problem, although it is irrational to make both bets in the combined decision problem.

The complaint against my decision rule assumes that if each member of a set of simultaneous decisions is rational, then the conjunction of their objects, if realizable, is a rational choice. The qualification about realizability is necessary to circumvent certain obvious problems. Suppose, for instance, that several acts have maximum utility, say, vacations in Hawaii, the Caribbean, and Corsica. In a decision between Hawaii and the Caribbean, Hawaii is a rational choice. In a simultaneous decision between the Caribbean and Corsica, Corsica is a rational choice. But in the combination of the two decision problems, the combination of choices, Hawaii and Corsica, is an irrational choice. It is impossible to spend one's vacation in both places. The objection's step from multiple rational decisions to the rationality of a decision to realize the conjunction of their objects has to be restricted to cases where the conjunction is realizable.

Even with the qualification about realizability, however, the objection's assumption is doubtful. To defuse the objection, I reject its assumption. To locate the trouble with the assumption, let me divide it into two subsidiary principles. The first, the *combination principle*, claims that if each member of a set of simultaneous decisions is rational, then the combination of decisions is rational. The second, the *conjunction principle*, claims that if a combination of simultaneous decisions is rational, then the decision to realize the conjunction of their objects is also rational. The conjunction principle is correct, but the combination principle is not.

The conjunction principle is correct because, given my idealizations about decision costs and the like, a combination of decisions is equivalent in relevant respects to a single decision to realize the conjunction of the decisions' objects. A combination of decisions to perform certain acts has in relevant respects the same outcome as the single decision to perform all the acts. Hence, under my idealizations, if the combination is rational, so is the equivalent complex decision. Whenever one member of a pair of decision equivalents is rational, the other is as well. If it is rational to make a set of decisions to perform certain acts, then it is rational to make the single decision to perform all the acts.

On the other hand, the combination principle is false. It overlooks coherence requirements that do not apply to simultaneous decisions taken one by one but do apply to their combination. Because of coherence requirements, the rationality of each of a set of decisions with respect to a certain decision situation does not guarantee the rationality of the whole set of decisions with respect to the same decision situation, including the same set of beliefs and desires.

To make my case against the combination principle, let me begin with some related points about coherence. Consider sets of subdecisions in a single decision problem. A subdecision selects an option from a subset of options. It is not a hypothetical decision that entertains a subset of options. Rather, it is a decision, in the context of the actual overall decision problem, about a subset of options. Its purpose is to reduce the scope of deliberations. One may hope to resolve the overall decision problem by making a series of subdecisions of reduced scope. Indeed, for ideal agents in ideal circumstances, a complete set of pairwise subdecisions between options entails a resolution of the overall decision problem. For example, suppose that in a decision problem the contending options are *a*, *b*, and *c*. One subdecision is between *a* and *b*. Another subdecision is between *b* and *c*. If *a* is adopted over *b*, and *b* is adopted over *c*, then the combination of subdecisions yields *a* as the resolution of the overall decision problem. Unfortunately, the rationality of each pairwise subdecision in a complete set does not guarantee the rationality of the whole set and the overall decision it yields.

To see this, consider preferences, which direct rational pairwise subdecisions. The combination principle extended to preferences claims that if each member of a set of preferences is rational with respect to the agent's state of mind, then the combination of those preferences is also rational with respect to the agent's state of mind. Some, for example, Dummett (1984: 32–35), use this principle for preferences to argue that cyclical preferences are rational in certain cases. They construct cases in which each preference in a set of cyclical preferences is rational taken alone and conclude that they are rational taken together. However, the combination principle for preferences is incorrect because it ignores coherence requirements, such as transitivity, that apply to sets of preferences. For example, imagine three boxes of chocolates. It may be rational to prefer the first to the second because the first has more cherries. It may be rational to prefer the second to the third because the second has more almonds. And it may be rational to prefer the third to the first because the third has more dark chocolates. But it is not rational to have all three preferences at once. The set of three preferences violates coherence requirements.[19]

The combination principle for subdecisions has a similar defect. A set of subdecisions that are rational taken one by one may be irrational taken together because they violate coherence requirements. Imagine, for instance, choosing among three boxes of chocolates and consider pairwise subdecisions between boxes of chocolates following the preferences stated. Each subdecision may be rational taken in isolation, but their combination is cyclical and irrational. They are incoherent and fail to yield a decision among all the boxes. Even if each subdecision in a set is rational taken by itself, it does not follow that the set of subdecisions is rational. Because rational subdecisions rest on preferences, coherence requirements govern subdecisions, just as they govern preferences.

Principles of coherence similar to the principle of transitivity for preferences and pairwise subdecisions militate against the combination principle's application to resolutions of simultaneous decision problems, as in the example about the purchase of lottery tickets concerning rain. The interval for the probability of rain is [0.25, 0.75]. So it is rational to pay $0.60 for a ticket that pays $1.00 if it rains and nothing otherwise. Also, it is rational to pay $0.60 for a ticket that pays $1.00 if it does not rain and nothing otherwise. But it is irrational to buy both tickets at those prices because that ensures a net loss of $0.20. Although each decision to purchase a ticket is rational taken by itself, the combination of decisions is irrational because it guarantees a loss.[20]

The appeal of the combination principle may come from a specious analogy with belief. The corresponding principle for belief claims that if beliefs are individually rational, then they are collectively rational. This principle has some plausibility given strict standards of rationality for belief that take a person's evidence to determine completely an appropriate belief state for every proposition. Given such strict standards, evidence must determine a belief state for a proposition in a way that guarantees coherence with the belief states determined for other propositions. In that case, the principle for belief does not ignore coherence requirements. But because standards of rationality for single desires allow some latitude, they do not take coherence requirements into account. So the rationality of each of a set of desire states does not guarantee the coherence, and hence the rationality, of the combination of those states. Because rational decision depends on rational desire, the same holds for coherent decisions.

The quantization principle governs decision problems taken one by one. When several decisions are made in the same decision situation, the principle says whether each is rational with respect to that decision situation, but it does not say whether the combination of decisions is rational. To answer that question, one must apply the principle to the equivalent single complex decision. When I say that meeting my standard of rationality is sufficient for rationality, I mean that an option o that meets it, taken alone, is a rational decision in the decision situation. This follows ordinary usage. It is common to understand a decision problem as the selection of a single option from among those available in the decision situation. If some other decision is made first, the decision situation changes, so there is no commitment to o's remaining rational. Similarly, if some other decision is made simultaneously, there is no commitment to o's rationality when taken with that other decision. If simultaneous decisions are incoherent, at least one is irrational. My principle does not attribute blame for the incoherence to any particular decision. Nonetheless, it allows for some decision, perhaps o, to be at fault. It may turn out that although a certain option, taken alone, is rational in a decision situation, adopting that option is irrational in light of the other decisions also made in that decision situation.[21]

4.5.4. *Quantizations' Sufficiency*

Under this chapter's idealizations, compliance with the quantization rule is sufficient for a rational decision. Hence, in the nonquantitative case every necessary condition for a rational decision is a necessary condition for maximization of utility under a quantization. Take, for instance, the rule of dominance. It says to avoid options dominated by other options. According to the definition of dominance it adopts, one option *dominates* another if and only if it is better in some states and worse in none (provided that the states have nonzero probability and are causally independent of the options). The rule expresses a necessary condition for a rational decision in the nonquantitative case because compliance is a necessary condition for maximizing utility under a quantization. Given expected utility analysis, no dominated option maximizes utility under a quantization of belief and desire. The quantization rule subsumes the rule of dominance. Although avoiding domination

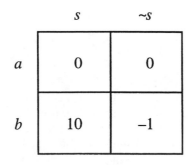

FIGURE 4.4. The maximin rule.

is a necessary condition of rationality, it is not a sufficient condition of rationality. Obeying the quantization rule, in contrast, is both necessary and sufficient for rationality.[22]

Because the quantization rule conflicts with any decision rule advancing a necessary condition of rational decision in nonquantitative cases unless that condition is also a necessary condition for utility maximization under a quantization, it conflicts with the familiar *maximin rule* proposed by Wald (1950: 18). That rule is formulated in terms of options' payoffs in states. These payoffs are the utilities for the option-state pairs. When probabilities of relevant states are completely indeterminate, it says to select an option whose minimum payoff is at least as great as any other option's minimum payoff, in other words, select a *maximin option*. Thus, for example, if a decision problem has the payoff matrix in figure 4.4, where *a* and *b* are options and *s* and ~*s* are states affecting payoffs, the minimum payoff for option *a* is 0 and the minimum payoff for option *b* is –1, so the maximin option is *a*. The maximin rule says to select *a*. It is intended to express a necessary and sufficient condition of rational choice given complete indeterminacy of probabilities.[23]

The payoffs used to identify a maximin option vary with the partition of states used to create a decision problem's payoff matrix. To avoid inconsistency from one partition to another, the rule must be restricted to cases in which utilities for option-state pairs are stable under suppositions about the manner of states' realizations. This ensures that finer partitions do not introduce new, lower minimum payoffs.

Also, the maximin rule rejects, as the quantization rule does, the combination principle for the rationality of sets of decisions. To see why it rejects the combination principle, consider an example. Suppose for simplicity that utilities reduce to monetary payoffs. Then, given a choice between not gambling and paying $1 for a gamble on *p* that yields $10 if *p* and nothing otherwise, the maximin choice is not gambling. Also, given a choice between not gambling and paying $1 for a gamble on ~*p* that yields $10 if ~*p* and nothing otherwise, the maximin choice is not gambling. However, accepting both gambles guarantees a profit of $8 and so is a maximin option with respect to a complex decision about the pair of gambles. So the maximin rule says that each decision to turn down a gamble is rational taken in isolation, but the complex decision to turn down both gambles is irrational.

Because the combination principle finds these judgments incoherent, the maximin rule rejects that principle.

Even given stable minimums and the combination principle's retreat, the maximin rule falters. It demands more than the quantization rule, which expresses a sufficient condition of rational choice. The maximin rule amounts to treating an option's minimum payoff as a certainty if the option were realized, whereas probability assignments treating that payoff as less than certain appear in some quantizations. Those quantizations sanction decisions that are not maximin decisions, and those decisions are reasonable. The stringency of the maximin rule is unjustified. There is no reason to follow that rule rather than decide in another way that maximizes utility under a quantization of probability and utility judgments. Compliance with the maximin rule is not necessary for rationality.[24]

The maximin rule for cases where probabilities of relevant states are completely indeterminate is often characterized as a cautious rule and is defended by trying to justify caution. Rawls (1971: 154–55) says that it is best supported in cases where, in addition to the absence of information supporting probability assignments, some option has a satisfactory minimum payoff and other options have woefully unsatisfactory minimum payoffs. This line of defense assumes that the decision maker is averse to risk, or at least ought to be averse to risk. Let me grant this assumption. Then the general line of defense is that the maximin option is less risky than other options and that this justifies its selection. This line of defense is weak, however, because the advantage the maximin option has with respect to risk is not sufficient to disqualify all other options. Still, in Rawls's cases, the defense gains strength because it may appear that the advantage the maximin option has with respect to risk is so great that it makes that option the rational choice.[25]

Let me pursue Rawls's attempt to formulate a more plausible, qualified version of the maximin rule. The maximin rule says to choose an option whose outcome of minimum utility is at least as great as any other option's outcome of minimum utility. It is advanced for cases where probabilities of relevant states are uninfluenced by options and completely unconstrained. Suppose that it is also formulated to avoid the problems mentioned earlier. First, it is applied with respect to a basic partition of states. Finer partitions do not change the options' minimums. Second, it is for decisions in isolation and does not intend its verdicts about them to carry implications about combinations of decisions. Finally, in accordance with Rawls's suggestions, it is for cases where one option guarantees a satisfactory outcome and others risk disasters so that, granting a strong aversion to risk, the maximin option enjoys a huge advantage from minimizing risk. Then the maximin option is the only rational choice. After adjusting payoffs for the maximin option's advantage with respect to risk, it dominates all other options.

Figure 4.5 illustrates the argument for the hedged maximin rule. It starts with a matrix presenting payoffs in terms of utilities for amounts of money won or lost. The probabilities of states are independent of options and completely indeterminate. Option *a* is the maximin option. Then the argument adjusts utilities to take account of other aspects of options' outcomes, in particular, risk. The example supposes that after taking account of option *a*'s advantage with respect to

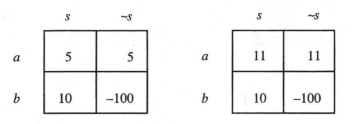

FIGURE 4.5. The hedged maximin rule.

risk, its payoff rises to 11 units in each state. In this case, the maximin option, *a*, dominates option *b*. It is justified by its risk-adjusted payoffs.

For vividness, the example stipulates the payoffs illustrating adjustment for risk. The argument for the hedged maximin rule only requires that payoffs make the maximin option dominate other options. It assumes that an agent values security so much that the maximin option receives a decisive security bonus.

Grant that for the cases described, risk reduction supports the hedged version of the maximin rule. How does the quantization rule fare in these cases? If a risk advantage justifies the maximin option in some decision problem, then that risk advantage justifies preferring the maximin option to other options. Outcomes take account of risk, and under every quantization the utilities of the maximin option's outcomes outpace their counterparts with other options, so the maximin option's utility is greater than other options' utilities under every quantization. Hence, utility maximization under a quantization of belief and desire requires the maximin option. In other words, the maximin rule when justified concurs with the quantization rule. If the maximin option is dominant given risk-adjusted payoffs, then only it maximizes utility under a quantization.

This treatment of the maximin rule illustrates a general point about decision rules that go beyond utility maximization under a quantization. Whenever such a rule is restricted so that it is justified, the justification generates preferences among options. Those preferences constrain utility maximization under a quantization so that it produces the same choice as the restricted rule. All reasons for decisions among options are also reasons for preferences among those options and so are registered by the quantization rule. Hence, alternative decision rules are unjustified when they demand more than the quantization rule and, when they are justified, demand no more than the quantization rule. In general, because the quantization principle comprehends all reasons for preferences among options, no reasons for decisions require more than it does. Compliance with the quantization principle is sufficient for a rational decision. Utility analysis, as expressed through quantizations, is the only guide to decision, even in nonquantitative cases.

Realism about Agents: Cognitive Limitations

The previous chapter advanced a decision principle for nonquantitative cases where agents are cognitively unlimited. This chapter attends to cognitive limitations. First, it proposes a decision principle for quantitative cases where agents have cognitive limitations. In some cases, an agent is uncertain of his own mental states, in particular, uncertain of his utility or probability assignments, and these states are inaccessible. In other cases, an agent can learn about his mental states, but at a cost in time and reflection. Next, the chapter proposes a decision principle for nonquantitative cases where agents have cognitive limitations. They can construct useful probability and utility assignments, but at a cost. Finally, the chapter addresses ignorance of a priori matters and considers the roles of substantive and procedural standards of rationality in nonideal cases.

The chapter promotes maximization with respect to available resources, assuming a reasonable effort to win resources. The assumption holds in virtue of an idealization the chapter retains, the idealization that an agent is fully rational, except possibly in the current decision problem, and makes no mistakes for which her decisions must compensate. In cases where an agent should, for example, gather information about her mental states before deciding, the idealization entails that she does this rationally.

When agents have cognitive limits, a decision's evaluation must consider decision costs. An agent may incur some costs by making a decision and other costs by preparing to make it. The principle of utility maximization (section 2.2) accommodates the costs of making a decision, as Weirich (1983b) observes. It takes options to be decisions rather than nonmental acts. As a result, the psychological cost of making a decision, the cost of forming and maintaining an intention to act, influences the utility of the option that decision constitutes. A utility-maximizing option has justified costs. This chapter attends to the costs of decision preparations, such as acquisition of information about relevant mental states and a priori matters. These costs influence evaluations of decision preparations.

My decision principles rely on some technical material about higher-order probability assignments. Readers wishing to skip it may move to chapter 6 without loss of continuity.

5.1. Unknown Mental States and Abilities

In quantitative cases, relevant probability and utility assignments exist. However, agents with cognitive limitations may not know their own probability and utility assignments, their basic intrinsic desires, and the options available to them. They may not have the input required for applications of the principles of utility maximization and expected utility. Ignorance about beliefs and desires may persist, despite incentives to overcome it, because of the difficulty of learning and maintaining awareness of psychological facts about oneself. Ignorance about options, possible decisions, may also persist. Because of psychological short-sightedness, one may not attain awareness of all one might decide in a current decision problem.

5.1.1. *Revised Idealizations and Decision Problems*

Suppose that agents have limited access to the psychological data for utility analysis but nonetheless know all a priori truths, including the principles of utility analysis and the logical and mathematical truths relevant to their application. Also, suppose that agents can apply utility analysis without cost so that, given the necessary input, they have no excuses for failing to maximize utility.[1]

Section 2.4's formulation of expected utility analysis prepared for eventual accommodation of limited access to beliefs and desires. It took the utility for an option-state pair to be a conditional utility, $U(o$ given $s)$, rather than the utility of a conditional outcome, $U(O[o$ given $s])$, where O is an operator yielding outcomes. $U(o$ given $s)$ is the utility of o's outcome given s, or $U(O[o]$ given $s)$. Using this utility instead of the utility of a conditional outcome is advantageous in cases where an agent is uncertain about his utility assignment. Given such uncertainty, the assumption that s may carry relevant information about his utility assignment. $U(o$ given $s)$ takes into account all the information carried by the assumption that s, even information about the agent's desires. It reflects the desires an agent believes he has given s. On the other hand, $U(O[o$ given $s])$ rests on current information only. It uses only desires an agent believes he has. It is a nonconditional utility of an outcome derived from o given a condition. That is, although $O[o$ given $s]$, when obtaining the outcome of o, takes into account the assumption that s, the utility attached to $O[o$ given $s]$ does not take into account the assumption that s. That utility does not use assumptions to supplement current information about desires. Although $U(o$ given $s)$ equals $U(O[o$ given $s])$ under section 2.4's idealizations, the equality may not hold when agents have cognitive limitations, and then the former is generally more accessible.[2]

Using $U(o$ given $s)$ reduces but does not eliminate uncertainty about utility assignments. The assumption that s may leave the agent uncertain of his utility assignment for o. Then how should o's choiceworthiness be assessed? How should agents decide in case they lack the psychological data required for utility analysis and decision rules?

The answers depend on whether the missing data are accessible and, if so, how difficult to acquire. This section supposes inaccessibility. It claims that rationality depends on data in hand only, not on existent but unknown psychological states. What is rational given no additional psychological data is rational period. Section 5.2 supposes that the missing data are accessible, but at a cost. It claims that a rational decision depends on not only data in hand, but also on data that can be reasonably acquired. Psychological states initially unknown constrain rational decisions if reasonable investigation brings them to light.

5.1.2. *Higher-Order Utility Analysis*

Consider an agent who lacks information about her psychological states so that she cannot use utility analysis to discover which options maximize utility. She is ignorant of crucial probabilities and utilities and is unable to apply expected utility analysis, for instance. Although my principles of utility analysis and decision are evaluative, not procedural, an agent is generally not responsible for meeting standards she cannot apply. So I revise standards of utility analysis and maximization to suit her abilities.

Because uncertainty is the crucial element in such cases, probabilistic standards make sense for the evaluation of options. Although an agent may be uncertain of a crucial probability, she may have information about that probability's value. Then she should use this higher-order information to evaluate options. Her evaluation should use probabilities of probabilities and the like. These higher-order probabilities may be inaccessible also, but when they are available, an agent should use them.[3]

To evaluate an option, I recommend, when possible, applying the expectation principle at a higher level, that is, applying the expectation principle with respect to the possible results of some form of utility analysis. For instance, instead of computing the expected utilities of options, compute the expected values of the expected utilities of options. In general, to overcome ignorance of a datum needed for a utility analysis, use the set of possible values of the unknown datum and the probability of each possible value. For an unknown probability, the possible values are real numbers between 0 and 1 inclusive, and the probabilities of these possible values are probabilities of probabilities. Where an expected utility depends on n unknown probabilities and utilities, the procedure computes its expected value from its value given n-tuples of real numbers and a probability for each n-tuple.

In the calculation of an expected value of an option's utility, one must identify a form of utility analysis, sets of possible values for the missing data on which the option's utility depends according to the form of utility analysis, and a probability for each set of values. Suppose, for example, that an agent has to decide whether to take $1.25 or a lottery ticket that pays $4.00 if it is drawn, nothing otherwise. He does not know the probability he assigns to the ticket's being drawn, but knows that the probability that it is 1/2 is 1/2 and the probability that it is 1/4 is 1/2. Then, letting utilities of outcomes go by amounts of money, the ticket's expected utility is 2 with probability 1/2 and 1 with probability 1/2. The expected value of its expected utility is 1.5, which is greater than the utility of $1.25. So he should take the ticket.

Under chapter 2's idealizations, probabilities are known. Hence, probabilities of probabilities are 0s or 1s. So are probabilities of utilities and other data for first-order utility analysis. Higher-order utility analysis applies trivially in the ideal case. It reduces to first-order utility analysis. Higher-order utility analysis is a generalization of first-order utility analysis for cases where the data for a first-order analysis are unknown.

What is the status of expected value estimates of probabilities and utilities? Is the expected value of the probability of p also the probability of p? Do expected values of probabilities, estimates of probabilities, reduce to probabilities? Is the expected value of an option's expected utility the same as the option's expected utility? Are the quantity and its estimate two quantities with the same value? To answer these questions, I distinguish an agent's whole mind and the agent's conscious mind. An agent's *conscious mind* is the part of her whole mind immediately accessible to her. It does not include unconscious desires, for instance. Then I distinguish probabilities and utilities with respect to the agent's whole mind and with respect to the agent's conscious mind. In the cases I am treating, some propositions' probabilities and utilities with respect to the whole mind are inaccessible. The expected values of those probabilities and utilities are not the propositions' probabilities and utilities with respect to the whole mind—those are unknown. But are their expected values the propositions' probabilities and utilities with respect to the conscious mind?

The answer is no for probabilities. Evidence for the value of p's probability is not evidence for p and so does not ground a degree of belief that p. Where p's probability with respect to the whole mind is unknown, even if the conscious mind yields an estimate, p's probability with respect to the conscious mind should be suspended. Estimates of probabilities with respect to the whole mind are not probabilities with respect to the conscious mind.

On the other hand, evidence for the value of p's utility with respect to the whole mind grounds p's utility with respect to the conscious mind. Utility goes by available psychological quantities. So estimates of options' utilities with respect to the whole mind are the options' utilities with respect to the conscious mind. However, an option's utility with respect to the conscious mind according to a higher-order analysis need not equal its utility with respect to the whole mind according to a first-order analysis using actual but unknown probabilities and utilities. An option's utility with respect to the conscious mind may differ from its utility with respect to the whole mind.

A similar point applies to an option's expected utility, of course. Its expected utility with respect to the whole mind need not equal its utility with respect to the conscious mind. An agent may be ignorant of the option's expected utility with respect to the whole mind, which may depend on unknown values of probabilities for option-state pairs. If crucial probabilities are inaccessible, they do not yield the option's utility with respect to the conscious mind. That quantity depends on the estimated value of the option's expected utility with respect to the whole mind.

The option's utility with respect to the conscious mind is its estimated expected utility with respect to the whole mind.

Sometimes an option's utility can be computed using higher-order expected utility analysis when it cannot be computed using first-order expected utility analysis. More precisely, one may be able to obtain the option's utility with respect to the conscious mind although one cannot obtain its utility with respect to the whole mind. Even if probabilities and utilities are inaccessible, options' utilities can be calculated with respect to what is accessible and then used to direct decisions. The calculations may use estimates of probabilities and utilities with respect to the whole mind but still yield genuine utilities with respect to the conscious mind.

When crucial probabilities and utilities are not accessible, rational agents rely on what is accessible. They follow this decision rule:

> *Accessible utility maximization.* Adopt an option of maximum utility with respect to the conscious mind.

This rule maintains that a decision rational given accessible data is rational period. A rational agent makes do with information on hand. The rule expresses a standard of evaluation and a goal of rationality. To be rational, agents meeting this chapter's idealizations must comply and other agents must aspire to comply.

The rule attends to accessible probabilities and utilities rather than probabilities and utilities actually entertained because probabilities and utilities not entertained may nonetheless influence decisions. Entertaining probabilities and utilities clutters the mind and helps only when necessary to adjust their influence. Under this section's idealizations, agents entertain accessible probabilities and utilities as needed.

The options among which utility is to be maximized are the options the agent considers. Under my idealization of full rationality, the agent reviews her options rationally. If she fails to consider an option because of limited mental power, she is not culpable in any way. Rationality does not demand that she extend the scope of her deliberations. Furthermore, in contrast with the case for missing probabilities and utilities, estimation is pointless for missing options. Her asking whether some possible decision is perhaps an option has no value. If she entertains the decision, she knows she can adopt it. The cognitive deficiencies this chapter introduces do not block that simple inference.

How is this section's decision rule related to chapter 2's rule of utility maximization for ideal agents in ideal circumstances? An agent who is perfectly situated has access to all psychological data relevant to utility maximization with respect to the whole mind. In that case, utility with respect to the conscious mind agrees with utility with respect to the whole mind. Therefore, chapter 2 conflates the distinction between the two types of utility. Nonetheless, its decision rule aims at utility maximization with respect to the whole mind. That is the more basic goal of rationality. Its primacy explains why utility maximization with respect to the conscious mind uses estimation procedures that aim at utility maximization with respect to the whole mind.

In nonideal cases, the two types of utility may diverge. Then this section's decision rule tracks utility with respect to the conscious mind because it is accessible. The rule agrees with chapter 2's rule in ideal cases and goes beyond that rule in nonideal cases. So it is a generalization of chapter 2's rule, not just a more precise specification of that rule. Utility maximization with respect to the conscious mind generalizes utility maximization restricted to perfectly situated agents.

Higher-order utility analysis is a way of calculating an option's utility with respect to the conscious mind when it differs from its utility with respect to the whole mind. It is a utility principle intended to complement the decision rule ordering utility maximization with respect to the conscious mind.[4]

In my example, the chance for each possible value of the lottery ticket's expected utility is a pro or con, according as the possible value is positive or negative, and the chance's utility is its probability times the possible value. Adding the chances' utilities yields the option's utility with respect to the conscious mind. Higher-order expected utility analysis is justified as a way of separating considerations that neither omits nor double-counts anything relevant. Just as section 2.4 claims that an option's expected utility is its utility, this section claims that the expected value of an option's expected utility is the expected value of its utility and is its utility with respect to the conscious mind.[5]

My decision rule's reliance on higher-order utility analysis is justified by the primary goal for decision: maximizing informed utility. An estimate of an option's expected utility with respect to the whole mind is an estimate of an estimate of the option's fully informed utility, or an estimate of that utility. Given uncertainty about the external and internal worlds, the estimate of an option's expected utility is the appropriate estimate of its fully informed utility, and maximizing the estimate is the appropriate way of pursuing the goal of maximizing fully informed utility.

When first-order quantities are unknown, higher-order expected utility analysis is distinct from first-order expected utility analysis. It is not just first-order expected utility analysis applied with respect to a partition of states encompassing the possible values of the unknown data. Take, for example, the case of the lottery ticket. Let t stand for the proposition that the ticket is drawn. The agent may try to compute the ticket's expected utility with respect to this fourfold partition of states: $t \& P(t) = 1/2$, $t \& P(t) = 1/4$, $\sim t \& P(t) = 1/2$, $\sim t \& P(t) = 1/4$. But the data are missing for a first-order analysis using this partition. If the agent had the probabilities of these four compound states, the probability that the ticket is drawn would be the sum of the probabilities of the first and second states. Hence, the probability that the ticket is drawn would be known, contrary to the hypothesis.

It may seem that the agent must know the probabilities of the compound states because, for example, $P(t/P(t) = 1/2) = 1/2$ and, because $P(P(t) = 1/2) = 1/2$, it follows that $P(t \& P(t) = 1/2) = 1/4$ according to the probability law that $P(t \& P(t) = 1/2) = P(t/P(t) = 1/2) \times P(P(t) = 1/2)$. But it is not the case that $P(t/P(t) = 1/2) = 1/2$. Along with $P(t \& P(t) = 1/2)$, the conditional probability is unknown. Miller's Principle (1966), which states that $P(s/P(s) = x) = x$, does not apply to the conditional probability, a probability ratio, when the ratio has unknown factors. It may fail in that case.[6] The inclination to apply it rests on the false impression that a proposition's conditional probability is the probability that the proposition would have if the condition were learned. The conditional probability is not a hypothetical probability but a ratio of actual nonconditional probabilities and does

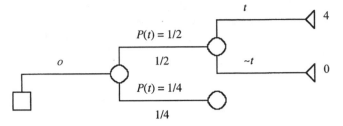

FIGURE 5.1. Higher-order utility analysis.

not always equal the corresponding hypothetical probability, as Weirich (1983a) shows.[7]

Consider the partial decision tree in figure 5.1. It displays a procedure for computation of option *o*'s expected utility. To construct the tree, one may start with a tree for a two-state partition and then replace its terminal nodes with chance nodes. In the expanded tree, conditional expected utility analysis, presented in Weirich (2001a: chap. 4), yields the utilities of outcomes at the original tree's replaced terminal nodes. The branches involving *t* and ~*t* analyze the utility of *o*'s outcome given the state $P(t) = 1/2$ if *o*.

Completing figure 5.1's tree, if possible, yields a first-order analysis of *o*'s utility. How may this proceed? Consider, for example, the probability to enter in the branch for *t*. It is, given *o*, $P(t$ given $P(t) = 1/2)$. Probabilities under an assumption, such as $P(t$ given $P(t) = 1/2)$, are not in general equal to standard conditional probabilities; they are not in general the same as ratios of nonconditional probabilities, as section A.6 explains. But because both propositions involved in $P(t$ given $P(t) = 1/2)$ are states, and the supposition of the condition tracks evidential relations, this probability equals $P(t/P(t) = 1/2)$, as Weirich (1985b) shows. Unfortunately, the latter probability is unknown, because, as noted, Miller's Principle does not apply. So the probability at the branch for *t* is unknown, and the first-order expected conditional utility analysis cannot be carried out.[8]

The first-order analysis using $P(t/P(t) = 1/2)$ is justified according to section 2.4. Because the conditional probability is a ratio, the first-order analysis may be reduced to an analysis using the compound state: t & $P(t) = 1/2$. When this first-order analysis can be conducted, the second-order analysis must agree with it. So when $P(t/P(t) = 1/2)$ and $P(t/P(t) = 1/4)$ are known and thus $P(t)$ is known, the first- and second-order analyses must yield the same utility for *o*. Let me verify that they do. Suppose, for example, that $P(t)$ is known to be 1/2. The second-order analysis concludes that $U(o) = 1/2 \times 4$, or 2, because then $P(P(t) = 1/2)$ equals 1. The first-order analysis also concludes that $U(o) = 1/2 \times 4$, or 2, because then $P(t/P(t) = 1/2) = P(t$ & $P(t) = 1/2)/P(P(t) = 1/2) = 1/2$. $P(t/P(t) = 1/4)$ is undefined under my assumption because then its condition has probability o, but it may be dropped from the first-order utility analysis because in general, states with probability o may be dropped. The case in which $P(t)$ is known to be 1/4 is similar.

One knows in advance that the two levels of utility analysis will agree when $P(t)$ is learned and the first-order analysis can be conducted. But one does not know in advance whether $P(t/P(t) = 1/2)$ will be 1/2 or undefined (as a result of division by zero) when $P(t)$ is learned. A similar situation occurs prior to learning which state obtains among those in a fine-grained partition for a first-order expected utility analysis. After learning which state obtains, one knows that an option's expected and informed utility will agree, but one does not know in advance the future value of the option's expected utility. It depends on the state learned.

5.1.3. *Higher-Order and Ersatz Utility Analyses*

Higher-order utility analysis is equivalent to certain procedures for estimating the values of missing data, say, missing probabilities or utilities, and applying utility analysis using those estimates. Even though an estimate of a state's probability with respect to the whole mind need not equal its probability with respect to the conscious mind, the estimate may be used in an expected utility analysis to obtain an option's utility with respect to the conscious mind. So, for decision purposes, an estimate of the probability's value with respect to the whole mind may be taken as the probability with respect to the conscious mind.

For instance, in my example concerning the lottery ticket that pays $4.00 if drawn, the agent reaches the right decision if she maximizes expected utility with respect to the conscious mind, taking the probability of the ticket's being drawn with respect to the conscious mind as its expected value with respect to the whole mind, that is, $(1/2 \times 1/2) + (1/2 \times 1/4)$, or 3/8. Given this value for the probability, the ticket's expected utility is $3/8 \times 4$, or 1.5. That is, using the estimate of the probability of the ticket's being drawn, the ticket's ersatz first-order expected utility is 1.5. This is the same as the expected value of its expected utility, its utility with respect to the conscious mind according to higher-order expected utility analysis. According to section 5.1.2's second-order expected utility analysis, the ticket's expected utility is 2 with probability 1/2 and 1 with probability 1/2, so the expected value of its expected utility is 1.5.

The estimate of the probability is not the probability of the state. The probability of the state is unknown and is known not to have the same value as the estimate. Moreover, the estimate is not the state's probability with respect to the conscious mind. That probability is suspended, as section 5.1.2 observes. Nonetheless, the estimate of the missing probability yields the right decision when one decides *as if* it were the probability of the state.

Use of expected value estimates of missing probabilities and utilities provides another general form of utility analysis, *ersatz* expected utility analysis, in which estimates serve as ersatz probabilities and utilities. This form of utility analysis for utilities with respect to the conscious mind neither omits nor double-counts considerations and gives considerations their proper weights when adding them to obtain an option's utility. The probability estimate times the utility of an outcome is the utility of the chance for the outcome given ignorance of the probability itself.[9] Because conditions are nonideal and the agent cannot compute the option's utility using expected utility analysis — the components exist but are unknown — the expected utility's estimate is the option's utility with respect to the conscious mind, not just an estimate of it, even though the option's utility with respect to the whole mind computed using actual values in place of estimates of probabilities and utilities would have a different value. The expected utility's estimate is the option's utility with respect to the conscious mind, although not the option's utility with respect to the whole mind.

I have introduced higher-order utility analysis and ersatz utility analysis through examples. Let me now formulate them precisely and demonstrate their equivalence. I do this only for second-order expected utility analysis using second-order probabilities of unknown first-order probabilities and for ersatz first-order expected utility analysis using estimates of unknown first-order probabilities. The definitions and proofs for other forms of higher-order and ersatz first-order utility analyses follow the same pattern.

Consider a second-order expected utility analysis. It is a method of estimating an option's first-order expected utility. Estimates of expected utilities are used to rank options just as actual expected utilities are. An option's estimated expected utility yields its actual utility given ignorance of probabilities for option-state pairs.

According to a second-order expected utility analysis estimating the results of an n-state first-order expected utility analysis in a case where only probabilities are unknown,

$$U(o) = \Sigma_i P_o(P_o(s) = p_i)\Sigma_j p_{ij}U(o \text{ given } s_j).$$

P_o is probability given the option o. Also, s and p_i are ordered n-tuples. $P_o(s) = p_i$ stands for $P_o(s_1) = p_{i1}$ & $P_o(s_2) = p_{i2}$ & ... & $P_o(s_n) = p_{in}$. The index i orders possible n-tuples of probabilities for the n states, and the index j orders the n states.[10]

An ersatz first-order expected utility analysis uses estimates of missing probabilities rather than genuine higher-order probabilities. Nonetheless, it also yields an option's utility with respect to the conscious mind. It advances the following formula for that utility:

$$U(o) = \Sigma_j[\Sigma_k P_o(P_o(s_j) = p_k)]U(o \text{ given } s_j)$$

The index k orders the possible values of $P_o(s_j)$. The formula inserts estimates exactly where the missing probabilities would appear in a first-order expected utility analysis.[11]

The two forms of utility analysis need not conditionalize the probability of a state given an option according to a possible value, using the condition that a particular possible value of the probability is correct. The probability of the state given the option *according to* a possible value is on a priori grounds probabilistically independent of the possible value's correctness, in contrast with the probability of the state *given* that a possible value is correct (see n. 8). Because agents are cognizant of a priori truths, probabilities according to possible values are independent of possible values' correctness.

As the start of this section showed, second-order and ersatz first-order expected utility analyses are equivalent in the case of the lottery ticket that pays $4.00 if drawn. The two forms of utility analysis are also equivalent in general. Appendix B generalizes the forms of analysis, shows that they agree, and explains how to establish their consistency with other forms of utility analysis.

Some tempting estimates of missing data fail to produce results equivalent to higher-order and ersatz utility analyses. Take, for instance, a form of estimation for probabilities, inspired by Jeffrey (1983: 199), that treats the choice of an estimate as a decision problem.[12] It recommends choosing a viable estimate that maximizes expected utility, where an estimate's expected utility depends on the option to which it leads and the expected value of the expected utility of that option. In more detail, it recommends picking a probability estimate as follows. First, consider only the viable estimates for the probability. These are the epistemically possible values for the probability. Then select the estimate that maximizes expected utility given that the estimate will be used in an expected utility analysis of options. I assume that the choice of an estimate has no influence on options' utilities.[13]

To illustrate use of these estimates, take a case in which an agent is ignorant of a probability crucial for a first-order expected utility analysis. Suppose he has higher-order probabilities concerning its possible values. The procedure says to use as an estimate of the missing probability the possible value that maximizes expected utility given the estimate's use in an expected utility analysis used to choose an option. In the case of the lottery ticket that pays $4.00 if drawn, using this estimate yields the same decision as higher-order expected utility analysis. First, the agent computes the expected value of picking 1/2 as the estimate of the missing probability. If it is picked, then the ticket's expected value is taken to be $2.00, and the ticket is selected rather than $1.25. The estimate's expected utility is the expected value of the ticket's expected utility, namely, 1.5. On the other hand, picking 1/4 as the estimate leads to an expected value of $1.00 for the ticket, so taking $1.25 is selected instead. This estimate's expected utility is the expected value of the expected utility of $1.25, namely, 1.25. Hence, the procedure to choose a viable estimate of maximum expected utility recommends choosing 1/2, and this estimate leads to buying the ticket, the decision generated by higher-order and ersatz utility analyses.[14]

Unfortunately, the estimation procedure leads to the wrong recommendation in other cases. Suppose that there are three salient options: o_1, o_2, o_3. And suppose that a probability needed for a first-order expected utility analysis is missing. It has only two epistemically possible values. Given one possible value, o_1 maximizes expected utility. Given the other possible value, o_3 maximizes expected utility. The expected value of the expected utility of o_1 is greater than the expected value of the expected utility of o_3, so the procedure recommends o_1. However, it may turn out that o_2 maximizes expected value of expected utility and so is the recommendation of a higher-order expected utility analysis. For example, suppose that o_1 is a bet that pays $1.00 if heads comes up on a coin toss, otherwise nothing; that o_3 is a bet that pays $1.00 if tails comes up on the coin toss, otherwise nothing; and that o_2 is a bet that pays $1.00 if anything but a heart is drawn from a standard deck, otherwise nothing. The (subjective) probability of heads with the coin is unknown, but in the extreme case I imagine is known to be either 1 or 0 with the probability of each value being 1/2. Then, given that the probability is estimated to be 1, o_1 has maximum expected utility, and the expected value of its expected utility is 1/2. Also, given that the probability is estimated to be 0, o_3 has maximum expected utility, and the expected value of its expected utility is 1/2. Now, apply the rule to pick the estimate that leads to the option with the highest expected value of expected utility. It says to pick either o_1 or o_3. But the expected value of the expected utility of o_2 is 3/4. My higher-order rule to maximize expected value of expected utility says to pick o_2. Because o_2 is the right choice, I favor higher-order expected utility analysis and maximization of utility according to it rather than the alternative estimation and decision procedure. The alternative does not sufficiently utilize information about the probabilities that estimates are correct.

The alternative procedure makes the kind of mistake made by the agent who picks the act that will probably maximize fully informed utility rather than the act that maximizes expected utility. Such an agent, driving on a two-lane country road, may decide to pass on a hill because probably no traffic is oncoming over the top, even though the risk of a head-on collision makes the expected utility of passing lower than the expected utility of waiting to pass. This agent's estimation procedure is not attuned to its purpose. It is not suited to guide decision, but rather opinion about outcomes. Rational deliberation for decisions takes account of all goals. Opinion formation, pros and cons reasoning for beliefs, registers only epistemic goals. Inserting estimates recommended by epistemic goals into decision rules may not promote deliberational goals. Different estimates suit deliberational and epistemic projects.[15]

Some decision procedures simply invoke the idea that when crucial data are unknown, one should use estimates. This is sensible advice but vague. Everything depends on the method of estimation. Simple approximations or guesses are unsatisfactory. One must have substitutes for the missing data that maximize one's chances of making the right decision according to first-order expected utility analysis. My method uses higher-order expected utility analysis to obtain estimates of options' expected utilities, or expected value estimates to serve as ersatz probabilities and utilities. I advocate higher-order and ersatz expected utility analyses because they have a clear justification using section A.3's principle of pros and cons. Divergent methods of utility analysis based on other estimation procedures do not have such a justification. No sound estimation procedure is independent of the principle of pros and cons. That is why the basic forms of utility analysis justified by that principle continue to serve as guides to decision even when their application faces obstacles.

5.1.4. *Higher-Order Quantizations*

Although I recommend higher-order utility analysis in cases where ignorance thwarts first-order utility analysis, I recognize that higher-order utility analysis is not always possible in such cases. Sometimes the information required, for example, information about higher-order probabilities, is not on hand and is inaccessible. Then an agent should decide according to a preference ordering of options that is compatible with a quantization of his data about his beliefs and desires. This quantization principle incorporates higher-order utility analysis. Such analysis restricts probability and utility values in ways that quantizations register.

My higher-order quantization principle is an analog of chapter 4's quantization principle, which treats nonquantitative cases where probabilities and utilities are nonexistent, not just unknown. It is similarly justified because deciding in ignorance of quantitative probabilities and utilities is analogous to deciding in their absence. The decision principle is motivated by the general advice to make the most of resources. On my view, quantitative methods for the ideal case should guide use of resources. Those methods should regulate quantizations of available beliefs and desires. Then these quantizations should in turn regulate decisions.

5.2. Acquisition of Missing Input

Section 5.1 considered cases where missing psychological data are out of reach. This section considers cases where they are accessible given some effort. For instance, an agent may be able to apply a representation theorem such as Savage's (1972: chap. 3) to infer probabilities and utilities when they exist but are unknown. Plainly, relevant probabilities and utilities should be obtained before a decision is made if the cost is not prohibitive. How may a decision maker determine whether gathering the missing data is worthwhile despite its cost?[16]

I assume that the decision maker knows that the missing information is accessible and knows its possible contents and their probabilities and the cost of obtaining the information, that is, the cost of introspection and reflection sufficient for obtaining it. Given this knowledge, he can calculate whether obtaining the information is worthwhile. To make the calculation, he has to take into account the benefit to be derived from having the information. The benefit is the expected increase in the expected utility of his decision if he makes it using the information. For example, if he lacks the probability of a lottery ticket's being drawn, he calculates the decision he would make without the information, using the procedures already described. He notes the expected value of the expected utility of that decision. In the example of the lottery ticket that pays $4.00 if drawn, without new data the agent picks the ticket, and the expected value of the expected utility of that decision is 1.5. Next, the agent supposes that he has the missing data. He then calculates the expected value of the expected utility of the decision he reaches using the missing data. In my example, if he learns the probability of winning is 1/2 and so picks the ticket, then the expected utility of his decision is $(1/2 \times 4) + (1/2 \times 0) = 2$. If he learns the probability is 1/4 and so takes $1.25 instead of the ticket, the expected utility of his decision is 1.25. Because for each of the two possible probability values, the probability of learning it is 1/2, the expected value of the expected utility of his decision given acquisition of the missing probability is 1.625. This quantity is higher than the expected value of his decision's expected utility if he does not acquire the missing probability. He should therefore acquire the missing probability if its cost is less than the expected increase in expected utility. Hence, in my example, the agent should acquire the missing probability if its acquisition's cost in terms of utility is less than $1.625 - 1.5 = 0.125$. This procedure for deciding whether to acquire missing psychological data shows how utility analysis serves as a guide to decisions even when it does not apply straightforwardly.[17]

The procedure just advanced is familiar from statistics books, for example, Chernoff and Moses (1959: chap. 1) and Pratt, Raiffa, and Schlaifer (1995: chap. 6). It is commonly used to direct acquisition of information about the external world.

For example, it might be used to determine whether a doctor should perform additional diagnostic tests on a patient before prescribing a treatment. My procedure just applies familiar advice about data acquisition to the acquisition of data about the agent's internal world. It is justified by the primary decision goal of maximizing informed utility.

Application of my procedure may face a regress. Perhaps the second-order psychological data needed to calculate whether it is worthwhile to acquire some missing first-order psychological data are also missing. Then one needs an assessment of the utility of acquiring the second-order data. The costs of acquiring them are taken into account along with the costs of acquiring the first-order data. The problem of missing data could ascend to the third level, and so on. However, because costs keep rising with the addition of the costs of retreating to a higher level, it eventually becomes clear, even without calculation, that it is too costly to continue the ascent. If it becomes clearly too costly to continue the ascent beyond level n, then one should decide about acquiring the information for an nth-order analysis without acquiring the information for an analysis at the next level. Information costs thus terminate the regress.[18]

Now suppose that after completing an analysis of a data acquisition problem, the result is that one should not acquire the missing data. Then one should make a decision on the basis of the data one already has. That is, one should adopt an option that is rational given no additional data. Whether or not one gathers information before deciding, eventually one decides according to information on hand. The principle of accessible utility maximization (section 5.1.2) says to maximize utility with respect to the conscious mind, that is, information on hand. The principle presumes fully rational agents and so rational gathering of psychological data.

This section does not revise the principle of accessible utility maximization. It just clarifies the presumption that the agent has rationally gathered psychological data. In particular, this section does not advance a new rule for a two-decision sequence, the first decision concerning information gathering and the second concerning acting on the information gathered. The principle of accessible utility maximization treats decisions at a moment, not sequences of decisions, but it covers a sequence of decisions about information and action because it applies to decisions to gather information as well as decisions to act using information gathered. This section just makes that decision principle a more useful guide by explaining how to meet its presumptions about information.

5.3. Nonexistent Probabilities and Utilities

The next topic is decision making when an agent has not formed the quantitative probabilities and utilities needed to compute an option's utility and, in addition, has cognitive limitations that impose a cost on the formation of those probabilities and utilities. Because the required probabilities and utilities do not exist, the cases treated are nonquantitative, as in chapter 4. Because forming probabilities and utilities has a cost, they resemble cases in which gathering information about probabilities and utilities has a cost, section 5.2's topic.

This section's recommendation for the formation of probabilities and utilities is similar to section 5.2's recommendation for the discovery of probabilities and utilities. An agent should generate input for utility analysis if feasible and beneficial. When critical probabilities or utilities are unformed but formable with thought, the agent should do the thinking required to form them, as long as the benefits justify the formation costs. The costs and benefits are assessed in the same way as for the acquisition of missing psychological data. Once probabilities and utilities have been formed to the extent warranted, an agent should then make a decision that maximizes utility under a quantization, following chapter 4's rule. Thus, the recommended decision procedure is to form probability and utility judgments to the extent justified by the costs and benefits of forming them and afterward to apply the quantization rule.

The recommendation for the formation of probability and utility judgments may be divided into three steps. The first step is to determine the set of decisions that are rational given no new probability and utility judgments. This is the set of decisions compatible with a quantization of current probability and utility judgments. The next step is to determine the costs and expected benefits of forming additional probability and utility judgments. I assume that the costs are known. The expected benefits are calculated using estimates of the results of the judgments' formation, as section 5.2 used estimates of missing psychological data to calculate the expected benefits of acquiring that data. The third step is conditional. If the expected benefits justify the costs of forming the critical probability and utility judgments, the agent should form them and then decide. If not, he should decide without them. What is rational without new judgments is rational period in this case.

Sometimes, of course, the data for evaluating judgment formation are missing, and then the agent has to decide whether to generate them. He should approach this second-order decision in the same way as the first-order decision. That is, he should compare the costs and expected benefits of forming or acquiring the relevant second-order data. The mounting costs of data generation squelch the threat of infinite regress.

This decision procedure may be elaborated to take account of cases in which some useful probability and utility judgments are formed but unknown and others are unformed. One must then combine the various procedures introduced. Evidently, the agent has to proceed in stages, sometimes forming new judgments, at other times learning about judgments already formed. The stages may acquire just part of the missing psychological data, rather than all of it, and afterward recalculate the value of acquiring more missing data in light of the newly acquired data. New stages arise until none of the formation and acquisition procedures lead to further changes.

I describe rational decision procedures because of their bearing on comprehensive evaluations of decisions, my main topic. A decision's comprehensive evaluation looks at the decision procedure that produced the decision. An agent who makes a comprehensively rational decision tries to reach a good position for deciding. If warranted, she follows a decision procedure that includes discovering and forming relevant probabilities and utilities before reaching a decision.

5.4. Ignorance of A Priori Matters

Up to now, I have assumed that agents know all a priori truths. Suppose cognitive limitations create ignorance of some a priori truths. How should utility and decision rules be revised? One problem is that such rules are a priori, so cognitive limitations may create ignorance of them, or ignorance of a priori truths grounding their application. Ignorance of the revised rules or their application may excuse agents' violations of the rules.[19]

Agents with limited a priori knowledge are said to have "bounded rationality." This terminology takes rationality to be the faculty of reason. Boundedly rational agents have an imperfect cognitive faculty that limits their access to a priori truths. They need not be irrational in any way. They may fully conform to all standards for agents with their limitations. Consequently, a boundedly rational agent may be fully rational. This section supposes that agents are fully rational, except possibly in the resolution of current decision problems. It considers how such agents should cope with their ignorance of a priori matters.

An evaluation of an agent's decision when he may lack relevant a priori information should examine his preliminary efforts to acquire relevant a priori information. An agent's decision is rational if the agent first acquires relevant a priori information to the extent warranted and then adopts an option estimated to maximize utility under a quantization of probability and utility judgments according to his a priori information. Under my idealization that agents are fully rational, they extend their a priori information as much as warranted. So a decision is rational if, in light of the agent's a priori information, it aims at maximization of utility. This standard offers a sufficient condition of rationality rather than a necessary condition. It allows for excuses arising from ignorance of standards of rationality.

Deciding without full information about relevant a priori matters is rational if it results from a pair of decisions guided by maximizing principles. First, the agent decides not to acquire relevant a priori facts, such as the contents of possible decisions and the results of calculating expected utilities, because of excessive acquisition costs. Second, the agent makes a decision that, according to available a priori information, is estimated to maximize utility under a quantization of probability and utility judgments.

This method of evaluation is just a sketch. It does not specify a method of estimating utility maximization, although, evidently, the method must be one reasonable in light of the goals of deliberation. My main point is that ignorance of a priori matters should be treated as ignorance of a posteriori matters. The costs and benefits of acquiring missing information should direct the agent's deliberations. I treat the acquisition of a priori information just as section 5.2 treated the acquisition of psychological data.[20]

To clarify the standard for adequate acquisition of a priori knowledge, I add a few supplementary points. As noted, for any standard devised, an agent may lack a priori knowledge of it, or a priori knowledge required for applying it, and so may excusably violate the standard. A standard cognizant of this difficulty calls on an agent to use current a priori knowledge to calculate the cost of acquiring additional a priori knowledge. Once new a priori knowledge is acquired, the value of acquiring additional a priori knowledge is reassessed. The process of reassessment continues until it prompts no further acquisitions of a priori knowledge. The agent pulls himself up by his bootstraps, as it were.

Skyrms (1990a: chap. 2) introduces rules of deliberation for boundedly rational agents. He recommends deliberation in stages and revision of one's tentative decision at a stage if a subsequent stage generates new relevant a priori information. Deliberation continues until one's tentative decision becomes stable and so becomes one's final decision. These procedures illustrate a type of bootstrapping to acquire a priori information. They treat only expected utility calculations, however. I imagine extending them to all sorts of a priori matters.

My bootstrapping standard is for the evaluation of decisions; it is not a standard that an agent must apply to make a rational decision. Although the standard of evaluation takes into account the agent's perspective, it may step outside that perspective. The agent's ignorance of a priori matters may hinder his assessment of the acquisition of additional a priori information. He asks whether acquiring relevant a priori information is worth the effort. His response draws on his limited a priori information. An outsider's evaluation of an agent's decision may use all a priori facts, not just facts in the agent's possession. An outsider may use complete a priori information to assess the agent's efforts to acquire relevant a priori information. Thus, the outsider's and the agent's evaluations may differ. My standard is for an outsider's evaluation of an agent's decision. The outsider's evaluation does not proceed by bootstrapping but rather assesses the agent's attempts at bootstrapping.

My standard covers cases in which the agent's initial a priori knowledge includes knowledge of the standard, but also covers cases in which the agent is initially ignorant of the standard and remains ignorant of it. Ignorance of the standard may, but does not always, excuse violations. Violations are unexcused, for example, when reasonable bootstrapping would have generated knowledge of the standard.[21]

5.5. Substantive and Procedural Standards

Obviously, I have not treated all problems caused by cognitive limitations. Also, many of my suggestions are just sketches. Before concluding this chapter, let me make some brief, general points about using procedural standards of rationality to handle cognitive limitations.

The standards this chapter presents are substantive standards that describe the contents of rational decisions. Procedural standards evaluate decisions according to the process that yields them rather than according to their contents. To illustrate, take a nonideal case where deliberation has a cost. The agent must decide when to terminate deliberations. Termination maximizes expected utility when the cost of further deliberation is greater than its expected benefits. But comparing the cost and expected benefits of further deliberation is further deliberation and has a cost, too. If further deliberation is not worthwhile, the agent should not conduct the deliberations needed to verify that this is so. Therefore, the agent must sometimes decide without making calculations that would help him decide. In these cases, the rationality of a spontaneous decision depends on the agent's habits of spontaneous decision. If he has acquired good habits, his decision is rational whatever its content. Some of the standards of rationality for terminating deliberation in nonideal cases are procedural rather than substantive.

Sometimes procedural standards may be replaced with substantive standards. For example, take the procedural standard that a rational decision is one that results from a rational deliberation procedure. This may be replaced with the substantive standard that a rational decision is one that results from a deliberation procedure that maximizes utility in a higher-order decision about deliberation procedures and so, in the ideal case, a decision that maximizes utility. However, sometimes procedural standards are uneliminable. Suppose that an agent has formed any basic goals rationality requires and then forms additional, compatible basic goals. Consider, for instance, this procedural standard for their formation: formation after reflection and experience. No substantive standards may replace it; rationality is purely procedural in its domain.

Procedural standards arise at all levels of idealization. They guide the formation of basic goals even for ideal agents. But procedural standards have a larger and larger role in decision theory as it rolls back idealizations. As just remarked, when thinking has a cost, procedural standards determine whether a decision made spontaneously, when spontaneity is rational, is a rational decision. I expect other procedural standards, uneliminable ones, to come into play as other idealizations are removed.

This chapter and the previous chapter added psychological realism to decision theory by removing idealizations about an agent's cognitive resources. The decision principles obtained given the new, more realistic assumptions, yield a more general decision theory. The more general theory yields four main conclusions:

(1) Quantitative principles are the basic guides to rational decision making. No independent, nonquantitative principles such as the maximin principle supplement them. Principles for nonideal cases stem from principles for quantitative cases.

(2) Rationality requires only maximization with respect to information in hand and so requires utility maximization with respect to the conscious mind. It uses as an option's utility an estimate of its utility with respect to the whole mind.

(3) Using estimates of probabilities and utilities in place of missing probabilities and utilities must be carefully controlled. Higher-order utility analysis using probabilities of probabilities and the like is more reliable than substitution of estimates of probabilities and utilities in first-order utility analysis. Only carefully selected estimates of probabilities and utilities are suitable replacements for probabilities and utilities.

(4) Adjusting for agents with bounded rationality about a priori matters is best accomplished by taking account of the cost of acquiring a priori knowledge.

Realism about Agents: Mistakes

The decision theory chapter 2 presents is for fully rational ideal agents. These agents enter decision problems having fully attained the goals of rationality for beliefs, desires, and past decisions. They have not made mistakes in the sense of having fallen short of the goals of rationality. Although they are fallible—that is, although it is possible for them to make mistakes—they have not made any mistakes. No mistakes shape the circumstances of their current decisions, in particular, the input for applications of utility analysis. Furthermore, the agents will not make mistakes in the future, and they know they are mistake-free, except perhaps in the current decision problem. Consequently, they need not worry about deciding in a way that compensates for errors elsewhere.

Another way to make my decision theory more realistic is to strip away the idealization that agents have not fallen short of the goals of rationality, that they have not made mistakes. Humans generally come to a decision problem burdened with errors. Even agents without cognitive limitations may bring mistakes to their decision problems because cognitive ability does not entail rationality. This chapter considers how to apply the rule of utility maximization when an agent has made mistakes prior to his decision problem, or knows he will make mistakes afterward. It treats agents both with and without cognitive limits.[1]

The agents I consider may, for example, have mistaken probability and utility assignments, or fail to consider all their options. The chapter shows how compensation for such errors affects standards of rationality. It formulates goals for resolving mistake-generated conflicts between the goal of maximizing expected utility and other goals of rationality. Its compromise goals ground principles evaluating decisions for rationality.

6.1. Accommodating Mistakes

Mistakes are departures from ideals of rationality. A false or unjustified belief is a mistake because it falls short of the ideal of knowledge. Granting that a concern for one's happiness is part of the ideal for desires, an agent without that concern makes a mistake. An agent's ignorance of his mistakes may excuse them but may not if the ignorance is culpable. For instance, a decision made in ignorance of the utility-maximizing option may be irrational because the oversight is not itself excused.

Mistakes relevant to utility maximization may concern options, probabilities, utilities, and decision principles. In examples I assume the accuracy of the traditional catalogue of mistaken beliefs, desires, and deliberative errors but acknowledge that items in the catalogue are controversial. My principles of rationality for mistaken agents do not depend on the catalogue's accuracy.

When an agent enters a decision problem having already made mistakes, evaluation of a decision faces a hard issue. Suppose some circumstances of the decision are results of the agent's mistakes. Does a rational decision fit the circumstances as they are, mistakes and all, or does it fit the circumstances that would obtain if the mistakes were corrected? Does it maximize utility with respect to corrected circumstances?

I distinguish two sorts of mistake that bear on the application of the principle of utility maximization. Some mistakes directly affect the input of the principles of utility analysis. These are mistakes in degrees of belief or desire, or mistakes in the set of options considered. An agent's degrees of belief may violate the probability calculus, or disregard evidence. Or he may have degrees of desire that violate utility laws, or rest on irrational goals; perhaps he has a pure time preference for some present satisfaction over a greater future satisfaction. Or he may fail to consider all his options, or consider as options acts not certain to be performed if chosen. When the input for utility analysis is mistaken in these ways, is a rational decision governed by utility analysis using actual input or corrected input? If an inattentive decision maker considers an inappropriate set of options, one that omits the attractive options, maximizing utility among the options considered may differ from maximizing utility among the options he would have considered had he been attentive. What type of maximizing forms the standard of rationality?

Other mistakes do not directly affect the input for utility analysis but may still significantly affect an agent's decision problem. An agent may have painted himself into a corner, for example. In general, some of the relevant states of the world, payoffs, probabilities of states, and so on may be influenced by past mistakes of the agent or mistakes he knows he will make. Is a rational decision governed by utility maximization applied to decision circumstances taken as they are, or does it compensate in some way for circumstances caused by the agent's mistakes?

Take, for instance, a case in which an agent irrationally develops an addiction. Later, he must decide between a small gain and a larger gain that comes if he acts contrary to his addiction. The probability that he will obtain the larger gain if he tries may be low. Should principles of utility maximization be applied to options taking his circumstances as they are, or after correction for his irrationally acquired addiction? Will they recommend trying for the larger gain, or settling for the smaller one?

Aristotle (1947: 358) regards culpability as infectious. A drunken man is responsible for his misdeeds even though he cannot help himself, because there was a time when he could have, when he could have decided not to drink more. A man who makes a mistake because he is drunk is still culpable because he could have avoided being drunk. Are other mistakes infectious as well? Does a man who decides on an inauspicious action because he misassigned probabilities decide irrationally because he could have correctly assigned probabilities? Should an agent be blamed for a bad decision even though he chooses well given his circumstances, because there was an earlier time when he could have taken steps to improve his decision circumstances?[2]

In some problem cases, goals for decisions conflict with other goals of rationality. For example, the members of a basketball team should not dwell on their team's losses before a game with their conference's first-place team. To bolster confidence, and thus enhance performance, the team's members should recall their victories and the opposing team's losses. They should cultivate a belief that they will win, statistical evidence notwithstanding. In this case, the goal for decisions about the cultivation of beliefs conflicts with the goal for beliefs. The goal for decisions recommends the cultivation of unsupported beliefs, whereas the goal for beliefs recommends only beliefs that the evidence supports. When a decision rests on defective beliefs cultivated for pragmatic reasons, what are the appropriate standards for the decision? Do they ignore the beliefs' deficiencies?

An issue similar to evaluation of decisions resting on mistakes has already arisen and been resolved. Recall the standard of maximizing utility. Section 2.3 asked how it should apply in cases where agents are fully rational but not fully informed. One might apply the standard of utility maximization using assessments of utility that are fully informed about the options' outcomes. Or one might apply it using assessments of utility that rely on the agent's beliefs about the options' outcomes. Section 2.3 argued that the standard of rationality should use assessments of utility that rely on the agent's beliefs. Although the primary goal of rational decision is maximization of fully informed utility, given uncertainty the appropriate secondary goal for pursuit of the primary goal is maximization of utility assessed with respect to the agent's beliefs. Likewise, although a goal of rational decision is maximization of utility given error-free circumstances, it may turn out that given mistakes, the appropriate way of pursuing this goal, and through it the primary goal, is maximization of utility given actual circumstances. On the other hand, the case of uncertainty differs significantly from the case of mistakes. Generally, a mistake is a self-created impediment to decision goals, whereas uncertainty is usually not self-created. This disanalogy may call for a different approach to the evaluation of decisions given mistakes.[3]

This chapter's objective is a general principle of compensation for mistakes. To evaluate decisions by agents who make mistakes, it must explain when to correct or partially correct the agents' circumstances before applying the standard of utility maximization. This chapter considers various proposals and revises them to obtain a satisfactory principle. My principle expresses a basic standard that organizes evaluations. Although it does not answer all questions, it answers some. Because the issue is large, any progress is rewarding.

Two ways of applying utility maximization given mistakes initially come to mind and have already appeared in my presentation of the problem mistakes pose. The first is to apply utility maximization taking circumstances as they are, mistakes included. The second is to apply utility maximization after correcting for the agent's mistakes. These two methods may, of course, conflict because the options that would maximize utility if the agent were error-free need not be the options that maximize utility given his mistakes.

The proposal to take circumstances as they are is reinforced by recalling that standards of rationality for an agent's decision consider the agent's capabilities. A rational decision need not meet all pertinent goals of rationality. Some short-comings are excused. When they are, a decision may be rational despite falling short of the ideal. For example, it is a goal of rationality in typical cases to decide so that utility is maximized. But circumstances sometimes pardon failures to meet this goal. For instance, a shortage of time for deliberation may cause a mistake. Then a decision falling short of the goal may still be rational. If the shortfall is excused in light of the circumstances, the decision is rational. A decision's being rational does not entail that it meets all goals of rationality. The standard for decisions where mistakes have been made is less stringent than the goals of rationality. It takes account of excuses. When mistakes are excused, being rational is not the same as meeting goals of rationality.

Because this chapter's standard of evaluation aims not at ideal rationality, but at ordinary rationality—which takes account of excuses for falling short of the ideal—it may seem that utility and decision principles should be applied taking circumstances as they are. It may seem that ordinary rationality demands no more than a good effort at utility maximization, taken with respect to the agent's circumstances, mistakes and all.

However, the principle to overlook the agent's mistakes and maximize utility given the agent's actual circumstances, is too forgiving. Sometimes a rational decision requires rectifying mistakes. For instance, take a case in which a decision to travel by train rather than by plane rests on an irrational belief that the plane will crash. The decision is irrational even if it follows by utility maximization from the agent's beliefs and desires. Or consider a case in which an agent chooses to become a doctor after considering only the law as an alternative. If the agent is a talented artist and fails to consider careers in art, then, if a career in art has maximum utility, his decision to enter medicine is irrational even if it maximizes utility among careers he considers. Finally, take an agent who knows he will do something irrational in the future. To compensate for his future mistake, he now decides on an act that does not maximize utility, except given his future mistake. That decision is irrational if the future mistake is easily avoided.

Let me turn to the second proposal. Its principle is to maximize utility with respect to the agent's circumstances corrected for mistakes. This principle, in contrast with the first, is too unforgiving. An agent may have made mistakes that are now incorrigible, so that it is wrong to judge his present decisions by what would be the case if they were corrected. For instance, if a driver has irrationally taken the wrong road, a current decision about how to reach his destination should not be guided by what is rational given that mistake's absence. It is wrong to apply utility maximization to the circumstances he would be in if he had not made the mistake. The road it would have been rational to take had he not erred need not be the road it is rational to take now. He may now need a road heading east to compensate for his having mistakenly turned west, whereas had he not made that mistake he would have now needed a road heading north.

I conclude that neither simple method of applying utility maximization is satisfactory. To begin seeking a compromise, I revise the principle that calls for correcting mistakes. A plausible revision says that a decision is rational only if it rests on a correction of corrigible mistakes. This revision quickly runs aground. An agent may have cognitive limitations that excuse some of his mistakes. Then some of his departures from the ideals of rationality may not be irrational. For instance, he may assign degree of belief 0.8 to some logical truth p because he fails to see that it is a logical truth, and he may be excused for this mistake because of his lack of logical perspicuity. Suppose, then, that he is unwilling to pay $0.90 for a gamble that pays $1.00 if and only if p is true. His decision is rational despite resting on a mistake. When a decision rests on corrigible mistakes that are excused, it may be rational even if it does not maximize utility given correction of those mistakes.

Another revision comes to mind. When mistakes are excused, taking circumstances as they are works. It may seem that before deciding, an agent need only remedy inexcusable mistakes. So perhaps my decision principle should call for the maximization of utility with respect to circumstances corrected for mistakes that are both corrigible and inexcusable. Unfortunately, this principle founders, too. An inexcusable mistake may be in the remote past. Then it may be the basis of a rational decision despite being corrigible and inexcusable. An agent with cognitive limitations need not search the remote past for mistakes (perhaps laziness in third-grade arithmetic class). A thorough search demands too much effort.

Also, some incorrigible mistakes are inexcusable and must be removed before calculating the rational decision. Take a failure to cultivate the habit of attending to the right options. A decision affected by this mistake may be irrational despite the incorrigibility of the mistake. For example, if, because of mistakes in cultivating habits of attention, an agent overlooks his best options, even a decision that maximizes utility among options considered may be irrational. This is illustrated by the case of a pilot who fails to consider the right options during an emergency because he failed to take emergency training seriously. Although lack of time makes his mistake incorrigible, a decision based on the mistake is still irrational. A decision that maximizes utility among the options considered is not a rational decision if it misses the options it is rational to consider after effective emergency training.

Let me stop revising decision principles for a moment. Perhaps difficulties arise because of unclarity about the type of evaluation sought. Evaluation of decisions by errant agents is complex. Perhaps to obtain adequate principles one must distinguish types of evaluation. An analogy between my problem and a similar problem in ethics suggests a distinction. The conflict between utility maximization applied with respect to actual circumstances and utility maximization applied with respect to corrected circumstances is similar to the conflict in ethics between objective and subjective standards of morality. Both sorts of conflict arise from agents' mistakes. For example, an objective standard of ethics is not to engage in an unjust war. A subjective standard is to follow one's conscience. Suppose that one believes a war is just and that participation is obligatory, so that following one's conscience requires participation. Still, the war may in fact be unjust so that participation is contrary to the objective standard. In this case, it is common to say that participation is *subjectively* right but *objectively* wrong.

Perhaps a similar distinction organizes evaluation of decisions resting on mistakes. Suppose, for instance, that an agent has unlimited cognitive power but makes a mistake in moving from his evidence to degrees of belief so that his degrees of belief are irrational. One way of applying utility maximization recommends an option that maximizes utility with respect to revised, rational degrees of belief and desire. Another way of applying utility maximization recommends an option that maximizes utility with respect to actual, irrational degrees of belief and desire. Suppose that the two ways of applying utility maximization conflict. Perhaps one should then distinguish objective and subjective rationality and maintain that the decision that maximizes utility with respect to corrected degrees of belief is objectively rational and that the decision that maximizes utility with respect to actual degrees of belief is subjectively rational.

This approach soon loses its appeal. A distinction between objective and subjective rationality does not provide a good resolution of the conflict between the two ways of applying utility maximization. First, it is hard to motivate a distinction between objective and subjective rationality. Suppose one says that a subjectively rational decision meets objective standards according to the decision maker's beliefs. What does this conception of rationality register that objective rationality misses? Objective standards take account of the decision maker's beliefs. All standards of rationality attend to her beliefs and desires. They all concern her decision's fit with her beliefs and desires, that is, its support or justification by her beliefs and desires.

Second, the distinction between objective and subjective standards of rationality does not resolve the conflict between the two methods of applying utility maximization. It does not suffice to assign the two methods to distinct types of evaluation. Classifying one objective and the other subjective does not obviate the need for a compromise. A decision's objective rationality, for instance, may depend partially on its meeting certain subjective standards. Then its objective evaluation presumes some way of combining objective and subjective standards. This combination of standards calls for a compromise between the two methods of applying utility maximization.

To clarify this point, first consider ethical evaluation. One may be tempted to say that an act's evaluation for objective rightness ignores subjective standards of rightness. However, subjective standards may have a crucial role in determining whether the act is objectively right. In some cases, it turns out that the subjective standard of following one's conscience has objective priority over conflicting objective standards. For instance, it is an objective standard to keep promises, except given certain conditions for release. Suppose a person's conscience tells him that he ought to break a promise because keeping it would aid in the commission of a murder. But suppose that as a matter of fact, keeping the promise would be harmless. Then keeping the promise meets the objective standard, and breaking it meets the subjective standard. If breaking the promise would not matter much, the subjective standard has objective priority. Breaking the promise is objectively right even though it conflicts with the objective standard of keeping promises because it complies with the subjective standard of following one's conscience. In this case, the objective value of following one's conscience outweighs the objective value of keeping one's promise so that on balance, what is objectively right agrees with the subjective standard of following one's conscience. Here, following one's conscience agrees with the objective standard of maximizing objective value. The conflict between the objective standard of keeping promises and the subjective standard of following one's conscience is objectively resolved in favor of the subjective standard. The application of objective standards does not ignore subjective standards.

Similarly, if an irrational belief is deeply rooted and would be hard to correct, an "objectively" rational decision may maximize expected utility with respect to it rather than corrected beliefs. That is, an "objectively" rational decision may be a decision that meets the "subjective" standards. Just as in ethics, objective evaluation does not ignore subjective standards, so also in decision theory "objective" evaluation does not ignore "subjective" standards. Even if one makes a distinction between objective and subjective rationality, one still must explain the interaction of objective and subjective standards for decisions. In particular, one still must strike a compromise between the two ways of applying utility maximization.

6.2. Evaluation's Scope

I have pursued several dead ends. Now I start a successful route. This section continues to explore various types of evaluation, but takes a more rewarding direction. The next section returns to correction of mistakes. The final section evaluates decisions by agents who make mistakes. It resolves the conflict between the two ways of applying utility maximization.

Distinguishing types of evaluation clarifies applications of utility maximization in cases where agents make mistakes. More important than distinguishing evaluations according to subjective and objective perspectives is distinguishing evaluations according to comprehensiveness. Ethics commonly distinguishes evaluations this way. A person may perform the right act but for the wrong reasons. When this happens, I say he acts wrongly even though his act is right. The adverbial construction indicates an evaluation of the manner of action, in particular, the motive from which the act arises, as well as the act itself. To act rightly, a person must perform the right act for the right reasons. Hence, ascertaining whether a person acts rightly calls for a more comprehensive evaluation than ascertaining whether his act is right.

When evaluating decisions for rationality, one must distinguish the comprehensiveness of evaluations in a similar way. A person may select a rational act but for irrational reasons. So he may decide irrationally even though the content of his decision is rational. The act selected may be rational to select although the agent's decision to perform that act is irrationally made. The decision may be irrationally made because of the reasons for it or the pedigree of those reasons. The adverbial construction indicates an evaluation of the manner of decision, including motive, as well as the content of the decision. To decide rationally a person must pick the right act for the right reasons. To decide rationally an agent must meet standards more comprehensive than those for his decision's content.

When an evaluation is limited to a decision's content, I say that the decision is either rational or irrational. When an evaluation is extended to the reasons for the decision, I say, when speaking carefully, that the decision is made either rationally or irrationally. The adverbial construction typically signals evaluation of a decision's content and manner only, but it can also express an even broader evaluation comprehending the decision's content, manner, and input, that is, the decision and all the reasons for it. I give it this more comprehensive sense.

The adverbial construction is sometimes awkward. To avoid it, people say, speaking informally, that a decision is either rational or irrational even when they have a comprehensive evaluation in mind. They rely on context to make the evaluation's scope clear. To make scope explicit even when adverbial expressions are inconvenient, I introduce some additional terminology for discussing decisions to perform acts. Because an evaluation of a decision by itself (that is, the mere formation of an intention to perform an act) goes by the decision's content (that is, the act intended), when I want to evaluate the decision by itself, I speak of the *act* selected. I say that the act is a rational or irrational selection. For ideal agents in ideal circumstances, the act selected is rational if and only if it maximizes utility. For nonideal agents, or for ideal agents in nonideal circumstances, the act selected may be rational despite failing to maximize utility because its deficiency is excused.

When I want to evaluate a decision along with the reasons for it, I distinguish two cases corresponding to the two types of reason for a decision. One type of reason is the decision's being the recommendation of a certain decision procedure, such as utility maximization. When I want to evaluate the decision procedure as well as the decision itself, I speak of the *choice* made. I say that the choice is rational or irrational. This term draws attention to the method of selection as well as its upshot.

The other type of reason for an agent's decision is the agent's decision situation, which provides the input, taken broadly, for her decision procedure. Her decision situation includes the immediate input for decision procedures, such as the probabilities and utilities that expected utility maximization requires. It also includes other relevant circumstances, for instance, the agent's options, considered or not, and the possible states of the world. These are relevant evaluative factors because an agent has some control over these circumstances and may exercise her control in mistaken ways. For the most comprehensive type of evaluation, an evaluation of the decision situation, decision procedure, and decision reached, I speak of the agent's *decision*. I say that the decision is rational or irrational. This term arises from the observation that a decision procedure is more comprehensive than a choice procedure. For example, a choice procedure takes options as given, whereas a decision procedure may introduce options previously unconsidered.

In brief, a decision (unless null) has a content and instantiates a method of choice, and the method of choice it instantiates rests on reasons (unless it is gratuitous). One may think of the act chosen as the content; the choice as the method of choice together with the act chosen; and the decision as the act chosen together with the method of choice and the reasons for it.

To illustrate my terminology, suppose that an agent selects the right act in the wrong way. This happens if, for example, in an important decision where deliberation is in order, he selects by whim the very act that it is rational for him to select. Then I say that the act is a rational selection but the choice is nonetheless irrational. Next, suppose that an agent has irrational beliefs about the risks of air travel but otherwise is indifferent between train and air travel. If he decides to travel by train because this mode of transportation has greater expected utility given his beliefs about air travel, his choice is rational. But I say that his decision is irrational because of the mistaken beliefs on which it rests. It is possible for the act selected and the agent's choice to be rational although his decision is irrational. If an agent selects the right act in the right way, the act and choice are rational. But if the input for the method of selection is irrational, it is still possible for his decision to be irrational. A decision resting on irrational beliefs is not irrational in every case—the effect of defective input on a decision's evaluation is complex—but in my example, the irrational beliefs generate an irrational decision.[4]

Let me clarify a point. The distinction between choices and decisions as objects of evaluation is just a distinction in evaluative scope. A decision and the choice realizing it are not distinct entities but the same entity—formation of an intention to act, or realization of an option—evaluated first comprehensively and then narrowly. Chapter 2 identifies options with possible decisions. Nonetheless, when I say that an option is rational, I do not necessarily mean that it is rational according to a comprehensive evaluation. An option is also a possible choice. The type of evaluation intended for an option depends on context. My terminology's implications for evaluative scope do not extend from choice and decision to other terms for an option those terms denote.

This chapter seeks standards for comprehensive evaluations of decisions. That is, it seeks principles for determining whether an agent decided rationally, or on the right act for the right reasons. When I say a decision is rational, I mean the decision's content, process, and input pass muster. In contrast with standards for choices, which take present circumstances for granted and so are noncomprehensive, my standards for decisions take nothing for granted and so are comprehensive. They consider whether present circumstances involve mistakes for which some compensation is in order. For instance, a decision maker may have some irrational beliefs about the options she is considering. Although the standards for her choice are nonetheless applied with respect to her actual beliefs, the standards for her decision consider the beliefs she ought to have as well as her actual beliefs. A choice among her options may be good although the resultant decision is bad because the genesis of the choice has bad elements. Comprehensive standards for decisions look to the origin of her choice as well as the choice itself.

Besides distinguishing evaluations according to scope, it is also important to distinguish them according to their presumptions. Some evaluations of decisions are made subject to conditions. One may, for instance, say that a decision was rational *given* the agent's beliefs. This means roughly that the decision met appropriate standards of rationality taking the agent's beliefs for granted, that is, putting aside complications that arise if the agent's beliefs contain mistakes. The mistakes in his beliefs, if any, are accepted or overlooked by the evaluation of his decision. Such evaluations of rationality given a condition ignore mistakes included in the condition. This interpretation of conditional rationality is not the only one in use, but it is common and I adopt it.

Imposing a condition typically makes an evaluation less comprehensive. Evaluating an agent's decision given his basic goals makes the evaluation less comprehensive by putting aside an evaluation of the agent's basic goals. A comprehensive evaluation may still impose a condition, say, an idealization, that does not grant mistakes. Also, a nonconditional evaluation may fail to be comprehensive, say, if it targets only an agent's choice procedure or ignores some of an option's consequences. Comprehensive and nonconditional evaluations may differ, but I generally treat evaluations that are both comprehensive and nonconditional (except for idealizations) and so usually do not attend to the distinction.

It would be useful to formulate fully the logic of conditional rationality, and I hope to do this in future work. However, some crucial points are already plain. Conditional rationality, as I take it, does not obey the rule of detachment. A decision's rationality given a condition does not imply that if the condition obtains the decision is rational. For example, an agent's decision may be irrational even though it is rational given his beliefs. This may happen because his beliefs contain mistakes that infect his decision, mistakes its conditional evaluation puts aside.[5]

Utility analysis furnishes a standard of conditional rationality as well as a standard of nonconditional rationality. To calculate what is rational given an agent's circumstances, one may use expected utility analysis (section 2.4). One need only make analyses relative to the conditions under which judgments of rationality are to be made. The judgments of conditional rationality waive mistakes those conditions may contain.

Making a decision's evaluation conditional typically makes it less comprehensive. If a decision is rational given the agent's reasons, then the act chosen is a rational selection, but there are no implications about the rationality of the agent's reasons. The decision procedure and its input are irrelevant for the decision's conditional evaluation. Evaluation of the agent's reasons does not matter when the agent's reasons are given as a condition for evaluating her decision. In my terminology, an agent's choice is rational if and only if her decision is rational given its circumstances.

A decision's rationality given its circumstances depends on the outcome it generates. But a decision's rationality, its comprehensive and nonconditional evaluation, depends on much more than the outcome it generates. A decision may be irrational, not in virtue of its consequences, but in virtue of its pedigree. It may be irrational because it follows from an irrational decision procedure, or because the decision procedure operates with irrational input. In other words, an agent may decide irrationally, even though his decision maximizes utility, because he reaches his decision for the wrong reasons.[6]

Besides evaluating an agent's decision given his circumstances, one may evaluate his decision procedure given his circumstances. Evaluating his decision procedure calls for broader evaluative scope, because the decision procedure includes method as well as result. Suppose that the agent has made some mistakes, but these mistakes are corrigible. They may, for instance, be mistaken probability assignments. Does the calculation of rational behavior given his circumstances take into account the possibility of correcting his mistakes before deciding, or does it assume that those mistakes are not corrected? If one wants a decision procedure that is rational given his circumstances, the condition is construed so that it takes account of the possibility of correcting mistakes. On the other hand, if one wants a decision that is rational given his circumstances, the condition is construed so that it ignores the possibility of correcting mistakes if the mistakes are in fact not corrected. When taking the agent's circumstances as a condition, I take past mistakes as accepted or as open to correction according to the breadth of the object of evaluation. They are taken as open to correction when a decision procedure is evaluated, but not when only its result is evaluated.

I distinguish between acceptance of an agent's mistakes and acceptance of a failure to correct them. Both evaluation of a decision and evaluation of a decision procedure given an agent's circumstances accept the agent's mistakes. But the acceptance of his mistakes does not entail an acceptance of a failure to correct them, not if there is an opportunity to correct them. So evaluation of a decision procedure given the agent's circumstances does not accept the agent's failure to correct his mistakes. But evaluation of a decision given circumstances where the agent fails to correct mistakes accepts both the mistakes and the failure to correct them. I understand conditional rationality to take the agent's mistakes for granted without accepting a failure to correct them. That is, it takes the mistakes as decision circumstances, but in evaluating a decision procedure does not forgive a failure to correct those mistakes. It forgives a failure to correct them only when evaluating a decision by itself and after putting aside the opportunity for their correction. Evaluation given the agent's circumstances discredits a decision procedure that bypasses easy correction of mistakes for immediate utility maximization in current uncorrected circumstances.[7]

Next, let me clarify a few points about the usage of evaluative terms. When saying what an agent should decide, I usually take "should" to be directed by standards of rationality. Because I recognize multiple standards of rational evaluation, I must either introduce corresponding senses of should, or else let should be directed by one standard and tolerate disharmony with other standards.

Should has different usages in ordinary language corresponding to different standards of evaluation. Consider, for instance, the usage of should in ethics. In a sense, it is true that one should never repent: one should never do wrong and so should never have occasion to repent. Should here is used to express a nonconditional and comprehensive standard of conduct. A violation indicates present unwarranted repentance or else past wrongdoing. Nonetheless, it is true that if one does wrong, then one should repent. Here, should is used to express a conditional and noncomprehensive standard, one for rectifying mistakes. In cases where an agent has done wrong, he should repent even though it remains true in the first sense that one should never repent.

In expressing judgments of rationality, should is used in similarly distinct ways. In one usage, a decision that should be made is just a rational decision, comprehensively evaluated. According to this usage, should is directed by a standard that assesses decision content, process, and input. In another usage, a decision one should make is just a rational choice, noncomprehensively evaluated.

Although ordinary usage makes should equivocal, I use it univocally to express the verdict of noncomprehensive standards for rational choice. The prevalent usage, I think, indicates how to proceed given all the mistakes one has made, and I follow this usage. Accordingly, a decision an agent should make is one rational according to noncomprehensive standards that take his mistakes for granted. When I say what an agent should decide, I mean what decision is rational given his circumstances. The evaluation is narrow. Mistakes are waived.

Because I interpret should this way, I sever the connection between should and comprehensive standards of evaluation. Evaluations that are comprehensive and nonconditional may differ from the less comprehensive conditional evaluations governing should. This may happen when the agent's input for a rational decision procedure contains some incorrigible but inexcusable mistakes. Because it is too late for the agent to correct those mistakes, a decision that is rational given his mistakes is a rational choice. But that decision may be irrational. In deciding rationally given his mistakes, he may still decide irrationally. The nonconditional standards for his decision evaluate it comprehensively according to content, process, and input for the process.

In cases where comprehensively and noncomprehensively rational decisions differ, the decision an agent should realize is not a rational decision, comprehensively evaluated. It is paradoxical to say that an agent should make a decision that is not rational. But the assertion means only that an agent should make a decision, rational on noncomprehensive standards waiving mistakes, that is not rational on comprehensive standards not waiving mistakes. The paradox is superficial and easily resolved.

To have another, less puzzling, means of expressing the distinction between what the agent should decide and a rational decision, I introduce a parallel distinction between *recommending* a decision and *rating* a decision. Rating a decision takes into account the history or pedigree of the decision and may declare the decision irrational because it rests on mistakes. Recommending a decision takes the history of the decision for granted and advances a decision that is rational given its history. Because rating and recommending treat mistakes differently, it may turn out that a recommended decision is not rated as rational. This may happen because incorrigible, inexcusable mistakes make certain decisions irrational even if they are rational responses to those mistakes. For instance, if an agent has an irrational belief that serves as the basis for a decision, the decision may be recommended even though it is irrational. The recommended decision accepts the agent's mistakes and so applies a noncomprehensive standard. Although the standards for ratings look to the past as well as to the future, the standards for recommendations are forward-looking only.

6.3. Correction of Mistakes

As section 1.1 observed, principles for deciding rationally may be applied to guide a decision, or to evaluate a decision after it has been made. When an agent has made mistakes, the two applications differ significantly. If an agent who has made mistakes uses decision principles for guidance, they tell him to take account of the possibility of correcting mistakes before making his decision. For instance, if he has misassigned probabilities, the principles may suggest correcting the assignment of probabilities before deciding. They suggest not just decisions but decision procedures, which may have several steps preceding the application of a choice rule. But if one uses decision principles to evaluate a decision already made, they obviously do not advise correcting mistakes before deciding. The time for such advice is past.

This chapter's objective is a comprehensive standard for evaluation of decisions. However, a comprehensive evaluation of a decision already made must consider whether the agent took appropriate steps to correct mistakes before deciding. As a preliminary for comprehensive evaluation of decisions already made, this section considers what cognitively unlimited and cognitively limited agents should do to correct mistakes. As a by-product of investigating mistake correction, I obtain some principles about rational decision procedures, principles expressing noncomprehensive standards of evaluation. These principles call for a suitable effort to remedy mistakes before applying utility analysis, that is, sensible decision preparation.

Suppose an agent without cognitive limitations has nonetheless made some mistakes. This sort of case is possible because such an agent may fail to use the resources she has for avoiding mistakes. She may be irrational even though she has the means of attaining all ideals of rationality. Because of irrationality, she may fall short of the ideals and so may make mistakes in my sense. For example, she may misassign probabilities. For an ideal agent, such misassignments are inexcusable but possible.

An appropriate first step for this cognitively unlimited agent is to correct all the corrigible mistakes that bear on the current decision. If, for example, relevant probabilities have been misassigned, they should be corrected before proceeding. For cognitively unlimited agents, these corrections have no cost; there is no obstacle to making them. This advice about decision procedures yields the following rule for decisions:

> Decide in a way that maximizes utility after correcting relevant corrigible mistakes.

This rule is a guide to rational choice. It recommends a two-step decision procedure. If it is followed, the result is a rational choice. If it is ignored, the choice is irrational because irrationally made even if its content is rational, and even if it is a choice that would maximize utility after corrections. Although a nonideal agent may not see mistakes and know how to correct them, an ideal agent is perfectly able to follow the rule.

The rule considers mistakes corrigible by the agent, not by external factors. The student with artistic talent who is deciding on a career but considering only law and medicine may have his attention drawn to another possibility if he meets an artist who describes her work. That is fortuitous, external correction of his mistake. In contrast, he can correct his mistake himself by conducting a study of his options. The rule holds an agent accountable for mistakes he can correct himself.

How does one correct a mistake? One way is to remove the mistake. An agent can correct an irrational belief by eliminating it. Another way is to render the mistake harmless or to correct for the mistake. Without removing it, one may compensate for it, as wearing eyeglasses compensates for bad eyesight without removing it. Past mistakes cannot be removed, but they are corrigible if one can compensate for them. Similarly, an agent may correct for a bad desire. Perhaps he wants to smoke although he knows it is not healthful and is averse to having the desire. Although the desire persists, his aversion to having the desire may make him on balance desire not to smoke or may make him decide contrary to his desire to smoke. The mistake is corrigible in the relevant sense even if it cannot be removed.

Suppose that section 6.1's traveler, who rides the train out of an irrational fear of flying, becomes a rail enthusiast because of his ride. He falls in love with a train's comfortable seats, spacious aisles, freedom of movement, and displays of scenery. If he decides between train and air travel again, is a decision to take the train irrational? To avoid irrationality, must he reinstate goals he had before panic led him to travel by train? The answer is no. Correction of a mistake does not require a return to conditions before the mistake. Because the traveler's new passion for train travel is not irrational, it need not be expunged before the traveler can make a rational decision. Moreover, when the traveler decides on transport again, his earlier mistake is incorrigible and not pertinent. He need not correct for it before deciding.[8]

Following my two-step decision procedure does not ensure a comprehensively rational decision. Incorrigible mistakes, because inexcusable in the case of a cognitively unlimited agent, are not forgiven by comprehensive evaluations of decisions. Incorrigible mistakes on which a rational choice rests may make that choice an irrational decision. My decision procedure leads to a rational choice, but not necessarily a rational decision.

What mistakes may be incorrigible? Perhaps a mistake has influenced the states, options, or consequences that are relevant in a decision problem. A cognitively unlimited agent may have irrationally promised the impossible. Every way of extricating himself may be defective. He may choose well among his options but cannot correct his poor set of options.

Two other sorts of mistakes in the past have a structural effect on decision problems in the present and may be incorrigible. They are both mistakes of decision preparedness. First, an agent may have mistakenly acquired a disposition to choose in a certain way, say, to be greedy. This disposition may be relevant to the outcomes of options in his current decision problem, say, a negotiation problem in which responses to his offers depend on perceptions of his motives. But it may be too late to change the mistaken disposition before making the decision. Even if, assuming compatibilism, the agent can, in the relevant noncausal sense, choose contrary to the disposition, it may be causally settled that he will not. So it may be that his mistaken disposition is incorrigible in the relevant causal sense.

Second, one must sometimes decide spontaneously without making decisions about how to decide. Ordinary agents must do this to avoid the costs of making metadecisions. Even cognitively unlimited agents must do this to avoid an infinite regress of decisions. Although a cognitively unlimited agent can effortlessly find an option of maximum utility, she cannot without infinite regress reflect on how to make each decision she makes. So even if reflection is costless, she must sometimes decide without it. If she is fully rational, she has developed good habits for spontaneous decisions that maximize utility. But if she is not fully rational, she may have bad habits for spontaneous decisions and may sometimes fail to maximize utility as a result. Bad habits for spontaneous decisions are not corrigible prior to decisions they influence. If by mistake one has a tendency to make spontaneous decisions poorly, that is, to miss options of maximum utility, this cannot be corrected prior to one's decision. Even an agent with a perfect mind cannot instantaneously alter her habits for spontaneous decisions and so cannot correct mistakes prior to resolving a current decision problem. Whatever she decides now must rest on habits acquired earlier. Even decisions to correct bad habits have to rest on those habits. In cases where an agent's decision arises from bad prior decisions, dispositions, or habits, the decision may be irrational even if the mistakes are incorrigible.

Next, I consider agents with cognitive limitations. Whereas a cognitively unlimited agent can become aware of her mistakes if she reflects, this is not necessarily so for a cognitively limited agent. A cognitively limited agent should nonetheless review his situation before making a decision and correct mistakes that are corrigible. For example, in certain cases, an agent may see that he has a tendency to make some mistake in the future. Correction of the mistake, as I understand it, prevents the mistake. It produces resolve not to make the mistake or otherwise eliminates the tendency to make the mistake. Ulysses, when he sailed near the Sirens, eliminated his tendency to err (assuming that his approaching the Sirens would have been an error) by having himself bound to his ship's mast.

Because of the costs of review and correction, the extensiveness of the correction process should be proportionate to the importance of the decision. An agent should invest only a warranted amount of effort in the correction of relevant mistakes. As a rule of thumb, the correction process should concentrate on important mistakes in the immediate past because these mistakes have the most influence on a current decision and because probing deeply into the past is costly. For example, rationality may require a job seeker to review recent assessments of the prospects for employment at places where he may apply. But it may not require him to review the emergence of his career goals during his youth. From the perspective of a current decision, prior matters lose weight with each step back in time. In typical cases, as one recedes into the past correction costs rapidly exceed benefits. Also, although ignorance of mistakes may not excuse them, the correction process should concentrate on rectifying mistakes clearly identified. This increases the likelihood that changes are genuine corrections. Moreover, the correction process should be alert to the danger that correcting some mistakes will generate new, greater mistakes.

An appropriate decision directive for cognitively limited agents, one incorporating my recommendations about decision procedures, is the following:

> Decide in a way that maximizes utility after a reasonable effort to correct relevant corrigible mistakes.

This principle proposes a two-step decision procedure which, if followed, yields a rational choice, but not necessarily a rational decision. It subsumes the principle earlier advanced for cognitively unlimited agents because their reasonable efforts correct all relevant corrigible mistakes. Notice that the principle does not ask whether mistakes are culpable. It cares only about correcting mistakes, not evaluating mistakes.

Although a rational choice maximizes utility with respect to actual circumstances, mistakes and all, a rational decision procedure is a two-step process that begins with a reasonable effort to correct mistakes and then maximizes utility. An option one should realize is a rational choice, at least when "should" has my interpretation and indicates directions for making the best of present circumstances. A decision procedure one should follow is a rational decision procedure. When it is possible to correct relevant mistakes before proceeding with a decision, rational decision procedures correct relevant mistakes that are corrigible with reasonable effort. Before deciding, one ought to make a reasonable effort to correct corrigible mistakes, just as one ought to make a reasonable effort to obtain accessible data and form achievable probability and utility judgments.

The nature of a reasonable effort to correct a relevant corrigible mistake depends on the mistake's significance or gravity and the abilities and circumstances of the agent. Suppose a person about to buy a house recalls having failed to inspect the basement. In normal circumstances, she should check it before closing the deal. However, if she has a building inspector's report that the house is in good condition and returning to the house would involve a long and expensive flight, then correcting the oversight may require unreasonable effort.

This section's principles explain how to prepare for a decision and, in particular, how extensively to search for mistakes before deciding. But I am interested mainly in postdecision comprehensive evaluation of a decision. I still need a principle for comprehensively evaluating decisions influenced by mistakes. A comprehensive evaluation considers how decision preparations were conducted and how the final decision was reached. If an agent decides without having made a reasonable effort to remedy mistakes, she adds complacence to the mistakes forming the context of her decision. If she makes a reasonable effort to correct mistakes, some mistakes may nonetheless remain. Even if all corrigible mistakes were corrected, some of the incorrigible mistakes remaining may be inexcusable and discredit her decision. It may be an irrational decision, comprehensively evaluated, because of defective input for her decision procedures, however rational they are. A rational decision may thus differ from a rational decision procedure's product. A decision may be irrational even though it is rational given mistakes that remain after a reasonable effort to correct mistakes. In particular, if an agent has cognitive limits, a reasonable effort to correct mistakes may not rectify all mistakes and so may not dispose of the problem of evaluating a decision made in the context of mistakes.

The next section takes these possibilities into account and formulates a general principle for comprehensive evaluation of decisions.

6.4. Comprehensive Evaluation of Decisions

The literature on rational decisions does not routinely specify an evaluation's comprehensiveness, or circumstances taken for granted, if any. As I interpret the literature, however, its evaluations are generally noncomprehensive. In my terminology, it evaluates choices rather than decisions. Put another way, it advances principles for evaluating decisions taking the agent's circumstances for granted. The agent's circumstances, even if they are influenced by his mistakes, are taken as given. My search for principles of comprehensive, nonconditional evaluation of decisions thus departs from the literature's main research program. The principles this section advances are extensions, not rivals, of the literature's leading proposals.

This section seeks principles that conform to intuitions about deciding rationally as opposed to intuitions about the contents of rational decisions. It evaluates a decision in terms of its content and also the reasons for the decision, the decision process and its input. For guidance, it appeals to common intuitions about deciding rationally and deciding for the right reasons. In some cases, however, intuitions may diverge because of subtly different conceptions of rationality. This section's decision principle articulates one common conception of rationality.[9]

A decision's comprehensive evaluation is more complex than a choice's noncomprehensive evaluation. It must resolve the following issue: In considering whether an agent has decided rationally, how far back into the history of the decision must one probe? More precisely, which past mistakes must be corrected to obtain an acceptable framework for making a decision? It must also answer an analogous question about anticipated future mistakes. The principle I advance uses the concept of an *acceptable* mistake. This is roughly a mistake that rationality forgives. Later examples and general points clarify the concept, but I do not define acceptability precisely. Thus, the principle advanced may be regarded as a program for future work.

I propose the following principle for comprehensive, nonconditional evaluation of decisions by agents who make mistakes:

> *Principle of acceptability.* A rational decision maximizes utility with respect to circumstances in which unacceptable mistakes are corrected.

The principle advances a necessary condition of rationality. Because it is for after-the-fact evaluation of a decision, it is not stated as a directive, in contrast with section 6.3's principles for decision procedures. A rational agent aspires to make a rational decision and so meet the necessary condition, but barriers may force settling for a more modest goal. The principle is a generalization of the principle of utility maximization for nonideal, errant agents.

The principle of acceptability advances a necessary condition of comprehensive rationality given some idealizations. Although the agents to which the principle applies may err, they are ideal in some respects. They have quantitative probability and utility assignments and know them. They may be ignorant of some a priori matters but know the standard of utility maximization and are perfectly able to meet it. After reasonable efforts to correct ignorance, remaining ignorance about a priori matters at least does not block compliance with the principle. Also, their decision problems are ideal in some respects. As before, the basis of comparison of options is stable, and an option of maximum utility exists. Their decision problems are ideal except for the complications their mistakes cause. The principle does not assume that agents know their mistakes, however. Acceptability itself sorts out the role that ignorance of mistakes plays in a decision's evaluation. Ignorance of a mistake may make, but does not invariably make, the mistake acceptable.

The principle of acceptability assumes that the appropriate form of utility maximization applies to the set of options the agent considers after correction of unacceptable mistakes. Given the assumption, the principle does not need the idealization that agents are cognitively unlimited and can consider all options. It applies to cognitively limited and unlimited agents alike. It requires all to correct the set of options under consideration if it is too narrow. Section 7.5 discusses corrections of this sort.

Both realized and unrealized options may be rational. An option is rational if it would meet all applicable standards of rationality if it were realized. Its actual rationality depends on its having a certain type of hypothetical rationality. If a possible decision is realized, it satisfies my principle's necessary condition of rationality if unacceptable mistakes are corrected and it maximizes utility. If it is not realized, it meets the condition if, were it realized, unacceptable mistakes would be corrected and it would maximize utility.[10]

I call a rational decision a *solution* to a decision problem if the agent is ideal. The decision's rationality, of course, assumes correction of unacceptable mistakes. Realizing a solution may not yield a rational decision if unacceptable mistakes have not been corrected. The type of hypothetical rationality a solution has is not enough to guarantee its being actually rational, not when the hypothetical conditions of its rationality are not met.[11]

According to my principle, conditional and nonconditional rationality agree under certain circumstances. An assessment of a decision's rationality given the agent's mistakes in effect assumes that the mistakes are acceptable, or, more precisely, accepts the mistakes. If in fact the mistakes are acceptable, then rationality agrees with rationality given the agent's circumstances. Acceptable mistakes have no effect during a move from noncomprehensive to comprehensive standards of evaluation. If all mistakes are acceptable, rational choice and rational decision agree.

Section 6.2 distinguishes between recommending and rating a decision. Rating uses a comprehensive standard of rationality. Recommending uses a non-comprehensive standard of rationality taking current circumstances for granted. Recommending accepts all mistakes, even unacceptable ones. If current circumstances include only acceptable mistakes, rating and recommending agree. Correction of unacceptable mistakes makes recommending a decision concur with rating a decision.

My principle employs a technical concept: acceptability of mistakes. Although basic and undefined, it needs an introduction. As its companion, utility, does, acceptability needs examples and a broad theoretical context to give it substance. The rest of this section explains acceptability briefly. The next chapter addresses fine points. The introductory material furnishes an "implicit definition" of acceptability although not a definition in the standard sense of necessary and sufficient conditions of application that explain the concept precisely.

As stated, a mistake is acceptable just in case rationality forgives it. An agent is not obliged to correct acceptable mistakes before resolving a current decision problem. Rationality requires a reasonable effort to correct unacceptable mistakes only. Although rationality does not oblige an agent to correct incorrigible, unacceptable mistakes, such mistakes may make a decision fall short of comprehensive standards of rationality. Ordinary language expresses claims about acceptability in assertions about conditional rationality. To say that a decision is rational given a condition is to say that it is rational assuming that the condition involves only acceptable mistakes. This rough characterization of acceptability indicates its role in decision theory. It identifies mistakes that do not influence a decision's assessment for comprehensive and nonconditional rationality.

Excusability and incorrigibility influence acceptability, but neither is decisive because inexcusable mistakes, say, in the remote past, may be acceptable and because incorrigible mistakes, say, about the cultivation of habits of attention, may be unacceptable. Because rationality is context-sensitive, the acceptability of mistakes is context-sensitive, also. In some decision situations standards are higher than in others. Whether a mistake is acceptable depends on the agent's circumstances and capabilities. For example, it depends on the circumstances in her control, her ability to correct mistakes, and her cognitive resources. It also depends on the nature of the mistake—for example, its gravity, remoteness, the cost of its correction, and so on—and the nature of the decision problem. Some mistakes are not pertinent to a decision problem and so are acceptable. Because acceptability is context-sensitive, the principle of acceptability applies to cognitively limited and unlimited agents alike.

I advance no precise, general rule for using factors such as excusability to classify mistakes as acceptable or not. I rely on intuitions about cases and a few rules of thumb. First, an agent's future mistakes are seldom acceptable because he is usually able to correct them even if he will not. Second, for cognitively unlimited agents significant, inexcusable, corrigible mistakes are unacceptable because they can be corrected without cost. Third, if a reasonable effort to correct mistakes has been made, and all remaining mistakes are excused, then all remaining mistakes are acceptable. That is, excusable mistakes remaining after reasonable proofing are acceptable. As a corollary, I obtain the maxim that excusable, incorrigible mistakes are acceptable.

Applying the principle of acceptability to this chapter's examples yields results agreeing with intuition. Take the case of the traveler who rides the train because of an irrational fear of flying. His decision about transport is not rational because his belief that the flight he booked will crash is an unacceptable mistake. It is contrary to his evidence and unexcused. Similarly, the student who chooses a career after considering only law and medicine decides irrationally because considering only those two options is not an acceptable mistake. It is unexcused and corrigible by a thorough study of his options. To flesh out Aristotle's case, suppose that a drinker drives into town to pick up groceries. Before shopping, he stops for a drink and then forgets why he came to town. Empty-handed, he decides to go back home. His decision is irrational. It rests on an unacceptable even if incorrigible mistake. His forgetfulness is not excused, assuming that he knew about the danger of losing sight of his errand if he stopped at a bar.

On the other hand, a worker who paints herself into a corner and then decides to exit across the freshly painted floor decides rationally if she maximizes utility. Her earlier mistake is incorrigible and not pertinent to her decision problem: to walk across the wet paint or wait for it to dry. Even if her earlier mistake is inexcusable, it is acceptable from the perspective of her current decision problem. Similarly, an agent who maximizes utility among options she considers when pressed for time decides rationally. The time pressure excuses her failure to consider all options. It makes her mistake acceptable. At least, it does if it is severe and the decision unimportant, for example, if she is double-parked in front of the video store and so elects to rent the first film that grabs her attention.

Chapter 1 presents cases in which agents decide contrary to preference. How does the principle of acceptability apply to them? The diner who forgoes the last piece of pie decides contrary to his preferences but in accord with his values. After correcting his preferences to fit his values, his decision maximizes utility. Still, his decision is not comprehensively rational because he has not corrected his preferences. His mistaken preferences are unacceptable mistakes that contaminate his decision. His decision is hypothetically rational but not actually rational. An ideal advisor recommends his decision's content but also recommends preference correction before reaching that decision.

Next, consider the college student who mistakenly believes she wants to go to medical school instead of pursuing a career in literature. Strictly speaking, the principle of acceptability does not cover this case because its idealizations include awareness of relevant probabilities and utilities. However, let me generalize the principle for cases with limited access to probabilities and utilities by incorporating the principle of accessible utility maximization (chapter 5). For an evaluation of the student's options using the extended principle, the crux is whether she is culpably ignorant of her true desire. If her mistaken belief is rational, then a decision to go to medical school is rational. It agrees with her estimate of her true desire and maximizes utility with respect to her conscious mind. If her belief is irrational, then it contaminates that decision. To decide rationally, she must correct the irrational belief and then maximize revised utility by opting for literature.[12]

Careful application of the principle of acceptability quiets threatening cases. Suppose an agent with an irrational fear of flying faints as he is boarding his plane. When he revives, he has no memory of his fear. He collects himself and flies to his destination without further incident. His decision to proceed with his plan to fly maximizes utility after correction of unacceptable mistakes. It is rational according to my principle even if the quelling of his fear was fortuitous and not the result of reasoning. Is the principle of acceptability too lenient with this traveler? Should it demand reasoned correction of mistakes?[13]

An evaluation of the traveler's deliberations may downgrade them because they did not eliminate his irrational belief, and, in any case, awards him no credit for the belief's elimination. However, an evaluation of his decision should not hold against it mistakes without influence. Even if his deliberations are faulty, their defects do not harm his decision. So those mistakes count as acceptable in its evaluation. Because no unacceptable mistake affects his decision, it is rational.

The principle of acceptability is just a framework for a theory of comprehensive evaluation of decisions. A complete theory supplies more details about acceptability than I have provided. Because my introduction leaves acceptability vague, applications of my principle for evaluating decisions may not be clear-cut. Nonetheless, the principle and my introduction of acceptability organize thoughts about rationality in contexts where agents make mistakes. They clarify the logic of evaluation and its reliance on the distinctions between rationality and conditional rationality, and between decision and choice. As the next chapter demonstrates, despite the need for fleshing out, the principle of acceptability has enough substance to generate many interesting results. Furthermore, even though the principle involves the vague concept of acceptability, it states precisely the connection between acceptability and rationality. The two concepts hang together, matching each other in their vagueness. The principle itself is exact despite the incomplete interpretation of its key concepts.

Acceptability's Consequences

This chapter explores consequences of the principle of acceptability and applies the principle to controversial decision problems. The first section treats mutually justifying and self-justifying mistakes. The second section examines dilemmas of rationality. The third section treats Newcomb's Problem. The fourth section addresses both irresolute and stubborn execution of plans. The final section investigates cases where agents fail to consider all their options.

7.1. No Mutually Justifying or Self-Justifying Mistakes

Using my account of acceptability, I show that the principle of acceptability prevents mutual justification and self-justification of mistakes. Consider first mutual justification of mistakes, or judgments that it is rational to make some mistake now to compensate for some other mistake in the future and rational to make that mistake in the future to compensate for the mistake made now. To explain how my principle prevents these judgments, I apply it to a challenging case Feldman (1986: 52–57) constructs. Suppose that one has an illness for which there are two medicines, A and B. The treatment is to take the same medicine on each of two occasions; mixing medicines is harmful. Given that medicine A works better, it is best to take it on each of the two occasions. The agent knows that it is fully in his power to take A on both occasions. But he also knows he will take B on one occasion and so plans to take B on the other occasion to compensate. Then, on each occasion, he has a reason to take B. Nonetheless, it is not the case that on each occasion his decision to take B is rational. To support this verdict, my evaluation of a decision takes account of the reasons for the decision. The reasons for reaching the decision are just as important as the act selected. According to my principle, it is irrational to decide now to compensate for a future decision that compensates for the present decision. The future decision is presently corrigible. Because of its corrigibility, it is not an acceptable mistake. Hence, I evaluate the present decision with respect to a context where the mistake is absent. Deciding to take A is the rational decision in that context. Hence, only it can be rational in a comprehensive sense. If the agent will take B on the second occasion, then he should take B now. That is the rational choice and also the rational decision given his circumstances. Nonetheless, the decision to take B now is not comprehensively and nonconditionally rational.

The analysis of this example displays the general case against mutually justifying mistakes. Imagine a pair of mistakes such that each compensates for the other. Grant that each is rational given the other. Nonetheless, they are not both comprehensively rational; for at least one, comprehensive rationality requires its correction. At least one mistake is unacceptable because corrigible and unexcused.

My principle similarly prevents self-justification of mistakes. Suppose that a decision falls short of the ideals of rationality and so is a mistake. It cannot nonetheless be rational because making the decision is a way of compensating for making the decision. Nonideal circumstances do not generate such excuses. Take, for instance, a case in which an agent's mistaken decision has been foreseen by his guardian angel, who has adjusted the circumstances of his decision so that it maximizes utility but still achieves a lower level of utility than an alternative decision would have achieved in the original circumstances. The agent knew prior to his decision that his guardian angel would adjust circumstances to make his decision utility-maximizing. The fact that the decision maximizes utility in the circumstances the angel creates does not make the agent's decision rational, however. My principle concurs. It rules that the agent's decision is irrational if a different decision would have maximized utility given the correction of unacceptable mistakes, and the mistaken decision itself counts as an unacceptable mistake because it is corrigible and inexcusable. Correcting for the mistaken decision, I obtain the original circumstances, and the alternative decision maximizes utility in those circumstances. So it is the rational decision in those circumstances. Therefore, only it can be comprehensively rational in the actual circumstances.

7.2. Dilemmas

The principle of acceptability states a demanding necessary condition of rationality. One consequence of the principle is the possibility, in nonideal cases, of *dilemmas of rational decision*. That is, decision problems in which, given the constraints of the agent's situation, whatever he decides and however he decides, his decision is irrational. Although some option maximizes utility given correction of unacceptable mistakes, that option may fail to be rational. If unacceptable mistakes are not corrected, for instance, then although that option is rational given correction of mistakes, its rationality is hypothetical, not actual. Because of infectious mistakes, no option is a rational decision. The defective input for decision rules contaminates their output. Predecision recommendations may advise a decision that would be rational if, counterfactually, mistakes were corrected. But postdecision evaluations commend a decision only if it is rational in actual circumstances.[1]

In a dilemma the constraints of the agent's decision problem make relevant only options' realizations that hold fast everything not in the agent's control. Thus, a dilemma may arise even if some option is a rational decision under a realization that supplies the agent with new information, has him prepare better for his decision problem, or externally removes mistakes.

Mistakes that an agent can correct with reasonable effort do not yield a dilemma. Correcting them, the agent can reach a rational decision. Incorrigible mistakes are another matter, however. The decision problem holds them fast. They may generate a dilemma if they are unacceptable, so that a rational decision requires their correction.

Dilemmas arise from different types of incorrigible mistakes. To illustrate one type of dilemma, consider a pilot who fails to train for emergencies. In the event of a hijacking, he does not know that the most prudent course is to stay in the cockpit and keep its door locked. A hijacking occurs, and he plans to enter the passenger cabin to confront the hijackers. His plan maximizes utility with respect to his defective utility assignment. If he were to decide to stay in the cockpit with the door locked, he would not maximize utility. That option maximizes utility only with respect to a corrected utility assignment responsive to knowledge he culpably neglected to acquire. During the hijacking, he cannot correct his utility assignment and so cannot make the right decision for the right reasons.

To illustrate another type of dilemma, consider an airline passenger who knows that the danger of a water landing is not negligible but ignores safety instructions he has heard before. He should have listened to them because he knows that the refresher would make relevant options come to mind more easily in that emergency. The emergency arises, and he thinks only of bolting to the front exit or proceeding there cautiously. He does not think of using the rear exit and taking his seat cushion with him as a flotation device. Deciding on that course has maximum utility, however. Hence, if he maximizes utility among options he considers, he adopts an inferior option. On the other hand, lacking time for a review of options, if he were to decide to move to the rear exit with his seat cushion, he would make that decision gratuitously, out of the blue, without regard for reasons. He would realize the utility-maximizing option but by accident and not because it is utility-maximizing. The realization of an option, a possible decision, involves considering the option. But if the utility-maximizing option were realized, holding the passenger's decision situation constant, comparison with other options would not be a reason for its realization. If it were adopted in the current decision situation, it would not meet comprehensive standards. It would rest on an infectious mistake.

The pilot is culpably ignorant of the best option. That option maximizes utility with respect to his corrected but not his current utility assignment. The passenger, in contrast, is culpably inattentive to options. His utility assignment does not need correction. Still, he needs to consider the right option if he is to realize it for the right reasons. In both cases, it is impossible for the agent to make a rational decision, even given allowances for cognitive limitations. If he maximizes utility among the options he considers, he follows a rational decision procedure but feeds it irrational input. If, without reflection, he adopts an option that maximizes utility given correction of unacceptable mistakes, he adopts a rational option but for irrational reasons. Whatever he decides, either his decision's content, his decision procedure, or the input for his decision procedure makes his decision irrational from a comprehensive point of view.

In my examples each agent can make a decision that is rational given his circumstances. This is just a decision supported by his reasons in his circumstances, even if those reasons and circumstances are the result of mistakes. So, in my terminology, he can make a rational choice. Some choice, noncomprehensively evaluated, is rational. In fact, in every decision problem some method of selecting an act is rational and some act is rational. Some act's selection proceeds from a selection process and input that are rational taking mistakes for granted. In other words, there are no dilemmas of rational choice, or rational decision content. This is the *principle against dilemmas of rational choice*.

Nonetheless, in my examples, because the reasons available for the agent's decision include unacceptable mistakes, the closest he can come to meeting standards of rationality is picking a rational act for reasons irrational because of their pedigree, or picking an irrational act for rational reasons. Even if the agent decides on a rational act using a rational selection process, he decides irrationally because the input for the selection process is defective. His decision must fall short in some way; no decision he can make meets the ideals of rationality. Moreover, because the reasons on which he might base a decision include unacceptable mistakes, his decision's falling short of the ideals of rationality is not excused. That is, whatever the content of his decision, his decision falls short of standards of rationality that take account of excuses. His decision, whatever it is, is irrational.

Agents who have made mistakes may face dilemmas of rational decision under comprehensive evaluation of decisions, even if they face no dilemmas of rational choice under noncomprehensive evaluations of choices restricted to content and procedure, that is, even if in every decision problem, for every type of agent, some option is a rational choice. As my examples show, there are dilemmas of rational decision in which every decision is irrational—with respect to content, procedure, or pedigree—even if there are no dilemmas of rational choice.

Dilemmas of rational decision may arise even for a cognitively unlimited agent. Such an agent may be hampered by incorrigible errors. For example, if she makes spontaneous decisions poorly, then a justifiably spontaneous decision, whatever its content, may be irrational. The decision rests on irrational habits of spontaneous decision. These habits cannot be corrected prior to her decision. They may infect every possible decision and so create a dilemma of rationality. Among cognitively unlimited agents, only the fully rational, because error-free, are exempt from dilemmas of rationality.

The possibility of dilemmas of rational decision and the impossibility of dilemmas of rational choice have a paradoxical consequence. Suppose an agent faces a dilemma of rational decision. Because of past incorrigible, inexcusable mistakes on which a current choice must rest, every choice yields an irrational decision. Still, some choice is one that the agent should make (in the ordinary, making-the-best-of-things sense). Then it turns out that the agent should make a choice that yields an irrational decision. This follows because what the agent should choose goes by rules of rational choice, not rational decision. She should make a certain choice (an ideal spectator would recommend that she does), even though the choice rests on defective reasons.

On reflection, the conclusion is not surprising. Ought implies can. No decision the agent can make is comprehensively rational. So it is false that she ought to make a rational decision. Although there is a decision she can and should make, that decision is not comprehensively rational. It is only noncomprehensively rational, a rational choice.

Let me compare my treatment of the rational evaluation of decisions to familiar treatments of the moral evaluation of acts. My view about rationality, applied to morality, allows for moral dilemmas, taken as cases where, whatever an agent does, he acts immorally. If he has acted immorally in a way that influences his current circumstances, it may be impossible for him to do the right act for the right reasons. For example, if he has hardened himself to the suffering of others, it may be psychologically impossible for him to help the needy out of a motive of charity. Then, in a situation where helping the needy is the right act, he cannot act in a way that is thoroughly moral. That is, it is psychologically impossible given his current character to do the right act for the right reasons. However, acting morally, in a comprehensive sense, is something he could have arranged to do by earlier character development. So he is culpable for his dilemma.[2]

In contrast, there are no dilemmas of moral obligation. "Should" and "ought" in the ordinary sense go by conditional morality and evaluate acts noncomprehensively. Even if an agent cannot avoid acting immorally, some act is permissible, or moral, given her circumstances. Not everything she can do is something she ought not do. The principle that "ought implies can" guarantees this result. For suppose that none of an agent's possible acts is permissible. Then she cannot avoid doing something she ought not do. By the principle, it is not the case that she ought to avoid doing something she ought not do. That is, it is not the case that she ought not do something that she ought not do. This is absurd. Hence, some act is permissible.

Theorists disagree about the standard of evaluation that directs the term ought. If an ideal directs it, then an agent ought to do the right act for the right reasons. For ought so interpreted, there must be a sense of can according to which the agent can do the right act for the right reasons even if such a course of action is not psychologically possible. The sense of can must look to the past and how it might have been different. I put aside the past-regarding senses of ought and can. I take ought as future-oriented. But which future-oriented standards direct it? Much of the relevant literature concerns moral standards rather than standards of rationality. To compare my view with others, I briefly consider various types of utilitarianism.

One may distinguish *individualistic* and *collectivistic* future-oriented standards according to whether their evaluations of an agent's act take other agents' future mistakes for granted. Sequences of acts of an agent and other agents, with future errors by the other agents, bring out the difference. The individualistic standard says to perform an act whose outcome has maximum utility. This directive is responsive to other agents' future errors. The collectivistic standard says to perform an act in a multi-agent sequence whose outcome has maximum utility. In other words, do your part in the collective act that maximizes utility among worlds realizable by collective action. This directive is not responsive to other agents' future errors. To illustrate, suppose that an agent can commit one murder to prevent another's committing two murders. The collectivistic standard says that he ought to do his part in the best joint plan: don't commit the murder. The individualistic standard says that he ought not be myopic: he ought not do his part in the best joint plan if others won't do their parts. It says that he ought to compensate for other agents' future departures from the best plan: he ought to commit the murder.

The individualistic standard for ought divides according to its extension to sequences of acts of a single agent. A *dissociative* version of the standard assigns an agent's future stages and acts the same status as future stages and acts of another person. This version of the standard takes an agent's future mistakes for granted, just as the individualistic standard takes other agents' future mistakes for granted. An *integrative* version of the standard treats an agent's temporal stages as collectively integrated. It treats an agent's future mistakes the way the collectivistic standard treats other agents' future mistakes. It does not take them for granted. It tells an agent to perform the first of a sequence of maximizing acts. To illustrate, suppose that an agent may avoid murder throughout the future, but unless he commits one murder today he will commit two murders tomorrow. Then the dissociative standard says to commit one murder today, whereas the integrative standard says the opposite. The integrative standard says to start today to shun murder throughout the future.

As I interpret ought, it is directed by standards conditional on actual circumstances, mistakes and all. It is future-oriented, but I leave open whether the appropriate future-oriented standards are individualistic or collectivistic and, if individualistic, dissociative or integrative. Figure 7.1 depicts the relationship of these distinctions concerning a standard of morality.

These distinctions clarify issues concerning moral action in the face of future immoral acts. Utilitarianism takes an act's moral status to depend on its meeting moral obligations. It is therefore future-oriented. Different ways of being future-oriented yield different forms of utilitarianism, however.

Suppose that an agent knows that he will perform an immoral act. And suppose that doing A now is best given that future mistake, but not otherwise. Is A moral? Feldman (1986: 52–57) and Zimmerman (1996: chap. 6) take morality to go by world-utilitarian standards—in my scheme of classification, integrative standards. Accordingly, A is not moral. The moral course is to avoid A and the future mistake.

```
              standard of morality
                  /      \
      past-regarding      future-oriented
                          /        \
              collectivistic    individualistic
                                /        \
                      integrative      dissociative
```

FIGURE 7.1. Classification of a moral standard.

On the other hand, Goldman (1976), Sobel (1976), and Jackson and Pargetter (1986) take morality to go by conditional utilitarian standards—in my scheme of classification, dissociative standards. They say that A is moral because, given the agent's future mistake, it is best.

The analogue of my view about rationality yields a utilitarian standard between these extremes. It takes utility maximization to express a moral ideal but does not judge an act solely by this ideal. It accommodates excuses for failing to meet the ideal. According to it, an act is moral only if it maximizes utility given correction of unacceptable mistakes. Hence, in the example, if the agent's future mistake is excused and acceptable, A is moral, other things being equal. Also, the future mistake, even if inexcusable, may be acceptable with respect to the agent's present decision if the agent can correct the mistake only with tremendous effort, not warranted given the present decision. The mistake, although corrigible, may be corrigible not by a simple volition, but only by eradicating a tenacious habit. Then A is moral, other things being equal, even though the mistake that makes it maximizing is inexcusable. However, if the future mistake is corrigible with reasonable effort and not excused, and so is unacceptable, then A is not moral. The moral course is avoiding A and the future mistake.

7.3. Irrationality Rewarded

To further clarify comprehensive evaluation of decisions by agents who make mistakes, let me apply my principle to Newcomb's Problem, presented by Nozick (1969). In this problem, an agent chooses to have either the contents of one box, or the contents of two boxes. The first box contains either $1 million or nothing. Given a prediction that the agent will take just it, it contains $1 million; otherwise, it contains nothing. The second box contains $1,000. The agent knows all this and also knows that the predictor is usually right.[3]

Some argue that the agent should take just the first box because then he is likely to gain $1 million. But the rational choice is to take both boxes, because what the agent chooses does not alter the boxes' contents and, whatever the first box's contents, he is $1,000 ahead if he takes both boxes. The dispute is fueled by the ambiguity of the phrasing of Newcomb's Problem. The usual question is: What is rational? But this question does not specify the standards of rationality to apply. Are the standards comprehensive or noncomprehensive? Also, the question does not specify the object of evaluation. Is it the act, choice, or decision? These distinctions are important if the agent enters the problem having made some mistakes.[4]

Suppose that the predictor relies on observing an agent's disposition to choose either the first box or both boxes. The disposition, I imagine, is some predecision psychological state of the agent that either causes him to choose the first box or causes him to choose both boxes when placed in Newcomb's Problem. The disposition's presence before the choice causally determines the choice, although other choices are still options for the purpose of evaluating his choice. Once the disposition arises, it persists. The laws of psychology prevent the agent from choosing contrary to it. An agent's having a disposition to choose a certain way in

Newcomb's Problem makes it true that if he were in Newcomb's Problem he would choose that way. Nonetheless, the agent is free to choose contrary to the disposition in the sense of freedom relevant to choice. He might have chosen differently than he will; he might have had a different decision disposition. To evaluate his choice, I compare it to other choices he might have made. During these comparisons, I do not suppose any change in the background for the choice, including the agent's disposition. So the suppositions on which the comparisons rest suspend the causal connection between his disposition and his choice.

Now suppose that an agent knows well in advance that he will face Newcomb's Problem. And suppose that he can cultivate either a one-boxing or a two-boxing disposition at negligible cost to himself. It is rational for him to cultivate the disposition to be a one-boxer because one-boxers almost always become rich. It is rational to cultivate this disposition even though it is irrational to choose just one box.[5] Because Newcomb's Problem rewards irrationality, it is rational to cultivate a disposition to make an irrational choice. If the agent fails to cultivate a one-boxing disposition, then he makes a mistake in the formation of decision dispositions. Because of the mistake, there is some inclination to say that if he takes both boxes, his decision is irrational—irrational because it proceeds from a mistake. But his decision is actually rational. My theory provides the following explanation.

The two-boxer's mistake about decision dispositions does not concern input for utility analysis, but rather the circumstances of his decision. It results first in the agent's having a disposition to two-box and then, if the predictor detects his disposition, in the first box's being empty. I claim that forming a two-boxing disposition is irrational, but the choice the disposition produces is rational. This seems paradoxical. How can a decision to take both boxes be rational if it proceeds from a mistake about the cultivation of a decision disposition, a mistake that is incorrigible but still inexcusable?

The answer is that the choice to take both boxes is strictly dominant. It is the rational choice in both actual circumstances and corrected circumstances. The disposition that is rational to cultivate, the disposition to take the first box only, is a disposition to choose in an irrational way. So two-boxing is the rational decision even if (1) the two-boxer's mistake about decision dispositions is inexcusable, (2) one evaluates his decision with respect to corrected circumstances in which he has a one-boxing disposition, and (3) there is $1 million in the first box. The mistaken disposition does not affect the application of utility analysis. If an agent has failed to cultivate a one-boxing disposition and enters Newcomb's Problem with a disposition to take both boxes, then, applying utility analysis to the corrected circumstances in which he has a disposition to take just the first box, the rational choice is still to take both boxes. And applying utility analysis to the actual circumstances in which he has a disposition to take both boxes, the rational choice is still to take both boxes. Either way, the rational choice is to take both boxes. Although his mistaken disposition affects the circumstances of his decision, it does not change the recommendation of utility analysis. It does not affect the option that maximizes utility. Therefore, lacking significance for the evaluation of decisions, the disposition is an acceptable mistake. Because it is an acceptable mistake, it need not be removed and so does not infect a decision that stems from it.

It is rational to cultivate a disposition to take just the first box, and the decision that disposition yields is irrational. But what about the disposition itself? Is it rational or irrational? The issue is resolved once the disposition is more fully specified. If it is the disposition to do what produces good news, then it is irrational. But if it is the disposition to decide irrationally in cases where irrationality is rewarded, then the disposition is rational. In other words, the issue is resolved once the content of the disposition is given, along with the disposition's input and output. This is a case where the evaluation of a disposition to decide a certain way depends on the content of the disposition as well as the decision reached. It depends on the mechanism that realizes the decision.

Correcting a bad two-boxing disposition yields circumstances in which the agent chooses one box. The choice he makes is irrational given his circumstances, however. Taking only the first box is irrational in any circumstances despite following from a disposition rational to form. Defenders of one-boxing's rationality make the understandable mistake of treating a decision that proceeds from corrected circumstances as rational, whereas to be rational it has to be rational in those corrected circumstances.

In Newcomb's Problem, at the time of choice it is too late to form a one-boxing disposition that will influence the boxes' contents. The case is different prior to the time of choice. Because rationality is unrewarded in Newcomb's Problem, a rational person will prepare, if possible, by, say, taking a one-boxing pill that makes him irrationally choose just one box. This preparation is rational although one-boxing is irrational. To say what a rational person will do in Newcomb's Problem, one must distinguish between decision and choice, and say whether standards are comprehensive. The rational choice is two-boxing. But a rational person with time for preparation will choose just one box. Two-boxing is rational given the agent's decision situation. But it rests on an irrational failure to cultivate a one-boxing disposition.[6]

Being a rational person in situations where not all goals of rationality can be met calls for abandoning some goals of rationality, but in a way that serves the goal of greatest overall rationality. Prior to entering Newcomb's Problem, it is rational to form the disposition to one-box. It is more important to have the rational disposition than to make the rational choice. So a rational agent has the one-boxing disposition and chooses one box. In worlds where an agent knows an irrational choice is rewarded, he cannot have a rational disposition and also make a rational choice. Rationality demands the best package of disposition and choice. In Newcomb's Problem, it involves an irrational choice.

With crucial distinctions in place, the dispute about Newcomb's Problem becomes a dispute about evaluation of decisions given mistakes. The disagreement about the status of two-boxing arises from a disagreement about the acceptability of the mistakenly formed disposition to take both boxes. The view that a two-boxing disposition is unacceptable, because inexcusable even if incorrigible, prompts the judgment that two-boxing is irrational. If two-boxing rests on an unacceptable, uncorrected mistake about dispositions, the decision to take two boxes is irrational when comprehensively evaluated. On the other hand, the view that a two-boxing disposition is an acceptable mistake prompts the judgment that two-boxing is rational. If two-boxing rests on an acceptable mistake, two-boxing is both a rational choice and a rational decision. My position is forgiving about the mistaken disposition and unforgiving about one-boxing.[7]

Let me emphasize that on any resolution of the mistaken disposition's status, two-boxing is a rational choice, the right recommendation on noncomprehensive standards, a rational decision given the agent's circumstances. In contrast, one-boxing is an irrational choice, the wrong recommendation on noncomprehensive standards, an irrational decision given the agent's circumstances. Hence, the main case for judging two-boxing irrational is not comparison with one-boxing but comprehensive evaluation of a decision to take both boxes.

Suppose that, contrary to my view, a two-boxing disposition is an unacceptable mistake. Then an agent with a two-boxing disposition faces a dilemma of rational decision. For him, no decision is thoroughly rational. A mistaken disposition or choice contaminates each decision. The decision to which his disposition leads is irrational because it rests on an unacceptable mistake. The alternative decision is irrational because it incorporates an irrational choice. On the other hand, an agent with a one-boxing disposition faces no dilemma. One-boxing is an irrational decision. It follows from a rational disposition but involves an irrational choice. The alternative decision to take both boxes is a rational option, however. If a one-boxer were to choose against his disposition, his decision would be comprehensively rational.

It is debatable whether a two-boxing disposition is an acceptable mistake. To cover all the bases, I have described the consequences of taking a two-boxing disposition as an unacceptable mistake. On my view, however, a two-boxing disposition, although an inexcusable mistake, is acceptable. It is insignificant, with respect to standards of rationality, because it does not alter the rational choice. Accordingly, the decision to take both boxes is rational when comprehensively evaluated despite resting on a mistake. Therefore, two-boxing is both a rational choice and a rational decision.

7.4. Mistakes in Execution of Plans

Planning theory concerns the adoption of plans. A plan calls for a sequence of acts, including perhaps conditional acts or strategies. Each act's performance is independent of earlier acts' performances in the sense that its performance requires a choice even if the earlier acts have already been performed. Adopting a plan is forming an intention to perform the sequence of acts that constitute the plan. The intention may not be carried out. Events may frustrate a plan, or an agent may abandon a plan. This section considers mistakes in the execution of plans. Suppose an agent irresolutely abandons a plan, or stubbornly persists with its execution. When are such mistakes unacceptable? When do they influence comprehensive evaluations of decisions about a plan's stages?

Generally, persevering with a plan is the best way to reach the long-term objectives that prompted the plan. Abandoning or changing a plan is usually inferior to persevering. For example, if one wants to go to Chicago and plans to fly, then upon arrival at the airport it is generally better to persevere than to adopt a new plan to take the train to Chicago. Vacillation is costly, as Good (1952: 111) observes. But why adopt a plan in the first place? To adopt a plan is to decide now about future acts. Why not put off decisions about future acts until the times for them arrive? Section 2.3's decision rule calls for utility maximization among possible decisions at a time. May it maximize utility to adopt a plan rather than postpone decisions about future acts?

Cognitively limited agents have good reasons to adopt plans. Adopting a plan is a way of achieving an extended act whose realization requires a sequence of momentary acts (in the case of a strategy, momentary acts responsive to future events). This way of realizing extended acts reduces deliberation costs for cognitively limited agents. Instead of deliberating about each momentary act in a sequence composing an extended act, as the momentary act's time arrives, an agent just continues to execute her plan to perform the extended act. Earlier deliberations settle her momentary acts throughout a period of time. Although moment-to-moment decisions may realize an extended act, because of the costs of deliberation cognitively limited agents profit from using plans to realize extended acts.[8]

Plans are occasionally justified in other ways. Ulysses planned to have himself tied to his ship's mast, and the ears of his crew stopped, before sailing near the Sirens. His plan removed choices he otherwise would have had. His plan prevented future mistakes he would have made. It accomplished something he would not have done making decisions moment by moment. In his case, planning overcame a clouded mind rather than deliberation costs.

This section assumes that agents are cognitively limited and benefit from planning typically because of savings in deliberation costs. I consider an agent who has adopted a plan and decides whether to execute a component of the plan. I ask whether his decision is rational taking account of mistakes he may make. Because I am not assuming full rationality, his decision's rationality is not settled by its maximizing utility with respect to his circumstances. Perhaps those circumstances involve unacceptable mistakes, mistakes involving the plan's adoption, his commitment to it, or departures from it. A comprehensive evaluation of his decision must weigh mistakes on which it rests.

According to chapter 2, given full information, a plan's execution is rational only if each momentary act comprising its execution is optimal. Given uncertainty, a plan's execution is rational only if each momentary act comprising its execution maximizes utility. In contrast, given uncertainty, a plan's adoption is rational only if its adoption maximizes utility. Its adoption's outcome typically but not necessarily includes the plan's execution. Because plans adopted may not be executed, the utility of a plan's adoption is not necessarily the same as the utility of its execution. A plan rational to adopt may be irrational to execute. Perhaps its adoption promises to deter an aggressor although its execution in fact includes pointless retaliation. Someone who resolutely executes a plan to retaliate if attacked acts irrationally if he is attacked and retaliation brings no benefits, even though the plan's adoption was rational because of the prospect of deterrence.

Suppose an agent has irrationally adopted a plan. Its irrational adoption counts as an unacceptable mistake. The execution of a component of the plan is rational only if it is rational given correction of that mistake and so, typically, only if it is rational independently of the plan.

A plan rationally adopted is rationally retained if no new relevant consideration arises, such as a change in the beliefs or desires supporting the plan. It is irrationally retained if it is unresponsive to relevant changes in circumstances. Irrationally retaining a plan is also an unacceptable mistake.

Under what circumstances is a plan irrationally retained? Constantly reviewing a plan squanders its savings in deliberation costs. Only salient changes should trigger a review. The appropriate level and type of responsiveness is achieved, not by deliberation, but by habits governing spontaneous review of plans. One should cultivate habits of spontaneously reopening deliberations at appropriate moments. Reopening deliberations too readily is the mistake of distraction or irresoluteness. Excessive resistance to reopening deliberations is the mistake of obstinacy or inflexibility. The optimal habit reopens deliberations when the benefits outweigh the costs. The benefits, like the benefits of gathering information, are increases in the expected value of maximizing utility. Calculating costs and benefits is costly. An optimal habit responds to them without calculation. Nonoptimal habits, easier to inculcate, respond to them less reliably. A rational agent develops the best habits his circumstances permit. A decision about execution of an act planned may be rational despite deliberation unjustified by benefits, or despite lack of deliberation justified by benefits. It is rational if the agent's habits of spontaneously reopening deliberation are rationally aimed at reopening deliberation if and only if justified by benefits.

This position on planning, although only a sketch, has some significant consequences. For example, because rational resoluteness aims at utility maximization taking account of the cost of deliberation, plans do not generate reasons for action that are independent of utility maximization. Planning by itself does not justify an act planned. Consider an example Bratman (1987: 23) uses to argue the contrary. He is driving to San Francisco. He knows both Highway 101 and Highway 280 go there. He is indifferent between them, but decides to take 101. After adopting this plan, when he reaches Page Mill Road, he has a reason to turn right toward 101 rather than left toward 280. Bratman suggests that his plan generates this reason independently of utility maximization. Both routes have maximum utility, but because of his plan, driving toward highway 101 is the rational choice upon arrival at Page Mill Road. My view is that only pursuing his plan to take 101 maximizes utility. At Page Mill Road he maximizes utility by not reopening deliberations about routes. Sticking to his plan maximizes utility given deliberation costs.[9]

Rabinowicz (in personal communication, May 26, 1998) uses a different type of example to argue that plans are a source of reasons independent of beliefs and desires. Someone slow to rise in the morning may resolve to get up on the count of ten. When he reaches ten, he hops out of bed. He is motivated by his intention to rise when the chosen moment arrives. In this example, the intention and its resolute execution are not a way of saving deliberation costs. The mere intention to rise on the count of ten, however, does not yield reasons for rising independent of utility maximization. Rather, the sleepyhead uses his habit of carrying out intentions, formed to save deliberation costs, to help him rise. He fears that reopening deliberations will be an occasion for rationalization and backsliding. Forming the intention maximizes utility. Also, the agent may have a desire to resolutely carry out his plans, other things being equal. His admiration for resolve then augments the desirability of rising on the count of ten. The formation of the intention and its execution because of habit and a desire to be resolute have explanations in terms of utility maximization.

In Bratman's and Rabinowicz's examples, adoption of a plan does not generate a reason independent of utility maximization for following the plan. Instead, it affects options' utilities so that utility maximization supports following the plan. Rational plans and their executions are utility maximizing.

Finally, consider an example Gauthier (1991: 24–25) uses to argue against straightforward utility maximization. An agent can gain a benefit by committing herself now to cooperate later, even though when it is time to cooperate she will already have the benefit, so that cooperating is only a cost. Should she commit herself now to cooperate later? Is it rational to resolutely plan to cooperate even though the plan includes a nonmaximizing future act? Gauthier endorses the plan and its execution. McClennen (1990: chap. 1) reinforces Gauthier's argument for resolute, nonmaximizing choices in such cases by emphasizing their advantages with respect to mechanisms compelling cooperation. However, the act of cooperation is irrational according to my standards because it is nonmaximizing. Moreover, the resoluteness that yields it is an unacceptable mistake. Rational resoluteness aims at moment-by-moment utility maximization. It is generated by sensitivity to deliberation costs, not sensitivity to rewards for irrationality. It may be rational to cultivate excessive resoluteness in circumstances where it is rewarded, but resoluteness insensitive to the benefits of reopening deliberations is irrational and unacceptable. Profit from a mistaken commitment to an irrational act does not make the mistake acceptable. A rational decision proceeds from correction of the mistaken commitment. The decision the mistaken commitment prompts is irrational. Profitless cooperation is an irrational decision on two counts. It involves an irrational choice and proceeds from an irrational commitment.[10]

7.5. Mistakes about Options

Next, let me apply my principle of evaluation, the principle of acceptability, to cases where an agent has made the mistake of failing to consider all options. I treat agents without cognitive limitations first and then agents with such limitations.

When an agent fails to consider all her options, her application of maximization rules has mistaken input. Because the input does not include all her options, she does not rank all her options according to utility. In the case of an ideal agent, who has no cognitive limitations, the mistake is corrigible. She can consider all options. She need only direct her attention to them. Moreover, considering all options takes her no time or effort. So she has no reason to restrict consideration of options. If she faces a decision that matters, where some gain or loss in utility is at stake, and she does not consider all options, then her mistake about options is not acceptable because it is significant, corrigible, and inexcusable. Her decision is then irrational according to my principle, which entails the irrationality of a decision resting on an unacceptable mistake. Her decision is irrational even if she decides by applying utility analysis to the options she considers and happens to select the option that does maximize utility among all options. In this case, the act realized is rational, and the choice is rational. But the decision is irrational. This is the verdict of my comprehensive standards because the manner of deciding is irrational. It follows the right procedure but rests on an unacceptable mistake.

Next, suppose that the agent lacks the cognitive capacity to consider all options and as a result overlooks the option that maximizes utility and fails to select it. We should not charge the agent with irrationality in all such cases. It may be rational to decide without considering the missing options, either because their consideration is impossible or too costly. The agent's cognitive limitations furnish an excuse for failing to consider all options before reaching a decision and thus for failing to select the option of maximum utility. My decision principle accommodates this excuse.

In a decision problem, an option is a decision, a mental act. On the other hand, an act arising from an option's realization may be nonmental. I take an agent's set of options to be the set of decisions that she can make at the time of decision. The relevant sense of "can" involves psychological possibility. So the agent's cognitive powers limit the set of options.

Can an agent realize an option unconsidered? Spontaneous decision is possible. Not every decision need be preceded by a review of options. However, a decision spontaneously realized is still an option considered. If an option is unconsidered throughout a decision problem, it is also unrealized.

Is an unconsidered option really in an agent's power? There is a sense in which an agent cannot adopt an option she does not consider. So it may seem that an option not considered is not really an option. However, in the sense relevant to evaluation of decisions, an agent can adopt an option not considered. She can do this by first considering the option and then forming an intention that realizes it. When I say that an option is a possible decision, I mean that there is a way for the agent to make the decision. I do not mean that there is a way for her to make the decision immediately without any mental preparation.

When an agent has cognitive limitations that prevent her considering all her options at once, it is still true for each option that she can consider it. Moreover, it is still true for each that she can adopt it if she considers it. So in the relevant sense, it is true for each option that she can adopt it. Although a psychologically possible decision may have no real chance of being realized if the agent fails to consider it, she nonetheless can realize it in the sense of psychological possibility that I adopt. Inattention does not disqualify options.

The type of consideration of options that is pertinent to utility maximization is comparative consideration of options in a set. Such comparative consideration furnishes reasons for realization of an option in the set. Even an option realized without deliberation may be supported by implicit comparisons with other options. The type of consideration of an option entailed by the option's realization is noncomparative. Realization of an option requires consideration of the option only as a product of the option's realization. Its gratuitous realization, for example, is independent of even implicit comparisons with other options. An agent's failure to comparatively consider an option does not disqualify it as an option.

These remarks about options leave the set of all options vague and ambiguous. The imprecision should be resolved in ways that improve normative decision theory. For instance, if it is unclear whether an agent can make a certain decision, but it is clear that a failure to make that decision would be excused even if it has maximum utility, then other things being equal, that decision should not be counted as an option. It is simpler if the theory makes being an option entail accountability. In general, unclear cases should be handled in a way that advances decision theory, but exactly how this should be done remains an open question.

For precision in treating cases where an agent fails to consider all options, first consider cases where cognitive limitations prevent consideration of all options, at least in the time period available for deliberation, so that there are good excuses for not considering all options before deciding. I suppose that the agent neither considers all options simultaneously nor considers them pairwise, keeping track of the top option reviewed. Despite these limitations, I assume that the agent still has an ability to calculate expected utilities instantaneously and without effort. I also assume that there are no problems accessing the relevant probabilities and utilities, that is, no problems of the sort chapters 4 and 5 discuss, so that there are no good excuses for failing to maximize expected utility among the options considered. This may be an unrealistic combination of assumptions because cognitive limitations excusing a failure to consider all options generally excuse a failure to maximize expected utility as well. But to isolate factors in the evaluation of decisions, I imagine cases where only a failure to consider all options is excused.

In these cases, theorists such as Riker and Ordeshook (1973: chap. 2) propose the principle to maximize expected utility among the options actually considered. This principle is too lax. Sometimes a person satisfies it but still makes an irrational decision. For example, as section 6.1 explains, a talented artist choosing a career decides irrationally if the only careers he considers are medicine and law, even if he maximizes expected utility when choosing between those two. He ought to consider careers that engage his artistic talent. Riker and Ordeshook's principle is reliable only in cases where agents are error-free, as in chapters 4 and 5. It does not govern cases where agents mistakenly overlook options.

I concede that a decision that maximizes expected utility among the options considered is rational given the options considered. This conditional evaluation goes by the options considered. But the nonconditional rationality of a decision requires, if not consideration of all options, at least consideration of an appropriate set of options. Irrationality in the consideration of options infects the decision itself. As illustrated earlier, mistakes in input for a good decision rule may make it recommend an irrational decision. One kind of mistake that does this is inattention to options one ought to have considered.

A choice among the options considered is rational if it maximizes utility among them. But a decision is evaluated more comprehensively than a choice. A choice's evaluation presumes a set of options considered. A decision's evaluation does not make such a presumption. Its evaluation has broader scope. Its rationality depends on the option realized, the reasons for the choice, and the pedigree of those reasons. Although the choice is rational, the decision may be irrational because of an inappropriate set of options considered.

My principle of acceptability evaluates decisions rather than choices. According to it, a rational decision maximizes utility after correcting unacceptable mistakes, and considering a set of options irrational to consider is an unacceptable mistake, one to be corrected when applying the principle. Because my principle evaluates decisions comprehensively and nonconditionally, it takes account of the deliberations leading up to a decision as well as the option realized. Applied to cases in which an agent fails to consider all options, it claims that a decision is rational only if it maximizes utility among the options considered and the set of options considered is rational to consider.

Let me emphasize that the general rule is not that whenever the preliminaries to a decision involve some irrationality, the decision itself is irrational. A transference of irrationality occurs when the set of options considered is irrational. It occurs then because the set of options considered is a major part of the decision process, on equal footing with the rule of choice employed. Consideration of an irrational set of options is therefore an unacceptable mistake. That makes it an infectious mistake in contrast with excusable, incorrigible mistakes.

How should one evaluate the set of options the agent considers? My proposal is to evaluate that set according to an evaluation of the habits of consideration that produced it. That is, I appeal to procedural standards of rationality. In brief, the options are rational to consider if and only if they enter consideration in the appropriate way. Moreover, they enter consideration in the appropriate way if and only if they enter consideration because of habits of consideration acquired through good use of opportunities for cultivating attention-focusing processes. Utility analysis appraises habits of consideration, so once again, it guides us although its application is indirect.

To elaborate these ideas, I distinguish two kinds of deliberation. Sometimes in the deliberation preceding a decision it is rational to reflect on the set of options under consideration and ask whether they exclude an important option. A case with this sort of reflection involves *complex* deliberation. In such cases, the options ultimately considered form a rational set only if the review process is rationally carried out. At other times, say, because of shortage of time, or because one must halt a regress of decisions about how to decide, it is rational to decide among the options under consideration without any review of those options. In contrast with the first type of case, I say that these are cases of *simple* deliberation. The standard for the rationality of the options considered in these cases is interesting because the set of options cannot be assessed via a review process. The only standard is the reason the set of options comes to mind spontaneously: habits of attention. I treat these cases, following Weirich (1986b).

Habits of attention produce the set of options that comes to mind spontaneously. Good habits of attention have a good chance of bringing to mind good options. This chapter's appendix characterizes them more precisely. For the set of options to be rational, one must have made satisfactory use of opportunities for cultivating good habits of attention. One may have squandered some opportunities, or have acquired some bad habits. One needs only a passing grade in this area. When the agent is fully rational so that she has never acted irrationally, then the rationality of the set of options she considers is ensured. When the agent is not fully rational and has sometimes acted irrationally, the rationality of the set of options she considers depends on whether her mistakes are acceptable. As section 6.4 stated, this depends on whether her mistakes regarding habits of attention affect her decision in a significant and immediate way and, as her mistakes are incorrigible, whether they are inexcusable.

A decision is rational in the comprehensive sense only if the set of options considered is rational and thus only if mistakes on which that set rests are acceptable. Because of cognitive limitations, failing to consider all options is an acceptable mistake when the options considered are either the result of a rational review process in complex deliberations, or the result of good decisions about the cultivation of attention-focusing processes in simple deliberations. In these cases, the mistake is excused; moreover, it is acceptable. However, these cases are not the only ones in which mistakes are acceptable. It is possible for a mistake to be acceptable in other cases because the mistake is remote or insignificant. Making good use of opportunities for cultivating habits of attention and reviewing options is sufficient but not necessary for acceptability. Elaborating this account of acceptable inattention to options is a topic for future research.

7.A. Appendix: Attention to Options

Good habits of attention to options are ones that have a good chance of yielding an option of maximum utility, or failing that, one of high utility, or failing that, one of middling utility, and so on. Also, because consideration costs are a factor, the good habits are ones that pass over options of high utility if their complexity makes the costs of considering them high. Let me say that the *fitness* of an option for consideration is its utility minus the cost of considering it. Fitness is utility adjusted for the cost of reflection, so maximizing fitness is maximizing cost-adjusted utility. The fitness of options creates levels of fitness in the set of all options. If some options have fitness 1 and the others fitness 2, then there are two levels of fitness. If all have fitness 1, 2, or 2.5, then there are three levels of fitness. I define the quality of a habit of attention, or attention-focusing process, in terms of its approximation to fitness maximization. I assume the quantities the assessment requires exist in the cases I treat.

Let $P(f_1)$ stand for the probability that among the options produced by an attention-focusing process, one of maximum fitness also has maximum fitness among all options. Similarly, let $P(f_2)$ stand for the probability that among the options produced, an option of maximum fitness has the degree of fitness of options at the second highest level of fitness among all options. Similarly for $P(f_3)$ and so on. Then, in a decision problem, the *quality* of an attention-focusing process p, $Q(p)$, is the probability-weighted average of the possible degrees of fitness of an option of maximum fitness in the set of options the process yields. That is,

$$Q(p) = \Sigma_i P(f_i) f_i.$$

The overall quality of an attention-focusing process is its expected quality in future decision problems.

Defined this way, the quality of an attention-focusing process indicates the process's expected level of success in its cognitive role. This is not the same as the utility of the attention-focusing process because its utility also takes account of noncognitive factors. Still, quality is obtained by an application of utility analysis. It is obtained (1) by restricting utility to a certain type of cognitive utility, that is, moving to a partial utility function defined in terms of cognitive goals, as in Weirich (2001a: chap. 2), and (2) by using expected utility analysis on the partial utility function applied to attention-focusing processes. That is, expected utilities are taken with respect to cognitive goals for attention-focusing processes and the probabilities of reaching those goals. Having good attention-focusing processes is a subsidiary goal for pursuit of the goal of considering a rational set of options, which is itself a subsidiary goal for pursuit of the goal of maximizing utility among all options, given an inability to consider all options.

Realism about Situations

Previous chapters treated decision situations where options' utilities may be unavailable but, having options' utilities, maximizing utility is straightforward. This chapter treats decision situations where, even having options' utilities, utility maximization falters. It treats nonideal decision problems instead of nonideal agents. First, it considers decision problems with an infinite number of salient options, none of which has maximum utility, as in the problem of picking your own income. Maximizing utility is impossible in such problems, and my decision rule must be generalized to cover them. Next, it considers decision problems where an option's assumption has implications about basic intrinsic attitudes or the relevant state of the world. In such problems, the basis for options' utility comparisons may be unstable and vary with the option assumed. This may happen in the problem of selecting one's values, for instance. The principle of utility maximization needs generalization to accommodate these problems also. This chapter replaces having maximum utility with a new, more general necessary condition for being a rational option. It also advances a rule for choosing among options that meet the necessary condition.

Treating nonideal decision problems adds generality and increases realism by enhancing decision theory's explanatory power. It broadens coverage of factors that make decisions rational (see chapter 3). Does it promote realism in other ways, too? Do any real decision problems have an infinite number of options? Do any involve unstable comparisons of options? I rely on common opinion about these empirical matters. Although an infinite number of options may arise under the idealization of unlimited cognitive power, in real cases the number of options is finite. Principles accommodating an infinite number of options nonetheless offer useful approximative coverage of some real problems, such as picking a number or picking a monetary gain below a certain amount.[1] Decision problems with unstable comparisons of options are real, as this chapter's and the next chapter's illustrations show. Removing the idealization of stability adds realism by improving coverage of such cases.

8.1. Reinstated Idealizations

Rational decision making does not always have the goal of realizing an option of maximum utility. In cases where no option has maximum utility, the goal of maximization is inappropriate. The absence of a maximum is not simply an impediment to a pertinent maximization goal. Because pursuing utility maximization is impossible when no option has maximum utility, the goal of maximization lacks force and ceases to guide decisions. Earlier chapters adopted idealizations to table decision problems where maximizing utility is not an appropriate goal. In particular, one idealization assumed the existence of an option maximizing utility with respect to stable utility comparisons. This chapter dispenses with that idealization and introduces decision principles that express goals of rationality more general than utility maximization.

In contrast with chapters 4–7, this chapter does not treat difficulties for utility maximization that arise because of errors or insufficient resources. It treats difficulties that arise because of the structure of decision problems without a stable top option. To facilitate their treatment, the chapter reinstates idealizations that preceding chapters removed. It considers only cases in which an agent is cognitively ideal, has quantitative probability and utility assignments, and is fully rational except possibly in the decision problem at hand. The assumption about the agent's rationality entails that she enter the decision problem in a fully rational state of mind and anticipate full rationality afterward. She knows she complies with all standards of rationality before and after her decision problem.

My task is generalizing the decision rule to maximize utility. I do not reconsider any principles of utility analysis. In particular, I do not change expected utility analysis (section 2.4), a method of calculating an option's utility. Although by generalizing the decision rule to maximize utility, I thereby also generalize the decision rule to maximize expected utility, I do not generalize expected utility analysis itself. It already applies to options in decision problems without a stable top option. Without modification, it may be used in conjunction with a generalization of the decision rule to maximize utility.

Section 7.2's principle against dilemmas of rational choice guides my generalization of decision rules. According to it, in every decision problem some choice is rational. That is, some choice is rational taking for granted the decision situation, including mistakes, if any. Under this chapter's idealization that agents are ideal and fully rational, they are error-free. Hence, the principle's condition that mistakes are taken for granted is unnecessary. A rational choice noncomprehensively evaluated is also a rational decision comprehensively evaluated. Therefore, the principle against dilemmas of rational choice yields a similar, restricted principle against dilemmas of rational decision. Because errors do not hamper fully rational ideal agents, in every decision problem they face, some decision is comprehensively rational, not just rational taking for granted their decision situations. In every decision problem, some option is both a rational choice and a rational decision. The distinction between decisions comprehensively evaluated and choices noncomprehensively evaluated is unnecessary given this chapter's idealizations.

8.2. No Maximum Utility

Consider a case with an infinite number of options where, for each option, another has greater utility. Take, for example, Savage's case (1972: 18) about fixing your yearly income at an amount less than $100,000, or Pollock's case (1984: 417) about immortals deciding when to drink a bottle of wine that improves every year without end. No option has maximum utility in these cases. So it is impossible to maximize utility. The rule to maximize utility does not say what to do.

Cases where it is impossible to maximize utility do not constitute counter-examples to the decision rule to maximize utility. As it is usually taken, the decision rule is restricted to cases where it is possible to maximize utility. The rule needs generalization, not correction. How should the generalization go? Which options are rational when no option maximizes utility? Decision problems with no option of maximum utility are not cases in which anything goes. Not all ways of deciding are rational. Some standards of rationality apply, and a rational decision meets them.

The most general decision rule is to select an option that is maximally supported by the reasons bearing on the decision, that is, an option for which the reasons are as weighty as the reasons for any rival. A maximally supported option is not always an option with maximum utility—not if all options lack maximum utility. When no option has maximum utility, options may be equally well supported even though some have more utility than others. The rule of maximal support, although completely general, is vague and difficult to apply. To yield a more definite decision rule for cases where no option has maximum utility, it needs supplementation by a theory of support. I use the general rule, together with some principles of support, to obtain my new decision rule.

When no option has maximum utility, all options are on equal footing in the sense that for each another has greater utility. But they need not all be equally well supported. Some but not all options may meet the agent's aspirations. For instance, some options may produce losses, whereas others produce gains. Given an aspiration to achieve gains and avoid losses, only the options producing gains are satisfactory. Only an option satisfactory in light of the agent's aspirations is a rational choice, as Simon (1955, 1959, 1982) suggests.

The proposal to "satisfice" arises from the observation that most reasons for an option concern the satisfaction of desires. The reasons for options conflict because different options satisfy different desires. The principle to pick an option with maximum utility is a way of resolving these conflicts. The principle to pick an option with satisfactory utility is another, more general way. The principle to maximize utility follows from the principle to satisfice given that only options of maximum utility have satisfactory utility when an option of maximum utility exists. Context determines the aspiration level, and for an ideal agent the aspiration level reaches the maximum available when a maximum exists.

Rules for setting the aspirations level that defines satisfactory options are crucial for applications of the principle to satisfice. The rules appeal to basic intrinsic attitudes and feasibility, but need not be specified for my purposes. The fully rational, ideal agents I treat comply with the rules whatever they are. My only substantive assumption is that aspiration levels adjust to circumstances so that at least one option is satisfactory. This assumption allows satisficing to be a necessary condition of rational choice. Because in every decision problem some option is a rational choice, taking satisficing as necessary for a rational choice requires the existence of a satisfactory option in every decision problem.

The principle to satisfice has different purposes for Simon and for me. Simon proposes satisficing as a decision procedure, a rival of maximization. He sanctions nonmaximizing decisions in cases where maximizing is possible, claiming that maximizing is too difficult for humans with only bounded rationality. As section 1.2 explains, I take maximization as a standard of evaluation and handle practical considerations by having it take account of decision costs, as in chapter 5. This section drafts satisficing as a standard of evaluation to generalize the principle of maximization for cases where maximization is impossible. It proposes satisficing for ideal agents with unbounded rationality, agents for whom deliberation is instantaneous and cost-free.

Both the principle to satisfice and the principle to maximize derive from the same general principle of maximum support. That an option is satisfactory is a reason for it. That one option has more utility than another is a reason to prefer the first. These reasons do not discredit each other; both have weight wherever they arise. Having satisfactory utility is a reason that complements reasons bearing on maximization. Rather than undermining those reasons, it comes to their aid when they are insufficient for reaching a decision. It helps in the special case in which all options are on the same footing with respect to reasons concerning maximization because for each option another has higher utility. My general principle of maximum support treats the two types of reasons together. Maximum support normally goes by comparisons, but it appeals to classifications involving satisfactoriness in special cases where comparisons are inconclusive.

Generalizing the principle of utility maximization to obtain the principle to satisfice accommodates cases without an option of maximum utility. The principle to maximize utility needs further generalization, however, for cases where utility comparisons are unstable. That is, although satisficing replaces utility maximization as a more general necessary condition of rationality, I need a still more general necessary condition of rationality for cases of instability. The next section formulates such a condition.

8.3. Shifting Grounds for Utility Comparisons

The decision principle to maximize utility relies on comparisons of options' utilities. An agent's utility assignment is subjective and dependent on information. In addition to depending on desires rather than values, it depends on beliefs rather than facts. In unusual cases, an agent's utility assignment changes with the option assumed. It changes because an option's assumption has implications about basic goals or carries information about relevant states of the world. The principle to maximize utility must be generalized for cases with an unstable basis for utility comparisons of options.

8.3.1. *Dynamic Decision Problems*

Section 2.1 pointed out that an act's performance may affect basic goals. The phenomenon of sour grapes, discussed by Elster (1983), provides an illustration. An agent may seek some prize but fail to attain it. On realizing that the prize is out of reach, he may lose his desire for it. Perhaps he wants to study medicine but after failing to gain admission to medical school concludes that he does not want to study medicine after all. Lack of confidence provides another illustration. An agent may distrust his own judgment so that sometimes, immediately upon making a decision, he repudiates the desire that prompted it. Success turns to ashes in his mouth. Perhaps he does not want to belong to any club that accepts him. Perhaps his soup tastes bland but as soon as he adds a little salt, doubting himself, he concludes that he has made it too salty. I say that a decision problem is *dynamic* when an option's assumption has implications about basic goals. The word dynamic often indicates that time introduces relevant changes, but I use it to indicate that an option's assumption introduces relevant changes.

When basic goals change with the option assumed, the basis of utility comparisons is unstable. How should options be compared? Which utility assignment is an appropriate basis of comparison? I return to these questions shortly but for now just make a preliminary observation. If the effect of decisions on basic goals is foreseen, rationality requires that deliberations take account of it. One needs a decision principle that attends to anticipated changes in basic goals.

An agent may also anticipate that realizing an option will affect his information about states of the world that determine options' outcomes. Suppose that he anticipates that an option's realization will causally influence those states. The formula for an option's expected utility handles this information. No new issues arise. Suppose, however, that he anticipates that an option's realization will not causally influence the states but nonetheless will provide relevant information about them. For example, suppose that an agent has the task of identifying the color of a ball he draws from an urn. The light is dim, and he knows that in dim light green objects look blue to him. He also knows that the balls in the urn are nearly all green. When he draws a ball from the urn, a decision to classify it as blue is unstable. Given the decision's realization, the agent has evidence that it is mistaken and the ball is green. The decision does not causally influence the ball's color. Still, it provides evidence about the ball's color. Next, suppose that an agent is answering a multiple-choice question on a topic he has not studied. He knows that the question makes incorrect answers appealing to uninformed respondents. So, if he picks an answer, he acquires evidence that it is wrong although his decision does not cause it to be wrong. For an example involving an act less cerebral than identifying and answering, suppose I am at a baseball field standing in the batter's box trying to hit major league pitching. The balls pitched are very fast, and to have any chance of hitting one, I must start my swing before the pitch. If I decide to swing at a ball when I see it thrown, the very decision is evidence that it is too late to hit the ball. The decision, if instantaneous, does not cause it to be too late but provides evidence that it is too late. The decision is a sign but not a cause of failure. Finally, suppose that deciding to seek happiness is good evidence that one will not find happiness. Then that decision is unstable. Once made, the reasons for it no longer support it. This happens even if the decision does not cause its lack of success but just indicates a personality type fated for unhappiness. The formula for expected utility does not take account of noncausally grounded evidence that undermines support for decisions. Rational deliberations must take account of it, however. One needs a decision principle that attends to such anticipated changes in information.

Expected utility analysis explains how options' utilities depend on information. Because of this dependency, the principle to maximize utility requires a specification of the information with respect to which utilities are to be computed. In particular, one needs to know with respect to which body of information one should compute utilities when a choice itself carries relevant information. Various informational specifications come to mind. One possibility is to use the information the agent has during deliberation. Another possibility is to use the information the agent has at the time of decision. Obviously, the difference is important only if relevant information arrives during the transition from deliberation to decision. This does not happen usually. But it does happen in some theoretically significant cases. For instance, in games of strategy an agent's decision provides information about the other agents' decisions, and information about their decisions affects his options' utilities.

Strictly speaking, an agent cannot decide using the information he will have at the time of decision. During deliberations, he does not have that information. Even if he knows what that information will be given an option, he does not have that information unless he knows he will adopt that option. During deliberations an agent has second-order information about the information he has at the time of decision if he adopts a certain option. He anticipates having such and such information if he adopts this or that option. An option's assumption carries information rather than provides it.

Earlier, I classified a decision problem as dynamic if an option's assumption has implications about basic goals. I also classify a decision problem as dynamic if an option's assumption carries information that changes utilities. In general, a decision problem is *dynamic* if and only if some option's assumption affects its utility. It is plain that rational decision making in dynamic problems takes account of anticipated changes in basic goals and information upon an option's adoption. How should it take account of them?

Given full information, rationality aims at a decision supported by desires at the time of decision, including desires the decision generates. Desires controlling choice should not seek a decision that serves them but rather one that serves desires at the time the decision is made. Given incomplete information, rationality seeks a decision that serves beliefs and desires at the time of decision. To be rational, an agent's decision has to be supported by all his information, including his information about desires given his decision and including his second-order information about the information he has given his decision. His decision has to be supported by the information he anticipates having given his decision, or, more precisely, because that information may not be certain, his decision has to have maximum support given his decision. During deliberations, I call a possible decision *self-supporting* if it has maximum support under supposition of the decision. This rough characterization of self-support suffices for this section's broad points about it. Subsequent sections explicate the idea more precisely.

The argument for self-supporting decisions is simple and compelling. An objective of rational decision making is a choice supported by beliefs and desires at the time the choice is made. Adopting a self-supporting option is the best way to pursue this objective. Rational deliberation uses available second-order information about the beliefs and desires one has given an option's adoption to achieve self-support. If one maximizes utility only with respect to first-order beliefs and desires during deliberations, one's decision fits beliefs and desires one has prior to one's choice. That is, one's decision fits beliefs and desires that are out of date at the time the decision is made. Past beliefs and desires do not justify a decision. Only current beliefs and desires can do that. Adopting a self-supporting option is the best way to avoid decisions regretted as they are made.[2]

I distinguish success goals and cognitive goals for decisions. The goal to maximize fully informed utility, the "factually objective" counterpart of subjective utility, is a success goal (see section 3.1.4). The goal to maximize utility is cognitive. Cognitive goals are subordinate to success goals. They express secondary goals aimed at promoting primary, success goals when obstacles arise. Self-support is a cognitive goal, a generalization of the cognitive goal of utility maximization for dynamic decision problems. The primary, success goal it serves is making a decision that is self-supporting with respect to fully informed utility. This success goal is a generalization of the goal to maximize fully informed utility. It encompasses cases with unstable comparisons of options.

Deciding according to utility comparisons is sensible only when the basis of utility comparisons is constant from option to option. In cases where the assumption that an option is adopted affects relevant beliefs and desires, and affects them differently from option to option, the basis of comparisons changes from option to option. Utility comparisons are not decisive when they vary this way. To yield a dependable ranking of options, utility comparisons must be made with respect to the same relevant beliefs and desires. Only then are they made with respect to a single standard of comparison. The principle to maximize utility, therefore, has to be restricted to cases in which the supposition that an option is realized does not affect relevant beliefs and desires, or affects them the same way for each option.

To reinforce this point, consider the justification of the principle to maximize utility. The principle follows, as a special case, from the more general principle of maximum support, which says to pick an option maximally supported in light of the reasons for and against each option. The reasons for and against an option are relative to one's beliefs and desires. They change as those beliefs and desires change. To yield a dependable ranking of options, utility comparisons must be made with respect to fixed beliefs and desires. When beliefs and desires vary from option to option, the principle of maximum support attends to the variation and generalizes the principle of utility maximization to obtain the principle of self-support.

What is the relation between the goals of self-support and utility maximization? Is the goal of self-support subordinate to the goal of utility maximization? Does it come into play only when utility maximization is blocked? Expected utility analysis is the chief way of computing options' utilities. Sometimes, ignorance of probabilities of states given options stands in the way of maximizing expected utility. This happens in games of strategy. Often, an agent does not know the probabilities of her opponent's strategies. Because her strategies do not causally influence his strategies, if she were to adopt a strategy she still would not know the probabilities of his strategies. Missing relevant probabilities thwart the goal of maximizing utility. How should one pursue that goal when relevant probabilities are unavailable? From a broader perspective, the question is: How should one seek maximum fully informed utility, the success goal, when there is not even enough information to maximize utility?

In such decision problems the agent may know the probabilities of relevant states under the assumption that an option is adopted. This indicative assumption has evidential rather than causal import (see section A.6). It enriches the basis of the agent's probability assignment and may enrich it to the point where probabilities are assigned to relevant states. In a game, an agent may know that if she adopts a certain strategy, her opponent is likely to have anticipated it and will adopt countermeasures. Given the informational value of an option's assumption, it is sensible to adopt an option supported on the assumption that it is adopted. That is, it is sensible to adopt a self-supporting option.

Reflecting on this path to self-support, seeking a self-supporting option may seem to be a way of seeking an option of maximum utility when information is sparse. The goal of self-support may therefore seem subordinate to utility maximization. However, utility maximization is simply impossible in cases without a stable top option. Appearances notwithstanding, adopting a self-supporting option is not a way of approximating utility maximization. Self-support is not a fall-back goal. It is a more general replacement goal. The goal of self-support is a general cognitive goal, articulating rational pursuit of the success goal in all sorts of cases with all sorts of obstacles. Self-support is a more general goal than utility maximization. It is not just a goal for cases where impediments block utility maximization. It is not subordinate to utility maximization.[3]

The directive to make a self-supporting choice generalizes the directive to maximize utility by adjusting it for dynamic problems. It subsumes utility maximization in nondynamic decision problems where options' utilities are stable and known, because then self-support amounts to utility maximization. The directive to maximize utility is sound only for decision problems that are not dynamic. Maximizing utility is not a general goal but a restricted goal, one restricted to cases where some option has maximum utility and the utility ranking of options does not change as the option assumed changes.

To obtain a more specific version of the directive to adopt a self-supporting option, one needs an account of self-support. The next section offers a preliminary account of self-support. The following sections improve it.

8.3.2. *Ratification*

During deliberations, an agent may be uncertain about the information she would have if she were to realize an option. She is certain that she would know which option she has realized, because options are decisions, but she may be uncertain about the additional information that would accompany her decision and so may be uncertain about her probability assignment if she were to make the decision. Given this sort of uncertainty, an obstacle to maximizing utility at the time of choice, a plausible subsidiary goal in deliberations is to realize an option that has maximum utility on the assumption that it is realized. That is, maximize with respect to an option's assumption rather than with respect to actual information at the time of the option's realization. An agent has the resources needed to maximize utility with respect to the information she anticipates having at the time of choice, more precisely, to adopt an option that has maximum utility on the assumption that it is adopted. According to my idealization about the availability of relevant current probabilities, the probabilities of states under an option's assumption are available, even if the agent's information given the option is uncertain. These probabilities are current conditional probabilities, not future probabilities given a condition. They are available to guide attempts to maximize utility at the time of choice.

One plausible generalization of the principle to maximize utility thus says that a rational decision is an option that has maximum utility on the assumption that it is adopted. It holds an agent accountable to only the information she has during deliberations, although its goal is maximization with respect to information at the time of choice. An option that has maximum utility on the assumption that it is adopted is said to be *ratifiable*. So the foregoing generalization of the principle to maximize utility is the same as the principle to adopt a ratifiable option.[4] Stating it as a directive, it reads as follows:

>   *Ratification*. Adopt an option that maximizes utility given its adoption.

The principle of ratification is a principle of self-support for options; a ratifiable option supports itself in the sense that under its assumption it maximizes utility. The principle demands that an option have a certain type of self-support. Sometimes the principle of ratification is taken to be distinct from the principle to maximize utility, but it is a generalization of that principle obtained by computing utilities with respect to beliefs and desires one anticipates having at the time of choice. When no relevant changes are anticipated, as in nondynamic decision problems, the principle of ratification reduces to the principle to maximize utility. Where there is uncertainty, expected utility yields utility. The principle of ratification then says to adopt an option that maximizes expected utility given that it is adopted.[5]

Problems with the goal of ratification, or picking an option that maximizes expected utility given the option's realization, arise in special decision situations where no option has maximum expected utility, or expected utility comparisons of options vary with the option assumed. In the latter case, it is possible that some option maximizes expected utility but no option maximizes expected utility on the assumption it is adopted. The principle of ratification is a good first step toward generalization of the principle to maximize utility. It draws attention to information carried by the assumption that an option is realized. But it needs amendment to deal with cases of two types: (1) cases where no option is ratifiable and (2) cases where more than one option is ratifiable. In these cases, the principle to pick a ratifiable option does not say which options are rational choices.

My revision of the principle of ratification proceeds in two stages. First, I introduce a principle that provides a more general necessary condition of rationality than ratification. Then I introduce a principle for choosing among options that meet this necessary condition. To revise the principle of ratification for cases without ratifiable options, I introduce a kind of self-support weaker than ratification, one that is possible in every decision problem. Then, for cases with multiple self-supporting options, I introduce a method of choosing among those options. It compares self-supporting options and recommends an option that is at least as good as the others according to the comparisons.

8.3.3. *Cases without Ratifiable Options*

Section 8.2 treated some cases without a ratifiable option, cases in which the options' preference ranking is infinite and has no top. Dynamic decision problems with a finite number of salient options may also lack a ratifiable option. Take, for example, Skyrms's (1982: 705–6) case of the Mean Demon. An agent chooses one of two boxes and keeps its contents. Each box contains either $1,000 or nothing. A mean demon controls the contents of the boxes. If he has predicted (*a*) that the agent will choose box A, he has put nothing in box A and $1,000 in box B. If he has predicted (*b*) that the agent will choose box B, he has put nothing in box B and $1,000 in box A (see figure 8.1). The agent is certain that the demon has predicted correctly. Her information about her choice is her sole source of information about the substance of his prediction and the contents of the boxes. In this case, whatever she chooses, she has evidence that the other choice has higher utility. No choice is ratifiable. What should she choose?[6]

Intuitively, an option is self-supporting just in case it is unopposed on the assumption that it is adopted. Other options may be better than it, but they do not constitute genuine opposition if still other options also undermine them and do

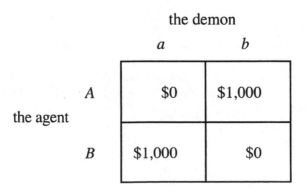

FIGURE 8.1. The Mean Demon.

not lead to a firm replacement for the original option. To handle cases without a ratifiable option, I introduce a new account of self-support that elaborates this idea. Its formulation requires some technical terms.[7]

I say that there is an *incentive to switch* from one option to another if and only if, given the first, the second is preferred. In my example there is an incentive to switch from A to B and from B to A. A sequence of two or more options is connected by a *path of incentives* to switch, or more briefly, is a path of incentives, if and only if for each pair of adjacent options there is an incentive to switch from the first to the second. The sequence $A, B, A, B, \ldots$, for example, is a path of incentives. A path of incentives *terminates* if it is finite and not extendible. The path $A, B, \ldots$ does not terminate. In the case of the Mean Demon, both options start nonterminating paths. Take choosing box A, for example. If the agent chooses it, she has evidence that B would be better. But if she chooses box B instead, she has evidence that A would be better. So the path of incentives away from A leads back to A; it cycles infinitely and does not terminate. Similarly, the path away from B does not terminate.

I say that an agent *pursues an incentive* to switch from one option to another if and only if, given the first, she adopts the second if her choice is either the first or some option to which she has an incentive to switch given the first. An agent cannot pursue every incentive generated by an option that generates multiple incentives. She has to be selective. I assume that a rational agent pursues some incentive starting a terminating path if there is one. Also, relentless pursuit of incentives is cognitively futile if an agent is on an infinite path of incentives. I assume that a rational agent stops pursuit of incentives at some options on the path to avoid futile pursuit of incentives. Hence, I assume that a tree of paths of incentives is first pruned to a single path and then truncated if the pruned path is infinite. Once this is done for all trees, paths of pursued incentives are all that remain. Focusing on pursued incentives lets an agent take account of information about her own choice dispositions in assessing options for self-support.[8]

In my example, the agent cannot pursue both the incentive from A to B and the incentive from B to A without cycling indefinitely. She may pursue either the incentive from A to B, or the incentive from B to A, or neither. The last is a possibility even though she must choose either A or B. Choosing A, for instance, does not entail pursuing the incentive from B to A. It could be that given B, if her choice were either B or A, she would not choose A.

According to my account of self-support, an option is self-supporting if and only if it does not start a terminating path of pursued incentives. An option may start a terminating path among pursued incentives even if it does not start a terminating path among all incentives. This may happen if an infinite path it starts is truncated. Because all paths of pursued incentives terminate, I may simplify my account of self-support. An option is self-supporting if and only if it does not start a path of pursued incentives. In the Mean Demon, after truncating the infinite path $A, B, A, \ldots$, only the last option of the path's remaining segment is self-supporting. Only it fails to start a path of pursued incentives. Every occurrence of the incentive to switch from it to its rival is removed. No rule for truncation requires making either A or B the last option of the remaining segment because the reasons for and against *A* are exactly similar to those for and against *B*. Hence, either option may be a self-supporting option depending on the agent's pursuit of incentives.

Self-support is a necessary condition of rationality. Expressing this necessary condition as a directive yields the following principle:

Self-support. Realize a self-supporting option.

Complying with the principle of self-support is a cognitive goal for decisions. Self-support registers the implications for beliefs and desires of an assumption that an option is adopted. The goal of self-support is a goal of fit between a choice and beliefs and desires. It enjoins a type of coherence—namely, support of the choice by beliefs and desires, including those generated by the choice itself.[9]

Self-support is necessary for rationality only if every decision problem has a self-supporting option so that requiring one generates no dilemmas of rational choice. No decision problem may arise in which all options are disqualified as rational choices on the grounds that each fails to be self-supporting. It is simple to prove that every decision problem has at least one self-supporting option. First, note that no option can fail to be self-supporting unless some option is self-supporting. For to fail to be self-supporting, an option has to start a terminating path of pursued incentives. The terminus of such a path is an option that does not start any path of pursued incentives. It starts no terminating path of pursued incentives and hence is self-supporting. Then observe that not every option can fail to be self-supporting, and so some option must be self-supporting, whatever the decision problem.

In the Mean Demon situation, any choice indicates a failure to pursue an incentive. The choice made does not generate any path of pursued incentives and so is self-supporting. But the failure to pursue the incentive is rational, and the decision is comprehensively rational, only if the principles for pursuit of incentives have been observed. The rules for rational pursuit of incentives prevent a decision from being self-justifying.[10]

The rules for pursuit of incentives also ensure conformity between the principle of self-support and section 8.2's principle of satisficing in cases where the options' preference ranking has no top. In such cases, each option starts a nonterminating path of incentives. Not all incentives are pursued, however. After eliminating unpursued incentives, not all options start terminating paths. Hence, not all options in a set without a top are self-supporting. Pursuit of incentives determines which options are self-supporting. A rule for pursuit of incentives requires pursuing incentives until reaching a satisfactory option. Therefore, unsatisfactory options start terminating paths of pursued incentives given my idealizations. Only satisfactory options are self-supporting and so rational choices.

Paths of incentives fail to terminate if they cycle, as in the case of the Mean Demon, or progress indefinitely without repeating options, as in the case of choosing your own salary. Neither type of nonterminating path generates any real opposition to the initial option. An option that starts either type of path is nonetheless self-supporting if, after pruning and truncating trees of incentives, it fails to start a path of pursued incentives. In the case of the Mean Demon, the reasons for each option have equal weight and either or both may be self-supporting, depending on the incentives to switch that the agent pursues. The case of choosing your own income has infinitely many self-supporting options, namely, the satisfactory options beyond which incentives are not pursued.

Self-support is strictly weaker than ratification. Every ratifiable option is self-supporting. A ratifiable option starts no path of incentives and hence no terminating path of pursued incentives. The principle of self-support extends ratification's generalization of utility maximization to better accommodate dynamic decision problems.[11]

8.3.4. *Cases with Multiple Self-Supporting Options*

Next, consider cases in which several options are self-supporting but are not equally good choices from an intuitive point of view. Take, for example, Skyrms's (1982: 706) case of the Nice Demon. It involves a choice between two boxes, as in the case of the Mean Demon. If the nice demon predicts (*a*) that the agent will pick box A, he puts $2,000 in box A and nothing in box B; and if he predicts (*b*) that the agent will pick box B, he puts $1,000 in box B and nothing in box A (see figure 8.2). In this case, choosing A and choosing B are both ratifiable and so self-supporting. Choosing either furnishes evidence that it was predicted and that it maximizes utility. Neither generates any incentive to switch and hence any terminating path of pursued incentives. The two options are not equally good decisions, however.

An ideal agent prepares herself for decision problems like this. Having foresight and being fully rational, she is ready for decision problems with multiple self-supporting options. In advance she cultivates a disposition to choose the self-supporting option that results in the best outcome. The demon, who bases his prediction on the agent's disposition to choose a certain option, predicts the choice the disposition yields. The choice issuing from the disposition then produces the best outcome. So in my example, a rational ideal agent chooses A. She chooses A not simply because it is self-supporting (another option is also self-supporting), but in virtue of a disposition formed in accord with rational decision policies. She chooses A as a result of having rationally formed a disposition to choose A. Because a fully rational ideal

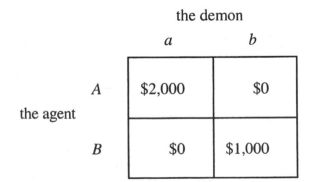

FIGURE 8.2. The Nice Demon.

agent chooses A, I conclude that it is the rational decision, evaluated comprehensively. Under my idealizations, it is the rational decision because it is the self-supporting option that proceeds from a rational choice disposition. Rational choice dispositions are the source of rational decisions, comprehensively evaluated, in cases with multiple self-supporting options given my idealizations.

The selection principle I advance is for ideal cases. It relies on the usual idealizations about agents but also the idealization that the utility of a disposition to realize an option in a decision problem equals, given the decision problem, the option's utility and, because the disposition ensures the option's realization, the option's self-conditional utility. The last equality holds because $U(o) = U(o, o)$ given o's realization. The idealization about dispositions is a justificational idealization. It simplifies explanations of a decision's rationality by putting aside cases in which the reasons for a disposition to realize an option are independent of the reasons for the option it yields.[12]

Let me state my selection principle more precisely. The utility of an option o_i on the assumption that it is performed is $U(o_i$ given $o_i)$. Given my idealizations, an option's self-conditional utility represents the utility of a decision disposition issuing that option. An ideal agent, who maximizes utility when forming decision dispositions, forms a disposition to adopt an option that maximizes self-conditional utility among self-supporting options. So my selection principle says that a rational option has that property (where such maximization is possible). Expressed as a rule, the principle issues the following directive:

> *Selection.* Choose an option o_i that maximizes $U(o_i$ given $o_i)$ among self-supporting options.

Under my idealizations, the selection principle expresses a necessary condition for rational choice that supplements the necessary condition of self-support. In my example, an option's self-conditional utility is the same as its utility given that it is predicted. Accordingly, $U(A$ given $A) > U(B$ given $B)$, and A is the rational choice.

The selection principle arises from a search for appropriate utility comparisons. Anticipated utility comparisons at the time of decision are not satisfactory because they vary with the option supposed realized. To find appropriate utility comparisons, one must adopt a vantage point that the agent has earlier in her life. I propose going back in time to the point where she has control over all the relevant features of her decision situation that are ever in her control. Her options are compared from this perspective. Certain options are ruled out because they are not self-supporting options. From the options remaining, I settle on one that is a product of rational use of her influence on her decision situation. For a fully rational ideal agent, such an option is rational when comprehensively evaluated.[13]

My selection principle may seem to condone one-boxing in Newcomb's Problem (see section 7.3). The one-boxer recognizes the advantage of having a one-boxing disposition. A rational ideal agent comes to a decision problem with the disposition to pick the option that pays more if predicted. She knows that the predictor will observe this disposition and make his prediction accordingly. A foresighted agent has formed a one-boxing disposition and acts on it. The one-boxer does not pursue her incentive to switch to two-boxing. So for her, one-boxing does not start a terminating path of pursued incentives. It is self-supporting. Moreover, it maximizes self-conditional utility among self-supporting options.

This application of the selection principle takes it out of its element. The principle applies to ideal agents who are fully rational. It selects a self-supporting option only under the assumption that self-support obtains with respect to rational pursuit of incentives. Taking all incentives into account, one-boxing starts a path of incentives terminating with two-boxing. So the incentive to switch to two-boxing should be pursued. For a fully rational agent, one-boxing starts a path of pursued incentives that terminates with two-boxing. For a fully rational agent, one-boxing is not self-supporting and so does not maximize self-conditional utility among self-supporting options. In Newcomb's Problem, only two-boxing is self-supporting with respect to rational pursuit of incentives. A one-boxer does not meet the selection rule's idealization of full rationality. Although forming a disposition to one-box is rational, the one-boxer is not fully rational entering her decision problem, after the prediction fixes the boxes' contents. Nonpursuit of the incentive to switch to two-boxing is irrational. Also, the disposition to one-box is irrational to have because it precludes a rational choice.

Suppose that self-conditional utility governs pursuit of incentives by governing the truncation of infinite paths of incentives. A rule for pursuit of incentives says to stop pursuit of incentives at a place of maximal self-conditional utility among members of the path. Then, in the Mean Demon situation, both options are equally good stopping points for pursuit of incentives. Both maximize self-conditional utility. Each has the same utility on the assumption that it is performed, namely, $U(\$0)$. However, in a modified version of the decision problem in which the demon puts \$10 under box A if he predicts B and puts no money under box B if he predicts A, rational pursuit of incentives stops with box A because A then has maximum self-conditional utility (see figure 8.3). Accordingly, the selection rule recommends A. This result agrees with intuitions about rational choice.

Given the foregoing rule for pursuit of incentives, my selection rule also handles challenging decision problems devised by Skyrms (1984: 84–86) and

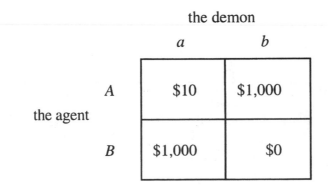

FIGURE 8.3. The asymmetric Mean Demon.

the demon

		a	b	c
	A	$0.1	$0	$0
the agent	B	$0	$10	$200
	C	$0	$100	$20

FIGURE 8.4. The Shell Game.

Rabinowicz (1985). These problems are similar, and I treat only Skyrms's Shell Game. Figure 8.4 depicts the decision problem. It involves an agent and a predicting demon, as in the cases of the Mean Demon and the Nice Demon. The demon's possible predictions *a*, *b*, and *c* concern the agent's options A, B, and C, respectively. In the Shell Game, just one option is ratifiable, namely, A. But C is intuitively the rational option because its realization produces evidence that the agent will receive $20, whereas any other option's realization produces evidence that the agent will receive less. My decision principles confirm that C is the rational option. The opposition to C, namely B, is itself opposed by C. So a path of incentives moving from C to B goes back to C. Because C maximizes self-conditional utility in the path of incentives, it is the rational stopping point for pursuit of incentives in the path. Hence, given the agent's rationality, it starts no terminating path of pursued incentives, although B does. Thus, C is self-supporting despite the incentive to switch that it generates. Ranking the self-supporting options, A and C, by self-conditional utility, C beats A. So it is the rational option.

The Shell Game is useful for distinguishing two views of my principle of self-support. According to one view, compliance is a cognitive goal for cases where the goal of ratification cannot be met. It is a goal for cases where the goal of ratification is unattainable. When both goals can be met, ratification takes precedence. According to the other view, self-support is a cognitive goal for all decision problems. It replaces the goal of ratification even where that goal can be met.

The view that self-support is a fall-back, subsidiary goal ignores cases like the Shell Game. In the Shell Game, there are multiple self-supporting options, but only one ratifiable option. The rational choice is not the ratifiable option. It is another self-supporting option. This result of my selection principle shows that ratification is not a general goal of rationality to which the goal of self-support is subordinate. The goal of self-support does not serve, but rather replaces, the goal of ratification.

The selection rule, to maximize self-conditional utility among self-supporting options, must be generalized to handle cases where no maximum exists. Take the case of choosing your own income. In that problem, suppose that incentives are not pursued past satisfactory options and, consequently, all satisfactory options are self-supporting. No satisfactory option maximizes self-conditional utility, however. For each there is another with higher self-conditional utility. My selection principle does not distinguish among the satisfactory options. For such cases I generalize the selection principle. Recalling section 8.2's principle to satisfice, I propose the following:

> Pick an option whose self-conditional utility is satisfactory among self-supporting options.

In my example, self-conditional utility is utility because options' utility comparisons are stable. So an option with satisfactory self-conditional utility is just an option with satisfactory utility. Because satisfactory options are self-supporting, my new principle recommends a satisfactory option, just as section 8.2's principle of satisficing does.

The aspiration level that options must meet to be satisfactory adjusts to the agent's opportunities. Satisfactoriness is defined with respect to an attainable aspiration level that rises to the maximum attainable level, if there is one. In cases with a top option, only the top option is satisfactory. Satisficing is thus a more general selection criterion than maximizing self-conditional utility among self-supporting options. When an option meets the latter criterion, it also meets the former. Satisficing yields a self-supporting option of maximum self-conditional utility whenever there is a maximum and otherwise yields a self-supporting option with satisfactory self-conditional utility.

Given rational pursuit of incentives, which requires pursuit of incentives up to a satisfactory option, my generalized selection principle is compatible with the principle to realize a satisfactory option. The latter principle is restricted to decision problems in which options' utility comparisons are stable. In dynamic decision problems, my generalized selection principle supersedes that principle. My generalized selection principle is its extension to dynamic decision problems.

8.3.5. *Objections and Replies*

My generalization of the principle to maximize utility proceeds in two stages. First, it advances the principle of self-support, which says to pick a self-supporting option. Next, it advances a selection criterion for cases with multiple self-supporting options, a criterion calling for maximum or satisfactory self-conditional utility. Combining stages and putting aside cases without a maximum, my generalization, the selection principle, says to maximize self-conditional utility among self-supporting options. It expresses a necessary condition of rational decision for fully rational ideal agents. This section responds to some objections.

The first objection concerns cases without ratifiable options, such as the case of the Mean Demon. I claim that the selection principle governs these cases, whereas some theorists claim that such cases are beyond the pale of decision theory. Jeffrey

(1983: chap. 1) says that cases without ratifiable options are pathological. He does not think that decision principles can be extended to them. Harper (1986) claims that principles of rational decision break down when there are no ratifiable options. He relies on mixed strategies as a means of obtaining ratifiable options in cases where no pure strategies are ratifiable. Sobel (1994: chap. 11) says that when there are no ratifiable options, no option is rational, although on his view, this does not entail that every option is irrational.[14]

I maintain that cases without ratifiable options are difficult, but not untreatable. As Richter (1984: 395–96) observes, we have intuitions about rational decisions in such cases. Principles of rationality may be formulated to generalize those intuitions. Furthermore, even if our current conception of rationality did not apply to cases without ratifiable options, we would want to extend that conception to encompass those cases. Our conception of rationality would be more fruitful if it were completely general, so that, as the principle against dilemmas of rational choice requires, in every decision problem there is a rational choice. To make standards of rational choice accommodate cases without ratifiable options, I adopt the principle of self-support as a replacement for the principle of ratification.

The second objection is that deciding on the basis of self-support in cases such as the Nice Demon is contrary to Principles Alpha and Beta concerning contraction and expansion of the set of options available. Take Principle Alpha, for instance. It says that an option recommended given one set of options should also be recommended given a subset that contains it. But an optimal self-supporting option given one set of options need not be an optimal self-supporting option given a subset that contains it. The subset may exclude the opposition to a self-defeating option so that the option becomes self-supporting in the subset. If that option also has higher self-conditional utility than optimal self-supporting options in the original set, then, given the subset, the selection principle no longer recommends those options even if the subset contains them.

My reply is that Principles Alpha and Beta, unless amended, are not justified in dynamic decision problems. In these problems, the availability of options affects the preference ranking of options in the universal set of options by altering the set of self-supporting options even if it does not change information about the states of the world that determine the options' outcomes. Principles Alpha and Beta are justified only in cases where the preference ranking of options in the universal set is stable with respect to the availability of options. When the preference ranking changes with the availability of options and changes justifiably because of a change in the grounds of preference, which include self-support, the argument for those principles collapses.[15]

The third objection is that the selection principle for cases with more than one self-supporting option conflicts with intuitive judgments about rationality. Take, for example, the case of the Nice Demon, which figure 8.5 repeats. Both *A* and *B* are self-supporting options. So, according to the selection principle, the rational decision is the option that maximizes self-conditional utility, namely, *A*. But suppose that prior to making a decision the agent knows that the demon has made prediction *b*. The agent assigns a probability of 1 to prediction *b*. Then, the objection claims, the rational decision is *B*, not *A*.[16]

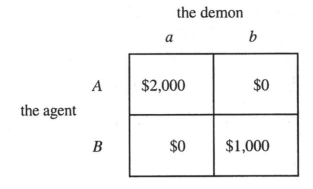

FIGURE 8.5. The Nice Demon.

Under the idealization that agents are fully rational, such cases cannot arise, because the agent's probability assignment indicates a mistake. The agent must have either mistakenly formed the disposition to choose B or mistakenly assigned a probability of 1 to prediction *b*. For the sake of definiteness, imagine that the probability assignment stems from a mistaken disposition to choose B, and let me minimally relax the idealization of full rationality to allow for this mistake. I use chapter 6's methods of handling mistakes to extend my principles to this case and check their verdict against intuition.

Section 6.4 presents a standard of comprehensive rationality for cases where an agent enters a decision problem having already made mistakes. The main proposal for these cases is that a rational decision follows from rational decision procedures in the circumstances that obtain after unacceptable mistakes are corrected. To apply this proposal, one must ascertain whether the disposition to choose B is an unacceptable mistake.

The idealizations for the selection principle include that the utility of a disposition to make a decision equals the decision's utility and its self-conditional utility. So, to apply the principle, my example assumes that a disposition and the decision it produces have exactly the same relevant consequence, namely, a particular monetary payoff. Although a disposition causes a prediction by the demon and a decision by the agent, these consequences are matters of indifference to the agent except insofar as they affect her monetary gain. Hence, the disposition and the decision it yields have the same utility.

The disposition to choose B was formed prior to the decision problem and is incorrigible, and this counts in favor of its being an acceptable mistake. On the other hand, despite the agent's disposition to choose B, she is free to choose A in the sense that A is an option in the decision problem. Moreover, if she were to choose A, her decision disposition would have been different. So in the decision problem, the agent is accountable for her disposition to choose B. As long as the disposition has not manifested itself, and choosing A is still in the agent's power in the sense that it counts as an option, the disposition is an unacceptable mistake.[17]

In the agent's decision problem, the time for correcting her disposition to choose *B* is past. She cannot correct that disposition. Hence, the disposition's unacceptability makes the agent's decision problem a dilemma of rationality. No option is comprehensively rational. Realizing *A* is unproductive. It yields $0, whereas realizing *B* yields $1,000. On the other hand, realizing *B* manifests an irrational disposition. Although realizing *B* is a rational choice, that is, rational taking the mistaken disposition for granted, its rationality is conditional only. It is not a comprehensively rational decision.[18]

To apply the selection principle, a principle of comprehensive rationality, one must use it to identify the decision problem's solution, the decision of a fully rational ideal agent in that decision problem (see section 6.4). Identifying this decision requires correcting unacceptable mistakes.

The disposition to choose *B* is incorrigible—that is, the agent cannot correct it—but one may imagine a hypothetical situation in which the disposition is corrected. Suppose, then, that the disposition to choose *B* is corrected. The supposition yields a case in which the agent has a disposition to choose *A*. *A* and *B* are still both self-supporting, and *A* maximizes self-conditional utility. So *A* is the rational decision. More precisely, if it were chosen, the choice disposition having been corrected, then it would be rational. Its rationality is just hypothetical because in fact, the mistake is not corrected and no decision is comprehensively rational. However, its hypothetical rationality makes it the decision problem's solution.

Notice that the solution is independent of the agent's decision disposition. According to my principles, whenever a mistaken decision disposition is an unacceptable mistake, a decision problem's solution is independent of the agent's disposition. The solution is just the self-supporting decision that stems from the rational disposition. Such independence is appropriate. Without it, some mistakes would be self-justifying. In my example, a decision is rational if and only if the disposition producing it is rational both to form and to have. So, if it were possible for a disposition to produce circumstances that would make the decision it yields rational, it would justify itself. My principles rule out this possibility. They make it the case that even if a disposition changes circumstances so that given the new circumstances the decision it yields maximizes utility, the decision it yields may still be irrational in the comprehensive sense and so fail to be a solution.

The fourth objection is that the selection rule violates the principle of strict dominance, which condemns an option worse than another in every state provided that states are causally independent of options and the preference ranking of options has a top. This objection first observes that a strictly dominated option may turn out to be self-supporting. It may even maximize self-conditional utility among self-supporting options, in which case the selection rule recommends it. Then the objection argues that because choosing a strictly dominated option flouts incentives, self-support and self-conditional utility are not appropriate criteria of rationality. Rabinowicz (1989) presents an example to bring out the point. Figure 8.6 presents his example modified to attack the current version of the selection rule.[19]

As in my other examples, states *a*, *b*, *c*, and *d* are a reliable forecaster's predictions of the corresponding act by the agent. All options start paths of incentives, but none of those paths terminates. Option *A*, for instance, starts the path *A*, *D*,

	a	*b*	*c*	*d*
A	1	9	2	9
B	0	8	1	8
C	4	10	0	4
D	6	0	0	0

FIGURE 8.6. Self-support and self-conditional utility v. dominance.

A,..., but that path does not terminate. Suppose that if an option generates multiple incentives to switch, the agent pursues the incentive to switch to the alternative of maximum utility, except in the case of C, from which she pursues the incentive to switch to B. Also, suppose that she stops pursuit of path A, D, A, D,...at option A and stops pursuit of path B, C, B, C,...at option B. These stipulations conform with the rules of rational pursuit of incentives that section 8.3.3 sketched. Then A and B are the only options that do not start terminating paths of pursued incentives. These two options are the self-supporting options. Among the self-supporting options, B maximizes self-conditional utility. Thus, the selection rule recommends B. But A strictly dominates B.[20]

As shown, it is possible for a strictly dominated option to fail to generate a terminating path of incentives, although the dominated option starts a path to the dominating option, because an agent may fail to pursue that path. The strictly dominated option may, then, be self-supporting and may even maximize self-conditional utility among self-supporting options so that the selection rule recommends it. The objection holds that the selection rule errs in recommending a self-supporting option that is strictly dominated.

One way of replying to the objection is to tighten the rules for rational pursuit of incentives. The selection principle never disagrees with the principle of strict dominance if, for instance, the rules allow pursuing only incentives away from an option that go to an alternative of maximum utility given the option. The objection arises only because I permit a path of pursued incentives to go from an option to any alternative whose utility is greater given that option. I do not take this line of reply because articulating and justifying the rules for rational pursuit of incentives is a large enterprise best left for another occasion. Instead, I discredit the principle of strict dominance's complaint against the selection principle.

The complaint has two forms arising from two interpretations of the principle of dominance. If the principle of dominance is taken as a principle of utility comparison, then the objection is that because A dominates B, A has greater utility than B, and so B is not a rational choice. If the principle of dominance is taken as a principle of choice, then the objection is that because A dominates B, B is not a rational choice. This form of the objection bypasses the claim about utilities.

Let me begin with the objection that uses the principle of dominance as a principle of utility comparison. This principle derives from expected utility analysis applied to quantizations of beliefs and desires. If all the states of some partition are causally independent of two options, and the first option has higher utility than the second in all states, then it has higher expected utility and so higher utility. Because this principle of dominance derives from expected utility analysis, it is subject to the same qualifications as expected utility analysis. In particular, its judgments that one option has higher utility than another are relative to the information used as a basis of comparison, just as expected utility comparisons are. As section 8.3.1 argues, in dynamic decision problems the relevant expected utility comparisons are made with respect to the information obtained given the assumption that an option is realized. So in dynamic cases, one needs a conditional form of the principle of dominance. Assuming causal independence of options and states, the following principle emerges: If one option has higher utility than another in every state and so strictly dominates the other, then it has higher utility than the other no matter which option is assumed.[21]

I accept the principle of dominance taken as a principle of utility comparison, but hold that a utility comparison is a conclusive reason for choice only in non-dynamic cases where the assumption that an option is realized does not change the basis of utility calculations. In dynamic cases where the appropriate information for utility calculations changes from option to option, higher utility given any option is not a sufficient reason for choice. In such cases, an option is not necessarily proscribed if, on the assumption that it is realized, another option has higher utility. As argued, not all incentives to switch are sufficient reasons to abandon an option. Sometimes rationality permits adopting an option despite an incentive to switch.

Because Rabinowicz's example presents a dynamic decision problem, A's domination of B is not a conclusive case against B. B has less utility than A on the assumption that B or any other option is realized. But B's having less utility does not provide a decisive reason against it. Utility comparisons are not decisive in dynamic problems.

Next, let me consider the objection that uses the principle of dominance as a principle of decision. According to this principle, provided that a top option exists and states are causally independent of options, if one option has higher utility than another in every state, then it is more choiceworthy than the other, even in dynamic cases. My reply to this version of the objection is to reject its decision principle. Even though A dominates B in my example, A may be less choiceworthy than B because the decision problem is dynamic.

To argue for the decision principle of dominance in dynamic cases, some may point out that if one option strictly dominates another, then no matter whether the first or second option is assumed, the first has higher utility. In reply, I reiterate that utility comparisons are insufficient reasons to reject an option in dynamic cases.

In dynamic cases, utility comparisons are not conclusive because the grounds for them shift. So an argument for a decision principle that rests on these utility comparisons is not conclusive either. An incentive to switch from B to A has no greater force because it is an incentive to switch to a strictly dominating option; the incentive may still be an insufficient reason to switch, as in other cases, such as the Mean Demon.[22]

In dynamic cases self-support should be considered along with utility comparisons. Because a dominated option may be self-supporting, a dominated option may be a rational choice in a dynamic problem. In my example, even though A dominates B, the criterion of self-conditional utility puts B ahead of A in choice-worthiness. Dynamic decision problems have novel features, and one should expect novelties in the decision principles that govern them.

Applications to Game Theory

Game theory is a valuable tool for investigating the interactions of people. Chapter 8's decision principles contribute to game theory because decision problems in games often have the dynamic characteristics those principles address. Their application to games demonstrates progress toward realism.

Given the standard idealizations that agents are cognitively ideal, fully rational, and fully informed about their game, an agent's choice in a game of strategy typically provides relevant information about other agents' choices, the states that determine his choice's outcome, so that his decision problem is dynamic. Utility comparisons are unstable. Making a move that looks best may provide information about the moves of other players that makes other moves look better. This chapter illustrates the self-support and selection principles' application to games of strategy. It shows that the principles overcome obstacles facing a decision-theoretic justification of familiar tenets of normative game theory. The principles make significant progress with the explanation of equilibrium in games. In particular, they explain the strategic reasoning of agents participating in an equilibrium.

9.1. Games of Strategy

An important project of normative game theory is a decision-theoretic justification of solutions to games. This requires showing that agents following principles of rational individual decision making, such as the principle to maximize expected utility, adopt their parts in a game's solution. Success is crucial because intuitions about solutions, and in general, intuitions about standards of rationality for groups of agents, are insecure without the backing of basic decision principles.

Classical game theory takes a solution to a game to be a *Nash equilibrium* (1950b). This is a *profile of strategies*, a combination of strategies for the agents, such that each strategy is a best response to the others.[1] Many game theorists have attempted to show that principles of individual rationality lead the agents in a game to a Nash equilibrium. Several approaches are current. Some authors, for example, Kalai and Lehrer (1993) and Vanderschraaf (2001: sec. 3.1), attend to what agents in repeated games learn to expect from each other. Some, for example, Aumann (1987) and Aumann and Brandenburger (1995), attend to ways of extending and co-ordinating the initial information agents have about each other. Some, for example, Harsanyi and Selten (1988: chap. 4), Binmore (1990: sec. 6.3), and Skyrms (1990a), attend to the bounded rationality of agents, in particular, their limited abilities for processing information.[2] And some, for example, Harper (1988, 1991), attend to refinements of the rules of individual decision making.

I address games of strategy, that is, games in which an agent's adopting a strategy gives him some evidence about the strategies of other agents. This chapter argues that for games of strategy, the best approach is the last, the one focusing on refinements of decision rules. This section's argument is indirect. It shows that the other approaches are inadequate for games of strategy. Section 9.2's argument is direct. It uses the self-support and selection principles to derive the realization of Nash equilibria in certain games of strategy.

Concentrating on games of strategy quickly narrows the field of viable approaches to the justification of solutions. An appeal to learning in a series of games, for instance, is not appropriate for games of strategy. It relies on nonstrategic principles, in particular, inductive principles for inferences from past to future decisions. As a result, it cannot treat an isolated play of a novel game of strategy and so cannot treat games of strategy in general.

An appeal to extended and coordinated initial information about agents, say, each agent's knowledge that they all assign the same probabilities to their strategies, is also unsatisfactory for games of strategy. This approach shows that given certain assumptions about agents' information concerning other agents' choices, equilibrium strategies maximize expected utility. But arguments starting with these informational assumptions do not provide a strategic justification of an equilibrium. They leave the crucial strategic information about choices unexplained. A strategic justification of an equilibrium shows how the agents' strategic reasoning takes them from basic information about the game to their equilibrium strategies. It shows how an agent reasons about the reasoning of others to learn about their choices. If an argument relies from the start on agents' knowledge of other agents' choices, or probability assignments to their strategies, then its account of the agents' reasoning is not strategic. Section 9.2.3's discussion of Aumann and Brandenburger (1995) elaborates this point.

Consequently, only two approaches to games of strategy are initially promising: an appeal to bounded rationality and an appeal to refinements of the rules of individual decision making. Skyrms's (1990a: chap. 2) justification of Nash equilibrium illustrates the appeal to bounded rationality. He notices that shortages of information about other agents often block applications of the principle of utility maximization to decision problems in games of strategy. Surprisingly, these obstacles are especially formidable in ideal games, where agents' rationality is unbounded, because strategic reasoning struggles to gain a foothold when all are gifted at outwitting others. To clear the way for utility maximization, Skyrms assumes that agents are not ideal and have bounded rationality. Then he shows how agents maximizing utility individually realize a Nash equilibrium. He assumes that bounded rationality obliges an agent to deliberate in stages, making tentative plans and revising them, until the grounds for revision are exhausted. Given certain assumptions, he shows that an agent's deliberations eventually settle on a Nash strategy, his part in a Nash equilibrium. A theorem establishes that in certain games, a Nash equilibrium arises from the application of expected utility analysis to the stepwise deliberations of boundedly rational agents.

The chapter's appendix offers a detailed account and evaluation of Skyrms's theorem about Nash equilibrium. Despite the theorem's significance for game theory, it does not explain why a Nash equilibrium is a solution to a game of strategy. According to it, realization of a Nash equilibrium depends on the cognitive limits of agents. It does not show why agents without those limits should realize a Nash equilibrium. Achieving a solution is an aspiration of ideal agents as well as cognitively limited agents. Explaining why a solution is a Nash equilibrium thus requires showing how certain goals of rationality for both ideal and nonideal agents lead to Nash equilibrium. The theorem does not do this.

Because of its assumptions, Skyrms's theorem does not provide the sort of justification of Nash equilibrium I seek. However, Skyrms advances his theorem for another purpose, namely, to show how the dynamics of deliberation may yield a Nash equilibrium. His main aim is not to explain why a game's solution is a Nash equilibrium. To point out the theorem's deficiency for my purpose is not to criticize it for his purpose.

The shortcoming of Skyrms's theorem as a justification of Nash equilibrium haunts any derivation of Nash equilibrium from an appeal to bounded rationality. Such derivations do not explain why a solution is a Nash equilibrium. Hence, I take the only remaining approach to an explanation: I use refinements of the principle of utility maximization to derive Nash equilibrium in certain games of strategy. The next section shows that the self-support and selection principles provide a good account of strategy in games. They support the realization of a Nash equilibrium in a way that explains why a solution is a Nash equilibrium. They express a goal of rationality that all rational agents aspire to attain. In the games treated, its attainment amounts to the realization of a Nash equilibrium.

9.2. Self-Support and Games of Strategy

I take a game as a decision problem facing a group of agents. Being concrete rather than abstract, a game's features include more than its representations indicate. They include psychological facts about the agents such as their pursuit of incentives, not just the outcomes of strategy profiles a payoff matrix displays.

This section treats games with a finite number of agents with a finite number of pure strategies, as opposed to mixed or randomized strategies.[3] Agents' strategies are executed in the same period of play and are causally independent. When considering an agent's strategy and the strategies of other agents, for convenience, I call the other agents' strategies responses to the agent's strategy. Nonetheless, strictly speaking, their choices are causally independent. This feature of a game justifies its normal-form representation, which does not depict stages of play but just agents' payoffs from combinations of pure strategies. Also, agents adopt strategies independently and may not form coalitions to coordinate strategies, so the games are noncooperative. For brevity, I often leave it understood that the games of interest are finite and noncooperative, and simply call them *normal-form* games after their type of representation. Some authors also call them strategic-form games. These games constitute a commonly studied type of game of strategy, and the proposal that their solutions are Nash equilibria has many adherents.

I assume that the agents in the normal-form games treated are ideal and fully rational. In contrast to the agents in Skyrms's cases, the agents in my cases are unboundedly rational and deliberate instantaneously. Also, the agents' decision situations are ideal except for an instability of options' utility comparisons, which strategic considerations cause. The principles of self-support and selection address the dynamic decision problems the instability generates. The instability does not block attainment of goals of rationality, but calls for generalization of those goals. Because of the idealizations, I call the games treated *ideal* normal-form games of strategy. First, I summarize points in Weirich (1998) about the existence of equilibria, and then I add observations about the realization of equilibria. The observations added are limited in scope, serving mainly to illustrate my decisions principles' application to games.

9.2.1. *Solutions and Equilibria*

Game theory investigates solutions and equilibria of games. A solution may be defined objectively in terms of success or subjectively in terms of rational beliefs about, and desires for, success. Similarly, equilibria may be defined objectively or subjectively. The objective and subjective definitions are closely linked, however. Because ideal agents in ideal circumstances are successful if rational, in ideal cases the two types of definition agree. In ideal cases, an outcome that is a solution and equilibrium in the objective sense is also a solution and equilibrium in the subjective sense.

I focus on solutions and equilibria defined subjectively. Accordingly, a *solution* is a profile of jointly rational strategies, and an *equilibrium* is a profile of jointly self-supporting strategies. Because self-support is necessary for rationality, being an equilibrium is necessary for being a solution.

Joint rationality and self-support are defined conditionally. The strategies in a profile are *jointly* rational and self-supporting if and only if they are rational and self-supporting given the profile's realization. This makes joint rationality and self-support relative to a profile's realization. Hence, as I generally take them, solutions and equilibria are *relative* as well as subjective.

Subjective but nonrelative accounts of solutions and equilibria define them nonconditionally as profiles of strategies in which each strategy is rational and self-supporting. Objective accounts of solutions and equilibria define them in terms of payoffs resulting from strategy profiles. They are then independent of agents' assignments of probabilities to strategies. For example, a Nash equilibrium is defined objectively as a profile of strategies in which each strategy is payoff-maximizing given the other strategies. This definition makes Nash equilibrium objective in the sense of being independent of beliefs about the strategies realized, even if payoffs are utilities and so dependent on desires. The definition makes Nash equilibrium relative, however, because each strategy in a qualifying profile is payoff-maximizing given the profile, but not necessarily given the game's actual outcome.

On some accounts of nonrelative equilibria and solutions, an equilibrium is the same as a solution. According to these accounts, self-support and rationality are both just maximization of utility. According to my decision principles, however, an equilibrium may not be a solution. A strategy's self-support requires that it not start a terminating path of pursued incentives. So a nonrelative equilibrium is a profile of strategies none of which starts a path of this type. A nonrelative solution is a profile of strategies in which each agent's strategy maximizes self-conditional utility among the agent's self-supporting strategies. Being part of a nonrelative solution requires more than being part of a nonrelative equilibrium.

Idealizations for games license the conflation of some distinctions. As an idealization, agents are commonly taken to know the game, to choose rationally, and to be *prescient* about others' responses. Prescience gives an agent knowledge of the response to each of his strategies.[4] Given that agents are informed about the game and each other, the difference between objective and subjective solutions may be conflated, and similarly for equilibria, because subjective incentives follow objective payoffs. In particular, assuming prescience, rationality and self-support given a profile may be taken as rationality and self-support given knowledge of the profile. Because I adopt the usual idealizations, I generally conflate the distinction.

In an ideal game, an agent knows that other agents will make a rational response to his decision and to the decisions of each other. Given the idealizations, an agent's decision provides information about the others' decisions even if it does not have any causal influence on their decisions. This added information affects the agent's assignment of utilities to his options. A strategy that maximizes utility on the assumption that one choice is made may not maximize utility on the assumption that another choice is made. As a result, it may be impossible to maximize utility with respect to information a choice provides. Alternatively, there may be several options, not all equally rational, which would each maximize utility with respect to the information it provides. As chapter 8 shows, agents may lack ratifiable options or have multiple ratifiable options. These possibilities generate questions about the existence and realization of equilibria. The next two sections use my decision principles to reply.

9.2.2. *Existence of Equilibrium*

This section considers the existence of equilibrium in ideal normal-form games. To begin, take the normal-form game called Matching Pennies. The game has two players. They simultaneously display a penny, which they may turn either heads up or tails up. The Matcher wins if the pennies are both heads up or both tails up. The Mismatcher wins if one penny is heads up and the other is tails up. Figure 9.1 depicts the game's structure. A box for a pair of strategies, one for each player, represents a possible outcome of the game. The numeral in the box's lower-left

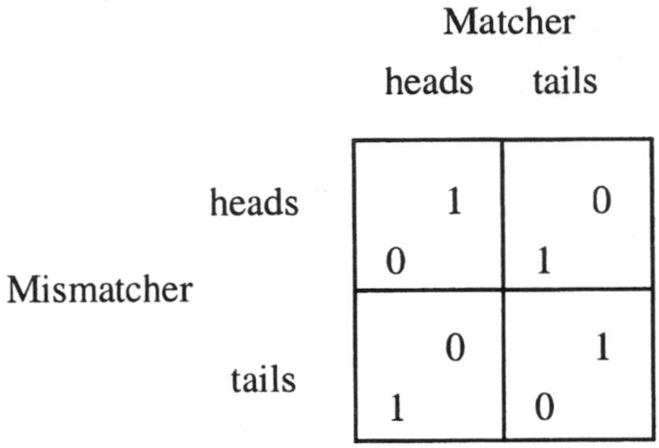

Matcher

heads   tails

	heads	tails
heads	1 0	0 1
tails	0 1	1 0

Mismatcher

FIGURE 9.1. Matching Pennies.

corner represents the payoff for the Mismatcher in that outcome, and the numeral in the box's upper-right corner represents the payoff for the Matcher in that outcome.

Suppose that mixed strategies are barred. Then the game has no Nash equilibrium because no strategy profile is such that each component is a best response to the other. In every profile, one agent does better switching strategy given the other agent's strategy. For example, in the profile according to which the Matcher shows heads and the Mismatcher shows tails, the Matcher does better by switching given his opponent's strategy. In the profile specified he loses, but he wins if he switches from heads to tails while his opponent shows tails.[5]

The game of Matching Pennies reveals that some normal-form games lack Nash equilibria. Furthermore, some ideal normal-form games lack *subjective Nash equilibria*. These equilibria are defined in terms of incentives rather than payoffs. A subjective Nash equilibrium is a profile of strategies such that no agent has an incentive to switch strategy given the other strategies. An ideal version of Matching Pennies without mixed strategies lacks a subjective Nash equilibrium. Each agent can predict the other's choice given his own choice. Because incentives follow potential gains, a profile is a subjective Nash equilibrium if and only if it is a Nash equilibrium. Hence, the absence of Nash equilibria entails the absence of subjective Nash equilibria.[6]

Figure 9.2 uses arrows to indicate the agents' incentives to switch strategies, given profiles, in an ideal version of Matching Pennies. Because each strategy profile generates an incentive to switch for some agent, no profile is a subjective Nash equilibrium. The absence of a subjective Nash equilibrium in such games creates a problem. How can the agents be jointly rational? I hold that although the agents cannot both win the game, they can both be rational and, moreover, can be jointly rational. The standards of rationality make adjustments for their circumstances.

A subjective relative equilibrium, recall, is a profile of jointly self-supporting strategies. Taking self-support as ratifiability makes an equilibrium so defined a subjective Nash equilibrium. For a profile of jointly ratifiable strategies is a profile in which no agent has an incentive to switch strategy given the other strategies. However, taking self-support as the absence of terminating paths of incentives

Matcher

heads   tails

heads

Mismatcher

tails

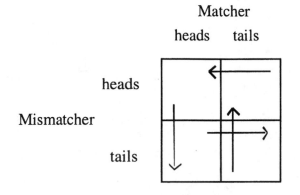

FIGURE 9.2. Incentives.

makes the characterization of equilibrium yield another type of subjective relative equilibrium I call *strategic equilibrium*. It is defined in terms of incentives relative to a profile. A strategic equilibrium is a profile of strategies none of which starts a terminating path of pursued incentives, incentives relative to the profiles reached by pursuit of incentives. In contrast with the incentives defining nonrelative equilibrium, the incentives defining strategic equilibrium are relative to entire profiles, not just an agent's strategy.

The existence of a nonrelative equilibrium follows from the existence of a nonrelative solution, and the latter's existence follows from the principle against dilemmas of rational choice (section 7.2), which says that an agent has a rational choice in every decision problem. The combination of the agents' rational strategies is a nonrelative solution. The existence of a strategic equilibrium is a more complex matter but still demonstrable, as the next paragraph indicates.

The principle of self-support is weaker than the principle of ratification. It is more easily satisfied jointly by the agents in a game. Profiles of jointly self-supporting strategies therefore exist even where profiles of jointly ratifiable strategies do not. In fact, every ideal normal-form game has a profile of jointly self-supporting strategies, or a strategic equilibrium. For a profile's strategies fail to be jointly self-supporting only if some profile of jointly self-supporting strategies opposes them. Consequently, there must be some profile of jointly self-supporting strategies. Weirich (1998: chap. 5) fills out this brief proof of the existence of a strategic equilibrium.

In Matching Pennies, the strategic equilibria depend on the agents' pursuit of incentives. Suppose, by way of illustration, that in a particular concrete version of the game the Matcher pursues his incentives whereas the Mismatcher forgoes hers, a rational policy for her because pursuit of her incentives is endless and futile. Then figure 9.3 depicts the agents' pursued incentives. The strategic equilibria are (H, H) and (T, T). These profiles do not start a terminating path of pursued incentives for any agent.

The strategic equilibria depend on the agents' psychology, their pursuit of incentives. Rules sketched in section 8.3.3 govern pursuit of incentives and so indirectly control the emergence of strategic equilibria. Although in Matching

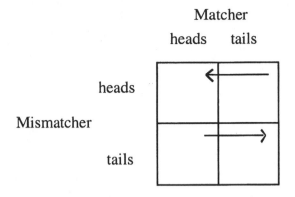

FIGURE 9.3. Pursued incentives.

Pennies any outcome may be a strategic equilibrium, which outcomes are strategic equilibria in a concrete version of the game depends on the agents' actual pursuit of incentives. Because in the example, Matcher knows Mismatcher forgoes pursuit of her incentives, rationality requires him to pursue his incentives. They start terminating paths. An agent may fail to pursue an incentive only if it is an insufficient reason to switch strategies because, for instance, it starts a path that cycles back to the original strategy.

This section takes a step toward realism concerning strategic reasoning. My generalization of the principle of utility maximization, the principle of self-support, yields my generalization of subjective Nash equilibrium, strategic equilibrium. Every subjective Nash equilibrium is a strategic equilibrium, but some profiles that are not subjective Nash equilibria are strategic equilibria. Being a strategic equilibrium is necessary for being a solution. Because strategic equilibria exist in all ideal normal-form games, agents in them can meet this standard for a solution. Providing this attainable standard contributes to realistic decision theory.[7]

9.2.3. *Realization of Equilibrium*

Next, I consider the realization of equilibria, a subject that the self-support and selection principles illuminate. For simplicity, I treat games that have a Nash equilibrium and in which self-support reduces to ratification and strategic equilibrium reduces to subjective Nash equilibrium, which, given my idealizations, reduces to Nash equilibrium. In these games, the realization of a Nash equilibrium may be explained in various ways. I seek an explanation that rests on rational decision making by the individual players.

The realization of a nonrelative equilibrium is simple. It results when each agent complies with the principle of self-support and chooses a self-supporting strategy. A nonrelative equilibrium may not be a relative equilibrium, however. Its strategies may not be jointly self-supporting, or each self-supporting given the whole profile of strategies. Realization of a relative equilibrium calls for coordination.

Because Nash equilibria are relative equilibria, explaining their realization requires explaining the coordination their realization involves.

My project is to use general decision principles to support game-theoretic principles about the realization of Nash equilibria. To do this for normal-form games, I need decision principles that achieve coordination without communication. Rationality alone has to bring all the agents to a Nash equilibrium. Moreover, it has to bring them to the same Nash equilibrium in games with multiple Nash equilibria.

Deliberations in normal-form games fall into a whirlpool of strategic reasoning. An agent, to obtain his strategies' utilities, that is, their expected utilities, must assign probabilities to other agents' strategies. Their strategies are the relevant states of the world. His strategy has no causal influence on their strategies, so expected utility analysis focuses on their nonconditional probabilities. But in ideal games, an agent's probability assignments to his own strategies and other agents' strategies are interdependent. His strategies' utilities and their probabilities are also interdependent. This interdependence blocks application of the principle to maximize utility. It makes strategies' utilities indeterminate and so makes the results of utility maximization indeterminate. Applying the principle of utility maximization under a quantization provides insufficient direction, too, because the range of indeterminacy generally is very broad. Intuition suggests that in ideal normal-form games, there are reasons utility maximization ignores. One needs new decision principles to cover the dynamic decision problems these games create.[8]

Fortunately, the probabilities that my decision principles require are easier to obtain than the probabilities that expected utility maximization requires. They exist more easily because they are probabilities given an option rather than nonconditional probabilities. The condition gives a probability assignment an extra bit of information. For example, take the probability that given a certain choice, an agent's opponents will adopt such and such strategies. The agent's choice gives him evidence about other agents' choices. My principles use his choice as additional information for probability assignments to other agents' choices.

In the cases I treat, my principle of self-support reduces to the principle of ratification. The principle of ratification says to make a decision that maximizes utility on the assumption that it is made. It uses all the information available in games, including second-order information about the information one has if one adopts a certain strategy. The conditional utilities the principle compares register the information a decision carries about the outcomes of decisions. The probabilities of other agents' strategies given the assumption of an agent's strategy may be determinate even if information given the assumption is not determinate because unanticipated relevant information might come with the decision. In these cases, the probabilities of other agents' strategies given the assumption may be weighted averages of their probabilities given possible bodies of information if the agent's strategy is realized (see section 8.3.2).

The principle of ratification is not a panacea. It classifies a strategy as ratifiable or not according to the utilities of alternative strategies under the assumption that the strategy is adopted. Although these conditional utilities are easier to obtain than the corresponding nonconditional utilities, they may be indeterminate in some cases. An agent's probability assignment to other agents' strategies may be indeterminate even given one of his strategies. Such deeper-going indeterminacy blocks application of the principle of ratification as well as the principle of utility maximization. So that I may use the principle of ratification, I restrict this section to games where the information available generates the conditional probabilities and utilities necessary for the principle's application.[9]

In an ideal game where agents know their own choices, the principle of ratification's advantage is its power to explain the deliberations leading to those choices. It can explain those choices, whereas the principle of utility maximization cannot. The principle of utility maximization must assume the choices to derive them, whereas the principle of ratification derives the choices from assumptions about probabilities and utilities conditional on choices. In ideal games, the agents' knowledge of their choices derives from their knowledge of the game's solution, a solution computed from strategies' conditional utilities, not from strategies' non-conditional utilities.

As a tool for justifying the realization of Nash equilibria, the principle of ratification is more promising than the principle of utility maximization. An agent in a game of strategy can use the principle of ratification to reach a decision without first predicting other agents' decisions. Knowledge of choices is a conclusion, not a premiss of deliberations. Because the principle uses conditional rather than nonconditional utilities, it can break the circle of strategic reasoning. As a result, the principle can provide decision-theoretic support for the realization of Nash equilibrium.

My justification of the realization of Nash equilibrium, an illustration rather than a general justification, covers only certain ideal games, in particular, games with a unique Nash equilibrium or a unique *Pareto optimal* Nash equilibrium, that is a Nash equilibrium such that no other Nash equilibrium is at least as good for all agents and better for some agents. To review crucial assumptions, in ideal games agents are rational and so, under my assumptions, choose ratifiable strategies. They also know the payoff matrix so that their incentives correspond to opportunities for payoff increases; their objective and subjective incentives agree. Moreover, agents are prescient; they know other agents' choices given each of their strategies. My justification also assumes that other agents' responses to an agent's strategies meet certain stipulations of the proofs to follow. My limited objective is to show that, given all my assumptions, ratification generates Nash equilibrium.[10]

First, I treat games with a unique Nash equilibrium. I show that the principle of ratification leads the agents to that equilibrium. Let me begin with an example that illustrates the proof's steps. Imagine an ideal game with agents Row and Column and only two salient strategies for each agent. Suppose their game has the incentive structure in figure 9.4. The unique Nash equilibrium of this game is (R_1, C_1). Suppose that the agents reply to each other's strategies as follows. If Column adopts C_1, Row adopts R_1, and if Column adopts C_2, Row adopts R_2. Column adopts C_1 whatever Row chooses. Because the game is ideal, each agent knows the other's response to his strategies. Because each picks a ratifiable strategy, Row picks R_1 and Column picks C_1. Each picks his part in the Nash equilibrium. Given my assumption about responses, ratification yields Nash equilibrium.

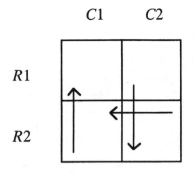

FIGURE 9.4. A unique Nash equilibrium.

Now consider the general case. Imagine an ideal game with a unique Nash equilibrium. Because the game is ideal, each agent knows the response to each of his strategies; each is prescient about the others. Suppose he knows that the response to his Nash strategy is the remainder of the Nash equilibrium. His Nash strategy is thus ratifiable. Also, the game's payoff matrix guarantees that for any non-Nash strategy, some profile containing it specifies strategies for other agents such that given those strategies for them he does better switching strategy. I suppose that such a profile provides the other agents' response to the non-Nash strategy. Given the agent's knowledge of their response and the game's payoff matrix, that strategy is not ratifiable; given the foreseen response, he prefers another strategy. Because the game is ideal, all agents are rational and adopt ratifiable strategies. Hence, given my assumptions about their responses, they all adopt their Nash strategies and realize the Nash equilibrium.

In some games, an agent may adopt a strategy expecting to contribute to a certain profile's realization, but that profile may not be realized because others fail to do their parts. In an ideal game, where agents are prescient, they are not surprised this way. Hence, if the agents realize a profile of ratifiable strategies, each strategy is ratifiable given the profile. The strategies are jointly ratifiable and form a subjective Nash equilibrium. Under my idealizations, the Nash equilibrium realized is also a subjective Nash equilibrium.

My derivation of Nash equilibrium breaks the circle of strategic reasoning. It uses prescience, or knowledge of responses to strategies, to derive choices. It does not start with knowledge of choices, obtained in some unexplained way despite the circle of strategic reasoning. Because my derivation of Nash equilibrium relies on aspirational idealizations, such as the rationality of the agents, it explains why an objective solution is a Nash equilibrium. It shows why realization of a Nash equilibrium is a goal of rationality for all agents. However, because my assumptions involve justificational idealizations and restrictions as well as aspirational idealizations, the derivation only establishes that realization of a Nash equilibrium is a restricted goal of rationality. It guides agents in circumstances meeting the assumptions. Delineating the general goal of rationality is a job for future research.

	C1	C2
R1	2 2	0 0
R2	0 0	1 1

FIGURE 9.5. A unique Pareto optimal Nash equilibrium.

Next, I treat ideal games with a unique Pareto optimal Nash equilibrium. I show that the selection principle generates that equilibrium. To start, consider an example that illustrates the proof's steps. Imagine a game for two agents, Row and Column. Each has just two salient strategies. Figure 9.5 depicts the game's payoff matrix. The Nash equilibria are ($R1$, $C1$) and ($R2$, $C2$), and the first is the Pareto optimal one. Imagine that the agents make the following responses to each other. If Column adopts $C1$, Row adopts $R1$, and if Column adopts $C2$, Row adopts $R2$. Similarly, if Row adopts $R1$, Column adopts $C1$, and if Row adopts $R2$, Column adopts $C2$. Because the agents are prescient, they know the responses to their strategies. Hence, each of an agent's strategies is ratifiable, but for Row, $R1$ maximizes self-conditional utility among ratifiable options, and for Column, $C1$ maximizes self-conditional utility among ratifiable options. So the selection principle leads each agent to do his part in the unique Pareto optimal Nash equilibrium.[11]

To treat the general case, suppose that an ideal game has multiple Nash equilibria and that one is Pareto superior to the others. Suppose that for each Nash strategy, the response is the remainder of the Nash equilibrium to which it belongs, and, if it belongs to multiple Nash equilibria, the remainder of one of those, the remainder of the Pareto optimal Nash equilibrium if that equilibrium is among the multiple Nash equilibria to which it belongs. Then each Nash strategy is ratifiable. Also suppose that for each non-Nash strategy, the response is the remainder of some profile that generates an incentive to switch. The game's payoff matrix and the agents' knowledge of it guarantee the existence of such a profile. Then only Nash strategies are ratifiable. Because agents are rational, each conforms to the selection principle and so, under my assumptions, maximizes self-conditional utility among ratifiable strategies. Although each Nash strategy is ratifiable, only the Nash strategies in the unique Pareto optimal Nash equilibrium maximize self-conditional utility among ratifiable strategies. Hence, the Pareto optimal Nash equilibrium is realized. The selection principle explains its realization.[12]

Does the rationality of participation in the Pareto optimal Nash equilibrium depend on whether agents have rival strategies that guarantee an acceptable outcome? Consider, for example, the game known as the Stag Hunt, which figure 9.6 depicts. Will safety push the agents to the inferior Nash equilibrium ($R2$, $C2$)? No,

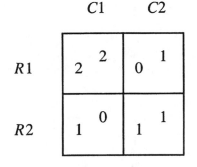

FIGURE 9.6. The Stag Hunt.

under the idealizations adopted, each agent is sure that the other participates in the Pareto optimal Nash equilibrium (R_1, C_1). In contrast with the framework of theorists such as Harsanyi and Selten (1988: chap. 4), the agents, being ideal, are not subject to performance errors.

Although most theorists treat the realization of Nash equilibrium in nonideal games where agents have bounded rationality, some treat ideal games. Aumann and Brandenburger (1995: 1161), for instance, point out that if all agents know the profile realized and all maximize utility, then a Nash equilibrium is realized. Only in a Nash equilibrium does each agent maximize utility given knowledge of that profile. This demonstration of a Nash equilibrium's realization, part of a larger project to identify minimum epistemic conditions sufficient for a Nash equilibrium's realization, does not attempt to explain how rational ideal agents realize a Nash equilibrium. Suppose that the agents enter the game not knowing directly the profile realized. How do they use their knowledge of the game and each other to infer the profile realized? What reasoning leads the agents to a Nash equilibrium? The demonstration does not answer such questions. Aumann and Brandenburger say, "The viewpoint adopted here is . . . *descriptive*. Not *why* the players do what they do, not what *should* they do; just what *do* they do, what *do* they believe" (1174–75, their emphasis).

My demonstration of a Nash equilibrium's realization, using ratification in place of utility maximization, has the advantage of explaining how all agents know the profile realized and maximize utility with respect to their knowledge. Their knowledge of the profile realized follows from their knowledge of responses to their strategies and the ratifiability of the profile's strategies. All maximize utility in realizing the profile, but they reach this profile by applying the principle of ratification.

In my demonstration, the agents do not start with knowledge of the profile realized. They start with only knowledge of responses to their strategies. They do not have the means to maximize utility directly. They lack direct access to probabilities of other agents' strategies. They have these probabilities only given supposition of one of their own strategies. Each agent seeks a strategy that maximizes utility given its realization. Each infers the profile realized. Thus, my demonstration not only establishes, but also explains, the realization of a Nash equilibrium. It presents the reasons that lead agents to a Nash equilibrium.[13]

My account of the realization of equilibria is explanatory but still incomplete. There is much more to do. A complete account covers all games with multiple equilibria, removes or derives the assumptions about responses, removes the assumption that self-support reduces to ratifiability, derives the idealization about prescience from more basic idealizations concerning the agents' common knowledge of the game and their rationality, and eventually removes idealizations about the agents and their situations. Moreover, it moves beyond normal-form games of strategy and treats types of equilibrium for other games. My restrictions and idealizations are provisional. They are imposed just for the sake of illustrating my decision principles' power to resolve certain problems in game theory, in particular, their power to break the circle of strategic reasoning. The derivations of Nash equilibrium they yield explain why an objective solution is a Nash equilibrium in a certain class of games. They show that realizing a Nash equilibrium is a goal for rational agents with either unlimited or limited cognitive abilities, a goal realized in certain ideal cases.

Game theory explores its decision-theoretic foundations from diverse perspectives. Investigations differ according to types of equilibrium studied, games treated, decision principles assumed, and theoretical objectives. This chapter shows how to make progress in game theory by generalizing the decision principles at game theory's base. The principles of self-support and selection revise characterizations of equilibria and solutions to make them exist more widely. They also explain the realization of equilibria. Their realism advances game theory by solving the dynamic decision problems that games of strategy create. They unify decision theory and game theory by creating a decision-theoretic foundation for game theory.

9.A. Appendix: Games of Strategy and Bounded Rationality

How does this chapter's method of justifying realization of a Nash equilibrium compare with other methods? As mentioned, its distinctive feature is an appeal to individuals' strategic reasoning to explain the rationality of their participation in a Nash equilibrium. To bring out this feature's significance, I examine a contrasting approach to Nash equilibrium.

Some methods of deriving a Nash equilibrium's realization in a game of strategy from principles of rationality governing the agents in the game appeal to the bounded rationality of the agents. That is, they appeal to various limits in the agents' cognitive abilities. As an illustration of these methods, this appendix considers Skyrms's (1990a: chap. 2) method of deriving Nash equilibrium, which is prominent in philosophy. I argue that the method's reliance on the agents' bounded rationality prevents it from explaining why a game's objective solution is a Nash equilibrium. Other methods relying on bounded rationality have the same shortcoming. I attend especially to the assumptions of Skyrms's method and classify them using chapter 3's taxonomy, extending section 3.A's study of controversial assumptions in the theory of decisions and games.

9.A.1. *Skyrms's Theorem about Deliberational and Nash Equilibria*

Skyrms addresses several types of equilibrium and several types of game, but I examine only his justification of Nash equilibrium in finite normal-form non-cooperative games. His method of providing decision-theoretic foundations for Nash equilibrium begins with an account of the deliberations of agents with bounded rationality. As he envisages such agents, they deliberate in stages instead of all at once. They use the results of one stage of deliberation as additional information for the next stage. Because agents in games of strategy try to take account of each other's deliberations, the results of an agent's deliberation in one stage often provide evidence about other agents' strategies. The agent can then use this evidence in his deliberation's next stage. The agents in section 5.4 use a similar bootstrapping method for the general acquisition of a priori knowledge.

In a little more detail, Skyrms's agents proceed as follows. An agent begins deliberation with an initial assignment of probabilities to his strategies and those of other agents. Using the probabilities for others' strategies, he finds a strategy for himself that maximizes expected utility. Typically, he then increases that strategy's probability. He does not increase its probability all the way to 1 because he is aware that his probability assignments are tentative. They do not accommodate all relevant considerations, so he expects revisions as his deliberations proceed. Next, the agent revises his probability assignment for other agents' strategies in light of his new probability assignment for his own strategies. Then, using the revised probabilities, he recalculates the expected utilities of his own strategies and readjusts their probabilities. The process of revision thus takes place in stages, with each stage used as input for a rule of bounded rationality that brings the agent to the next stage. This process continues until the probabilities of the agent's strategies do not lead to any further revision in his probability assignment for other agents' strategies. When all the agents reach this stopping point, they achieve a joint deliberational equilibrium. In suitable conditions, this joint deliberational equilibrium is a Nash equilibrium.

Figure 9.7 illustrates a possible course of deliberations for the game of Matching Pennies, in which two agents simultaneously display pennies, one seeking a match in the sides displayed and the other a mismatch (see section 9.2.2). In the figure, Agent 1 seeks a match and Agent 2 seeks a mismatch. The agents know each other's initial probability assignments and updating rules, so they know each other's probability assignments at every stage of deliberations. Deliberations start with each agent assigning a probability of slightly more than 0 to playing heads. Agent 2 then starts to increase the probability of heads, seeking a mismatch. After the probability of Agent 2's playing heads exceeds 0.5, Agent 1 begins to increase the probability of heads also, seeking to obtain a match. When the probability of his playing heads exceeds 0.5, Agent 2 begins to decrease the probability of heads. Mutual adjustment of probability assignments leads to the joint deliberational equilibrium in which each agent settles on the mixed strategy of playing heads and tails with equal probability. Their mixed strategies form a Nash equilibrium.

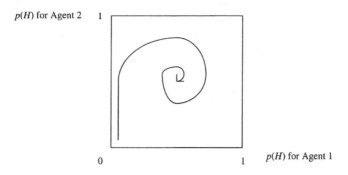

p(H) for Agent 2   1

0   1   p(H) for Agent 1

FIGURE 9.7. The course of deliberations in Matching Pennies.

Skyrms shows a theorem with the following form. Under certain assumptions, "A joint deliberational equilibrium on the part of all the players corresponds to a Nash equilibrium point of the game" (1990a: 29). This result has intrinsic interest because it shows how a Nash equilibrium in a game may arise from the agents' deliberations. But the theorem is not an adequate foundation for the theory of normal-form games. The justification it provides for Nash equilibrium has two drawbacks. First, the justification does not support the classical hypothesis of Nash equilibrium. Second, the assumptions on which it rests are too restrictive. I will explain these drawbacks in separate sections.[14]

9.A.2. *The Theorem's Role in Classical Game Theory*

Skyrms (1990a: 26–27) says that his theorem provides a justification of classical game theory's hypothesis about Nash equilibria. This hypothesis says that given suitable assumptions, the solution to a normal-form game is a Nash equilibrium.[15] Hence, to justify the hypothesis in a deliberational framework, it must be shown that given suitable assumptions, rational deliberators end up at a Nash equilibrium, that is, each does her part in the equilibrium.

Skyrms's theorem shows that given certain assumptions, rational agents reach a joint deliberational equilibrium if and only if they reach a Nash equilibrium. But the theorem's assumptions provide no guarantee that the agents reach a joint deliberational equilibrium. Under the assumptions, whether the agents reach a joint deliberational equilibrium depends on their initial probabilities and their rules for revising probabilities. For instance, agents who revise probabilities using a non-continuous rule may not reach a joint deliberational equilibrium even though one exists. They may skip over it (1990a: 32). Furthermore, in the game of Matching Pennies, "Aristotelian" deliberators, who revise probability assignments according to the continuous rule $dp(H)/dt = EU(H) - EU(T)$, may fail to reach a joint deliberational equilibrium (80–81).[16] Given almost every initial probability assignment, they circle the 50–50 Nash equilibrium, as in figure 9.8. Because the theorem's assumptions do not guarantee a joint deliberational equilibrium, the theorem provides only partial justification of the classical hypothesis about Nash equilibrium.

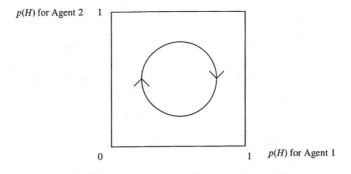

FIGURE 9.8. Matching Pennies with Aristotelian deliberators.

It supports Nash equilibrium only in cases where the agents reach a joint deliberational equilibrium.

Skyrms also claims to have given Nash equilibrium "the sort of justification that von Neumann and Morgenstern [1947] desired" (1990a: 29). As he points out, von Neumann and Morgenstern wanted to justify a Nash equilibrium in terms of each agent's thoughts about other agents' thoughts about his strategy (13–14). That is, they wanted a justification in terms of strategic reasoning. Skyrms's justification meets this criterion but still falls short of von Neumann and Morgenstern's hopes about the type of justification for Nash equilibrium.

In Skyrms's (1990a: 33) model of deliberation, agents reach a Nash equilibrium by adjusting their probability assignments in light of their knowledge of other agents' probability assignments. So Nash equilibrium is supported by strategic reasoning, even if the reasoning occurs step by step instead of all at once. Nonetheless, Skyrms's justification of Nash equilibrium lacks a feature that von Neumann and Morgenstern sought. An essential part of their rationale for Nash equilibrium was the foresight of agents' reasoning about strategies. They wanted a justification that appeals to agents' computational perspicuity. But Skyrms's justification makes no appeal to computational perspicuity; it succeeds for short-sighted agents. In characterizing the deliberators in his examples, he says, "These players follow their noses in the direction of the current apparent good, with no real memory of where they have been, no capability of recognizing patterns, and no sense of where they are going" (152). His model does not require that the deliberators be as simple-minded as this, but the justification of Nash equilibrium he gives succeeds for such deliberators. As he observes (58, 152), his model of deliberation resembles the evolutionary models of animal behavior proposed by Maynard Smith (1982). It does not require looking ahead to future stages. It has a dynamics suited to mindless organisms as well as humans.

Furthermore, Skyrms's method of justification cannot be extended to agents with computational perspicuity, such as the ideal agents of classical game theory. For the bounded rationality of agents is an essential feature of his model of deliberation. Someone arguing the contrary might claim that ideal agents may be accommodated by letting the time interval between the stages of deliberation go to zero, so that the stages are not temporally distinct. One might argue that ideal agents go through all the stages in an instant and immediately settle on a Nash equilibrium. But Skyrms's model does not allow instantaneous deliberation. First, the stages of deliberation must be temporally distinct to allow for updating probabilities from stage to stage. If the stages were not temporally distinct, the revisions of probabilities made during a stage would not provide new information for the subsequent stage. So there would be no reason to update probabilities during that stage. Second, at a stage of deliberation, the probability that an agent assigns to one of his strategies is the probability for him that he will ultimately adopt the strategy (1990a: 29). This probability is subjective and defined in terms of the agent's preferences among strategies at the stage (8–11). But such preferences would disrupt the process of deliberation if the agent were ideal and the stages were contemporaneous. For if an ideal agent had preferences among his strategies at a stage of deliberation, he would act on those preferences at that stage. Subsequent stages would be otiose because they would not register new information.

Skyrms's justification of Nash equilibrium thus disappoints classical game theory in two ways. It not only succeeds for agents who grope their way toward equilibrium, rather than looking ahead to it, but it also fails for agents who see at once where calculations lead. Because classical game theory seeks a justification of Nash equilibrium that relies on computational perspicuity, it must look elsewhere.[17]

9.A.3.   *The Theorem's Role in Game Theory*

Ultimately, the value of Skyrms's theorem depends not on its contribution to classical game theory, but on its contribution to game theory. So I now consider the theorem from a broader perspective. I put aside the special concerns of classical game theory and evaluate the theorem with respect to the overall project of justifying solutions to games of strategy.

Skyrms's model of deliberation for agents with bounded rationality is obviously useful in applications of game theory to humans. Also, it is clear that his theorem exposes an interesting connection between joint deliberational equilibrium and Nash equilibrium. Moreover, the significance of this connection is supported by his investigations of its robustness (1990a: 62–86). However, the theorem's assumptions have several drawbacks for my purposes.

For theoretical appeal, the assumptions should meet the following standards. First, they should not be mere restrictions. As chapter 3 explains, they should be simplifying and idealizing assumptions that control for factors that explain rational behavior. Second, the assumptions should not conceal problems in justifying Nash equilibrium. In particular, it should be clear that the assumptions can be realized. Third, the assumptions should be alterable in ways that yield full solutions to all normal-form games, not just partial solutions to selected normal-form games with a certain type of agent. This section argues that the theorem's assumptions fall short with respect to these three standards.

Let me begin with a review of the theorem's assumptions. They appear in the following statement of the theorem: "In a game played by Bayesian deliberators with a common prior, an adaptive rule that seeks the good, and a feedback process that updates by emulation, with common knowledge of all the foregoing, each player is at a deliberational equilibrium at a state of the system if and only if the assignment of the default mixed acts to each player constitutes a Nash equilibrium of the game" (Skyrms 1990a: 33).[18] A common prior is a common assignment of probabilities to all the strategies of all the players. An adaptive rule that seeks the good revises the probabilities of an agent's strategies, after calculations of their expected utilities, so that only strategies with a higher expected utility than the agent's tentative mixed strategy receive a higher probability and so that the sum of the probabilities of such strategies increases. A feedback process that updates by emulation revises the probabilities assigned to other agents' strategies by replicating their revision procedures. Common knowledge of the process of deliberation entails that all know it, know that all know it, and so on. The default mixed act of a player is the randomized strategy that follows the agent's current assignment of probabilities to his pure strategies.

Taking Skyrms's theorem as a means of justifying Nash equilibrium in normal-form games, the role of an assumption is either to facilitate the attainment of joint deliberational equilibrium or to bring joint deliberational equilibrium into alignment with Nash equilibrium. My evaluation of the assumptions examines the way they fulfill these roles.

The first drawback is that some of the assumptions are mere restrictions: they are not simplifying assumptions or idealizations that control for factors that explain rational behavior (see section 3.1). To show that an assumption is a mere restriction without advancing an inventory of factors that explain rational behavior, I show that modifying the assumption in a way that has no significance according to a general theory of rationality (insofar as its contours are known) either blocks joint deliberational equilibrium or else upsets the alignment of joint deliberational equilibrium and Nash equilibrium.

Before arguing that some assumptions are in fact mere restrictions, let me clarify the standard of evaluation by explaining why some assumptions are not mere restrictions. Take the common knowledge assumption. It is an idealization because it controls an explanatory factor, namely, each agent's knowledge about others. Clearly, a general theory of rational behavior uses this factor to help explain rational behavior in strategic situations. An assumption that controls each agent's knowledge about others is therefore not a mere restriction. Likewise, the assumption of a common prior is an idealization because, in the context of the common knowledge assumption, it also controls each agent's knowledge about others. These assumptions are not mere restrictions, but rather justificational idealizations.

The other assumptions lack this sort of theoretical warrant. Take the assumption that all agents have the same adaptive rule for revision of probabilities. Because, as Skyrms allows, many adaptive rules are rational, this assumption is a mere restriction. It does not control for a basic explanatory factor. Also, consider the assumption that the adaptive rule seeks the good. This assumption excludes adaptive rules that permit raising the probabilities of strategies that are just as good as one's tentative mixed strategy. Because probability increases of this sort are not irrational, excluding adaptive rules that permit them is restrictive. Their exclusion does not serve to control a basic explanatory factor.

Moreover, the exclusion of the permissive adaptive rules is not merely a matter of technical convenience. It is necessary for the correspondence between deliberational and Nash equilibrium. To see this, consider a game with a unique Nash equilibrium that is not strict. Given a permissive adaptive rule, the agents may be at a Nash equilibrium but not achieve joint deliberational equilibrium. They may oscillate away from and back to the Nash equilibrium until lack of time forces them to halt deliberations, perhaps away from the Nash equilibrium.[19]

The assumption that the agents update by emulation is also a restriction. According to it, an agent's stage n deliberations about others replicate their stage n deliberations. It has the consequence that an agent learns about others' stage n deliberations during his stage n deliberations. But this feature of an agent's learning lacks theoretical motivation. Why should an agent learn about others' stage n deliberations during his stage n deliberations as opposed to his stage $n-1$ or $n+1$ deliberations? The symmetry of the agents' situations does not require their learning to be in step with deliberations rather than a step behind or ahead. It requires only that each agent's learning follow the same pattern. And rationality, although it requires gathering information about others, does not require that agents in stage n deliberations gather information about others by replicating their stage n deliberations as opposed to their stage $n-1$ or $n+1$ deliberations. Because predictions about others are subject to revision in later stages of deliberation, they need not stem from replications of any particular stage.

However, the timing of information about others is critical for the attainment of a joint deliberational equilibrium. If in a two-person case learning about the other agent falls a step behind deliberations, so that it is as if the agents take turns going through the stages of deliberation, joint deliberational equilibrium may move out of reach. In the game of Matching Pennies, for instance, each agent may end up oscillating perpetually between two mixed acts. When Agent 1, who wants a match, learns of an increase in the probability of heads for his opponent, he raises the probability of his playing heads. Then, when Agent 2 learns of this change, she lowers the probability of her playing heads. This triggers a decrease in the probability of Agent 1's playing heads, and so on. As a result, the agents do not reach the mixed acts that constitute deliberational and Nash equilibrium. They trace a box around the Nash equilibrium, as in figure 9.9, until time for deliberation ends.

A derivation of a Nash equilibrium explains why an objective solution to a game of strategy is a Nash equilibrium only if it shows why realization of a Nash equilibrium is a goal of rationality. This requires showing that ideal agents achieve Nash equilibrium. The assumptions of an explanatory derivation should be idealizations, moreover aspirational idealizations, that nonideal agents aspire to realize. If not all assumptions are aspirational idealizations, the derivation may still establish that realization of a Nash equilibrium is a restricted goal of rationality. This is what section 9.2 does. Nonetheless, under the restrictions, ideal agents should realize the Nash equilibrium. For ideal agents, Skyrms's assumptions block the realization of Nash equilibrium and so do not yield an explanation of an objective solution's being a Nash equilibrium. They do not yield a principle expressing a goal of rationality that may suggest further principles concerning appropriate pursuit of the goal when obstacles arise.

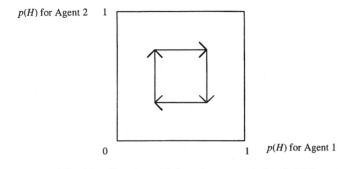

FIGURE 9.9. Matching Pennies with learning a step behind deliberations.

Next, I argue that some of the difficulties in justifying Nash equilibrium are hidden in the assumptions of Skyrms's theorem. They reappear as problems for the realization of the assumptions. Before applying this type of criticism to the theorem's assumptions, however, let me consider, for the sake of illustration, how it applies to an assumption that von Neumann and Morgenstern make in the course of their arguments for Nash equilibrium.

As section 9.2.3 noted, a difficulty in justifying Nash equilibrium is an apparent circularity in the reasons for solutions to games of strategy. What is rational for an agent depends on what is rational for the other agents, and that in turn depends on what is rational for the first agent. More specifically, for an agent to make a decision by applying the rule to maximize expected utility, he must assign probabilities to the strategies of his opponents. To assign probabilities to their strategies in a rational way, he must take account of their insight into his reasoning. In particular, his prediction of his opponents' strategies must take account of his opponents' anticipation of his own strategy. Hence, to make a decision, he must predict his opponents' strategies; but to predict their strategies, he must know what he will decide.

To overcome this problem, von Neumann and Morgenstern assume that each agent knows what the others will do. They argue that given this assumption, Nash equilibrium follows (1947: 147–48). However, the assumption of knowledge of strategies is unsatisfactory because its realization also faces a problem of circularity. It is not clear how the agents could gain this knowledge, given that each agent knows that the others' strategies anticipate his strategy. His knowledge of their strategies seems to require prior knowledge of his own strategy, and his knowledge of his own strategy seems to require prior knowledge of their strategies.

Some of Skyrms's assumptions are open to a similar objection. Take the assumption of a common prior probability assignment. It appears often in game theory as a convenient simplification but is unwarranted in an explanation of Nash equilibrium. It entails that each agent begin deliberations with an initial assignment of probabilities to his own strategies and those of others. How do the agents make this initial probability assignment? Just as there is an apparent circularity in the grounds for knowledge of strategies, there is an apparent circularity in the grounds for probabilities of strategies. The probabilities an agent assigns to his own strategies depend on the probabilities he assigns to others' strategies. And the probabilities he assigns to others' strategies depend on the probabilities he assigns to his own strategies. How can the agents make their initial probability assignments given this apparent circularity?

One reply is that the provenance of the initial probabilities is unimportant for normative game theory. The initial probabilities are subjective probabilities. Their origin is a psychological matter, not part of a theory of rationality. Normative game theory need treat only the revision of initial probabilities in light of the information deliberation provides.

This reply dismisses too quickly the problem of initial probabilities. Although the standard laws of subjective probability do not govern the formation of initial probabilities, one should not conclude that there are no epistemic constraints on initial probabilities. Strategic considerations indicate the contrary. If an agent assigns a high probability to one of his strategies, he thereby obtains evidence concerning others' strategies and so should not assign probabilities to their strategies arbitrarily. A justification of Nash equilibrium using initial probabilities must show that they can meet the pertinent epistemic constraints. The justification need not resolve all the problems surrounding the formation of initial probabilities, but it should at least resolve the apparent circularity in the grounds for initial probabilities.

One might also try to dismiss the problem of initial probabilities by appealing to the agents' bounded rationality. One might say that an agent's initial probabilities are just the probabilities he assigns before he begins to take account of strategic considerations. There is no circularity in the grounds for them because the strategic considerations that generate the apparent circularity do not arise until deliberations begin and then are accommodated by the process of probability revision. However, if the initial probabilities do not rest on strategic considerations, it is hard to see what they can rest on. In normal-form games, strategic considerations are all that the agents have to guide their initial probability assignments. Other factors are irrelevant by hypothesis. So even acknowledging the agents' bounded rationality, the problem of initial probabilities seems insoluble. Initial probability assignments appear to be ungrounded.

Section 9.2.3's account of the realization of a Nash equilibrium overcomes the circle of strategic reasoning. It assumes that each agent knows the other's strategies given a strategy of his. From this conditional knowledge, he derives his own choice and the choices of others using the self-support and selection principles. Because Skyrms's account adheres to principles of utility maximization not generalized for dynamic problems, it lacks the means of breaking the circle of strategic reasoning.

In addition to problems concerning the realization of Skyrms's assumptions individually, there are problems concerning their joint realization. Some of the assumptions appear to be psychologically incompatible. Under the assumption of updating by emulation, agents assign probabilities to strategies without looking ahead to the evidence that their assignments provide for those strategies. The assumption thus implies that certain intellectual powers are limited. In contrast, other assumptions imply that certain intellectual powers are unlimited. For instance, according to the common knowledge assumption, the agents know certain facts, know that all know these facts, and so on ad infinitum. Also, according to background assumptions, deliberation is cost-free (1990a: 29) and preferences are coherent in the sense of fully conforming to standard axioms of preference (11). Of course, the limited and unlimited intellectual powers implied by these assumptions are not logically incompatible because they are distinct powers. But they seem psychologically incompatible because the distinctions between them concern topics rather than the cognitive abilities distinguished in psychology. It seems, for instance, psychologically impossible for agents to have limits for computations about some topics and no limits for computations about other topics. In all likelihood, limits for computations about a topic stem from limited general computational abilities and thus psychologically entail limits for computations about all topics.

Furthermore, even if the assumptions concerning intellectual powers are psychologically compatible, it is restrictive to make those assumptions jointly. Taken together, the assumptions do not control for factors that play a role in the general theory of rational behavior. In particular, they do not control for factors that guide adjustments of standards of rationality for a nonideal agent. Given what is known about basic principles of rationality, standards of rationality for a nonideal agent depend on the agent's general cognitive abilities, and not on his topic-specific intellectual powers—because the latter may be limited by the agent's culpable neglect of topics. Therefore, although an assumption that fixes the level of general computational ability is not restrictive, a set of assumptions that fixes different levels of computational ability for different topics is restrictive.

To defend Skyrms's assumptions concerning intellectual powers, one may frame them differently. First, suppose that an agent has low cognitive ability in all areas. Next, suppose that he has the assistance of a team of experts specialized in different areas. Section 5.1.1 suggests a similar maneuver to explain a combination of ignorance concerning psychological matters with expertise concerning a priori matters. However, the new framework for Skyrms's assumptions is still restrictive. A fine-grained separation of computational powers according to topic is not as explanatorily useful as a general separation of ignorance concerning psychological and a priori matters.

The last problem with the assumptions of Skyrms's theorem is their inflexibility. They are not easily modified to obtain more precise and more general specifications of the solutions of normal-form games. For instance, as section 9.A.2 notes, it is impossible to adjust the assumptions to accommodate the classical case of agents who are computationally perspicuous. This limitation prevents Skyrms's methods from justifying general principles for normal-form games. Although such principles are works in progress, it is clear that they must treat cases of unbounded rationality as well as cases of bounded rationality.

There are also other ways in which Skyrms's assumptions are inflexible. For example, one would like to enrich the assumptions to obtain justifications of common hypotheses about a solution to a normal-form game with multiple Nash equilibria, in particular, the hypothesis that a solution is a Pareto optimal Nash equilibrium, that is, a Nash equilibrium such that no other Nash equilibrium is better for some agents and worse for none. But extending Skyrms's theorem in this direction is not possible. Skyrms shows that, given his model of deliberation, when there are multiple Nash equilibria, the equilibrium reached depends on the initial probability assignment of the agents (1990a: 34). Furthermore, it is a requirement of his model that agents lack computational foresight. So they must lack the ability to look ahead to see where their initial probability assignments will take them. Thus, they cannot reason their way to initial probabilities that will take them to a Pareto optimal Nash equilibrium. Given Skyrms's model, no idealization can be added to guarantee a Pareto optimal Nash equilibrium. The difficulty stems from a general problem with evolutionary models of strategic choice. As Elster (1989: 72–73) and others point out, evolutionary processes tend toward local maxima but not necessarily toward global maxima.

In addition, one would like to be able to adjust the theorem's assumptions to accommodate normal-form games without Nash equilibria. These games are commonplace when mixed strategies are not available, and a general account of normal-form games must address them. Even though their solutions are controversial, so that the appropriate direction for adjustment of the theorem's assumptions is unclear, avenues of adjustment should be available. But it is difficult to adjust the assumptions so that joint deliberational equilibria occur at plausible alternatives to Nash equilibria.

Such adjustments may appear unnecessary because, according to one of the background assumptions, deliberation has a time limit (1990a: 29, n. 3). When it is reached, deliberation stops and agents adopt their tentative mixed strategies or default acts, even if they are not at a Nash equilibrium. The time limit thus prevents agents from deliberating endlessly in the absence of a Nash equilibrium. However, the outcome imposed by the time limit is not a solution to a normal-form game. It is a product of exogenous factors, which are independent of the structural features of the game and strategic considerations. Consequently, to obtain solutions to games without Nash equilibria, adjustments of the assumptions are necessary.

One possibility is suggested by Skyrms's examination of Good's (1967) theorem on the value of new information. Skyrms notes that in games without Nash equilibria, deliberations do not meet the conditions of Good's theorem, and at some time deliberation ceases to be worthwhile; it no longer provides useful information. At that time, an agent adopts his default act (1990a: 102–3). So one might argue that solutions to games without Nash equilibria are given by limits on the productivity of deliberation. One might attempt to derive solutions from specifications of those limits.

However, this approach is unsatisfactory. First, there are problems with the stopping rule's implementation. It is not clear how agents unable to see where their deliberations are taking them can see that further deliberations are not worthwhile. Evaluating the productivity of further deliberations requires just the sort of foresight they lack. Second, the justification of a specific stopping rule requires more than the structural features of the game and the general characteristics of agents. It requires new, restrictive assumptions about the productivity of deliberations. Third, the outcomes generated by the proposal are heavily dependent on initial probabilities and thus fully inherit the arbitrariness of those probabilities. Suppose, for instance, that it is not worthwhile even to begin deliberations. Then the proposal simply yields the outcome given by the initial probability assignment, an outcome just as arbitrary as that assignment.[20]

To summarize, Skyrms's theorem illuminates the dynamics of rational deliberation by cognitively limited agents. If it is advanced as a justification of Nash equilibrium, however, its assumptions have a number of drawbacks. They lack theoretical motivation, face epistemological and psychological objections, and impede general results, in particular, results covering the classical case of ideal agents. As a result, the theorem does not explain why an objective solution to a game of strategy is a Nash equilibrium. It does not show that realizing a Nash equilibrium is a goal of rationality, one met by ideal agents in ideal circumstances.

Ideal to Real

The preceding chapters remove idealizations behind the decision principle to maximize utility. They weaken the principle's assumptions and generalize it in various ways. Having greater scope, the revised principles move closer to realistic decision problems, the sort people confront in their everyday lives, and enrich explanations of the rationality of decisions.

Chapters 4 and 5 remove the idealization that an agent consciously assigns precise probabilities and utilities to every option's possible outcomes. They treat cases in which agents lack probability and utility assignments, or do not have direct access to them. When an agent lacks the requisite probability and utility assignments, chapter 4 recommends adopting an option that maximizes utility under some quantization of beliefs and desires. The recommendation assumes that every relevant reason for an option influences beliefs and desires and so quantizations of them. No quantization overlooks any reason affecting an option's choiceworthiness. When an agent has probability and utility assignments but fails after reasonable efforts to discover them, chapter 5 recommends using higher-order beliefs about the assignments to make full use of information in hand. The higher-order analyses yield accessible utilities of options, which should direct utility maximization. The chapter also sketches methods of evaluating efforts to form and learn about probability and utility assignments and to acquire a priori knowledge useful for reaching a decision.

Chapters 6 and 7 remove the idealization that an agent is fully rational except perhaps in resolving his current decision problem. They entertain cases in which an agent enters a decision problem with irrational beliefs or desires, or knows he will make irrational decisions afterward. Comprehensive rationality in such cases depends on whether those mistakes are acceptable. If they are acceptable, then a decision is rational only if it is utility-maximizing taking the mistakes for granted. If they are unacceptable, then a decision is rational only if it is utility-maximizing given their correction.

Chapters 8 and 9 remove the idealization that a decision problem includes an option of stable maximum utility. Decision problems without a stable maximum arise in games of strategy, for instance. To generalize the principle of utility maximization, I use conditional incentives to analyze an option's being self-supporting and advance the principle to adopt a self-supporting option. This principle recognizes the futility of endless pursuit of incentives and does not require it. Investigation of noncooperative games shows that the principle grounds a type of equilibrium, strategic equilibrium, that exists more widely than Nash equilibrium does. The principle provides for solutions to games without Nash equilibria. A companion principle for choosing among multiple self-supporting options grounds equilibrium selection in games with more than one strategic equilibrium.

Chapters 4–9 advance independently generalizations of utility maximization. These generalizations arise from rolling back different idealizations and address distinct issues. They may be combined, however. The principle of acceptability, designed for errant agents, incorporates the standard of utility maximization but may use instead the more general standard of utility maximization under a quantization. Similarly, the principle of self-support relies on preferences but may use instead preferences after correction of unacceptable mistakes. Putting together all the generalizations yields a wide-ranging principle of comprehensive rationality: *A rational decision maximizes self-conditional utility among self-supporting options with respect to a quantization of conscious beliefs and desires after a reasonable effort to form and become aware of relevant beliefs and desires, acquire pertinent a priori knowledge, and correct unacceptable mistakes.*

The combination of my independent generalizations makes substantial progress toward realism. Still, it relies on idealizations supporting the generalizations it combines. It assumes that agents are perfectly situated for meeting the standard it advances. To move closer to a completely realistic decision theory, let me suggest some additional steps that seem promising and in any case raise topics of intrinsic interest.

Revising standards of rationality to compensate for an agent's mistakes confronts many issues. My principles need further elaboration to facilitate their application. They involve concepts, such as conditional rationality and acceptability of mistakes, that auxiliary principles should flesh out. The principle of acceptability does not identify and classify mistakes according to acceptability but instead presumes some way of doing that. It needs supplementation with an analysis of common mistakes and methods of correcting them. Consider, for instance, three common mistakes. First, an agent's aversion to risk may be stronger than warranted; it may lead to excessive caution. Second, an agent may too deeply discount satisfaction of future desires; this may prompt imprudent, short-sighted acts. Third, an agent may incorrectly assesses the benefit of resolutely carrying out plans; as a result, he may pointlessly vacillate. The literature offers thorough treatments of these three mistakes and may be mined for correctives. It furnishes accounts of rational attitudes toward risk, toward satisfaction of desires foreseen but not yet felt, and toward resolute execution of plans. Research on risk, time preference, and planning suggests ways of guiding applications of the principle of acceptability.

My treatment of games without Nash equilibria considers only noncooperative games. However, the concept of strategic equilibrium carries over to cooperative games, in which coalitions may form and adopt joint strategies. To extend the concept of strategic equilibrium to cooperative games, I need primarily an account of the incentives of coalitions. In future work, I plan to produce such an account and thereby construct a unified theory of equilibrium in cooperative and noncooperative games alike. Besides covering the existence of equilibria, the theory will cover the selection and realization of an equilibrium in games with multiple equilibria.

Some idealizations that chapters 4–9 retain are very strong, for instance, idealizations giving agents knowledge of relevant logical and mathematical truths. Removing these idealizations may require novel techniques, perhaps greater reliance on procedural standards of rationality. Contemporary epistemology, in particular, reliabilism, focuses on procedures of belief formation. It may inspire productive revisions of decision principles. Because epistemology has a long tradition of attention to standards of attainable rationality, its innovations may extend, with appropriate modification, to standards of attainable rationality in decision making.

Investigating empirical questions about people's decision problems and decision-making skills also promotes realism. Empirical studies flesh out claims that people have cognitive limits, often lack probability and utility assignments, make mistakes, and so on. Details can refine applications of decision principles. For example, assessments of the costs of decisions can guide identification of utility-maximizing options. Empirical studies can also direct efforts to remove more idealizations. They can show which idealizations most inhibit realism and suggest how to dispense with them. Empirical studies are a powerful ally for a normative decision theory aiming for realism.

Realistic decision theory presents many absorbing challenges. Fortunately, several areas of philosophy and allied fields offer abundant resources for meeting those challenges.

Appendix A: Optimization and Utility Maximization

Chapter 2 presents the principles of optimization and utility maximization. Its objective is to lay the foundation for a study of their idealizations and for a method of relaxing those idealizations. It postpones a full articulation of the principles because the techniques for generalizing them are versatile and do not rely on details. This appendix elaborates chapter 2's presentation of the principles. It addresses questions about an option's nature, the comparison set for an option's evaluation, and calculations of an option's utility. My glosses on the decision principles extend to their generalizations in chapters 4–9. They yield a more refined final product.

The appendix assumes chapter 2's idealizations for the principles. Agents are ideal and rational. Their situations are perfect for complying with the principles. The principle of optimization assumes full information, whereas the principle of utility maximization allows for uncertainty about options' outcomes.

A.1. Sets of Options

Chapter 2 applies optimization to momentary acts and utility maximization to a special type of momentary act: decisions. This section supports these versions of the principles. It explains the advantages of taking options as momentary acts and, given uncertainty, as decisions.

A.1.1. *Full Information*

To clarify the principle of optimization, one must say which acts it evaluates and which (possible) acts form the comparison set for an act evaluated. Assuming that the act evaluated is in the comparison set for it, the chief requirement is to specify for an agent the acts over which she should optimize. Some candidate sets are: all acts, all momentary acts, all extended acts, all intentional acts, and all acts not performed by performing other acts. The appropriate set depends on at least three factors. First, it depends on the principle's force: Does the principle express only a necessary condition of rationality, or also a sufficient condition of rationality? Second, it depends on the principle's idealizations: Does the principle, for instance, assume that an agent has unlimited cognitive power and direct control of all her acts? Third, it depends on the criteria of individuation and identity for acts: For example, are acts concrete, abstract, or hybrid events?

The features of an act that matter to standards of rationality, such as optimization, are related to responsibility. In particular, an agent's control over the act and awareness of her control over it matter. So chapter 2 applies optimization to the set of acts in an agent's direct control, basic acts, and adopts idealizations that ensure the agent's knowledge of that set. It adjusts the principle's force according to its characterization of acts.

To round out chapter 2's characterization of basic acts, consider some types of act. Acts may be simple or composite. A driver may change lanes and accelerate at the same time. Her act at the time is composite. Composite acts may be in an agent's direct control. So I do not require that basic acts be simple.

Acts may be specific or nonspecific. I may raise an arm. At the same time, I may raise my right arm high. The second act is more specific than the first. Both specific and nonspecific acts may be in an agent's direct control. So I do not require that basic acts be specific. Lewis (1981: 7) takes options to be maximally specific acts. But optimization advanced as a necessary condition of rationality can ignore an act's specificity without contravening Lewis's version of the principle. An option optimal among basic specific acts is optimal among basic acts.

Under my assumptions, agents directly control at a moment only acts at that moment. So I take basic acts as momentary acts and restrict the principle of optimization to them. Optimization is then relative to rival momentary acts.[1] Other comparison sets may also work, especially given adjustments in the principle's force, idealizations, and characterization of acts. This section examines and rejects just one alternative.

Should optimization also consider extended acts of some sort? Extended acts include following rules, policies, strategies, plans, and decision procedures. They include composite acts of self-direction, such as forming an intention to perform an act and then carrying out the intention, in particular, forming a resolution and then acting on it and also adopting a constraint on action and then adhering to it. Extended acts also include composite acts of self-influence, such as forming a disposition to act in a certain way and then acting in that way. Optimizing among extended acts thus covers proposals that section 1.1 mentions concerning plans, resolutions, and dispositions. This section briefly assesses and dismisses optimization among extended acts. For more discussion, see Gauthier (1986: chap. 6; 1998), Bratman (1987: chap. 2; 1998; 1999, pt. 1), McClennen (1990: chap. 1; 1998), Weirich (2001a: 84–86), and related essays in Mele and Rawling (2004).

Some features of human decision making recommend optimizing among extended acts. People commonly decide to perform extended acts. One decides to take a walk, for instance, and afterward does not think about each step. When grading a logic class's homework, one decides to deduct so many points for a misapplication of *modus ponens* and afterward follows the policy without reviewing the reasons for it every time one spots the mistake. Extended acts have many benefits. Adopting a plan and following it is the best way to perform a complex act. Without a plan, it is unlikely that one can cook dinner, build a canoe, or become a doctor. Coordination with others also depends on one's sticking to a plan adopted in concert with them. Taking a broad perspective on action makes good sense. Leaving action to spur-of-the-moment decisions runs the risk of missing opportunities because one overlooks the best options or misevaluates them. Following a plan also has lower cognitive costs than constantly surveying and assessing one's options. Because extended acts have a prominent, beneficial role in deliberations, it may seem sensible to optimize among them.

Despite the importance of extended acts, optimization works best applied only to momentary acts. This restriction does not entirely ignore extended acts, however. Momentary acts include decisions to perform extended acts. Execution of a strategy, for example, takes place over an extended period of time and is not in an agent's direct control. But a decision to adopt the strategy is momentary and a matter of direct control. The restriction excludes the strategy's execution but not its adoption.

Although agents justifiably deliberate about extended acts, they realize those acts by performing momentary acts. Momentary acts are the basic units of control and so should be the basic units of evaluation. The rationality of momentary acts explains the rationality of extended acts. Two points support this position. First, optimization among momentary acts is feasible for the agents I treat. Optimization, as I take it, is a standard of evaluation, not a decision procedure; momentary acts need not be the focus of deliberation to be optimization's target. One may optimize among momentary acts without deliberating about them. Also, even if cognitive limits make optimization among momentary acts too high a standard for humans, it is rational for ideal agents in ideal circumstances to optimize among those acts. Ideal agents can deliberate about momentary acts. They have the cognitive power to examine and evaluate every option. In ideal circumstances, they can identify optimal momentary acts. Chapter 2 treats ideal agents in ideal circumstances and for them proposes optimization among momentary acts. Its idealizations support optimization's concentration on momentary acts.

Second, the benefits of extended acts redound upon the momentary acts that constitute them. Consider, for example, the extended act of giving a toy to each child in a class. Because stopping short disappoints some children, the act's rationality seems to require optimization among extended acts occupying the same period. However, each step toward completion of the extended act is optimal given that the agent will complete the extended act, as one assumes when evaluating it. Similarly, if adopting and following a plan for cooking dinner has benefits, then so does each step of the plan. Each step, by contributing to the realization of the extended act, shares in producing the extended act's consequences. The benefits that justify a plan's execution typically justify the momentary acts that constitute the plan's execution. So optimizing among momentary acts generally agrees with optimizing among extended acts. In particular, optimization among momentary acts is not myopic. It does not counsel short-term optimization at the expense of long-term optimization. If passing up a benefit now brings a greater benefit in the future, then passing up the benefit now optimizes among momentary acts. The virtue of prudence accrues to the momentary acts that yield prudent extended acts.

One consequence of section 2.1.2's evaluating acts according to their outcomes is that any extended act performed has the same utility as each of its parts. It and each of its parts have the same possible world as outcome and so the same desirability. This does not hold for a counterfactual extended act, however. It may have a part that is performed. Perhaps the extended act was started but abandoned. The outcome of the part performed is the actual world, whereas the outcome of the unperformed extended act is some other possible world. The desirabilities of the two worlds may differ. So the desirabilities of the extended act and its part may differ.[2]

Clearly, taking optimization among acts to go by comparison of acts' worlds erases the distinction between short- and long-term optimization. Take an alleged case where a multistage act optimal among contemporaneous acts has a first stage not optimal among contemporaneous acts, a case where, for instance, by forgoing optimization among momentary acts now, one optimizes one's future. Such cases cannot arise given appraisal according to acts' worlds. If the possible world resulting from an allegedly nonoptimal momentary act is an optimal future, then the momentary act is really optimal, because its world contains its temporal sequel. Its generating an optimal future makes it an optimal momentary act.

Sometimes, comparison of decision theory with other theories suggests optimization among extended acts. Take ethical theory. Some moralists argue for rule-consequentialism over act-consequentialism. They argue for following rules that optimize among possible rules. This position may be appealing because people follow moral rules, such as rules prohibiting violence, and because the acts the rules mandate seem to have noninstrumental moral value. But similar reasons do not ground the rationality of optimization among rules. In typical cases, the standard of rationality for acts is instrumental. An act is rational if it promotes rational values. An act does not have noninstrumental rational value that supports following a rule that requires the act. Compare sparing another person pain with preventing pain to oneself. Morality may require sparing another person pain even if causing him pain spares many other people pain. On the other hand, rationality does not require preventing pain to oneself even if causing it prevents pain to oneself many other times. Acts of a certain type may have noninstrumental moral value that rules to perform that type of act inherit. But typically, acts do not have noninstrumental rational value that rules inherit.

Next, consider physics. Imagine one is studying a system of molecules that form a gas. Studying the system only at a moment is short-sighted. Understanding the system requires studying its dynamics, too. Similarly, it may seem that optimization among momentary acts overlooks a momentary act's connections with the past and the future. The analogy is imperfect, however. Optimization among momentary acts takes account of temporal context. If a connection with the past or future is valuable, then a present act derives value from establishing that connection. A momentary act's utility depends on the act's outcome including connections with the past and future. It takes a broad view stretching across time, not just a snapshot at a moment.

The reasons for optimizing among extended acts are either eliminated by idealizations or else are already covered by perspicacious optimization among momentary acts. Moreover, applying optimization to extended acts runs into serious difficulties. One proposal recommends a maximally extended act optimal among all acts occupying the same time interval. This recommendation yields the advice to lead the best life possible. Another proposal recommends optimizing among acts that start now, regardless of their duration. Both proposals face a powerful objection. Some extended acts optimal among acts occupying the same interval, or starting at the same time, include momentary acts not optimal among acts occupying the same moment. To execute one of these extended acts, at some time the agent must pick a momentary act worse than a rival momentary act. This is irrational for ideal agents ideally situated. An extended act can be executed only by executing its stages. If a stage is irrational, then so is the whole act, even if it is optimal in some comparison classes. The attractions of the whole do not make up for the flaws of the parts.

For example, suppose that an agent will choose between $1.00 and $2.00. If he will choose the lesser amount, a predictor of that choice gives him $5.00 before his choice. The agent's optimal extended act involves later choosing $1.00 rather than $2.00. But if, when the time comes, the predictor has already given him $5.00, he lacks a reason to take $1.00 rather than $2.00. Taking the lesser amount is irrational even if it is part of an optimal extended act. Given my idealizations, an extended act is rational if and only if each of its momentary stages is optimal with respect to acts that can be performed at its time.[3]

Optimization among momentary acts differs from optimization among extended acts in other cases in which an agent is rewarded because another predicts that he will perform an act nonoptimal among acts at the same moment. Suppose that a bully leaves alone a child he predicts will futilely combat an attack. Then the child gains from a disposition to deviate from optimization moment by moment. Even in such cases, the rational course is to optimize moment by moment because only the disposition to deviate brings benefits, not the deviation itself. Sections 7.3 and 7.4 argue this point further, evaluating separately dispositions and the acts they yield and also forming intentions and carrying them out. They treat cases in which a momentary act is irrational although it is part of an optimizing extended act.

In general, if optimizing among extended acts differs from optimizing among momentary acts, then at some moment it asks an agent to perform an act not best at the moment because it is part of a best extended act. It demands forgoing the best momentary act for some gain from the extended act. But evaluation of the best momentary act is comprehensive. That momentary act is best taking account of the gain from the extended act. So there is no reason on balance to forgo the best momentary act.

The strongest argument I know for forgoing optimization among momentary acts draws an analogy. Suppose that buying a red hat is optimal. One may buy a hat, although the act is not optimal because it is entailed by the optimal act. Similarly, the argument claims, one may perform a momentary act that is not optimal because it is entailed by an optimal extended act.

A disanalogy defeats the argument, however. Performing a nonoptimal momentary act rules out the optimal momentary act, although buying a hat does not rule out the optimal act of buying a red hat. The argument does not provide a reason to tolerate nonoptimal momentary acts.

Inconsistency results from advancing optimization for both momentary and extended acts. As the examples show, in some cases an optimal extended act contains a nonoptimal momentary act. The agent cannot realize a rival optimal momentary act and also the optimal extended act. Rationality cannot require both forms of optimization, and the balance of considerations supports applying optimization to momentary acts only.

A.1.2. *Uncertainty*

The principle of utility maximization is more general than the principle of optimization. It is designed for agents who may lack full information. Without full information an agent may not know which acts are in her direct control. To ensure that an agent is responsible for maximizing, the principle should be restricted to options she knows are in her direct control. I assume that an agent knows that her decisions, at least, are in her direct control. So I present the principle of utility maximization for decisions, a particular type of momentary act.[4]

Is my version of the principle too restrictive? Maximization among all acts an agent is certain she can perform, decisions and nondecisions alike, also keeps uncertainty in its place. Why apply maximization to decisions alone? Shouldn't the principle require an agent at a moment to maximize utility among all acts at the moment she is certain she can perform?

Simplification is one reason to apply utility maximization to decisions alone. The restriction does not sacrifice substance. It does not actually eliminate any act an ideal agent is certain she can perform. Such acts correspond to decisions. A nondecision an agent is certain she can perform may be represented by a decision to perform it. The decision may substitute for the nondecision because they are equally within the agent's control and have the same utility. Deciding is not obstructionist for ideal agents. Any act an agent can perform, except a spontaneous act, may be the product of a decision. If an agent is certain she can perform the act, she is certain she can decide to perform it and then carry out her decision. Also, decision is costless under my idealizations. A decision to perform an act has no relevant consequences besides the act and its consequences. Without decision costs, an act whose execution is certain has the same utility as a decision to perform that act. So the decision to perform the act may replace the act in maximization problems. The special case of a spontaneous act may be taken as the product of the null decision, a decision without content. A rational ideal agent in ideal circumstances assigns it the utility of maximizing among spontaneous acts at the moment. Consequently, considering all decisions amounts to considering each act whose execution is certain, and maximizing utility among decisions maximizes utility among those acts. Action problems reduce to decision problems.[5]

My idealizations justify focusing on decisions, but that focus has an independent warrant, too. Utility maximization is a necessary condition of rationality for ideal agents. Therefore, its restriction to decisions does not conflict with its extension to all momentary acts an agent is certain she can perform. No conflict arises if to be rational a decision, besides maximizing utility among rival possible decisions, must also maximize utility in a more inclusive set of momentary acts. My restricted principle is not threatened by the possibility that utility maximization governs momentary acts besides decisions.

Making decisions the comparison set for the principle of utility maximization conforms with tradition. The principle of utility maximization belongs to decision theory. Textbook examples explicitly treat acts but implicitly treat decisions to perform acts. The acts specified give the contents of the decisions considered. The examples assume that an act's consequences do not differ relevantly from the consequences of a decision to perform the act. Restricting utility maximization to decisions is convenient and sets the stage for dealing with decision costs.

A.2. Utility of Worlds

Broome (1991) presents three dimensions along which an option's utility may be divided into components. They are the dimensions of possible outcomes, time, and people. He considers the possibility of dividing an option's utility into components that concern sorts of good such as the realization of an agent's goals, say, fame and comfort, but does not think that the analysis can be achieved (25–26). Binmore (1998: 362–63) distinguishes direct utility that attaches to final ends from indirect utility that attaches to means. Direct utility focuses on outcomes, is insensitive to changes in information, and assesses realizations of goals. Indirect utility focuses on acts, is sensitive to changes in information, and assesses prospects for realizations of goals. In a decision problem, Binmore does not analyze indirect utility in terms of direct utility, nor does he analyze an outcome's direct utility in terms of the agent's final ends. He defines indirect utility, or utility tout court, in terms of choices so that an agent's deciding in a way that maximizes utility just amounts to deciding in a way that is consistent with the agent's other decisions (1994: 50–51). He does not think that utility can be interpreted so that an agent's utility assignment explains a decision's rationality (180–81).

Broome and Binmore describe a traditional method of analyzing a world's utility in terms of basic goals or final ends but do not flesh out that method. This section formulates the method precisely to explain a world's utility and, through it, an option's utility. A precursor is Keeney and Raiffa's (1976) method of assessing an option's outcome in terms of multiple objectives.

Given full information and other idealizations, section 2.1.2 claims that an act's utility equals the utility of the act's outcome, the trimmed world that would be realized if the act were realized. The utility of the act's world depends on an agent's basic intrinsic attitudes. To introduce these attitudes, I first consider intrinsic attitudes.

The intrinsic attitudes of interest are intrinsic desire, aversion, and indifference. These differ from their extrinsic counterparts in evaluating a proposition with respect to its logical consequences and not also other features of its realization, such as its causal consequences. Thus, a person's intrinsic desire to be wise attends only to the logical consequences of being wise (such as being prudent) and not also to wisdom's monetary rewards.[6]

An intrinsic desire is not a desire that is intrinsic, but rather a desire whose grounds are intrinsic features of its object's realization. A person's intrinsic attitude toward a proposition depends on not only the intrinsic features of the proposition, the proposition's logical consequences, but also the person's evaluation of those features. She evaluates the proposition's realization, the realization of its logical consequences. One person may intrinsically desire that the Cubs win the World Series while another person lacks that desire. Both nonetheless evaluate the same proposition, focusing on only its logical consequences. Moreover, a person may have an intrinsic and an extrinsic desire concerning the same proposition. She may intrinsically desire to be healthy because of health's logical consequences (such as life) and extrinsically desire to be healthy because of health's causal consequences (such as productivity). The type of evaluation affects the character of the attitude to the proposition, although the proposition itself is constant.

An agent's *basic* intrinsic desires, aversions, and attitudes of indifference are the attitudes that cause the agent's other intrinsic desires, aversions, and attitudes of indifference. For example, an agent's basic intrinsic desires to be healthy and to be wise may cause her intrinsic desire to be healthy and wise. An agent's basic intrinsic attitudes (BITs) are the foundation of her intrinsic attitudes and her utility assignment.[7]

In a rational ideal agent, intrinsic attitudes obey rules of coherence, and so intrinsic attitudes have a certain structure. In other agents, they are less regimented. Because causation may operate in various ways, anomalies may arise: (1) a person's extrinsic desire for money may prompt thoughts about having the wisdom to spend well; these thoughts about wisdom may then produce an intrinsic desire for wisdom; (2) an agent's intrinsic desire for health may lead to thoughts about having the wisdom to live well, which then produce an intrinsic desire for wisdom; (3) a person may think about health and then wisdom and consequently intrinsically desire wisdom more strongly; as a result, he may think about wisdom and then health and consequently intrinsically desire health more strongly. The symbiotic relation between the intrinsic desires may ratchet up their intensities in a mutually supportive way. Are these three anomalies trouble for the view that BITs are a causal foundation for other intrinsic attitudes (ITs)?

The foundational thesis is this: BITs are sufficient sustaining causes of other ITs, and no ITs are sufficient sustaining causes of any BIT. A sufficient cause is a complete cause, not just a contributing cause. A sustaining cause's effect ends as soon as the cause ceases. The cause is contemporaneous with its effect, not just prior to its effect. As a table holds up a vase at the same time the vase is restrained from falling, BITs are contemporaneous with the intrinsic attitudes they cause.

None of the three anomalies refutes the view that BITs are a causal foundation for intrinsic attitudes. They are not cases in which a BIT has as a sufficient sustaining cause some other intrinsic attitudes. They present causes that are not intrinsic attitudes or are not sufficient sustaining causes. Even the case of ratcheting up strengths of intrinsic desire is not a counterexample because a sufficient sustaining cause of a BIT must fully account for the BIT's intensity. No pair of basic intrinsic attitudes is such that each attitude is a sufficient sustaining cause of the other.[8]

A rational ideal agent's BITs are typically independent of information because they assess logical consequences, not empirical consequences. However, suppose that such an agent is ignorant about some a posteriori matters. In some cases, new information, without providing grounds for a change in BITs, may trigger a revision of BITs. BITs are revisable without reason even if the revision process must be judicious. For a rational, fully informed ideal agent, supposition of an act's performance may involve a similar ungrounded change in BITs. It is possible, therefore, that if an act were performed, the agent's utility assignment to worlds would change. For example, joining a group may lead to adopting its values. How should one interpret the utility of an act? Should it assess the act according to current BITs, or according to the BITs the act generates? These generated BITs are hypothetical if the act is not performed and future if the act is performed.

Of course, a rational agent has an intrinsic desire for the realization of her other intrinsic desires and an intrinsic aversion to the realization of her other intrinsic aversions. These attitudes promote conformity between an assessment of an act's world with respect to current BITs and an assessment of that world with respect to BITs the act generates. However, conflicting intrinsic desires may arise. Suppose an agent is intrinsically averse to having a certain intrinsic desire, and consider an unperformed act in whose world the agent has that intrinsic desire and it is realized. In an assessment of the act's world, the intrinsic aversion conflicts with the general intrinsic desire for the realization of intrinsic desires. Because a current intrinsic aversion disapproves of the agent's intrinsic desire in the act's world, the world's utility is lower with respect to current BITs than with respect to BITs in the act's world. It therefore makes a difference whether one evaluates the act's world using current BITs or that world's BITs.

I use current BITs to assess all acts. To yield rational action, the principle of utility maximization needs an assessment of acts using current BITs. Rationality requires that current acts serve current BITs. An act's utility is therefore the current utility of its outcome, not the utility that the act's outcome would have if the act were performed. It is the current utility assignment to the act's world, not a hypothetical or future utility assignment in the act's world.[9]

What counts as a current BIT is ambiguous, however. Are the current BITs those that control an act's selection and obtain just prior to its performance, or those that obtain at the moment the act is performed? The difference matters because the act's performance may immediately create new BITs. Perhaps someone craving a cigarette is repulsed the moment he takes a puff.[10] I take the goal of rationality to be an act supported by contemporaneous BITs. The reasons for an act involve those BITs. Prior higher-order BITs controlling an act's performance should aim for an act supported by BITs when the act is performed. This account of rationality makes BITs a potentially unstable basis of acts' comparison. As one supposes various acts, BITs accompanying the act supposed may vary. Thus, the utility assignment evaluating acts may change from act to act. Chapter 8 addresses this complication. Earlier chapters put it aside by adopting the idealization of a stable basis of comparison for acts.[11]

Ordinary utility evaluates the total outcome of its object's realization. I sometimes call it *comprehensive utility*. An analog that evaluates just the logical consequences of its object's realization I call *intrinsic utility*. The intrinsic utility of a BIT's realization is the degree of intrinsic desire for its realization. This is positive in the case of an intrinsic desire, negative in the case of an intrinsic aversion, and zero in the case of an attitude of intrinsic indifference. I assume an agent with a finite number of BITs, all comparable, forming a causal foundation for intrinsic attitudes as specified. The intrinsic utility of an act's outcome, a possible world, is then the sum of the intrinsic utilities of the objects of BITs realized in that world. The next section supports this tradition-inspired summation principle.

A world's utility is its intrinsic utility because all aspects of its outcome are logical consequences. Because a world's intrinsic utility is the sum of the intrinsic utilities of the objects of BITs realized there, the world's utility is the same sum. Furthermore, an act's utility is its outcome's utility, the utility of the act's world. Transitivity of identity thus yields the following principle of utility:

> An act's utility is the sum of the intrinsic utilities of the objects of the BITs that would be realized if the act were performed.

This principle presumes that agents are ideal and ideally situated, in particular, fully informed. A fully informed agent knows the world that would be realized if the act were performed. This knowledge is presumed by the principle's assumption that an act's utility equals its outcome's utility, its world's utility. If the agent were not fully informed, she might not know the act's outcome and the act's utility might not equal its outcome's utility. The principle's application assumes the existence of quantitative intrinsic utilities, but its accuracy does not. In their absence, the principle does not apply and so is not violated.

The rest of this section responds to some worries about analyzing a world's utility according to the BITs it realizes. I suspect there are two sources of reluctance to embrace this method of analysis, which I call *intrinsic utility analysis*. First, additivity may seem to fail because of complementarity between realizations of BITs. Second, the analysis may seem nonoperational because intrinsic attitudes seem nonoperational. I address these concerns in order.

Cases of alleged counterexamples to additivity either misidentify BITs or else ignore BITs. Suppose that someone likes sardines and likes chocolate but does not like eating both together. Assuming that the only relevant BITs are gustatory, is this a counterexample to the summation principle? To answer, the BITs must be identified. In a normal case, the objects of BITs are the taste of sardines alone and the taste of chocolate alone. These BITs are not realized when both foods are eaten together.

Another case supposes that an agent has an intrinsic desire for leisure and an intrinsic aversion to having this intrinsic desire. Imagine a world in which both the desire and the aversion are realized, and imagine that the world's utility is not a sum of the intrinsic utilities of realizing them. This case is not troubling for the summation principle unless the two intrinsic attitudes are basic and the only basic intrinsic attitudes the world realizes. However, in a rational ideal agent, the sort to which the principle applies, the two attitudes are not basic. They are not causally independent. The intrinsic aversion to desiring leisure influences the intrinsic attitude to leisure.[12]

Next, take the objection that intrinsic attitudes are not operational. Operationist theories of meaning have been refuted.[13] The only plausible operationist standard is inferential. It insists on testability for theoretical entities. Intrinsic utilities meet the standard. In a rational ideal agent, one may identify an intrinsic attitude as one independent of information and a BIT as an intrinsic attitude not caused (in the way explained) by other intrinsic attitudes. Also, one may infer the intrinsic utilities of objects of BITs from the utilities of worlds, which are operationalizable in terms of preferences among gambles, as in Savage (1972: chap. 3). To illustrate the method of inference, grant that health and wisdom are objects of basic intrinsic desires and hence BITs. Suppose, moreover, that no other BITs exist. Then trimmed worlds treat only health and wisdom. Imagine that $U(H \&\ W) = 2$, $U(H \&\ {\sim}W) = U({\sim}H \&\ W) = 1$, and $U({\sim}H \&\ {\sim}W) = 0$. Using IU to stand for intrinsic utility, it follows that $IU(H) = IU(W) = 1$.

One may construct a representation theorem generalizing this pattern of inference. It states sufficient conditions for inferring intrinsic utilities of objects of BITs from utilities of worlds. The theorem assumes that intrinsic utilities of BITs yield intrinsic utilities of worlds in accordance with the summation principle. It also assumes that BITs have a rich, fine-grained structure. Start with basic intrinsic desires (BIDs). Suppose that for any n, there are n BIDs of equal intensity realized with no other BITs in a world of unit intrinsic utility. The intrinsic utility of realizing one of the n BIDs is therefore $1/n$. Suppose also that for any such BID, there are an indefinite number of other compatible BIDs of equal intensity and that every combination of m of them is realized with no other BITs in some world whose intrinsic utility is therefore m/n. As a result, for every positive rational number m/n, a world exists whose intrinsic utility equals that number. Then consider an arbitrary BID. By comparison of a world in which it is realized by itself with other worlds in which combinations of BIDs are realized by themselves, one can measure the intrinsic utility of a BID's realization as finely as desired. The same can be done for basic intrinsic aversions. The theorem thus concludes that if BITs have the structure described, then an IU function over worlds and realizations of BITs exists such that the intrinsic utility of a world is the sum of the intrinsic utilities of objects of BITs it realizes, and, taking intrinsic indifference as a zero point, the function is unique up to multiplication by a positive constant.[14]

A.3. The Principle of Pros and Cons

A general principle of utility analysis, the principle of pros and cons, supports the previous section's analysis of a world's utility. To obtain a proposition's utility, it says to list the pros and cons of the proposition's realization. Then, to indicate the importance of those considerations, attach utilities to them, positive or negative according as they are pros or cons. Finally, add the pros and cons using their utilities to obtain the proposition's utility. This principle of pros and cons is familiar, going back at least to Benjamin Franklin (1945: 280–81). The procedure it sketches needs elaboration in applications. Precision requires directions for listing pros and cons and attaching weights to them.

When applying the principle of pros and cons to obtain a proposition's utility, the first step is to separate considerations bearing on an evaluation of the proposition's realization. The separation of considerations must satisfy two conditions: (1) no consideration may be counted twice, and (2) no relevant consideration may be omitted. If these conditions are not satisfied, then adding the considerations' utilities may not yield the proposition's utility. For double-counting inappropriately boosts the utilities' sum and omission inappropriately lowers it.

It is difficult to divide relevant considerations so that none is omitted or double-counted. The more considerations entertained, the less likely is omission but the more likely is double-counting. Everyday deliberations typically fail to separate relevant considerations adequately. Someone buying a new car, for instance, may rate models according to styling, fuel economy, and other considerations. But if he likes aerodynamic sleekness, a factor affecting his rating for fuel economy also influences his rating for styling. Then adding his ratings implicitly double-counts that factor.

The second step in applying the principle of pros and cons is to obtain the utilities of considerations. A difficulty in this second step is making assessments of utility quantitative. In some cases, one consideration clearly has more utility than another, but not clearly a certain number of times more utility. Because of this difficulty, the principle of pros and cons seems impractical. Like most quantitative methods of treating the mental, it appears unrealistic. Quantitative methods may work for corporations single-mindedly seeking profit, but they seem ungrounded in other contexts.

This worry is not an objection to the principle of pros and cons, but a reservation about its range of application. Where the principle applies, the input for it is available; considerations have quantitative weights. I table the worry by idealizing when applying the principle. I assume circumstances that warrant the applications' quantitative aspects. Methods of utility analysis initially advanced under idealizations may be adjusted later, when the idealizations are removed.

To justify a form of utility analysis using the principle of pros and cons, I investigate the analysis's method of separating considerations and assigning utilities to them. First, I verify that it separates considerations in a way that neither omits nor double-counts any relevant consideration. Then I verify that it assigns considerations suitable utilities. Section A.2's analysis of a world's utility passes the test. Basic intrinsic attitudes (BITs) separate considerations without omission or double-counting. Also, the intrinsic utility of realizing a BIT is an appropriate weight for its realization. Adding the intrinsic utilities of objects of BITs realized in a world thus yields the world's utility. The analysis of a world's utility is a paradigmatic application of the principle of pros and cons.

The principle of pros and cons also supports expected utility analysis (section 2.4). The analysis separates considerations for and against an option according to subjective chances for the option's possible outcomes, as given by a partition of states.[15] Chances for good outcomes are pros; chances for bad outcomes are cons. Given an option's realization, the agent has a chance for each of its possible outcomes. The agent is certain to have the chances for the possible outcomes if he performs the option. Each chance obtains with certainty even if each possible outcome has only a limited probability of obtaining. The division of chances according to a partition of states guarantees that no chance is omitted or double-counted. Even if the relevant possible outcomes are the same for two states, the corresponding chances are different because the probabilities of the possible outcomes come from different states.

The utility of a chance for a possible outcome is the utility of the outcome multiplied by the outcome's probability according to the chance. Adding the utilities of the chances is a way of adding pros and cons. An option's expected utility, the sum of the products of the probabilities and utilities of its possible outcomes, therefore yields its utility.

A.4. Outcomes

Given full information, an act's utility assesses the act's outcome. But given uncertainty, an act's outcome may be unknown. More precisely, an agent may not know the world that would be realized if the act were realized, that is, the act's world. An implicit part of section 2.3's accommodation of uncertainty is a suitable interpretation of an act's outcome, the target of an act's utility assignment.

An act's world is a maximal consistent proposition. Because it may be unknown, its utility may be unknown as well. For an act's appraisal, one needs a utility that is known. Given uncertainty, one cannot take the act's utility as the utility of the act's world because the act's world may be any in the range of worlds where the act is realized. Instead, I take the act's utility to be the utility of the nonmaximal proposition that the act's world obtains. This proposition is true just in case the act's world is realized. Although the proposition's full expression, "The act's world obtains," contains a name of the act's world, the expression "the act's world," that expression does not specify the act's world. In contrast, the full expression of the proposition that is the act's world specifies all the details of the act's world. Given certainty, the utility of the act's world equals the utility of the proposition that the act's world obtains. But given uncertainty, they may differ. The utility of the proposition that the act's world obtains is the utility of a lottery over the worlds where the act is realized, not the utility of one of those worlds. Its utility is an estimate of the utility of the act's world. Although the act's world and its utility may be unknown, the proposition that the act's world obtains, and its utility, are known. I therefore take the proposition that the act's world obtains to express the act's outcome. This interpretation of an act's outcome makes its utility and the act's utility accessible despite uncertainty.[16]

My specification of an act's outcome makes it possible for agents to comply knowingly with utility rules despite uncertainty. In an application of a rule, an agent needs to know the propositions involved and their utilities. To achieve this end, I formulate each rule so that propositional variables are substitutional rather than directly referential. For example, the rule that an act's utility is the utility of its outcome, or $U(a) = U(O[a])$, is taken as a schema where a is a place-holder for a name of a proposition expressing an act rather than as a generalization where *a* has propositions as values. $O[a]$ is to be replaced by a name for the act's outcome, a name the routine O forms from a name for the act. As the previous paragraph explains, the routine yields a name that fully specifies a nonmaximal proposition, the proposition that the act's world obtains. An ideal agent knows the proposition under that standard name despite ignorance of the act's world. The proposition that the act's world obtains is itself fully specified even though it is about a maximal consistent proposition that is not fully specified. Because the act's outcome is fully specified, the agent knows the utility he assigns to it. He is in a position to make sure that its utility equals the act's utility.[17]

Accommodating uncertainty also brings attention to the objects of utility assignments, which, according to section 2.1.2, are propositions. I ascribe to the Russellian view of propositions, expounded, for example, by D. Kaplan (1989). It takes propositions as structured entities (and so not sets of possible worlds) and allows them to contain individuals (and so not just concepts of individuals). Sentences expressing propositions may contain directly referential terms that refer to individuals without the mediation of a Fregean sense. An example of a directly referential term is a variable under an assignment of a value to it. Granting that proper names are directly referential, "Cicero is Tully" and "Cicero is Cicero" express the same proposition because "Cicero" and "Tully" refer to the same individual.

An agent evaluates a proposition according to a way of grasping it, a way indicated in a context by a name of the proposition.[18] Strictly speaking, utility attaches to a proposition taken a certain way. Ways of grasping a proposition add grain to the objects of utility. My utility rules make the additional grain irrelevant by specifying a standard way of grasping a proposition. They fix the way a proposition is grasped to make the way of grasping it an otiose parameter. My rules assume that a propositional variable is replaced by a standard sentential name of a proposition, under which ideal agents grasp the proposition. A propositional variable is not replaced, for instance, by the name "Quine's favorite proposition." This descriptive name may denote the proposition that Cicero is Tully, but that proposition may not be grasped under the descriptive name, and so under that name an agent may not know its utility. An agent's responsibilities under standards of rationality concern propositions as the agent grasps them.

Also, in utility laws a propositional variable must be replaced uniformly by the same sentential name for a proposition. Otherwise, a proposition with two sentential names may receive two utilities, one for each of two ways the proposition is grasped. For instance, U(Cicero is Tully) may differ from U(Cicero is Cicero), even though "Cicero is Tully" and "Cicero is Cicero" express the same proposition, if the agent does not know that Tully is Cicero. Multiple occurrences of a single propositional variable in a utility law should not occasion questions about identity of propositions.

In contrast, occurrences of multiple variables in a utility law may generate such questions. Consider the two-variable utility law that $U(p) = U(q)$ if p and q are a priori equivalent. Under my interpretation, it says that the identity holds if it is an a priori matter that the names replacing p and q name equivalent propositions.

The law permits U(Cicero is Tully) to differ from U(Cicero is Cicero) because it is not an a priori matter that the proposition that Cicero is Tully is the same as, and thus equivalent to, the proposition that Cicero is Cicero.

In short, utility laws often function as if utility attached to sentences rather than propositions. I take utility to attach to propositions, nonetheless, because some sentences are ambiguous and indexical, so not sufficiently fine-grained. The same sentence may express different propositions in different contexts.[19] In addition, in some cases an agent knows that two sentential names for a proposition express the same proposition. In those cases, the agent's utility assignment is insensitive to the name used, and so sentences are too fine-grained.

Given my idealizations, rational ideal agents knowingly comply with utility rules in instances that uniformly replace propositional variables with standard sentential names of propositions and follow prescribed routines for constructing more complex propositional names from those sentential names. In particular, they comply with applications of the expected utility principle, $U(o) = \Sigma_i P(s_i$ given $o)U(o$ given $s_i)$, given transparent designations of options and states.

A.5. Intrinsic Utility Analysis

Expected utility analysis provides a reliable method of calculating an option's utility given uncertainty about the option's outcome. However, when agents are nonideal and in nonideal circumstances, it is often advantageous to have multiple ways of generating an option's utility. Conditions may block or impede application of one form of analysis but leave open another form of analysis. This section presents a new form of utility analysis. It draws on section A.2's method of analyzing a world's utility according to basic intrinsic attitudes (BITs) realized.

Given uncertainty, an option's utility is an estimate of, and not necessarily the same as, the utility of the option's world. Its value may depend on the utilities of many possible worlds. Nonetheless, intrinsic utilities are useful for analyzing an option's utility. The intrinsic utilities of BITs' objects and their probabilities of realization given an option yield an option's utility. The utility analysis treats realizations of an agent's BITs as possible results of an option o's realization. It assumes that there is an intrinsic utility of realizing each BIT and a probability of realizing each BIT if o were realized. To obtain $U(o)$ it then takes the intrinsic utility of each BIT's object, weights it by its probability given o, and adds the products as follows:

Intrinsic utility analysis. $U(o) = \Sigma_j P(\mathrm{BIT}_j$ given $o)IU(\mathrm{BIT}_j)$, where BIT_j ranges over the objects of all BITs.

In the analysis, unlike the probabilities of BITs' objects, the intrinsic utilities of BITs' objects need not be conditional on the option. The option's supposition does not influence their intrinsic utilities, assuming the stability of BITs, because intrinsic utilities depend only on logical consequences and o's realization does not change the logical consequences of a BIT's realization.

The assumptions for the principle of intrinsic utility analysis are similar to those for section A.2's analysis of a world's utility. The principle assumes the rationality of input probabilities and utilities and the absence of cognitive limits. Conformity with the principle is a requirement of rationality for agents meeting my idealizations.

The principle of pros and cons (section A.3) supports intrinsic utility analysis. An option's pros and cons are the chances it generates for realizations of BITs. Chances for realizations of basic intrinsic desires are pros; chances for realizations of basic intrinsic aversions are cons. The weights of these considerations are their utilities. The utility of a chance for the realization of a BIT is the probability of its realization times the intrinsic utility of its realization. The chances for BITs' realizations cover all relevant considerations without double-counting. Addition of the utilities of their chances of realization therefore yields the option's utility. Weirich (2001a: sec. A.3) shows that intrinsic utility analysis is consistent with expected utility analysis.

A.6. Conditional Probability and Utility

The principles of optimization, utility maximization, and expected utility entertain options and states not realized. How are those unrealized possibilities imagined? What features of the actual world do their suppositions preserve?

The principle of optimization (section 2.1) evaluates an act by evaluating the act's world, the world that would be realized if the act were realized. It matters that an act's world is entertained by supposing that the act *were* realized rather than that the act *is* realized. The *subjunctive* form of supposition is sensitive to the act's causal influence, whereas the *indicative* form of supposition is sensitive to the act's epistemic influence. The principle of optimization, being a principle of rational action, should be sensitive to an act's causal influence rather than its epistemic influence. In favorable circumstances, a rational act causes a good outcome rather than creates evidence of a good outcome.[20]

According to expected utility analysis (section 2.4),

$$U(o) = \Sigma_i P(s_i \text{ given } o) U(o \text{ given } s_i).$$

This principle also prompts questions about the appropriate way of supposing options and states. How should one interpret $U(o \text{ given } s_i)$, the utility of an option given a state? The role of the state is to provide information about the option's outcome. Thus, the conditional utility supposes the state indicatively to bring to bear the information it carries. On the other hand, the conditional utility evaluates the option to direct the agent's decision. It considers the option's causal consequences. It therefore supposes the option subjunctively. It seeks the outcome that would obtain if the option were realized. Because the option and state are supposed differently, an option's utility given a state should not be taken as the utility of the option and state conjoined. Conjoining the option and state to form a single object of utility makes it impossible to do justice to each. Moreover, the expected utility principle imposes no restriction on states. Hence, it has to handle cases in which an option and its negation serve as states. This means evaluating $U(o \text{ given } \sim o)$.

For generality, this utility should have a value, and intuitively it does, but intuitively $U(o \ \& \sim o)$ has no value, as Armendt (1988) observes. For these reasons, the utility of an option given a state is best taken as a primitive concept introduced by its role in utility theory.

How should one interpret $P(s_i$ given $o)$, the probability of a state given an option? In cases in which options may influence states, the probability of a state given an option should register the option's influence on the state rather than the evidence the option provides for the state. It should assess the state under a subjunctive supposition of the option. It should consider possibilities if the option were realized. I therefore take a state's probability given an option as a primitive quantity rather than, as in probability theory, as a ratio of nonconditional probabilities. According to the standard definition, a state's probability given an option registers the evidence the option provides for the state rather than its causal influence on the state. In contrast, I interpret $P(s_i$ given $o)$ so that it equals $P(s_i)$ unless o does not merely provide evidence for s but causally influences s.[21]

Section 2.4's formulation of expected utility analysis needs further refinement to fully register the attractive or unattractive effects of an option's influence on states. Multiplying $U(o$ given $s_i)$ by $P(s_i$ given $o)$ does not suffice. Although the probability takes account of the influence of o on s_i, the utility must be modified to take account of that influence. For example, suppose that the agent desires that o cause s_i. This desire does not boost $U(o$ given $s_i)$, even if the agent believes that o causes s_i. The indicative supposition that s_i makes the belief idle. The supposition makes s_i part of the background for entertaining o and so precludes o's causing s_i. Although $U(o$ given $s_i)$ entertains worlds, not just causal consequences, the supposition of s_i carries implications about causal relations and so directs evaluation to a set of worlds where o does not cause s_i. The conditional utilities used in expected utility analysis must have suppositions that direct evaluation to the right set of worlds.

To obtain a utility that registers the influence of o on s_i, I conditionalize on the conditional that s_i if o. I replace $U(o$ given $s_i)$ with $U(o$ given $(s_i$ if $o))$. The latter quantity is the utility of the outcome that obtains if the option *were* realized given that it *is* the case that the state *would* obtain if the option *were* realized. Even though the conditional is supposed indicatively, the conditional is itself subjunctive, and in it s_i is supposed subjunctively.[22] The change in type of supposition for s_i makes the revised conditional utility sensitive to o's causal influence on s_i. The complex condition is sensitive to o's causal influence on s_i, unlike the supposition that s_i obtains, with its implication in the context of $U(o$ given $s_i)$ that s_i obtains independently of the option realized. Because the supposition that s_i if o leaves it open that o causes s_i, the revised conditional utility increases if the agent believes and desires that o causes s_i. Using the subjunctive conditional as the condition for an option's utility accommodates cases in which the option has a desirable or undesirable influence on the state.[23]

Adopting these revisions yields an accurate, general form of expected utility analysis. According to it,

$$U(o) = \Sigma_i P(s_i \text{ given } o)U(o \text{ given } (s_i \text{ if } o)).$$

With respect to a partition of states $\{s_i\}$, the summation ranges over only s_i such that it is possible that (s_i if o). This restriction is necessary because utility is not defined with respect to an impossible condition. Given my interpretation of the suppositions involved, the restriction ignores only s_i for which $P(s_i$ given $o)$ equals zero. So ignoring those states would not affect an option's expected utility even if utilities conditional on them were defined.[24]

A.7. Informed Utility's Primacy

Section 2.3 uses the goal of maximizing informed utility to explain the goal of maximizing utility. Maximizing informed utility is the primary goal, it claims. Beebee and Papineau (1997: 238–43) argue for the reverse. They claim that maximizing utility is the primary goal of rational decision and that maximizing informed utility is a subordinate goal. They state their claim in terms of expected utility rather than utility, but one may identify the two. Also, rather than contrast informed and current utility, they contrast utility resting on single-case probabilities and utility resting on relative probabilities, novel probabilities standing between subjective and objective probabilities. In the cases I consider, however, utility resting on single-case probabilities is informed utility. Moreover, utility resting on relative probabilities, for my purposes, is not importantly different from current utility, which rests on subjective probabilities.

Beebee and Papineau support their claim about the primacy of the goal of maximizing current utility by using that goal to derive the goal of maximizing informed utility. For the derivation, they use Ramsey's (1990) and Good's (1967) theorem about expectations of expectations to derive the intermediate goal of gathering relevant information. They move from current utility maximization, to gathering information, to informed utility maximization. The crucial theorem shows that relevant information increases the expected utility of the option of maximum expected utility, the expected expected utility of the option adopted. Beebee and Papineau conclude that, given the availability of additional relevant information, gathering the information has higher expected utility than deciding without it.

An example displays the reasoning behind their argument. "Imagine you are presented with three sealed boxes. You know that a ball has been placed in one, and that the other two are empty, and that some chance mechanism has given each box the same 1/3 single-case probability of getting the ball. Felicity offers you her £3 to your £2, with you winning the total stake if the ball is in box 1. You can either accept or decline the bet now (option G, for 'go'), or you can look in box 3 and then accept or decline the same bet (option W, for 'wait-and-see')" (1997: 239). Notice that the chance mechanism has finished operating, so that the single-case probability that the ball is in a given box is an informed probability with the value 1 or 0 according as the ball is or is not in that box.

Take utilities to equal expected gains in pounds. The expected gain from G is £0 because you will decline the bet, its being disadvantageous given current information. The expected gain from W is £0.33 because if you see a ball in box 3 you will not bet, betting's then having an expected loss of £2, and if you do not see a ball in box 3 you will bet, betting's then having an expected gain of £0.50. Hence, W is preferable to G. In general it is better, if possible, to wait for additional relevant information before acting.

This derivation is inadequate for showing that the goal of maximizing utility is primary, however. It depends on the assumption that acquiring information relevant to meeting goals is possible and has negligible cost. Not all cases meet that assumption. For instance, acquiring information may overload the mind or trigger destructive emotions. When the assumption is not met, the goal of maximizing utility does not yield the goal of maximizing informed utility. Thus, the derivation incompletely grounds the latter goal.

Beebee and Papineau's derivation of the goal of maximizing informed utility also has another flaw. The step from current utility maximization to gathering information uses anticipated future utilities to calculate current utilities. To illustrate, return to the example. Because one knows that on looking in box 3 and seeing a ball the utility of betting on box 1 will be −2, one uses that value as the current utility of that outcome of W. This is sensible because the future utility is known to be informed, and maximizing informed utility is a goal. But the goal of maximizing informed utility may not be used to derive the goal of gathering information, if the latter is to be used to derive the goal of maximizing informed utility. It is circular to use the goal of gathering information, with its implicit appeal to the goal of maximizing informed utility, to carry out that derivation.

In the argument for the value of gathering information, it is crucial that future utilities are known to be more informed than current utilities. In the example, the mere fact that the future utility of betting on box 1 will have a certain value given some information that W's realization might yield is not a good reason to use that value as the current utility of that outcome of W. To illustrate, suppose that you look in box 3 and then decide whether to go, G, or wait, W. Imagine that you see a ball in box 3. Also suppose that you know that after waiting you will forget you inspected box 3 and think you saw a ball in box 1. After waiting, you will bet, the expected gain from betting's being £3 then. It would be a mistake to take that future expected gain as the current utility of that result of W. The future expected gain is less well informed than the current expected gain. Future utilities are good reasons for current utilities only if informed.[25]

To dramatize the inconclusiveness of Beebee and Papineau's derivation of the goal of maximizing informed utility, consider again its step from maximizing expected utility to maximizing expected expected utility. This step uses the principle that the goal of maximizing x justifies the goal of maximizing the expectation of x. This general principle instantiated to informed utility asserts that the goal of maximizing informed utility justifies the goal of maximizing expected informed utility, that is, maximizing utility. Hence, the reasoning their derivation assumes, generalized, grounds the reverse derivation.

Beebee and Papineau have not derived the goal of maximizing informed utility from the goal of maximizing current utility. Their derivation uses the goal they attempt to derive. Moreover, the goal of maximizing utility may be obtained from the goal of maximizing informed utility, contrary to their claims (1997: 242).

As section 2.3 explains, given standard idealizations, maximizing utility is the rational way to pursue the goal of maximizing informed utility. Maximizing informed utility is the primary goal of rational decisions.

Section 2.3's method of obtaining the goal of maximizing utility from the goal of maximizing informed utility takes probability as the guide of life. Given uncertainty, maximizing expected informed utility is sensible. It amounts to maximizing utility. In each particular case, the rational way of pursuing informed utility is to maximize utility. This derivation of the goal of maximizing utility is immediate, but the principle of expectation is basic and not a likely candidate for a deep-going derivation from a more fundamental principle.

Showing that one goal is derivable from another is an inconclusive demonstration of primacy because mutual derivation is possible. The usual way of stating the goal of maximizing utility comprehends the special case of full information so that the goal of maximizing informed utility follows from it directly. Given section 2.3's reverse derivation, mutual derivability follows. Derivability does not indicate which goal is primary.

To verify maximizing informed utility's primacy over maximizing utility, consider which goal explains the other. Consider how changes in utility assignments affect other utility assignments. Imagine that an agent wants a prize and wants a lottery ticket for it, too. Suppose that he were to cease desiring the prize. Would he continue to want the lottery ticket? No, it would lose its appeal. On the other hand, suppose that he were to cease desiring the lottery ticket. Would he continue to want the prize? Yes, in the most plausible scenario, he desires the prize but not the ticket because he thinks the ticket offers a negligible chance of winning the prize. The utility of the prize is primary and the utility of the ticket subordinate. In general, informed utility of possible worlds generates utility in accordance with expected utility analysis, and therefore informed utility is primary and ordinary utility subordinate. Maximizing the primary form of utility is a rational agent's basic goal.

Appendix B: Consistency of Calculations of Utilities

I have proposed several methods of calculating an option's utility. Are they are consistent? Verifying consistency is a good way of showing that my utility principles build an accurate, systematic theory. Weirich (2001a: appendix) verifies consistency in ideal cases. This appendix treats consistency in nonideal cases. It verifies the consistency of two methods of utility analysis in cases with unknown, inaccessible probabilities or utilities. The two methods, presented in section 5.1.3, are higher-order expected utility analysis and ersatz first-order expected utility analysis, that is, first-order expected utility analysis using estimates. The methods are generalized here by incorporating section A.6's generalization of expected utility analysis, which replaces $U(o$ given $s_i)$ with $U(o$ given $(s_i$ if $o))$.

B.1. Verification of Consistency

My way of demonstrating consistency, following Sobel (1989), is to specify a canonical method of computing utilities and then show that the various forms of utility analysis reduce to the canonical computation of utilities. The reduction requires canonical methods of obtaining all the input for the various forms of utility analysis. So, more fully, the canonical methods are, first, a canonical form of utility analysis and, second, a canonical way of obtaining input for the other forms of utility analysis from the input for the canonical form of utility analysis. This section specifies the canonical methods for ideal cases and then extends them to nonideal cases.

Sections A.2, A.5, and A.6 present detailed accounts of intrinsic and expected utility analyses. This section adopts their assumption of a finite number of basic intrinsic attitudes (BITs) and then, after trimming irrelevancies, a finite number of possible worlds. As the canonical method of computing utility, I take a combination of expected and intrinsic utility analyses, that is, expected utility analysis with respect to possible worlds and intrinsic utility analysis of worlds. According to this canonical method of computing utility,

$U(o) = \Sigma_i P(w_i \text{ given } o)\Sigma_{j \in \{ji\}}IU(BIT_j)$, where w_i ranges over possible worlds and $\{ji\}$ indexes the objects of the BITs realized in w_i.

In other words, an option's utility is a probability-weighted average of the sums of the intrinsic utilities of realizing BITs in sets of BITs that might be realized if the option were realized.

As canonical methods of obtaining input for all forms of utility analysis from probabilities of worlds and intrinsic utilities of objects of BITs, I adopt familiar methods. For expected utility analysis, I derive probabilities of states from probabilities of worlds in the usual way, and I derive utilities of the form $U(o$ given $(s$ if $o))$ by conditional expected utility analysis using worlds as states.

Verifying that compliance with section 5.1.3's methods of utility analysis is a goal achievable by fully rational agents requires verifying the methods' consistency in cases where agents are fully rational even if nonideal in ways envisioned by those methods, that is, even if agents do not know and cannot learn all probabilities and utilities they assign. Because the agents of interest are fully rational, the verification may assume basic coherence constraints for probability and utility assignments. I assume, in particular, that utility assignments conform to canonical analyses, and so, for instance, the utility of a world equals the sum of the intrinsic utilities of the objects of BITs realized there.

Weirich (2001a: appendix) shows that given the canonical method of calculating utility—and the canonical ways of computing input for other methods—my basic forms of utility analysis agree. It shows that expected and intrinsic utility analyses agree with the canonical method and so agree with each other. Utilities computable by the two forms of analysis have the same value.

My verifications of consistency involve canonical reasons for or against an option. The canonical reasons are combinations of probabilities and utilities. Specifically, I take a canonical reason to be the intrinsic utility of a BIT's realization in a possible world, after weighting the intrinsic utility by the probability of the possible world. That is, a canonical reason is a chance for a BIT's realization. The various forms of utility analysis employ various helpful ways of partitioning these canonical reasons. My proofs show that the analyses are consistent by showing that they constitute different ways of adding up the same canonical reasons in accordance with the principle of pros and cons (section A.3).

To motivate the extension of my canonical analysis to nonideal cases, I consider the role of canonical reasons in those cases. A higher-order expected utility analysis for cases with an unknown probability uses probabilities of the probability. It is a finer-grained analysis than first-order expected utility analysis. Higher-order expected utility analysis may be finer- and finer-grained without end—using probabilities of probabilities, probabilities of probabilities of probabilities, and so on. An agent with unlimited powers of attitude formation may have finer- and finer-grained reasons without end. A canonical reason, therefore, is not a top from which to work down, or a bottom from which to work up, but a middle from which to work out. A canonical reason is a benchmark reason, not a foundational reason; finer as well as coarser reasons also exist. Both addition and division of canonical reasons yield noncanonical methods of utility analysis. The noncanonical methods compute utilities either by adding up canonical reasons like marbles or by dividing them more and more thinly, like jam spread on toast.[1]

Given the possibility of reasons finer- and finer-grained without end, I take utility analysis to add weights of categories of reasons. The elements of a partition of reasons provide the categories. Utilities provide their weights. Categories of reasons receive weights rather than reasons themselves because reasons may be infinitely divisible so that their weights are infinitesimal. Adding the weights of canonical categories yields the weights of coarser categories. Dividing the weights of canonical categories yields the weights of finer categories, as, for example, dividing a unit into three equal parts yields as one part the quantity 1/3. Different additions of a quantity's division into parts yield the same sum no matter whether the parts are themselves sums of units or fractions of units. The consistency proofs show the same for weights of categories of reasons.

The categories are similar to events comprised of points in probability space. Probabilities are assigned to events taken as sets of points in an infinitely divisible probability space. Weights are assigned to categories comprised of points in an infinitely divisible space of reasons. One could use measure theory and integral calculus, as in probability theory, for adding an infinite number of categories of reasons. But for simplicity of technical methods, I assume a finite number of categories at every level of division of reasons into categories.[2]

I say that a coarser-grained analysis *subsumes* a finer-grained analysis. Thus, an analysis using a probability subsumes a finer-grained analysis using probabilities of the probability. My procedure for verifying consistency is to show that all forms of utility analysis either reduce to, or are subsumed by, the canonical analysis. Non-canonical analyses either partition the set of canonical reasons or partition the canonical reasons themselves and, consequently, by addition laws, conform with the canonical analysis.

In treating nonideal cases, one must allow for the nonexistence of the input and output for my methods of utility analysis. How can one use reduction to, or subsumption by, the canonical analysis to show consistency in cases where input or output utilities do not exist?

To begin an answer, note that the methods of utility analysis do not conflict when an output utility, say, $U(o)$, does not exist. In that case, being inapplicable, they make no claims about its value and so do not yield inconsistent values for it. Similarly, when the output utility exists but the input utilities do not, the methods of utility analysis make no claims and so make no inconsistent claims. My consistency check must cover only cases where the input and output quantities exist for a pair of methods so that both are applicable. Only in these cases does the possibility of inconsistency arise.

Most of the relevant cases may be treated by reduction to the canonical analysis. The only troublesome cases are those where the input for the canonical calculation of some utilities does not exist, but those utilities exist and serve as input for two analyses of an existing utility. Then it seems that one may not use the canonical method to show that the two analyses are consistent. For example, suppose that probabilities of worlds do not exist, but the input exists for two distinct expected utility analyses of $U(o)$, which also exists. How can one use the canonical method to show that the two expected utility analyses are consistent? The method requires the probabilities of worlds.

Where the input for the canonical method does not exist, I assume as a rule of rationality that the input for all utility analyses agrees with its calculation by the canonical method under some specification of input for the canonical method. That is, where probabilities of worlds or intrinsic utilities of objects of BITs do not exist, I assume that rational utility assignments nonetheless agree with canonical analyses under a hypothetical specification of those missing quantities. In other words, rational utility assignments are compatible with being derived canonically from probabilities of worlds and intrinsic utilities of objects of BITs. Therefore, to be rational, inputs for utility analyses must be *as if* computed in the canonical way. This assumption limits the range of cases, with fully rational agents, across which my methods of utility analysis must be consistent. It is similar to section 4.4's assumption that rational comparative probability and utility judgments are compatible with expected utility analysis under a quantization of them.

My assumption entails that where the input for a utility's analysis does not exist, the utility nonetheless agrees with the analysis under some specification of the input and, where the common input of two analyses of the utility does not exist, the utility agrees with both analyses under the same specification of their input. Given my assumptions about rationality, in cases where agents are fully rational, my utility analyses are consistent, even where the input for a canonical utility analysis is absent, because the analyses are all compatible given the canonical methods of obtaining their input.

The next section considers nonideal cases where an agent is fully rational but has unknown probabilities or utilities. Section 5.1.3's higher-order and ersatz utility analyses apply. How do my canonical methods constrain probabilities of an unknown probability and other input for analyses of utilities with respect to the conscious mind if probabilities of worlds and intrinsic utilities of objects of BITs exist but are unknown? This section's rationality requirement resolves the problem. According to it, probabilities of a probability and the like must agree, under canonical calculations, with some specification of probabilities of worlds and intrinsic utilities of objects of BITs. They therefore must yield coherent expected value estimates of unknown probabilities and utilities. The estimates must in turn yield expected values of expected utilities and ersatz expected utilities that yield options' utilities with respect to the conscious mind.

A finishing touch is needed. Strictly speaking, an analysis of an unknown probability using probabilities of the probability does not divide an unknown probability-reason into finer-grained reasons. The unknown probability is not a reason in the relevant sense; it has no deliberative force because it is unavailable. The analysis's estimate of the unknown probability is the corresponding reason, and probabilities of the probability are the reason's components. An ersatz expected utility analysis using the estimate divides that reason into component reasons that combine with utilities to assess canonical reasons with respect to the conscious mind.

To cover consistency in the next section's nonideal cases, I therefore extend the canonical analysis. I adopt as canonical a first-order expected utility analysis of

$U(o)$ using expected value estimates of missing quantities, that is, an ersatz expected utility analysis. For example, if a probability exists but is unknown, I use an estimate of it. These expected value estimates replace the unknown quantities for decision purposes. To illustrate, the extended canonical analysis for nonideal cases where probabilities are unknown advances this equality:

$U(o) = \Sigma_j[\Sigma_k P_o(P_o(w_j) = p_k)p_k]\Sigma_i IU(BIT_{ij})$, where p_k ranges over the possible values of $P_o(w_j)$ and BIT_{ij} ranges over the objects of the BITs realized in w_j.

The canonical analysis for the ideal case follows from this extension to the nonideal case because probabilities of probabilities are 0 or 1 when probabilities are known.

B.2. Consistency of Higher-Order and Ersatz Utility Analyses

Section 5.1.3 introduces higher-order and ersatz utility analyses for cases where quantities needed for first-order utility analysis exist but are unknown and inaccessible. In these cases, an agent is nonideal because unaware of his probability and utility assignments, but psychological opacity is his only limitation. He still knows all a priori truths and is fully rational. The two forms of utility analysis yield an option's utility with respect to the agent's conscious mind. This utility assignment motivates the agent's decisions.

Second-order expected utility analysis is a method of estimating an option's first-order expected utility, with respect to a partition with n states, in cases where only first-order probabilities are unknown. Let s and p_i be respectively ordered n-tuples of states and their probabilities given o, so that $P_o(s) = p_i$ stands for $P_o(s_1) = p_{i_1}$ & $P_o(s_2) = p_{i_2}$ & ... & $P_o(s_n) = p_{i_n}$. According to a second-order expected utility analysis,

$$U(o) = \Sigma_i P_o(P_o(s) = p_i)\Sigma_j p_{ij} U(o \text{ given } (s_j \text{ if } o))$$

where p_i ranges over possible n-tuples of probabilities for the n states and s_j ranges over the n states.

An ersatz first-order expected utility analysis using estimates of unknown probabilities computes the same utility using the same resources. According to it,

$$U(o) = \Sigma_j[\Sigma_k P_o(P_o(s_j) = p_k)]U(o \text{ given } (s_j \text{ if } o))$$

where p_k ranges over the possible values of $P_o(s_j)$. Is the second-order expected utility analysis consistent with this ersatz first-order expected utility analysis? To illustrate the issue and its resolution, let me first demonstrate consistency in a special case.

When the probabilities of states in a two-state, first-order expected utility analysis are unknown, a second-order expected utility analysis follows the tree in figure B.1. Here p is the probability of s given o according to the possible case $P(s) = p$, a mental state. $P(s)$ according to the case is the same whether or not the

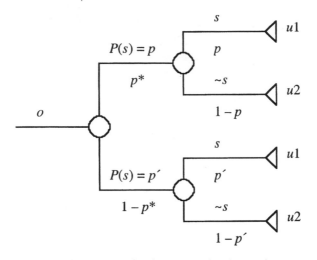

FIGURE B.1. A second-order expected utility analysis.

case obtains, so the probability according to the case is probabilistically independent of the case itself. The situation is analogous for p', the probability of s given o
according to the possible case $P(s) = p'$. Using this second-order analysis tree,
$U(o) = p^* [pu_1 + (1 - p)u_2] + (1 - p^*)[p' u_1 + (1 - p')u_2]$.

On the other hand, one may estimate the unknown probability of a state given
o as its probability-weighted average and use that estimate to conduct an ersatz
first-order expected utility analysis. The analysis follows the tree in figure B.2.
Accordingly, $U(o) = [p^*p + (1 - p^*)p']u_1 + [1 - (p^*p + (1 - p^*)p')]u_2$. By algebra,
the two calculations of $U(o)$ yield the same value.

To show the consistency of the two methods of utility analysis in general, I first
observe that because second-order estimates of the probabilities of worlds yield all
probability estimates for states, each method of utility analysis may be reduced to
an application that uses worlds for states. The reduction is similar to Weirich's
(2001a: sec. A.2) reduction of an arbitrary expected utility analysis of $U(o)$ to an
expected utility analysis of $U(o)$ using worlds.

Next, I show that with worlds as states, a second-order expected utility
analysis reduces to an ersatz first-order expected utility analysis using estimates of

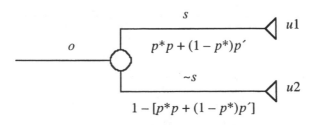

FIGURE B.2. An ersatz first-order expected utility analysis.

probabilities of worlds. Let w stand for the n-tuple of worlds and p_i stand for an n-tuple of probability values for the worlds. The reduction rests on the identity

$$P_o(P_o(w_j) = p_k) = \Sigma_i P_o(P_o(w) = p_i \,\&\, p_{ij} = p_k)$$

where $p_{ij} = p_k$ indicates that the probability of w_j according to p_i is p_k. According to this identity, the probability of a particular probability value for a world is the sum of the probabilities of the n-tuples giving the world's probability that value. The identity holds because the possible n-tuples of probabilities of worlds cover the possible values of the probability of a single world.

In virtue of the identity, for each world w_j,

$$
\begin{aligned}
\Sigma_k P_o(P_o(w_j) = p_k)p_k &= \Sigma_k[\Sigma_i P_o(P_o(w) = p_i \,\&\, p_{ij} = p_k)]p_k \\
&= \Sigma_k \Sigma_i P_o(P_o(w) = p_i \,\&\, p_{ij} = p_k)p_k \\
&= \Sigma_k \Sigma_i P_o(P_o(w) = p_i \,\&\, p_{ij} = p_k)p_{ij} \\
&= \Sigma_i \Sigma_k P_o(P_o(w) = p_i \,\&\, p_{ij} = p_k)p_{ij} \\
&= \Sigma_i P_o(P_o(w) = p_i)p_{ij}.
\end{aligned}
$$

The last step holds because if $p_{ij} \neq p_k$, then $P_o(P_o(w) = p_i \,\&\, p_{ij} = p_k) = 0$. Then, according to a second-order expected utility analysis,

$$
\begin{aligned}
U(o) &= \Sigma_i P_o(P_o(w) = p_i)\Sigma_j p_{ij}U(o \text{ given } (w_j \text{ if } o)) \\
&= \Sigma_i \Sigma_j P_o(P_o(w) = p_i)p_{ij}U(o \text{ given } (w_j \text{ if } o)) \\
&= \Sigma_j \Sigma_i P_o(P_o(w) = p_i)p_{ij}U(o \text{ given } (w_j \text{ if } o)) \\
&= \Sigma_j[\Sigma_i P_o(P_o(w) = p_i)p_{ij}]U(o \text{ given } (w_j \text{ if } o)) \\
&= \Sigma_j[\Sigma_k P_o(P_o(w_j) = p_k)p_k]U(o \text{ given } (w_j \text{ if } o)).
\end{aligned}
$$

The last sum, however, is the value of $U(o)$ according to an ersatz first-order expected utility analysis using estimates of unknown probabilities. Hence, the two forms of utility analysis agree.

Second-order utility analysis is also consistent with ersatz first-order expected utility analysis using estimates of unknown utility values. To illustrate, suppose that in a first-order expected utility analysis for an option o using the state s and its complement, the utilities for the two possible outcomes are, respectively, u_1 and u_2. Suppose that there are two possible values for u_1, namely u_1' and u_1'', having probabilities p^* and $1 - p^*$, respectively. In this case, a second-order expected utility analysis, assuming the states' independence of the option, yields that $U(o) = p^*[P(s)u_1' + (1 - P(s))u_2] + (1 - p^*)[P(s)u_1'' + (1 - P(s))u_2]$. An ersatz first-order expected utility analysis using the probability-weighted average of the utility as an estimate yields that $U(o) = P(s)[p^*u_1' + (1 - p^*)u_1''] + (1 - P(s))u_2$. By algebra, these quantities are the same.

To show consistency in general, I first observe that each form of utility analysis reduces to its application using the partition of worlds. The reduction follows the reduction for expected utility analysis in Weirich (2001a: sec. A.2). Then I show that the second-order analysis with respect to worlds agrees with the ersatz first-order analysis with respect to worlds. To simplify the demonstration, note that as Weirich observes, $U(o$ given $(w_j$ if $o)) = U(w_j)$ because a world comprehends an option realized in it. Also note that for each world w_j and possible value for its utility u_k,

$$P_o(U(w_j) = u_k) = \Sigma_i P_o(U(w) = u_i \ \& \ u_{ij} = u_k)$$

where w is the n-tuple of worlds, u_i is an n-tuple of possible utility values for worlds, i indexes n-tuples of possible utility values for worlds, and $u_{ij} = u_k$ indicates that the utility of w_j according to u_i is u_k.

Now, according to a second-order utility analysis,

$$
\begin{aligned}
U(o) &= \Sigma_i P_o(U(w) = u_i)\Sigma_j P(w_j \text{ given } o)u_{ij} \\
&= \Sigma_j P(w_j \text{ given } o)\Sigma_i P_o(U(w) = u_i)u_{ij} \\
&= \Sigma_j P(w_j \text{ given } o)\Sigma_i \Sigma_k P_o(U(w) = u_i \ \& \ u_{ij} = u_k)u_k \\
&= \Sigma_j P(w_j \text{ given } o)\Sigma_k [\Sigma_i P_o(U(w) = u_i \ \& \ u_{ij} = u_k)]u_k \\
&= \Sigma_j P(w_j \text{ given } o)\Sigma_k P_o(U(w_j) = u_k)u_k.
\end{aligned}
$$

Because the last sum is $U(o)$ according to an ersatz first-order expected utility analysis using utility estimates, both methods of calculating $U(o)$ agree.

I have shown that second-order and ersatz first-order expected utility analyses agree with each other. How can one establish that they are consistent with all other forms of utility analysis? One way is to reduce both forms of analysis to section B.1's canonical form of utility analysis, as it is extended to nonideal cases. The reduction is left as an exercise for the reader. It follows Weirich's (2001a: sec. A.3) reduction of expected utility analysis using a partition of worlds to the canonical form of utility analysis. Its main assumptions, which hold for the agents I treat, are that $U(w_j) = IU(w_j)$ and that $IU(w_j) = \Sigma_i IU(\text{BIT}_{ij})$, where i indexes the objects of the BITs w_j realizes.

Notes

Chapter 1

1. Not all decision principles require degrees of belief and desire. Some make do with comparisons of beliefs and comparisons of desires. Others make do with beliefs and desires. The quantitative approach extends the range of decision principles.

2. Speaking of utility maximization, Ramsey says, "The theory I propose to adopt is that we seek things which we want, which may be our own or other people's pleasure, or anything else whatever, and our actions are such as we think most likely to realize these goals (1931: 173).

3. Binmore (1994: 55) expresses the position this way (his emphasis): "A rational individual is only said to behave *as though* he were satisfying preferences or maximizing a utility function and nothing is claimed at all about the internal mental processes that may have led him to do so. A utility function, in the modern sense, is nothing more than a mathematically tractable means of expressing the fact that an individual's choice behavior is consistent."

4. The literature on satisficing advances various motivations for it. Winter (1964) claims that satisficing is needed to prevent an infinite regress of decisions about how to decide. As Winter does, Mongin (1994, 2000) questions optimization because it seems to lead to a regress about deciding how to decide. The regress assumes that before deciding, a rational agent applies a criterion of rational decision. This assumption errs. A rational decision must meet criteria of rationality, but the agent need not apply the criteria before deciding. At least sometimes, a spontaneous decision that meets the criteria of rationality is rational even though the agent has not applied the criteria to reach his decision. Sometimes, rationality may require application of criteria prior to a decision to ensure reflectiveness, but other times, it is enough to meet the criteria. Given the distinction between meeting and applying decision criteria, optimization does not force rational decision makers into a regress. So preventing regress is insufficient motivation for satisficing. See also Smith (1991).

Slote (1989: chap. 1) advances the principle to satisfice as a replacement for the principle to optimize. His argument for satisficing appeals to the virtue of having modest ambitions. However, optimizing can accommodate the value of modesty. A modest choice may optimize when all goods, including modesty, are considered even though it does not optimize when, say, only money is considered. Whenever modesty's utility is a decisive reason for an option, it also influences options' utilities so that satisficing does not contravene the principle to optimize. Satisficing motivated by modesty is not a rival of optimizing, just an alternative form of it. Hence, modesty is not a good reason for replacing optimization with satisficing.

The indeterminacy of options' utilities provides another motivation for satisficing rather than optimizing. Satisficing does not require comparisons of options. Giere (1979: 314) says that in decisions given uncertainty about states, one should pick a satisfactory option, an option with a satisfactory outcome in each state, if there is just one such option. The principle to satisfice, so presented, is not a rival of the principle to optimize. It is compatible with section 4.4's generalization of the principle to optimize. For more on satisficing and optimizing in nonideal situations, see Schmidtz (1992) and Byron (1998).

5. The behaviorist tradition in decision theory recognizes only preferences that yield acts given the opportunity. The ordinary concept of preference, however, recognizes inefficacious preferences. I use the ordinary concept of preference. According to it, preferring is favoring or liking better. For example, most people prefer pleasure to pain. People tend to choose following preferences, although exceptions arise. Special circumstances may prevent acting on a preference. Imagine an agent who prefers not to make choices. If an occasion for choosing according to this preference arises, he cannot choose according to it. Hence, his preference not to make choices is not accurately represented as a disposition to choose.

I adopt the ordinary concept of preference rather than the technical, behavioristic concept because it is more familiar. Most people gravitate toward it. Also, it yields a richer representation of agents' mental states and a fuller theory of rationality. Because it distinguishes preference from choice, it acknowledges principles of rationality connecting the two.

6. Rubinstein (1998) reviews economic literature on the decisions of nonideal agents. For an approach to realistic decision making that dispenses with more idealizations than I do, see Morton (1991) and, for comments on Morton's approach, see Weirich (1994a).

Chapter 2

1. *Propositions* are basic bearers of truth-values and are typically expressed by declarative sentences.

2. The propositions an agent uses to represent her acts are first-person action propositions. Some theorists treat a proposition of this type as a set of agent-centered possible worlds, pairs consisting of a world and an agent in the world. In contrast, I take such a proposition to be a structured entity with the agent as a component (see section A.4).

Using propositions to represent acts expresses an account of the individuation of acts. Acts are as finely individuated as the propositions that represent them. If I buy a red hat, I also perform the act of buying a hat. The two acts differ, even though both are realized by the same microphysical events. In a possible world where I buy a hat of another color, the utility of buying a red hat may be greater than the utility of buying a hat.

Acts have parts, but being part of an act is not the same as being a logical consequence of its propositional representation. Although buying a hat is part of buying a hat and gloves, buying a hat or closing the door is not part of buying a hat, despite being a logical consequence of buying a hat.

These points about acts explicate rather than analyze the ordinary concept of an act. They stipulate a view of acts fruitful for decision theory. In particular, taking acts to have propositional representations simplifies decision principles because propositions are the objects of beliefs and desires, which ground evaluations of acts. For an account of the ordinary concept of an act, see contemporary action theory, for example, Mele (2003).

3. Schick (1997: 56) argues for the intensionality of value. To accommodate it, he evaluates an act together with a way of understanding the act. Letting the object of evaluation be a proposition representing an act is another way of accommodating the intensionality of value.

4. Strictly speaking, the principle of optimization does not require a quantitative evaluation of each act. Comparisons of acts suffice (see section 4.1). However, section 2.1.3 converts the principle of optimization into the principle of utility maximization, and section 2.4 conjoins the latter with the expected utility principle. The combination assumes quantitative evaluation of acts. Because I need quantitative evaluations of acts eventually, I assume them at the outset instead of first introducing comparative utility and later quantitative utility.

5. According to a prevalent account of conditionals, the world that would be realized if an act were realized is the act-world closest to the actual world, that is, the act-world involving minimal change from the actual world. Typically, that world preserves the laws of nature (see section A.6). This account needs refinement for cases in which the act's world is indeterminate because, say, several act-worlds tie for closest. Lewis (1973: chap. 1) and Stalnaker (1981a, 1981b) address the issue. To simplify, I treat only cases in which an act's world is determinate.

6. A trimmed world specifies for each goal whether it is satisfied. All worlds in a set representing a trimmed world therefore have the same utility. However, if trimmed worlds realizing different goals have the same utility, then some set representing a trimmed world does not include every world with its utility.

7. A scale for temperature is an interval scale. The zero point and unit are arbitrary. A scale for length is a ratio scale. Only the unit is arbitrary. I take a scale for degrees of desire to be a ratio scale because I take indifference to be a nonarbitrary zero point. Nothing important hangs on this claim or the choice of zero point.

8. For more on degrees of desire, see Weirich (2001a: sec. 3.2.4). Many decision theorists define degrees of desire in terms of preferences, assuming rational ideal agents. Then degrees of desire represent preferences. However, conceptually separating degrees of desire and preferences adds realism. It acknowledges their divergence in agents not rational or ideal. It recognizes principles of rationality requiring their coherence.

9. Blackburn (1998: chap. 6) and Hubin (2001: 449–53) also appraise the consequences of defining utilities in terms of preferences. For nonideal agents, such definitions are especially restrictive. They assume that an agent has a rich structure of preferences. A nonideal agent's preference structure may not be rich. Cognitive limits may make it lean. Chapter 4 treats this case. Also, even given a rich preference structure, a nonideal agent may not form utilities according to it. The cognitive costs may be unreasonable. Chapter 5 treats this case.

10. Stocker (1990: chap. 10; 1997) argues against utility maximization. His argument is multipronged. The central tine claims, "We can justify an act, both morally and rationally, by showing that it helps bring about or constitute a good life, or good part of a good life, or a good project" (1997: 206). My acknowledgment of excuses for falling short of goals of rationality meets this objection. Because of excuses for failures to maximize utility, justifications involving goods short of utility maximization are possible.

11. Making a decision is a limiting case for decision procedures. It is a decision procedure without steps prior to the procedure's culmination. Even in the limit, a decision procedure may be self-defeating. A decision to perform an act may cause one not to perform it. For example, a decision not to think about an insult immediately frustrates its aim. A decision to impress one's friends may be counterproductive. A decision to maximize utility at every turn may fall short because it precludes genuine friendship and love. In such cases,

evaluation distinguishes a decision and its aim. Although performing an act may maximize utility among rival acts, deciding to perform it may not maximize utility among rival decisions. The rule to maximize utility in decision problems, where options are decisions, attends to self-defeat. A self-defeating decision causes its aim not to be realized, which counts against it in evaluations according to utility.

I thank Eric Wiland for stimulating discussion of self-defeating decisions.

12. A sequence of decisions is not in an agent's direct control because it requires his continuing to live throughout the period the sequence covers. However, a combination of decisions at the same moment—say, to buy a hat and to have its color be red—is in an agent's direct control. My decision principles recognize just one decision problem at a moment: what to decide at the moment. They treat a combination of decisions at the same moment as a resolution of the decision problem at that moment. I generally put aside combinations of simultaneous decisions, however. Given my idealizations, such a combination is equivalent to a single decision whose content is the conjunction of the contents of the combination's components. The single decision is rational if and only if the combination is. If the combination is rational, its components are. Section 4.5.3 entertains multiple simultaneous decisions as resolutions of distinct decision problems and examines the relation between the rationality of each and the rationality of their combination.

13. Hall and Johnson (1998) argue that the epistemic duty to believe all and only truths begets the epistemic duty to seek evidence. The relation that they claim holds between the two duties is similar to the relation that I claim holds between the goal of maximizing informed utility and the goal of gathering information.

14. After a certain possible gain, as possible gains increase, the probabilities of obtaining them drop faster and faster so that probability-utility products become negligible. Hence, the probability-weighted average of possible gains is finite. For example, take the possibility of gaining $1 trillion. The probability of that gain is less than a trillionth, so that the probability-utility product is less than 1 and negligible.

15. Christensen (2001: sec. 3) expresses a similar view of degrees of belief.

16. These versions of Kolmogorov's axioms are the basic structural laws: (a) $P(p) \geq 0$, (b) $P(p) = 1$ if p is an a priori truth, and (c) $P(p \vee q) = P(p) + P(q)$ if p and q are mutually exclusive a priori. They constrain probabilities that exist.

17. Some theorists, instead of defining degrees of belief in terms of an agent's overall preference structure, define them in terms of betting quotients. Proponents of the Dutch book argument for the probability axioms define an agent's degree of belief that p as, say, the lowest price in dollars at which the agent is willing to buy a gamble that pays $1 if p and $0 otherwise. Such definitions are just rough characterizations of an agent's degrees of belief. An agent's degree of belief that heads will turn up on a coin toss may arise from her knowledge of the statistical probability of heads. Although her degree of belief is 0.50, if she feels lucky she may be willing to pay more than $0.50 for a gamble that pays $1 if heads turns up and $0 otherwise. Putting aside definitions in terms of betting quotients allows a theory of degrees of belief to acknowledge and treat such cases.

18. Weirich (1986a) argues that some paradoxes of utility theory, such as Allais's paradox (1953), are the result of oversimplified forms of expected utility analysis, forms that omit relevant outcomes such as the risk involved in a gamble.

19. The outcomes that two states generate for an option may be the same if the outcomes are trimmed worlds and the states correspond to sets of untrimmed worlds. For example, suppose that w_1, w_2, w_3, and w_4 are untrimmed worlds. Let s_1 represent $\{w_1, w_2\}$ and s_2 represent $\{w_3, w_4\}$. Suppose that an option given s_1 and also given s_2 generates the trimmed world w_t. Perhaps it is entailed by w_1 and by w_3. Then it is the option's outcome in both states.

I allow states and outcomes to include an agent's acts, as do Jeffrey (1983), Aumann (1987), and Joyce (1999). Levi (2000: 393–96) objects. I save discussion of the issue for another occasion.

Chapter 3

1. This chapter's account of idealizations builds on the account in Weirich (1977: chap. 1; 2001a: sec. 1.3).

2. For a comparison of idealizations in physics and in economics, see Lind (1993). Hamminga and De Marchi (1994) offer a collection of articles on idealizations in economics.

3. Justification has many senses. I use the term so that justification of a decision amounts to explanation of its rationality but acknowledge that some senses of justification require objective or public reasons beyond those sufficient for rationality.

4. Savage (1972: sec. 5.4) and Jeffrey (1983: chap. 10) discuss the assumption of bounded utility. It facilitates the mathematical representation of preferences. Even if the assumption puts aside no realistic cases, it does not control for a factor in the explanation of a decision's rationality. Bounded utility may be correlated with explanatory factors but is not itself an explanatory factor. Explanatory principles must cover possible cases in which utility is not bounded.

5. Although a thorough explanation of the way principles for ideal cases provide guidance in realistic cases would be very worthwhile, it is not necessary here because such guidance is familiar. Science classes commonly point out the value of ideal laws of science in engineering problems.

6. The Divine Command Theory of Morality furnishes a classic example of a normative principle that is not explanatory. According to it, an act is immoral if and only if God forbids it. Even if this principle is true, it does not explain an act's being immoral. Presumably, God forbids acts because they are immoral, and acts are not immoral because God forbids them. Hence, an explanation of an act's immorality must say why God forbids the act.

7. Epistemic logic treats the influence of an agent's knowledge of her own rationality on her set of beliefs. For an introduction to epistemic logic, see Osborne and Rubinstein (1994: chap. 5) and Bacharach, Gerard-Varet, Mongin, and Shin (1997).

8. For example, the principle of ratification (section 8.3.2) relies on them.

9. The existence assumption's implications depend on the nature of probabilities and utilities. Defining probabilities and utilities in terms of preferences typically makes their existence require a rich preference structure. Because I take probabilities and utilities to be conceptually independent of preferences, my assumption about their existence does not reduce to an assumption of a rich preference structure. Section 4.2 discusses the prerequisites of probabilities and utilities given my interpretation of them.

Chapter 4

1. Lack of information is the principal impediment to probability and utility assignments, but other factors may also block them. Kusser and Spohn (1992) investigate cases in which the obstacle to utility assignments is uncongenial desires. For example, a person may want something because he enjoys it and enjoy it because he wants it. Then the existence of a quantitative utility for it demands a delicate equilibrium that may not obtain. See Weirich (1986a: 437–38) for a similar equilibrium problem involving risk.

2. Kyburg (1984: 17–18; 1997: 380–81) attributes magnitudes to objects but defines an object's having a magnitude as being a member of a class of objects bearing the same

quantitative relation to a unit of measurement. He does not take magnitudes as basic intrinsic quantitative empirical properties. In his view, quantities express empirical relations, but, in contrast with the view of Krantz et al. (1971: chap. 1), quantitative relations not reducible to comparative relations. For a historical survey of philosophical positions on magnitudes and quantities, see Berka (1983: chap. 3).

3. Goodman (1968) forcefully makes this point; see his chapter I on representation, section II.3 on exemplification, and section IV.8 on analog and digital representation.

4. Aversion to risk is distinct from diminishing marginal utility. It is aversion to a kind of indeterminacy of outcome. See Weirich (1986a).

5. The story of Buridan's ass shows that one can decide rationally without first forming preferences. I go a step further and claim that one can decide rationally without first forming any preference comparisons at all, not even indifference. Bratman (1987: secs. 1.3.2, 2.4) uses a discussion of Buridan's ass to make points about commitment to plans similar to my points about commitment to future decisions.

6. Chang (1997) collects essays on the problem of incomparability.

7. Millgram (1997) argues for a view similar to my view about the role of experience in the formation of basic intrinsic desires. He holds, "That practical reasoning, when it is done properly, is driven by experience: that part of practical reasoning is learning, from experience, what matters and what is important" (1). Also, Audi (2001: 133, 135) claims that rational intrinsic desires normally are rational because well-grounded in experience.

8. It is a goal of rationality to have full information, and from full information a complete probability assignment follows. However, goals are intensional objects, and not every consequence of a goal's realization is a goal.

9. See M. Kaplan (1996: chap. 1, sec. V) and Schick (1997: 45–47) for additional argumentation against the view that rationality encourages a complete preference ranking of gambles and thereby quantitative probability and utility assignments.

10. Levi (1986: sec. 7.5), Skyrms (1990a: 112), and Jeffrey (1992: 71, 86) take belief states to be represented by sets of probability functions. One picturesque way of representing the nonquantitative case is to say that the mind is divided between the various possible probability and utility assignments. Then the problem is too many quantitative assignments and not the absence of a quantitative assignment. See Lewis (1986a: 30–32) on "doublethink." For reasons n. 17 presents, I do not adopt this representation of the nonquantitative case. At any rate, representing belief states with sets of probability assignments does not change the main issue: What is a rational decision? Multiple assignments create the same quandary as missing assignments. Skyrms (1990a: 112–14) reviews some rules for making decisions when probabilities are indeterminate.

11. In the first rule, pain is not conceived of as a neurologically identified sensation-type bothersome in humans although perhaps not in Martians, but rather as a phenomenologically identified sensation-type bothersome in whomever it occurs. Another rule, related to the second, requires an intrinsic desire for satisfaction of one's other desires. Note that these rules constrain intrinsic desires, not extrinsic desires one has, all things considered.

12. Brandt (1979: chap. 6) proposes another procedural rule for intrinsic desires that brings reflection to bear. He says that rational intrinsic desires withstand cognitive psychotherapy.

13. I need not specify all constraints on probability and utility judgments because under my idealizations, an agent satisfies all of them whatever they are. Furthermore, under my idealizations, probability and utility judgments extended according to one form of utility analysis, such as expected utility analysis, also comply with all other forms of utility analysis. For instance, the utilities of options under one form of analysis must be the same as under

another form of analysis. In particular, as an expected utility analysis generates an option's utility, it must also conform to an intrinsic utility analysis of the option's utility (see section A.5). As an intrinsic utility analysis generates an option's utility, it must simultaneously influence utilities of option-state pairs so that an expected utility analysis generates the same utility for the option. So, if desirable, one may focus on extensions of probability and utility judgments according to one form of utility analysis, say, expected utility analysis. Each form of utility analysis surveys all relevant considerations.

14. See Harris (2001: 172–75) on the anguish of making decisions despite incomparability.

15. Richardson (1997: chap. 6) considers and rejects arguments that rational choice requires commensurability of options.

16. Hampton (1998: 264) considers taking outcomes broadly, or, as she says, "loading up" outcomes with everything that matters. She concludes that this tactic does not save Savage's (1972) expected utility theory from certain objections. I am not defending Savage's expected utility theory, which aims to derive probabilities and utilities from preferences. I am defending only my expected utility principle (section 2.4).

17. This is one reason I do not consider an agent's quantizations as divisions of her mind, as, for example, Lewis (1986a: 30–32) does. In a nonquantitative case, a quantization is not an actual or hypothetical state of mind, but merely a representation of an actual state of mind.

18. Some theorists do not give rational decision as much latitude as the quantization rule does. See, for example, Levi (1980: chap. 7), Gärdenfors and Sahlin (1982), and Bandyopadhyay (1994). My argument against their additional restrictions is that the reasons for them are already handled by utility under a quantization. For instance, Levi's rule for decision given indeterminacy, a version of the maximin rule for cases without complete uncertainty, assumes that utility under a quantization omits risk and his maximin rule registers the omitted risk. Because utility under a quantization attends to risk, however, the restrictions his maximin rule imposes are unjustified.

For a detailed discussion of the decision rule that Gärdenfors and Sahlin (1982) propose, see Weirich (2001b).

19. Lehrer (1989) distinguishes between comparative desire and preference. Although he allows comparative desire to be intransitive, he requires transitivity for preference. I do not maintain a distinction between comparative desire and preference, and require transitivity for both. For more on the principle of transitivity of preference, see Hurley (1989: secs. 4.2, 13.2), Broome (1991: sec. 5.4), Anand (1993: chap. 4), Maher (1993: chap. 2), Hansson (1993), Rawling (1997), and Sobel (1997).

20. I treat only decisions made at the same time. Coherence issues also arise for decisions made at different times. See the literature on diachronic Dutch book arguments for using conditionalization to update probability assignments, for example, Skyrms (1990a: chap. 5).

21. The rationality of a decision in a certain decision situation does not entail the rationality of that decision given other decisions made in the same decision situation. It may turn out that the decision is irrational given those other decisions because it does not cohere with them. This may happen even if the other decisions are actually made in that decision situation. Conditional rationality and irrationality do not obey the principle of detachment (see section 6.2).

22. For another example, consider an analogue of the rule of dominance inspired by section A.5's version of intrinsic utility analysis. According to it, each basic intrinsic attitude is a dimension of comparison. If, given full information, some option is at least as intrinsically desirable as another along every dimension and is more intrinsically desirable

along some dimension, then the rule says not to choose the other option. This comparative rule expresses a necessary condition of rational decision. Given intrinsic utility analysis, compliance is also a necessary condition for utility maximization under a quantization. Hence, the quantization rule subsumes this comparative rule, too.

23. The rule is called the *minimax rule* if stated in terms of losses rather than payoffs. Sen (1970: 138) proposes a lexicographic version of the maximin rule, the *leximin rule*, to break ties among maximin options. For simplicity, I treat only the maximin rule. My remarks about it carry over to the leximin rule.

24. Binmore (1994: 317–27) criticizes the maximin decision rule, too. He claims that expected utility maximization fully accounts for rational aversion to risk.

Social choice theorists such as Deschamps and Gevers (1978) suggest methods of characterizing the maximin rule in terms of general criteria for choice rules. Their work may be extended to rules of individual choice. However, the criteria for choice rules that characterize the maximin rule are strong and do not mount an effective argument for that rule. In particular, they ignore issues concerning separability highlighted by Allais's Paradox (1953).

25. Hubin (1980) and Ihara (1981) evaluate the maximin rule in light of Rawls's restrictions.

Chapter 5

1. Assumptions separating ignorance of mental and a priori matters are explanatorily fruitful and suitable justificational idealizations. However, it may seem that psychology joins the two types of ignorance. If an agent with no difficulty learning and applying a priori truths but with difficulty learning and applying truths about his own state of mind seems incongruous, imagine that the agent also has difficulty learning and applying a priori truths but has the aid of a perfect consultant or computer that applies all relevant a priori truths once he provides appropriate psychological data. In any case, my separation of the two types of ignorance is temporary. Section 5.4 relaxes the idealization about knowledge of a priori matters.

2. Weirich (1982) elaborates the advantages of using $U(o$ given $s)$ rather than $U(O[o$ given $s])$ in expected utility analyses in nonideal circumstances where desires are uncertain. Similar advantages recommend the conditional utilities that section A.6 uses in its refinement of expected utility analysis.

3. If possible worlds include missing probability values, so that a world's probability depends on the probability that a possible probability value is correct, paradoxes of higher-order probability arise, as indicated in Weirich (1983a: 87–89). Therefore, as a justificational idealization, I assume that the correctness of a possible probability value has no intrinsic utility, so that trimming worlds of irrelevant matters includes trimming them of probability values. Standard devices for blocking semantic paradox are also available.

For an introduction to the literature on higher-order probabilities, see Skyrms (1980b, 1984: 29–36), Gaifmann (1988), and Sahlin (1994). As this section does, Eells (1982: chap. 7) weakens the idealization that agents are certain of their probability and utility assignments. He uses second-order probabilities to represent an agent's uncertainty about first-order probabilities and utilities. He argues that, given some idealizations and restrictions different from mine, causal and evidential decision theory agree in cases with such uncertainty.

4. Consider a problem that section A.4 addresses. Suppose an option is expressed non-transparently, say, by the phrase, "the option my wife prefers," and so designated, the option's utility is not accessible to me because I do not know which option my wife prefers. Does higher-order utility analysis yield the option's utility with respect to the conscious mind? No,

that utility need not be an average of the utilities, with respect to the whole mind, of all the options my wife might prefer. It is the utility, with respect to the whole mind, of just one option my wife might prefer, the one she actually prefers. Higher-order utility analysis as this chapter advances it does not estimate utilities inaccessible because their objects are unclear.

5. This justification of higher-order expected utility analysis applies section A.3's principle of pros and cons with respect to accessible higher-order considerations. The principle of pros and cons ensures invariance among various forms of higher-order expected utility analysis. According to the principle, each form, applied to an option, yields the option's utility with respect to the conscious mind. The expected value of an expected utility is a utility with respect to the conscious mind. A similar result holds for even higher levels of analysis if all utilities are utilities with respect to the conscious mind. Hence, all levels of analysis yield the same value. Furthermore, the consistency checks in Weirich (2001a: appendix) for expected and intrinsic utility analyses carry over to these forms of analysis applied at a higher level, because each form of analysis has the same structure whether applied at the first level or at a higher level.

6. Miller's Principle (1966) is similar to the Principle of Reflection in van Fraassen (1984), but Miller's Principle governs probabilities at a single time, whereas the Principle of Reflection governs probabilities at two times.

The original version of Miller's Principle does not concern subjective probability but a connection between statistical and logical probability. Miller viewed it as a troublesome consequence of Carnap's theory of logical probability. See Jeffrey (1970) for a discussion of the principle.

7. For a case in which the equality does not hold, consider P(I have learned that Caesar liked cheese/Caesar liked cheese). It differs from P(I have learned that Caesar liked cheese/I have learned that Caesar liked cheese). The first ratio is near 0 because its numerator, P(I have learned that Caesar liked cheese and Caesar liked cheese), is near 0; I almost certainly have not learned that Caesar liked cheese. Yet the second ratio is 1 because its numerator, P(I have learned that Caesar liked cheese and I have learned that Caesar liked cheese), equals its denominator, P(I have learned that Caesar liked cheese).

8. Suppose that the tree uses the probability of t *according to* a possible case, such as $P(t) = 1/2$, rather than *given* the case. Then the tree can be completed. But t's probability according to a case is the same whether or not the case obtains. This sort of independence is inappropriate in expected utility computations, and so those computations should not use probabilities according to a case.

9. Section A.3's principle of pros and cons therefore justifies ersatz utility analysis.

10. Probabilities of probabilities are still probabilities of propositions, so I use P to stand for probability whether it attaches to a proposition about probability or some other type of proposition.

11. The index i, used earlier, cannot serve in place of k because two values for i, where p_i is an n-tuple of probability values, may yield two n-tuples with the same probability for s_j.

12. Jeffrey (1983) entertains an estimation procedure drawn from de Finetti. It involves setting odds for a bet that an unknown objective probability is in a certain interval. The estimation procedure I consider evaluates the odds set according to the expected utility of the bet they yield.

13. The procedure to choose the estimate that maximizes expected utility given the way it will be used to choose an option may be applied to estimates of utilities and basic intrinsic attitudes. The possible values of an estimate are real numbers for utilities and "yes" and "no" for possible basic intrinsic attitudes. However, the procedure is not well defined for estimates

of the genuineness of a possible option. One cannot obtain a possible option's expected utility in the case in which it is not a possible option.

14. Suppose that the procedure is liberalized so that it dispenses with the initial restriction to viable estimates. Any number in the interval [0,1] is a possible estimate of the ticket's probability of being drawn. All estimates below 3/8 have expected utility 1.25, and all those above 3/8 have expected utility 1.5. The estimate 3/8 itself has an expected utility that depends on how the tie to which it leads is broken. I suppose that the tie is broken so that the ticket is not bought given 3/8 as an estimate. Then the procedure says to use an estimate above 3/8 and leads to the decision to take the ticket. In terminology closer to Jeffrey's (1983: 199), it says to pick a probability estimate that maximizes expected utility, where the expected utility of an estimate p^* is defined as $EU(p^*) = \int EU(o_{p^*})dF(p)$, where o_{p^*} stands for the option chosen if p^* is used and F stands for the cumulative probability function over the possible values of p, the probability to be estimated. $EU(p^*)$ is thus the area under the curve for $EU(o_{p^*})$ plotted against p. The liberalized estimation procedure allows estimates that are not epistemically possible values. I put it aside for simplicity. The extra estimates allowed have the same expected utilities as the epistemically possible estimates, so their omission just amounts to the adoption of a tie-breaking procedure favoring the epistemically possible values. My forthcoming objections to the simplified procedure therefore also apply to the liberalized procedure.

Another alternative uses the estimate itself, rather than the range of possible probability values, to compute the expected utility of the estimate, taken as the expected utility of the decision to which it leads. This estimation procedure promotes wishful thinking in some cases.

15. Wagner (1999) uses the Two-Envelope Problem to argue that some surrogates for options' expected utilities are not good indications of options' choiceworthiness.

16. Good (1967) shows that acquiring relevant information is advantageous if there are no acquisition costs. If there are acquisition costs, it may not be advantageous. The costs of acquiring information about probabilities and utilities include all the undesirable consequences, such as the effort of concentration, the time taken from other activities, and the attention withdrawn from other problems. I postpone to another occasion formulation of methods of assessing those costs. In principle, information costs may be inferred from a rational agent's behavior. Being consistent, she will reflect about probabilities and utilities at least as much before a major decision as before a minor decision, other things being equal. As a rule of thumb, if she reflects about probabilities and utilities before a minor decision, her reflection costs are low.

17. If the costs and benefits of information gathering accumulate smoothly, the procedure says to gather information until marginal costs exceed marginal benefits.

18. Joyce (1999: sec. 2.6) advances a standard for halting deliberations. He has in mind human decision makers rather than the idealized agents this chapter treats, but his standard suggests an alternative for my ideal agents, too. According to Joyce, "The most we can reasonably ask of an agent is that she reflect on the decision problem she faces until she has good reason to think that further reflection would not change her views (at least not change them enough to affect her decision). At that point her job is to stop deliberating and solve the problem" (77). Instead of focusing on the possibility of a change in the agent's decision, my standard for stopping deliberations focuses on the costs of continuing deliberations and the probability and size of the benefits an agent might gain by continuing deliberations. An agent need not continue deliberations if the possibility of revising a tentative decision is so unlikely and of so little benefit that it does not offset the costs of continuing deliberations. As Joyce does, I think that stopping deliberations need not be supported by a conscious cost-benefit analysis. But unlike him, I think that the standard for stopping should address the

optimality of stopping rather than the possibility that continuing deliberations will change the agent's decision.

Smith (1991: 206–8) argues that in some cases, the maximin rule applied to deliberation recommends applying the maximin rule to resolve a decision problem without higher-order reflection about how to deliberate. As she does, I apply decision rules to deliberation to identify a stopping point for deliberation. However I apply the utility maximization rule rather than the maximin rule and take it as a standard of evaluation rather than as a decision procedure.

19. Another problem is that ignorance of a priori matters upsets the basis of utility assignments, intrinsic attitudes. Intrinsic attitudes evaluate propositions with respect to their logical consequences. Ignorance of these logical consequences makes intrinsic attitudes susceptible to change given acquisition of a priori knowledge. For example, consider the proposition that a certain intrinsic desire will be satisfied if Goldbach's conjecture is true. The intrinsic attitude toward the proposition may change if Goldbach's conjecture is proved.

20. Hacking (1967) revises Savage's theory of personal probability so that it treats the acquisition of a priori truths the same way as the acquisition of a posteriori truths. Another precedent is Garber's (1983) work on the problem of old evidence, a problem for Bayesian conditionalization. He also treats the acquisition of a priori knowledge as the Bayesian standardly treats the acquisition of a posteriori knowledge. He formulates procedures for nontrivially conditionalizing probability assignments with respect to a priori truths.

Lipman (1991) treats decisions about conducting computations to assist other decisions, keeping in mind the costs of computations. He argues that under weak assumptions, the regress of deliberations about how to decide reaches a level such that additional levels of deliberation do not alter the option that maximizes utility among options including methods of improving efforts at maximizing utility among options. In this sense, he solves the regress problem for acquisition of a priori information.

21. Suppose an agent makes a decision using a mistaken decision principle. Should we evaluate the agent's decision by his own lights? Should an evaluation of his decision proceed this way? First, identify standards of rationality that are neutral between the agent's principle and the correct principle. Then add the agent's principle to them and evaluate his decision with respect to their expansion. A problem for this procedure is the difficulty of finding a suitable neutral set of principles of rationality. No principles of Ur-rationality exist to govern the application of mistaken principles of rationality. I thank Timothy Williamson for this observation.

Chapter 6

1. Eells (1994: 39, 52) distinguishes between static and dynamic rationality. Static rationality evaluates an agent given her current resources. Dynamic rationality evaluates an agent also with respect to her history. Eells observes that Bayesianism is an explication of static rationality. This chapter moves beyond Bayesianism. It takes steps toward a theory of dynamic rationality in Eells's sense. It evaluates an agent's current decisions in light of the agent's history, including past mistakes. It generalizes Bayesian decision principles to make their evaluations more comprehensive.

2. Some versions of utilitarianism promote maximizing corrected utility because an agent's subjective utility assignment may arise from defective desires. Ideal utilitarianism, for instance, may be viewed in this light. Maximization of value may be taken as maximization of corrected utility.

3. The disanalogy exists only in the main. Some mistakes are not self-created. A student may inherit his teacher's mistakes about logic or statistics, say. Also, some uncertainty is self-created. An unlucky gambler may drink to forget his losses.

4. Should I distinguish scopes of evaluation more finely than I do? A decision in one sense is a mental act—the formation of an intention—and a decision in another sense is the product of such a mental act—an intention. It may seem important to explain whether an evaluation covers just the intention, or the intention together with its formation. This distinction in scope supplements my distinctions between the act intended, the selection process, and the selection process together with the grounds for it. That is, the distinction supplements my distinctions between act, choice, and decision. It divides a choice into an intention and the intention's formation (which differs from deliberations culminating in the intention's formation).

The supplementary distinction gathers steam from a presumption that standards of rationality differ for a mental act and its product. In particular, some may envisage procedural standards for formation of an intention that do not apply to the intention. But the formation of an intention is a simple mental act with no component mental acts. As a result, the only standard for it is the production of a rational intention. Because the mental act is simple, it cannot produce a rational intention, but in the wrong way. In this respect, it differs from a complex mental act such as solving a mathematical problem; one might obtain the right answer to the mathematical problem via mistaken calculations. Procedural evaluations that apply to complex mental acts do not apply to the formation of an intention.

Sometimes we seem to criticize a decision, taken as a mental act, in a procedural way. We say that it was hasty or ill-considered, that it was irresolute or, in contrast, obstinate. But from the strict point of view, these criticisms assert that a decision ought not to have been made, or ought not to have been changed, or ought to have been changed. They criticize the result of the decision and not the way the decision was achieved. Because the standards for the formation of an intention and the intention coincide, the supplementary distinction is superfluous. My distinctions between act, choice, and decision are sufficiently fine-grained for my purposes.

5. Broome (1998) discusses reasoning by which some beliefs rationally require additional beliefs and reasoning by which some intentions and beliefs rationally require additional intentions. The requirements are not detachable from the initial beliefs and intentions. In my terminology, the required beliefs and intentions are rational given the initial beliefs and intentions, but not necessarily rational tout court.

6. Not all his reasons need be ones he recognizes. Perhaps he thinks that he reached a decision by carefully comparing options when in fact he just adopted the first option he entertained. Then a reason for his decision is its quickly coming to mind even though he does not acknowledge that reason.

7. Recall that chapter 5 individuates decision procedures in a fine-grained way. Unreflective utility maximization differs from reflective utility maximization. The latter has costs the former lacks, the costs of reflection. Cognitive overload, say, may make it inferior to the former decision procedure.

8. I thank Don Hubin for bringing up this case. Intuition supports the view that rational change in basic goals is possible in such cases, but I do not propose general principles to govern it.

9. Section 1.1 claims that the disciplines share a single concept of rationality. One expects different opinions about its applications, however. These different opinions yield different conceptions of rationality.

10. Meeting the necessary condition may therefore depend on the time of a possible decision's assessment. In a predecision assessment, correction of mistakes may be part of a possible decision's supposition. In a postdecision assessment, after forgone opportunities to correct mistakes, it may not be part of the decision's supposition. Correction may require backward causation then. Although the possible decision's supposition entertains the nearest

world in which the decision is realized, and the actual world is constant, what counts as nearest to it may vary with context.

11. Identifying a decision problem's solutions confronts a problem. Corrected circumstances may be indeterminate if there are multiple methods of correction, for instance, multiple rational extensions of the set of options under consideration to correct its being too narrow. If there are many ways of correcting mistakes and they yield different utility rankings of options, it may be indeterminate whether an option is rational under counterfactual correction of mistakes.

12. A decision is rational only if it maximizes utility with respect to an agent's conscious mind. Mistakes she is not aware of tend to be excused. But an agent's decision may be irrational, say, because an unexcused mistake contaminates it, even if the agent justifiably believes that it is rational. An ideal agent is in a position to know of a rational decision that it is rational, whereas a nonideal agent may not be so favorably situated.

13. I thank Susan Vineberg for drawing my attention to such cases.

Chapter 7

1. For a discussion of the possibility of dilemmas of rationality, see Slote (1989: 99–115), Cubitt (1993), Mintoff (1997), and Priest (2002).

2. An alternative analysis broadens the relevant sense of "can" so that he can act morally in the comprehensive sense despite the psychological impossibility of so acting. Then the moral dilemma disappears. This response does not resolve dilemmas of rationality because rationality cannot ignore psychological limits.

3. For various perspectives on Newcomb's Problem, see, for example, Gibbard and Harper (1978), Campbell and Sowden (1985: pt. 1), Nozick (1993: 41–50), Sobel (1994: chap. 2), and Morton (2002).

4. Eells (1982: chap. 8) assumes that an agent is certain he will decide rationally and then shows that maximizing expected utility using standard conditional probabilities yields a recommendation to take both boxes. Eells's assumption regulates probability and utility assignments so that standard conditional probability agrees with causally sensitive types of probability taken with respect to conditions. Eells's version of the expected utility principle cannot be generalized to cases where the agent will make an irrational decision, however. It goes wrong in Newcomb's Problem when the agent lacks knowledge that his choice will be rational. Removal of Eells's assumption requires a radical shift to more causally discriminating versions of the expected utility principle, such as section A.6's version. See Sobel (1994: chap. 2) on Eells's approach to Newcomb's Problem.

5. Morton (2002: 111), for example, endorses two-boxing but also acquiring a disposition to one-box.

6. Gauthier (1986: chap. 6) recognizes the importance of decision preparations. He considers the choice dispositions that are rational to form and says that a disposition is rational if and only if the choice it yields is rational (182–84). Because he thinks a disposition to reciprocate cooperation in the Prisoner's Dilemma is rational, he thinks that a decision to reciprocate cooperation is rational. I agree that the disposition is rational. Nonetheless, the decision it yields is irrational; it is irrational given both actual and corrected circumstances. The rational disposition is a disposition to decide irrationally.

7. Other sources of disagreement about two-boxing are possible. The origins of intuitions about Newcomb's Problem are complex.

8. Bratman (1999: chap. 2) makes similar points about the role of planning for cognitively limited agents. Skyrms (1990a: chap. 6) discusses cognitive economies that support certain habits of choice.

9. If a decision to take 101 generates a reason for taking 101, that reason combines with other reasons for taking 101 to yield the utility of taking 101. If it tips the balance in favor of 101, then 101's utility is greater than 280's utility. Only 101 has maximum utility once utility assignments register the new reason. So decision-generated reasons do not count against utility maximization but rather change its direction.

10. Skyrms (1996: 38–42) also criticizes Gauthier's and McClennen's view that the rationality of a commitment to an act entails the rationality of the act.

Chapter 8

1. Using the infinite as an idealization is common in real cases where finite limits are hard to specify. Linguists, for example, assume that a speaker can generate an infinite number of sentences although human cognition imposes a finite limit. In the problem of picking a number, realism imposes limits on the set of options, but specifying the limits precisely is difficult. Evaluators and decision makers alike find it convenient to represent the problem with an infinite set of options. When a decision maker adopts such a representation, a full evaluation of her decision may require principles for problems that have such option sets.

2. A time lag between deliberation and choice grounds an argument for maximizing with respect to prechoice utilities. Given that thought takes time, asking that a choice fit beliefs and desires just before the decision reflects a demand for realism. An appeal to such a time lag, however, contravenes this chapter's idealization that thought is instantaneous.

3. The goal of self-support is a subgoal, although general (see section 3.1.4). The overall goal of rationality is more comprehensive. Because the goal of self-support is a subgoal, section 8.3.4 presents a principle for selecting a self-supporting option when several exist. This principle expresses an additional subgoal of rationality.

4. Versions of the principle of ratification appear in Jeffrey (1983: sec. 1.7), Harper (1985), and Weirich (1985a). Some versions use the assumption that an option is performed, and some use the assumption that it is chosen. Section 2.3 conflates this distinction by taking options in an action problem to be acts that are certain to be performed if chosen. Also, it takes the options in a decision problem to be possible decisions. Because this chapter treats decision problems with possible decisions as options, I use the assumption that an option is adopted or realized rather than performed or chosen.

In some situations, an agent knows that the only relevant information arriving with her decision is the content of her decision. So she knows that the utility an option will have if it is adopted is the same as its utility on the assumption that it is adopted. She can then ignore the distinction between (1) maximizing utility with respect to information at the time of decision and (2) adopting an option that maximizes utility on the assumption that it is adopted. Adopting an option that maximizes utility at the time of choice comes to the same thing as adopting an option that maximizes utility on the assumption that it is adopted. An interesting special case arises if the agent knows the information she will have if she adopts some option and knows she will adopt that option. Then she knows in advance the information she will have at the time of choice. So the information she has during deliberations is the same as at the time of choice, even though the choice is evidence about relevant states of affairs.

5. According to section A.6, conditional utility uses indicative supposition of a condition. So $U(o \text{ given } o')$ is the utility of o given that o' is realized. To evaluate this utility, one considers the prechoice circumstances if o' is about to be realized and then imagines the outcome if in those circumstances o were realized instead. To calculate this utility, one may apply utility analysis, for example, expected utility analysis. Because, according to section

A.6's version of expected utility analysis, $U(o) = \sum_i P(s_i$ given $o)U(o$ given $(s_i$ if $o))$, its application to the conditional utility says that $U(o$ given $o') = \sum_i P_{o'}(s_i$ given $o)U_{o'}(o$ given $(s_i$ if $o))$. For more details, see Weirich (1988: 579) on *holistic* expected utility.

When a condition's supposition is expressed in the indicative mood, it tracks evidential relations. When it is expressed in the subjunctive mood, it tracks causal relations. Notice that the principle of ratification uses a condition that involves an option's indicative supposition. It uses an option's indicative supposition to obtain beliefs and desires with respect to which options' expected utilities are computed. It assumes subjunctive supposition of options when computing their expected utilities, however. Thus, it yields the right decision in Newcomb's Problem (see section 7.3). Even though the indicative supposition of an option is relevant to the probabilities of states, so that Newcomb's Problem is dynamic in my sense, given any assignment of probabilities to states under an option's indicative supposition, two-boxing still maximizes expected utility.

The principle of ratification asserts that an option's evidential influence on states' probabilities has a role to play in rational choice. Although the conditional probabilities appearing in expected utility analysis should have a causal interpretation, as section A.6 explains—so that an option's expected utility registers only the option's causal influence on states—when selecting the body of information to use in computing an option's expected utility, one should include the option itself and so register its evidential influence on states before computing its expected utility. Despite its attention to an option's evidential influence, my version of the principle of ratification does not belong to evidential decision theory, which uses standard conditional probabilities in computing expected utilities. Because its calculation of expected utility proceeds according to causal decision theory, which uses causally regulated probabilities, the principle of ratification recommends two-boxing in Newcomb's Problem. It does not concur with the standard version of evidential decision theory, which recommends one-boxing, assuming the usual calculation of conditional probabilities in that problem.

6. For a classic example of the same type of decision problem, consider the problem of Death in Damascus in Gibbard and Harper (1978: sec. 11) or the Samarra Problem in Sobel (1998: chap. 2). These problems raise essentially the same puzzle: how to evade an appointment with Death. Although the Samarra Problem has older literary roots, I describe the case of Death in Damascus.

A man sees Death walking the streets of Damascus. Death tells the man he has an appointment with him at midnight but does not say where. If the man can avoid being at the appointed place, he will be spared. Terrified, the man tries to decide what to do. He knows that Death works from an appointment book and that the book is very accurate about the future whereabouts of people. He can stay in Damascus or go to the neighboring town, Aleppo. These are his only salient options. If the man decides to stay in Damascus, probably the appointment is in Damascus. If the man decides to go to Aleppo, probably the appointment is there.

In this case, whatever the man decides, he has evidence that the opposite decision would have been better. That is, whatever he decides, the opposite decision has higher utility with respect to the evidence his decision produces. Realizing this, he may vacillate during deliberation, first inclining to stay in Damascus, next finding that inclination a reason to go to Aleppo, then finding the inclination to go to Aleppo a reason to stay in Damascus, and so on. If he could decide by flipping a coin, he would at least have a 50% chance of avoiding Death. But I suppose that he cannot randomize his decision. In this case, no option is ratifiable. No option maximizes utility on the assumption that it is realized.

Sorensen (1987) argues that such cases of decision instability are impossible for ideal agents. Kroon (1990), on the other hand, defends their possibility. I side with Kroon.

My examples illustrate the possibility of decision instability. Although they do not explore the dynamics of an ideal agent's psychological states, they show that ideal agents may face decision problems without a ratifiable option. See Weirich (1998: 69–71) for further explanation.

7. My concept of self-support draws on Aumann and Maschler's (1964) ideas about objections and counterobjections in cooperative games.

8. An agent may comply with principles for pruning and truncating paths of incentives without deliberately applying those principles, just as she may comply with a decision principle without deliberately applying it.

9. The principle of self-support relies on an account of conditional incentives and hence conditional probabilities, which section A.6 treats.

10. The dependence of rational choice on pursuit of incentives is similar to the dependence of rational choice on beliefs and desires. An agent's psychological state affects rational choice in a decision problem. Just as principles of rationality regulate beliefs and desires and thus choice, principles of rationality regulate pursuit of incentives and thus choice. In a two-option decision problem, a choice settles some questions about pursuit of incentives, and rational pursuit of incentives settles rational choice. An analogue in non-dynamic two-option problems is rational preference's settling rational choice.

In a decision problem with several options, an agent violates the principle of self-support if her choice ignores a pursued incentive away from it. Such an incentive may exist because it depends on a hypothetical choice among a subset of options, not on the actual choice among all options. A rational resolution of the decision problem depends on compliance with the principle of self-support as well as rational pursuit of incentives. See Weirich (1998: 102).

11. Weirich (1999) offers a simple account of the principle of self-support, and Weirich (1998: chap. 4) offers a more complete account. The latter work makes three refinements. First, it strengthens the principle of self-support by allowing a path of incentives to terminate in a set of options. Second, it provides more precise and complete rules for pruning and truncating the incentive trees generated by options. Third, it distinguishes self-support defined in terms of paths of incentives, or *strategic* self-support, from self-support that takes account of reasons besides incentives. My formulation of the principle of self-support ignores reasons that are not incentives; it is a principle of strategic self-support. Strengthened versions of the principle may register reasons that are not incentives.

In general, an option is self-supporting if and only if it does not generate a sufficient reason to switch. An insufficient reason is one whose pursuit is cognitively futile. According to the principle against dilemmas of rational choice, and the necessity of self-support for rationality, every decision problem has an option that does not generate a sufficient reason to switch. For convenience, I assume that an option satisfying my principle of self-support satisfies the strengthened general principle. In particular, when the next section applies a rule for selecting a self-supporting option, it assumes that options self-supporting in my restricted sense are self-supporting in the general sense. It assumes that the options to which the selection criterion is applied are genuinely self-supporting and do not satisfy only my necessary condition for self-support, namely, failure to start a terminating path of pursued incentives.

12. The idealization's crucial consequence is that the top-ranked disposition's manifestation is the decision top-ranked according to self-conditional utility. The idealization may be weakened to that assumption, but the stronger idealization is more illuminating.

The idealization follows from other idealizations concerning cognitive power and full rationality. However, rather than fully explore the idealization's dependence on other idealizations, I just add the idealization explicitly.

Here is a quick sketch of the way the idealization follows from other idealizations. A disposition to realize an option in a decision problem grounds only the truth of the conditional that in the decision problem the agent realizes that option. Under the usual idealizations, a disposition has no relevant consequences besides the option. The disposition is cost-free because of the agent's cognitive power. Her full rationality precludes cases such as Newcomb's Problem that reward irrationality. It requires that the top-ranked disposition be rational to form and to have, being a product of rational pursuit of incentives. Hence, that disposition must issue in a rational decision. The comprehensive rationality of the disposition requires that result. For these reasons, the utility of a disposition to realize an option equals the option's self-conditional utility.

13. In Weirich (1988), the goal opt-l is for comprehensive assessment of rationality and the goal opt-c is for noncomprehensive assessment of rationality, rationality given circumstances including mistakes. Both are goals of rationality, but the second is conditional. The principle to maximize self-conditional utility among self-supporting options combines these two goals and itself expresses a goal of comprehensive rationality.

14. Sobel (1994: chap. 11) claims that to be rational an act must be ratifiable and maximize nonconditional expected utility just before choice. Even in cases where it is impossible to meet both goals, rationality requires meeting both. My disagreement with Sobel is partly terminological. Sobel holds that some acts that are not rational are also not irrational. In the case of the Mean Demon, he holds that although neither choice is rational, neither choice is irrational. For him, a choice is rational if and only if it meets all pertinent goals of rationality. His interpretation of rationality makes it an ideal unchanged by unfavorable circumstances. I interpret rationality so that it responds to unfavorable circumstances. As a result, even in cases such as the Mean Demon, I hold that it is possible to make a rational choice.

15. I reject Nash's (1950a) Independence Condition along with the conditions Sen (1970: 17) calls Alpha and Beta. See Luce and Raiffa (1957: 128–34) for some criticism of Nash's Independence Condition. This criticism also applies to Alpha and Beta; Alpha is Nash's Independence Condition. See also McClennen (1990: sec. 2.3), Eells and Harper (1991), Vallentyne (1991), Vickers (1995), Rawling (1997), Weirich (1998: chap. 4), and Sen (2002: chap. 3).

Much of decision theory is implicitly restricted to nondynamic decision problems. Besides Principles Alpha and Beta, representation theorems for probability and utility, such as Savage's (1972: chap. 3), assume that preferences are unaffected by the availability of options. This restriction is not very severe because most apparent cases of rational changes in preferences in response to changes in availability disappear when one takes a fine-grained view of consequences. If choosing an act from one set of alternatives has different relevant consequences than choosing the act from another set of alternatives, the act does not really constitute the same option in both contexts. However, even if one takes a maximally fine-grained view of consequences, there still are cases where a change in the availability of options causes a change in preferences because of a change in self-support and not because of a change in relevant consequences. So the representation theorems are effectively restricted to rational preferences in the context of nondynamic decision problems.

16. In this case, the self-supporting options are also ratifiable. Harper (1986: 33) proposes to choose among ratifiable options on the basis of their utility. See also Eells (1985) and Richter (1986) for a discussion of selection criteria.

17. The disposition to choose B designates two states, one psychological and one behavioral. If the agent were to choose A, the psychological state would not change, but it would lose its efficacy. It would not be a behavioral state that yields B.

18. I rely on the intuition that in this version of the Nice Demon, A is an irrational choice because it is unproductive. Extending the selection principle to this case confirms the intuition. In noncomprehensive evaluations of options, taking mistakes for granted, the selection principle's application requires careful appraisal of utilities conditional on options. $U(A$ given $A)$ involves indicative supposition of the condition that A is realized (see section A.6). This form of supposition depends on the epistemic perspective adopted. A perspective may be before or after the decision problem's resolution. It may be the agent's or an outside evaluator's. It may give priority to holding constant certain features of the decision problem. In my example, the right epistemic perspective prohibits backtracking to alter the agent's decision situation. It holds constant the monetary consequences of the options and entertains an erroneous prediction of the agent's choice. A's supposition is not new relevant evidence concerning A's monetary outcome because $P(b) = 1$. Thus, given A, the agent prefers B. A is not self-supporting. The selection principle rejects it.

19. In my view, conditional rationality is not simply a matter of utility maximization, so in my example, rationality given the agent's disposition is not simply a matter of utility maximization. The selection principle replaces utility maximization even as a criterion of conditional rationality. Rationality given the agent's mistaken disposition appeals to that principle of nonconditional rationality—the principle to choose an option that maximizes self-conditional utility among self-supporting options—but applies the principle under the assumption that the agent has the mistaken disposition. In my example, given the disposition to choose B, $U(A$ given $A)$ is $U(\$0)$, because given the disposition, box A is empty. The utility $U(A$ given $A)$ does not backtrack to correct the mistaken disposition that is given. So, given the disposition to choose B, $U(A$ given $A) < U(B$ given $A)$. Consequently, A is not self-supporting and does not maximize self-conditional utility among self-supporting options given the mistaken disposition. Given that disposition, B maximizes self-conditional utility among self-supporting options. It is just a coincidence that B also maximizes utility. Given the mistaken disposition, self-conditional utility equals utility in my example, although the equality does not hold in general.

19. Rabinowicz's (1989) example is designed to make the dominant option self-defeating and the dominated option self-supporting. This is impossible on the current account of self-support. If the dominant option starts a terminating path, so does the dominated option because there is a path from the dominated option to the dominant one. On the relationship of self-support and dominance, see also Rabinowicz (1988) and Sobel (1990).

20. Should one solve the decision problem in figure 8.6 by maximizing along the diagonal in which predictions match options? That procedure yields B, too. However, it ignores relevant considerations. Certainty that one will adopt B and that state b obtains does not make irrelevant the outcomes of other options in state b. Because in that state A and C have outcomes superior to B's outcome, reasons arise for adopting them instead of B. My decision principles attend to such reasons, as adequate decision principles must. Maximizing along the diagonal goes wrong in other decision problems, such as Newcomb's Problem, because it ignores such reasons.

21. Under a suitable independence assumption, this follows from the principle that if, given a condition, one option has higher utility than another option in every state, then it has higher utility than the other option given the condition. The independence assumption is that the utility of an option given a state if the option were realized is independent of the options. In my examples, a matrix cell's utility for an option and state is the utility of the option given the state if the option were realized. So the independence assumption says that the utilities in the cells do not change given the condition that an option is realized. This assumption is part of all my examples. If it were not met, the matrix representation of

a decision problem would not have enough information to solve dynamic decision problems. For to compute the utility of an option given a condition, one needs for each state the utility of the option given the state if the option were realized given the condition.

22. In nondynamic decision problems without an option of maximum utility, such as the case of picking your income, it is rational to pick a dominated option. These cases furnish independent reasons for concluding that dominance is not always a decisive factor in rational choice.

Chapter 9

1. The agents' options are called strategies because they often issue from strategic reasoning, not because they are invariably conditional acts.

2. Certain "refinements" of Nash equilibrium propose ways of identifying the Nash equilibrium realized by agents with bounded rationality, in particular, agents with a tendency to err. See, for example, Selten (1975), Myerson (1978), and Kohlberg and Mertens (1986) on perfect, proper, and strictly perfect Nash equilibrium, respectively.

3. Weirich (1998: chap. 5) lifts the restriction to a finite number of pure strategies.

4. Prescience may arise from the agents' common knowledge of their game and their rationality.

5. Is barring mixed strategies realistic? Yes, prohibiting use of randomizers suffices. Rapoport and Budescu (1992) and Budescu and Rapoport (1994) show that people cannot randomize in their heads, although they come closer to it in games than elsewhere.

6. In the ideal games I describe, the absence of a Nash equilibrium entails, moreover, the absence of an *equilibrium-in-belief*, another type of subjective equilibrium, which Vanderschraaf (2001: 47–50), for example, presents. Similarly, it entails the absence of a *rationalizable* profile, which Bernheim (1984) and Pearce (1984) define in terms of agents' possible probability assignments, that incorporates agents' actual probability assignments. See Weirich (1998: 215–17).

7. My move from utility maximization to self-support meets Sensat's (1998) objections to game theory.

8. Bicchieri (1993: chap. 2) and Sobel (1994: 303–13) review the difficulties facing explanations of a Nash equilibrium's realization. They also make some assumptions that exacerbate the difficulties. Bicchieri assumes games in which an agent's choice does not furnish evidence of other agents' choices (35). Sobel assumes hyperrational agents, who resemble ideal agents, but act only on considerations of rationality, whereas ideal agents may act on whims when these are not contrary to rationality. I do not make such assumptions.

9. An explanation of the conditional utilities, and the conditional probabilities on which they depend, may proceed in an n-person game from the response of $n-1$ agents to a first agent's strategy, to the response of the remaining $n-2$ agents to a second agent's strategy, and so on, until reaching the response of the single remaining agent to a next to last agent. See Weirich (1998: 155–58) for an example of this method.

10. I do not require that the response to an agent's strategy be a solution to the subgame obtained by fixing his strategy. There may not even be a Nash equilibrium in the subgame. So the responses need not be jointly ratifiable strategies. I assume that each agent is rational in the profile actually realized, but not necessarily in each hypothetical response to a strategy. Also, the responses of agents to each other may vary with the order in which strategies are supposed. In a game between agents Row and Column, strategy C_1 may be the response to strategy R_1 although strategy R_2 is the response to strategy C_1. C_1 is the response to R_1 just in case it is true that if R_1 is realized, then C_1 is realized. Responses need not be symmetrical because a hypothetical conditional need not entail its converse.

11. Regan (1980: 18) presents the following problem. Two agents committed to utilitarianism can cooperate in two ways, one of which is better in terms of total utility. In particular, each agent will do either act 1 or act 2. If they do not perform the same act, they achieve 0 units of utility. If they both perform act 1, they achieve 6 units of utility. If they both perform act 2, they achieve 10 units of utility. What should each do?

My theory solves this problem by appealing to decision preparedness. Prior to the problem, the agents ought to have formed the disposition to cooperate in the most beneficial way. Although each agent's cooperation in the less beneficial way maximizes utility given what the other does, and so is conditionally rational, the less beneficial form of cooperation shows that at least one agent has made a mistake in the cultivation of decision dispositions. In ideal circumstances, with prescience, the decision rational in a comprehensive sense is to do one's part in the most beneficial form of cooperation. This leads to the Pareto optimal Nash equilibrium.

Bacharach (1999) considers similar coordination games and argues that individualistic reasoning cannot generate the Pareto optimal Nash equilibrium. He correctly observes that the principle to maximize expected utility does not generate that equilibrium because realization of the inferior equilibrium may also satisfy that principle. However, he does not make a case against the selection principle. In cases meeting this section's assumptions, this principle of individualistic reasoning generates the Pareto optimal Nash equilibrium.

12. See Harper (1988, 1989, 1999), Skyrms (1990b), Shin (1991), Eells and Harper (1991), Weirich (1994b), Levi (1998), and Vanderschraaf (2001: sec. 2.3) for applications of ratification to games. Weirich shows that in an ideal normal-form game with a unique profile of jointly self-supporting strategies constituting a strict Nash equilibrium, if self-supporting strategies are all ratifiable strategies so that the principle of self-support reduces to the principle of ratification, then ratification justifies the realization of that Nash equilibrium.

Colman (2003: sec. 8.2) describes a type of reasoning, Stackelberg reasoning, similar to the reasoning I present for realization of a Pareto optimal Nash equilibrium. Stackelberg reasoning, however, is committed to evidential decision theory, whereas my principles belong to causal decision theory.

13. I attend to Nash equilibrium because it is game theory's primary type of equilibrium. Aumann (1987) introduces correlated equilibrium, a generalization of Nash equilibrium for games in which agents' strategies are correlated, and shows that it emerges from standard common knowledge assumptions given that agents have a common prior probability assignment to their strategies. Given a realization of a correlated equilibrium, no agent has an incentive to deviate unilaterally. If a correlated equilibrium is not realized, some agent fails to maximize utility with respect to his information, which includes his own choice. Aumann's result assumes that utility maximization, not ratification, is the standard of rationality. An agent who maximizes utility given knowledge of her own choice conforms with the principle of ratification but does not necessarily use the principle of ratification. She may not evaluate alternative strategies with respect to the information they generate. She may not take another strategy's ratifiability as a reason to deviate unilaterally.

Under standard common knowledge assumptions, Shin (1991) argues for realization of a correlated equilibrium and also a perfect equilibrium (see n. 2). He uses ratification as the standard of rationality, in particular, Jeffrey's (1983: sec. 1.7) account of ratification, which distinguishes decisions and their executions and evaluates an act on the assumption that it is chosen. His argument appeals to performance errors or "trembles." I do not use performance errors to explain realization of equilibrium because I take options as decisions (and so executed when adopted) and because I take agents to be ideal and without "trembling hands."

Aumann's and Shin's results differ from mine in games treated, decision principles invoked, assumptions concerning agents, and type of equilibrium realized. But the main difference is their theoretical objective. Their goal is to demonstrate the realization of an equilibrium. Mine is to explain the realization of the equilibrium realized. They do not present the strategic reasoning by which each agent settles on his part in a correlated equilibrium. Aumann says that he assumes that an agent knows her own choice, but does not assume that she uses her knowledge to infer others' choices (1987: 9). Also, he does not explain the origin of the common prior probability assignment or its updating. In examples, updating is a response to an arbitrator's recommendation of agents' parts in a joint strategy, but he does not explain the origin of the arbitrator's recommendation. In games with several possible correlated equilibria, the one realized depends on the common prior probability assignment and updating. An explanation of an equilibrium's realization explains these features too.

Skyrms (1989: 361) draws attention to the lacuna of Aumann's approach when comparing it with his own approach. He says, "Aumann's viewpoint is somewhat different from ours in that he does not consider the process of deliberation, but only its result. So there is no analysis of how the players jointly arrive at decisions where each maximizes his expected utility."

To clarify my theoretical objective, consider equilibrium for a ball in a basin with several low spots. It will settle in one. An explanation of its settling in one provides an account of its travels before coming to rest, however. Similarly, an explanation of an equilibrium's realization does not just show that an equilibrium is realized but also provides an account of deliberations leading to the equilibrium's realization. An explanation accounts for the agents' strategic reasoning and does not just characterize its outcome.

14. Skyrms advances variations of the foregoing model of deliberation that replace "adaptive" rules of probability revision with "inductive" rules that do not require an agent to assign probabilities to his own acts. See, for instance, Skyrms (1991). Because my appraisal of Skyrms's justification of Nash equilibrium is unaffected by this change in the rules of probability revision, I do not explore it.

15. Von Neumann and Morgenstern (1947: chap. 3) restrict this claim to two-person zero-sum games, in which for each strategy profile, the sum of the agents' payoffs is zero, and they use the term "equilibrium" rather than "Nash equilibrium" because Nash's work on equilibria followed theirs.

16. The notation $dp(H)/dt$ stands for the rate of change in $p(H)$ with respect to a change in t as the change in t approaches zero.

17. Binmore (1990: 155) distinguishes two categories of argument for Nash equilibrium: *eductive* arguments and *evolutive* arguments. Eductive arguments apply only to agents with a capacity for reasoning, in particular, a capacity for learning (see 197–204 and consider the label "eductive"), whereas evolutive arguments apply as well to primitive organisms. Classical game theory aims at a third type of argument—let me call it *strategic*—that relies on reasoning from information in hand, and not on the acquisition of information either in previous games or during the course of deliberations. Skyrms's argument is eductive because his agents reason and learn. But it is not strategic because it relies on the acquisition of information during deliberations.

18. It is assumed, in addition, that joint probabilities of acts are product probabilities (Skyrms 1990a: 33, n. 8). I follow Skyrms in relegating this assumption to the background.

19. A "Darwinian" deliberator revises the probabilities of the acts open to him according to the following rule: $p_2(A) = p_1(A)U(A)/U(SQ)$, where A is an act, SQ is the status quo or default act, and U is his utility function (Skyrms 1990a: 37). Darwinian deliberators are rational but fail to seek the good because they never increase the probability of a strategy

once it has a probability of zero. Their rationality, however, does not clearly show that the assumption that deliberators seek the good is a mere restriction. For, provided that Darwinian deliberators start with completely mixed strategies, they are also at a joint deliberational equilibrium if and only if they are at a Nash equilibrium (38). Thus, for these deliberators, a close correspondence between joint deliberational equilibrium and Nash equilibrium persists.

20. I presented a version of these comments at a symposium on Skyrms's (1990a) book, *The Dynamics of Rational Deliberation*, at the 1991 Pacific Division APA meeting. I thank Skyrms for his reply.

Appendix A

1. Optimization among momentary acts supports the familiar principle of dynamic consistency (which in turn supports the standard of subgame-perfect equilibrium for extensive-form games). This principle declares a sequence of acts rational only if each act in the sequence maximizes utility at the time it is performed. For a discussion of dynamic consistency, see Strotz (1956), Hammond (1988), McClennen (1990: sec. 7.4, chap. 9), Machina (1991), Rabinowicz (1995), and Gauthier (1997). The interpretation of dynamic consistency varies slightly among these authors, and not all adopt my interpretation exactly. Some reject the principle of dynamic consistency. For a criticism of the principle, see Velleman (1997: 45–50). See Skyrms (1996: 38–42) for a defense of dynamic consistency, or, using his term, modular rationality.

2. If it seems impossible for an actual and a merely possible act to share a stage, given that acts are concrete, let them have stages with the same propositional representation. Having the same propositional representation is all that matters in the end because desirabilities attach to propositions.

3. Sobel (1997) investigates pairwise preferences. A pairwise preference between two options is a preference between them given that choice is restricted to them. Sobel argues that cyclical pairwise preferences may be rational for ideal agents in ideal circumstances because the changing conditions of the pairwise preferences in the cycle change the grounds for preferences. Sobel (2001: sec. 5) argues that a perfectly reasonable and ideally knowledgeable agent with cyclical pairwise preferences may be financially ruined by a series of cyclical trades known as a money pump. Sobel's examples are cases where stepwise optimization among momentary acts yields an extended act nonoptimal among contemporaneous acts. Like my example, his examples argue that rationality counsels a series of acts, each of which optimizes among acts at the same time, rather than an extended act that optimizes among acts filling the same period. However, his examples rest on controversial assumptions. In particular, they rest on the assumption that rationality does not require changing the cyclical pairwise preferences that generate the money pump.

4. My application of the principle of utility maximization to decisions has motives similar to Jeffrey's (1983: 83) application of the principle to attempts or tryings and Joyce's (1999: 57) application of the principle to exercises of will.

5. The reduction is also suitable as an independently adopted idealization for the principle of utility maximization. However, if it were independently adopted, then whenever one removes the idealization that decisions are costless, one must also remove the idealization that the reduction holds. Decision costs may create a disparity between the utilities of top decisions and top acts of certain execution.

In my ideal cases, an agent knows that she will execute any decision she adopts. She also knows that she is fully rational except possibly in the current decision problem. These idealizations rule out situations in which utility maximization evaluates differently a decision and its execution. In nonideal cases such as Kavka's (1983) toxin puzzle, however, a maximizing decision may settle on a nonmaximizing act. A maximizing agent then adopts but does not execute the decision.

6. The term "intrinsic desire" is Brandt's (1979: 111). He uses it for a desire assessing intrinsic qualities in part. I use it for a desire assessing intrinsic qualities exclusively. My account of intrinsic desires follows Weirich (2001a: sec. 2.1).

7. Basic intrinsic desires are analogous in many ways to basic intrinsic values as described by Harman (1967), Feldman (2000), and Zimmerman (2001: chap. 5).

8. I thank Wlodek Rabinowicz and James Joyce for good questions about the causes of BITs.

9. A consequence of this view is that an agent may rationally perform an act she knows she will regret. See Weirich (1981) and, for an opposing viewpoint, Fuchs (1985).

10. In Racine's (1986: 16–17) *Phaedra*, Act I, scene 3, Oenone attributes similar fickleness to Phaedra:

> Her wishes war against each other still.
> 'Twas you who, full of self-reproach, just now
> Insisted that our hands adorn your brow;
> You who called back your strength so that you might
> Come forth and once more see the light.
> Yet seeing it, you all but turn and flee,
> Hating the light which you came forth to see.

11. Normally, I assume that BITs do not change as an act is performed. But my idealization allows BITs to change as long as they change the same way given any act. Hence, the idealization does not rule out moments when BITs change. It does not require that BITs be constant throughout an agent's life.

12. I thank Troy Nunley for illuminating discussion of cases involving higher-order intrinsic attitudes.

13. Weirich (2001a: sec. 1.4) reviews objections to operationism.

14. What types of input may a representation theorem use? This is an open question. Quantitative relations are too powerful given the objective of reducing the quantitative to the comparative. Preferences are too theoretical given strict operationist objectives. For a modest, standard inferential objective, however, one may use the input of the representation theorem sketched. Its input and assumptions are comparable to those of other, standard representation theorems.

15. To realize an x percent subjective chance of an outcome is to perform an act that yields that outcome with a subjective probability of x percent. The subjective chance is a result of the act, whereas the subjective probability is a degree of belief concerning the act's outcome. Having terms for both the chance and the probability aids exposition.

16. Section 2.1 takes an act's utility as the utility of the act's world merely for simplicity. To make a seamless transition from maximization given full information to maximization given uncertainty, one may recast section 2.1.3's principle of maximization so that it takes an act's utility as the utility of the proposition that the act's world obtains. Given full information, this is the same as the utility of the act's world. Then allowing for uncertainty does not change the formulation of the principle of maximization or its interpretation of an act's utility.

The problem of characterizing outcomes given uncertainty is related to the problem of small worlds introduced by Savage (1972: sec. 5.5) and recently discussed by Joyce (1999: sec. 3.3).

17. The rule identifying an act's utility with its outcome's utility, when applied to decisions, also identifies a decision's utility with its outcome's utility. The latter is the utility of the proposition that the decision's world obtains. This proposition expresses the decision's outcome. If a decision is carried out, its world includes the act selected and that act's temporal sequel.

18. See Crimmins (1992) for an analysis of belief according to which a person believes a proposition in a way, a way given by a context including words used to state the proposition believed.

19. To illustrate the problem, consider a case in which the utility of the proposition that George Bush speaks in Washington differs from the utility of the proposition that George Clooney speaks in Hollywood. Suppose that the sentence "George speaks here" expresses the first proposition on one occasion and the second proposition on another occasion. Attaching a utility to the sentence then conflates a crucial difference.

20. The indicative supposition of an act not performed may change the epistemic basis of the act's evaluation even given full information. But the effects of an act's indicative supposition are especially prominent given uncertainty, the topic of sections 2.3 and 2.4.

21. Consider the subjunctive conditional that if o were realized, then s_i would obtain. The conditional is true if both option and state are actual, but in counterfactual cases, its truth generally requires a causal connection between option and state. Suppose that one takes $P(s_i$ given $o)$ as the probability of the subjunctive conditional. This definition attends to causal influence but limits the existence of conditional probabilities unnecessarily, as Weirich (2001a: sec. 4.2.1) points out.

22. Lewis (1981: 11) introduces dependency hypotheses that he uses to compute an option's expected utility. The condition $(s_i$ if $o)$ resembles a dependency hypothesis.

23. For more support, see Weirich (1980; 2001a: sec. 4.2.2) and, for an opposing viewpoint, see Davis (1982).

24. Expected utility analysis may be extended to cases not meeting the assumption that the number of relevant worlds is finite. Then it may use infinite partitions and generate infinite utilities. The extension calls for calculus and nonstandard numerical analysis in the style of Robinson (1966), mathematics beyond my project's scope. See Skyrms (1995: sec. 3), Sobel (1996), Vallentyne and Kagan (1997: 7–9), and Vallentyne (2000) for applications of nonstandard numerical analysis to probability and utility theory.

25. Forgetting causes trouble for familiar diachronic principles of probability such as Conditionalization and Reflection. See, for example, Williamson (2000: 219) and Monton (2002). Williamson (sec. 10.2) argues that in general, an agent may violate the Principle of Conditionalization, which governs updating probability assignments as new evidence arrives, because she may not know all her evidence. An agent may not know what she knows.

Appendix B

1. An option's utility for an agent need not be taken as the most coarse-grained reason for the option. That utility may figure in an analysis of the option's utility for a group. Then it is just one factor in the option's group utility. The option's group utility may in turn be just one factor in the option's utility for a more inclusive group. Coarser and coarser reasons for the option may be generated without end as groups of stakeholders become more and more inclusive without end.

2. Accepting finer and finer partitions without end does not introduce a partition with an infinite number of members. One cannot form an infinite partition by taking one member from each of the finer and finer partitions. Suppose we try in the following case. Assume the unit interval of real numbers represents the whole set of reasons. Let a series of congruent

partitions of the interval be 2-fold, 4-fold, 8-fold, and so on. Select an interval from each partition, making sure that the interval selected from partition $n+1$ in the series has not been selected from the first n partitions. The selection produces intervals that do not overlap and whose widths are 1/2, 1/4, 1/8, ... The selection approaches an infinite partition of the unit interval, but never quite produces one.

Glossary

This glossary explains technical terms, distinctions, and principles that the text uses more than once.

Acceptable mistake. A mistake that rationality forgives.

Act. An event an agent realizes. An agent represents her possible acts with first-person action propositions. A decision she makes may have a proposition of this type as its content. See *choice* and *decision*.

Aspirational idealization. An idealization that removes an obstacle to a goal of rationality. Its status as aspirational is relative to that goal. See *justificational idealization*.

Basic intrinsic attitude. An intrinsic attitude not caused by other intrinsic attitudes, for example, an intrinsic desire not caused by other intrinsic desires. BIT abbreviates "basic intrinsic attitude."

Choice. An option's realization. The term signals an evaluation that takes context for granted. See *act* and *decision*.

Combination principle. A principle stating that if each member of a set of simultaneous decisions is rational, then the combination of decisions is rational. See *conjunction principle*.

Complex deliberation. Deliberation that includes an assessment of the suitability of the set of options under consideration. See *simple deliberation*.

Comprehensive utility. Rational degree of desire. It evaluates a proposition taking account of everything that would be true if the proposition were realized and is usually called utility tout court. See *intrinsic utility*.

Conjunction principle. A principle stating that if a combination of simultaneous decisions is rational, then the decision to realize the conjunction of their objects is also rational. See *combination principle*.

Conscious mind. The part of a person's mind immediately accessible to the person. It does not include unconscious beliefs and desires.

Decision. An option's realization. The term signals an evaluation that does not take context for granted. See *act* and *choice*.

Degree of belief. A number from 0 to 1 that indicates the level of a doxastic attitude ranging from maximally strong disbelief to maximally strong belief.

Degree of desire. A number that, when positive, indicates strength of desire; when negative, strength of aversion; and when zero, indifference.

Dilemma of rational decision. A decision problem in which no decision is rational in a comprehensive sense, taking account of its content, genesis, and pedigree.

Dynamic decision problem. A decision problem in which some option's utility varies with the option assumed to be realized.

Equilibrium of a game. A profile of jointly self-supporting strategies. See *solution of a game*.

Ersatz expected utility analysis. An expected utility analysis in which estimates serve as ersatz probabilities or utilities.

Expected utility of an option. A probability-weighted sum of the utilities of the option's possible outcomes. In ideal agents, it equals the option's utility. Section 2.4 presents my definition of an option o's expected utility: $\Sigma_i P(s_i \text{ given } o)U(o \text{ given } s_i)$, where s_i ranges over the members of a partition of states. Section A.6 adds refinements.

Extrinsic desire. A desire whose strength toward a proposition is an assessment of everything that would obtain if the proposition were realized. It is usually called desire tout court. See *intrinsic desire*.

Fitness of an option for consideration. The option's utility minus the cost of considering the option.

Idealization. An assumption of an explanatory principle concerning a phenomenon that identifies and controls for a factor in the phenomenon's explanation. See *restriction*.

Incentive to switch from one option to another. An incentive that obtains just in case given the first option the second option is preferred.

Indicative supposition. Supposition of a proposition that yields a possible world entailing that proposition and, to the greatest extent possible, the proposition that actual evidence supports. Such a supposition is usually expressed in the indicative mood. See *subjunctive supposition*.

Intrinsic desire. A desire whose strength toward a proposition is an assessment of just the logical consequences of the proposition's realization. See *extrinsic desire*.

Intrinsic utility. Rational degree of intrinsic desire. It evaluates a proposition taking account of just the logical consequences of the proposition's realization. See *comprehensive utility*.

Jointly rational profile of strategies. A profile of strategies in which each strategy is rational given the profile.

Jointly self-supporting profile of strategies. A profile of strategies in which each strategy is self-supporting given the profile.

Justificational idealization. An idealization that controls for a factor in the explanation of a decision's or a utility assignment's rationality but may not remove an obstacle to a goal of rationality. See *aspirational idealization*.

Maximin option. An option whose worst possible outcome according to a utility-comparison of outcomes is at least as good as the worst possible outcome of every other option.

Maximin rule. A rule for decision problems in which probabilities of relevant states are completely indeterminate. It says to select a maximin option. See *maximin option*.

Nash equilibrium. In a game, a profile of strategies, one for each agent, such that each agent's strategy maximizes his payoff given the other agents' strategies. See *subjective Nash equilibrium*.

Nonrelative equilibrium of a game. A profile of strategies in which each strategy is self-supporting.

Nonrelative solution of a game. A profile of strategies in which each strategy is rational.

Optimization. In an action problem, performing an act at least as good as any other possible act.

Option. A possible decision, a possible resolution of a decision problem.

Outcome. All that obtains if a proposition is realized, a possible world. $O[o]$ names but need not specify option o's outcome. $W[o]$ specifies o's outcome.

Pareto optimal profile of strategies. A profile such that no other profile has strategies at least as good for all agents and better for some agents.

Path of incentives. A sequence of two or more options in which for each pair of adjacent options there is an incentive to switch from the first to the second.

Perfect agent. An agent whose desires control action directly.

Possible world. A maximal consistent proposition. If it is trimmed of irrelevant matters, it just specifies for every intrinsic attitude whether that attitude is realized.

Prescience. An agent's knowledge of the response to each of his strategies in a game.

Principle against dilemmas of rational choice. A principle stating that in every decision problem, some option is a rational choice. It assumes noncomprehensive standards that evaluate only the option's content and the choice procedure.

Principle of acceptability. A principle stating that a rational decision maximizes utility with respect to circumstances in which unacceptable mistakes are corrected.

Principle of accessible utility maximization. A principle requiring adoption of an option of maximum utility with respect to the conscious mind.

Principle of ratification. A principle recommending a ratifiable option. See *ratifiable option*.

Principle of self-support. A principle requiring realization of a self-supporting option. See *self-supporting option*.

Principle to satisfice. A principle recommending adoption of the first satisfactory option discovered.

Probability. Rational degree of belief.

Profile of strategies for a game. A set of strategies containing exactly one strategy for each agent in the game.

Proposition. A structured concept with a truth value. It differs from an unstructured set of possible worlds.

Pursuit of an incentive. An agent pursues an incentive to switch from one option to another if and only if given the first, she adopts the second if her choice is either the first or some option to which she has an incentive to switch given the first.

Quantization. A probability and utility assignment compatible with an agent's beliefs and desires.

Quantization rule. A rule requiring an option that maximizes utility under some quantization of probability and utility judgments. See *quantization*.

Ratifiable option. An option that has maximum utility on the assumption that it is adopted.

Rating a decision. Evaluating a decision for rationality, taking account of the history or pedigree of the decision. The evaluation may declare the decision irrational because it rests on mistakes. See *recommending a decision*.

Recommending a decision. Endorsing the realization of a decision, taking for granted the history of the decision. The endorsement advances a decision that is rational given its history. See *rating a decision*.

Restriction. An assumption of a principle. It is called a mere restriction if it is not an idealization. See *idealization*.

Selection principle. A principle recommending an option that has maximum self-conditional utility among self-supporting options. See *self-supporting option*.

Self-supporting option. An option that has maximum support given its realization. It starts no terminating path of pursued incentives. See *termination of a path of incentives*.

Sensitivity analysis. An analysis assessing the extent to which a decision principle's recommendation is sensitive to variation in the input for the principle, such as probabilities and utilities of possible outcomes.

Simple deliberation. Deliberation yielding a decision among the options under consideration without assessment of the suitability of the set of options considered. See *complex deliberation*.

Solution of a decision problem. A decision that a fully rational ideal agent may make in the decision problem.

Solution of a game. A profile of jointly rational strategies. See *equilibrium of a game*.

State. A possible state of the world that, if it holds, may affect the outcome of a decision.

Strategic equilibrium. In a game, a profile of strategies none of which starts a terminating path of pursued incentives relative to the profiles reached by pursuit of incentives. See *termination of a path of incentives*.

Strategic self-support. Self-support defined in terms of paths of incentives. It differs from self-support that takes account of reasons in addition to incentives.

Subjective Nash equilibrium. In a game, a profile of strategies, one for each agent, such that no agent has an incentive to switch strategies given the other agents' strategies.

Subjunctive supposition. Supposition of a proposition that yields a possible world entailing that proposition and, to the greatest extent possible, causal laws and propositions holding in the actual world. Such a supposition is usually expressed in the subjunctive mood. See *indicative supposition*.

Termination of a path of incentives. The nonextendibility of a finite path of incentives.

Utility. Rational degree of desire.

Utility maximization. In a decision problem, realizing an option whose utility is at least as great as the utility of any other option. See *expected utility of an option*.

References

Allais, M. 1953. "Le Comportement de l'Homme Rationnel devant le Risque." *Econometrica* 21: 503–46. A complete version appears translated as "Foundations of a Positive Theory of Choice Involving Risk and a Criticism of the Postulates and Axioms of the American School." In *Expected Utility Hypothesis and the Allais Paradox*, M. Allais and O. Hagen, eds., pp. 27–145. Dordrecht: Reidel, 1979.

Anand, P. 1993. *Foundations of Rational Choice under Risk.* New York: Oxford University Press.

Anderson, E. 1993. *Value in Ethics and Economics.* Cambridge, Mass.: Harvard University Press.

Aristotle. 1947. *Introduction to Aristotle.* R. McKeon, ed. New York: Modern Library.

Armendt, B. 1988. "Conditional Preference and Causal Expected Utility." In *Causation in Decision, Belief Change, and Statistics.* Vol. 2. W. Harper and B. Skyrms, eds., pp. 1–24. Dordrecht: Kluwer.

Audi, R. 2001. *The Architecture of Reason.* New York: Oxford University Press.

Aumann, R. 1987. "Correlated Equilibrium as an Expression of Bayesian Rationality." *Econometrica* 55: 1–18.

Aumann, R., and A. Brandenburger. 1995. "Epistemic Conditions for Nash Equilibrium." *Econometrica* 63: 1161–80.

Aumann, R., and M. Maschler. 1964. "The Bargaining Set for Cooperative Games." In *Advances in Game Theory*, M. Dresher, L. Shapley, and A. Tucker, eds. *Annals of Mathematics Studies*, no. 52, pp. 443–76. Princeton, N.J.: Princeton University Press. Also in Kuhn (1997: 140–69).

Bacharach, M. 1999. "Interactive Team Reasoning: A Contribution to the Theory of Cooperation." *Research in Economics* 53: 117–47.

Bacharach, M., L. Gerard-Varet, P. Mongin, and H. Shin, eds. 1997. *Epistemic Logic and the Theory of Games and Decisions.* Boston: Kluwer.

Bacharach, M., and S. Hurley, eds. 1991. *Foundations of Decision Theory.* Oxford: Blackwell.

Bandyopadhyay, P. 1994. "In Search of a Pointless Decision Principle." In *PSA 1994*, vol. 1, D. Hull, M. Forbes, and R. Burian, eds., pp. 260–69. East Lansing, Mich.: Philosophy of Science Association.

Beebee, H., and D. Papineau. 1997. "Probability as a Guide to Life." *Journal of Philosophy* 94: 217–43.

Behn, R., and J. Vaupel. 1982. *Quick Analysis for Busy Decision Makers*. New York: Basic Books.

Berka, K. 1983. *Measurement: Its Concepts, Theories and Problems*. A. Riska, trans. Dordrecht: Reidel.

Bernheim, B. D. 1984. "Rationalizable Strategic Behavior." *Econometrica* 52: 1007–28.

Bicchieri, C. 1989. "Self-Refuting Theories of Strategic Interaction." *Erkenntnis* 30: 69–85.

———. 1993. *Rationality and Coordination*. Cambridge: Cambridge University Press.

Binmore, K. 1990. *Essays on the Foundations of Game Theory*. Oxford: Blackwell.

———. 1994. *Game Theory and the Social Contract*. Vol. 1, *Playing Fair*. Cambridge, Mass.: MIT Press.

———. 1998. *Game Theory and the Social Contract*. Vol. 2, *Just Playing*. Cambridge, Mass.: MIT Press.

Blackburn, S. 1998. *Ruling Passions: A Theory of Practical Reasoning*. Oxford: Clarendon Press.

Brandt, R. 1979. *A Theory of the Good and the Right*. Oxford: Oxford University Press.

Bratman, M. 1987. *Intention, Plans, and Practical Reason*. Cambridge, Mass.: Harvard University Press.

———. 1998. "Following Through with One's Plans: Reply to David Gauthier." In *Modeling Rationality, Morality, and Evolution*, P. Danielson, ed., pp. 55–66. New York: Oxford University Press.

———. 1999. *Faces of Intention*. Cambridge: Cambridge University Press.

Broome, J. 1991. *Weighing Goods*. Oxford: Blackwell.

———. 1998. "Practical Reasoning." Paper presented at the University of Lund, May.

Budescu, D., and A. Rapoport. 1994. "Subjective Randomization in One- and Two-Person Games." *Journal of Behavioral Decision Making* 7: 261–78.

Butler, J. 1950. *Five Sermons Preached at the Rolls Chapel*. New York: Liberal Arts Press.

Byron, M. 1998. "Satisficing and Optimality." *Ethics* 109: 67–93.

Campbell, R., and L. Sowden. 1985. *Paradoxes of Rationality and Cooperation*. Vancouver: University of British Columbia Press.

Chang, R., ed. 1997. *Incommensurability, Incomparability, and Practical Reason*. Cambridge, Mass.: Harvard University Press.

Chernoff, H., and L. Moses. 1959. *Elementary Decision Theory*. New York: Wiley.

Christensen, D. 2001. "Preference-Based Arguments for Probabilism." *Philosophy of Science* 68: 356–76.

Cohen, L. J. 1992. *Belief and Acceptance*. Oxford: Clarendon Press.

Colman, A. 2003. "Cooperation, Psychological Game Theory, and Limitations of Rationality in Social Interaction." *Behavioral and Brain Sciences* 26: 139–53.

Crimmins, M. 1992. *Talk about Beliefs*. Cambridge, Mass.: MIT Press.

Cubitt, R. 1993. "On the Possibility of Rational Dilemmas: An Axiomatic Approach." *Economics and Philosophy* 9: 1–23.

Davis, W. 1982. "Weirich on Conditional and Expected Utility." *Journal of Philosophy* 79: 342–50.

Deschamps, R., and L. Gevers. 1978. "Leximin and Utilitarian Rules: A Joint Characterization." *Journal of Economic Theory* 17: 143–63.

Dummett, M. 1984. *Voting Procedures*. Oxford: Oxford University Press.

Eells, E. 1982. *Rational Decision and Causation*. Cambridge: Cambridge University Press.

———. 1985. "Weirich on Decision Instability." *Australasian Journal of Philosophy* 63: 473–78.

———. 1994. "Bayesian Epistemology: Probabilistic Confirmation and Rational Decision." *Proto Soziologie* 6: 38–60.

Eells, E., and W. Harper. 1991. "Ratifiability, Game Theory, and the Principle of Independence of Irrelevant Alternatives." *Australasian Journal of Philosophy* 69: 1–19.

Ellsberg, D. 1961. "Risk, Ambiguity, and the Savage Axioms." *Quarterly Journal of Economics* 75: 643–69. Also in Gärdenfors and Sahlin (1988: 245–69).

Elster, J. 1983. *Sour Grapes*. Cambridge: Cambridge University Press.

———. 1989. *Nuts and Bolts for the Social Sciences*. Cambridge: Cambridge University Press.

Feldman, F. 1986. *Doing the Best We Can*. Dordrecht: Reidel.

———. 2000. "Basic Intrinsic Value." *Philosophical Studies* 99: 319–46.

Foley, R. 1993. *Working without a Net*. New York: Oxford University Press.

Franklin, B. 1945. *Benjamin Franklin's Autobiographical Writings*. C. van Doren, ed. New York: Viking Press.

Fuchs, A. 1985. "Rationality and Future Desires." *Australasian Journal of Philosophy* 63: 479–84.

Gaifman, H. 1988. "A Theory of Higher Order Probabilities." In *Causation, Chance, and Credence*, vol. 1, B. Skyrms and W. Harper, eds., pp. 191–220. Dordrecht: Kluwer.

Garber, D. 1983. "Old Evidence and Logical Omniscience in Bayesian Confirmation Theory." In *Testing Scientific Theories*, J. Earman, ed., pp. 99–131. Minneapolis: University of Minnesota Press.

Gärdenfors, P., and N. Sahlin. 1982. "Unreliable Probabilities, Risk Taking, and Decision Making." *Synthese* 53: 361–86. Also in Gärdenfors and Sahlin (1988: 313–34).

———, eds. 1988. *Decision, Probability, and Utility*. Cambridge: Cambridge University Press.

Gauthier, D. 1986. *Morals by Agreement*. Oxford: Oxford University Press.

———. 1991. "Why Contractarianism?" In *Contractarianism and Rational Choice*, P. Vallentyne, ed., pp. 15–30. Cambridge: Cambridge University Press.

———. 1997. "Resolute Choice and Rational Deliberation." *Noûs* 31: 1–25.

———. 1998. "Intention and Deliberation." In *Modeling Rationality, Morality, and Evolution*, P. Danielson, ed., pp. 41–54. New York: Oxford University Press.

Gert, Bernard. 1998. *Morality: Its Nature and Justification*. Oxford: Oxford University Press.

Gibbard, A., and W. Harper, 1978. "Counterfactuals and Two Kinds of Expected Utility." In *Foundations and Applications of Decision Theory*, vol. 1, C. Hooker, J. Leach, and E. McClennen, eds., pp. 125–62. Dordrecht: Reidel. Also in Gärdenfors and Sahlin (1988: 341–76).

Giere, R. 1979. *Understanding Scientific Reasoning*. New York: Holt, Rinehart & Winston.

Gigerenzer, G. 2000. *Adaptive Thinking: Rationality in the Real World*. New York: Oxford University Press.

Goldman, H. 1976. "Dated Rightness and Moral Imperfection." *Philosophical Review* 85: 449–87.

Good, I. J. 1952. "Rational Decisions." *Journal of the Royal Statistical Society*, Ser. B, 14: 107–14.

———. 1967. "On the Principle of Total Evidence." *British Journal for the Philosophy of Science* 17: 319–21.

Goodman, N. 1968. *Languages of Art*. Indianapolis, Ind.: Bobbs-Merrill.

Hacking, I. 1967. "Slightly More Realistic Personal Probability." *Philosophy of Science* 34: 311–25. Also in Gärdenfors and Sahlin (1988: 118–35).

Hall, R., and C. Johnson. 1998. "The Epistemic Duty to Seek More Evidence." *American Philosophical Quarterly* 35: 129–39.

Hamminga, B., and N. De Marchi, eds. 1994. *Idealization VI: Idealization in Economics.* Amsterdam: Rodopi.

Hammond, P. 1988. "Consequentialist Foundations for Expected Utility." *Theory and Decision* 25: 25–78.

Hampton, J. 1998. *The Authority of Reason.* Cambridge: Cambridge University Press.

Hansson, S. 1993. "Money Pumps, Self-Torturers and the Demons of Real Life." *Australasian Journal of Philosophy* 71: 476–85.

Harman, G. 1967. "Toward a Theory of Intrinsic Value." *Journal of Philosophy* 64: 792–804.

Harper, W. 1985. "Ratifiability and Causal Decision Theory." In *PSA 1984*, vol. 2, P. Asquith and P. Kitcher, eds., pp. 213–28. East Lansing, Mich.: Philosophy of Science Association.

———. 1986. "Mixed Strategies and Ratifiability in Causal Decision Theory." *Erkenntnis* 24: 25–36.

———. 1988. "Causal Decision Theory and Game Theory." In *Causation in Decision, Belief Change, and Statistics*, vol. 2, W. Harper and B. Skyrms, eds., pp. 25–48. Dordrecht: Kluwer.

———. 1989. "Decisions, Games, and Equilibrium Solutions." In *PSA 1988*, vol. 2, A. Fine and J. Lepin, eds., pp. 344–62. East Lansing, Mich.: Philosophy of Science Association.

———. 1991. "Ratifiability and Refinements." In *Foundations of Decision Theory*, M. Bacharach and S. Hurley, eds., pp. 263–93. Oxford: Blackwell.

———. 1999. "Solutions Based on Ratifiability and Sure Thing Reasoning." In *The Logic of Strategy*, C. Bicchieri, R. Jeffrey, and B. Skyrms, eds., pp. 67–81. New York: Oxford University Press.

Harris, G. 2001. "Value Vagueness, Zones of Incomparability, and Tragedy." *American Philosophical Quarterly* 38: 155–76.

Harsanyi, J., and R. Selten. 1988. *A General Theory of Equilibrium Selection in Games.* Cambridge, Mass.: MIT Press.

Horwich, P. 1987. *Asymmetries in Time.* Cambridge, Mass.: MIT Press.

Hubin, D. 1980. "Minimizing Maximin." *Philosophical Studies* 37: 363–72.

———. 2001. "The Groundless Normativity of Instrumental Rationality." *Journal of Philosophy* 98: 445–68.

Hurley, S. 1989. *Natural Reasons.* New York: Oxford University Press.

Ihara, C. 1981. "Maximin and Other Decision Principles." *Philosophical Topics* 12, 3: 59–72.

Jackson, F., and R. Pargetter. 1986. "Oughts, Options, and Actualism." *Philosophical Review* 95: 233–55.

Jeffrey, R. 1970. "Review of David Miller, 'A Paradox of Information,' and Related Essays." *Journal of Symbolic Logic* 35: 124–27.

———. 1983. *The Logic of Decision.* 2nd ed. Chicago: University of Chicago Press.

———. 1992. *Probability and the Art of Judgment.* Cambridge: Cambridge University Press.

Joyce, J. 1999. *The Foundations of Causal Decision Theory.* Cambridge: Cambridge University Press.

Kahneman, D., and A. Tversky. 1979. "Prospect Theory." *Econometrica* 47: 263–91. Also in Gärdenfors and Sahlin (1988: 183–214).

Kalai, E., and E. Lehrer. 1993. "Rational Learning Leads to Nash Equilibrium." *Econometrica* 61: 1019–45.

Kaplan, D. 1989. "Demonstratives." In *Themes from David Kaplan*, J. Almog, J. Perry, and H. Wettstein, eds., pp. 481–614. Oxford: Oxford University Press.

Kaplan, M. 1996. *Decision Theory as Philosophy.* Cambridge: Cambridge University Press.

Kavka, G. 1983. "The Toxin Puzzle." *Analysis* 43: 33–36.

Keeney, R., and H. Raiffa. 1976. *Decisions with Multiple Objectives*. New York: Wiley.

Kohlberg, E., and J. Mertens. 1986. "On the Strategic Stability of Equilibria." *Econometrica* 54: 1003–37.

Krantz, D., R. D. Luce, P. Suppes, and A. Tversky. 1971. *Foundations of Measurement*, vol. 1. New York: Academic Press.

Kripke, S. 1980. *Naming and Necessity*. Cambridge, Mass.: Harvard University Press.

Kroon, F. 1990. "On a Moorean Solution to Instability Puzzles." *Australasian Journal of Philosophy* 68: 455–61.

Kuhn, H., ed. 1997. *Classics in Game Theory*. Princeton, N.J.: Princeton University Press.

Kusser, A., and W. Spohn. 1992. "The Utility of Pleasure Is a Pain for Decision Theory." *Journal of Philosophy* 89: 10–29.

Kyburg, H. 1984. *Theory and Measurement*. Cambridge: Cambridge University Press.

———. 1997. "Quantities, Magnitudes, and Numbers." *Philosophy of Science* 64: 377–410.

Lehrer, K. 1989. "Metamental Ascent: Beyond Belief and Desire." *APA Proceedings* 63, 3: 19–30.

Leibniz, G. 1969. *Gottfried Wilhelm Leibniz: Philosophical Papers and Letters*. L. Loemker, trans. 2nd ed. Dordrecht: Reidel.

Levi, I. 1980. *The Enterprise of Knowledge*. Cambridge, Mass.: MIT Press.

———. 1986. *Hard Choices*. Cambridge: Cambridge University Press.

———. 1997. *The Covenant of Reason*. Cambridge: Cambridge University Press.

———. 1998. "Prediction, Bayesian Deliberation and Correlated Equilibrium." In *Game Theory, Experience, Rationality*, W. Leinfellner and E. Köhler, eds., pp. 173–85. Dordrecht: Kluwer.

———. 2000. "Review Essay on *The Foundations of Causal Decision Theory* by James Joyce." *Journal of Philosophy* 97: 387–402.

Lewis, D. 1973. *Counterfactuals*. Cambridge, Mass.: Harvard University Press.

———. 1981. "Causal Decision Theory." *Australasian Journal of Philosophy* 59: 5–30. Also in Gärdenfors and Sahlin (1988: 377–405).

———. 1986a. *On the Plurality of Worlds*. Oxford: Blackwell.

———. 1986b. *Philosophical Papers*, vol. 2. New York: Oxford University Press.

Lind, H. 1993. "A Note on Fundamental Theory and Idealizations in Economics and Physics." *British Journal for the Philosophy of Science* 44: 493–503.

Lipman, B. 1991. "How to Decide How to Decide How to . . . : Modeling Limited Rationality." *Econometrica* 59: 1105–25.

Luce, R. D., and H. Raiffa. 1957. *Games and Decisions*. New York: Wiley.

Machina, M. 1991. "Dynamic Consistency and Non-Expected Utility." In *Foundations of Decision Theory*, M. Bacharach and S. Hurley, eds., pp. 39–91. Oxford: Blackwell.

Maher, P. 1993. *Betting on Theories*. Cambridge: Cambridge University Press.

Maynard Smith, J. 1982. *Evolution and the Theory of Games*. Cambridge: Cambridge University Press.

McClennen, E. 1990. *Rationality and Dynamic Choice*. Cambridge: Cambridge University Press.

———. 1998. "Rationality and Rules." In *Modeling Rationality, Morality, and Evolution*, P. Danielson, ed., pp. 13–40. New York: Oxford University Press.

Mele, A. 2003. *Motivation and Agency*. New York: Oxford University Press.

Mele, A., and P. Rawling, eds. 2004. *Handbook of Rationality*. New York: Oxford University Press.

Miller, D. 1966. "A Paradox of Information." *British Journal for the Philosophy of Science* 17: 59–61.

Millgram, E. 1997. *Practical Induction*. Cambridge, Mass.: Harvard University Press.

Mintoff, J. 1997. "Slote on Rational Dilemmas and Rational Supererogation." *Erkenntnis* 46: 111–26.

Mongin, P. 1994. "L'Optimisation Est-Elle un Critère de Rationalité Individuelle?" ("Is Optimization a Criterion of Individual Rationality?") *Dialogue* 23: 191–222.

———. 2000. "Does Optimization Imply Rationality?" *Synthese* 124: 73–111.

Monton, B. 2002. "Sleeping Beauty and the Forgetful Bayesian." *Analysis* 62: 47–53.

Morton, A. 1991. *Disasters and Dilemmas*. Oxford: Blackwell.

———. 2002. "If You're So Smart Why Are You Ignorant? Epistemic Causal Paradoxes." *Analysis* 62: 110–16.

Myerson, R. 1978. "Refinements of the Nash Equilibrium Concept." *International Journal of Game Theory* 7: 73–80.

Nash, J. 1950a. "The Bargaining Problem." *Econometrica* 18: 155–62. Also in Kuhn (1997: 5–13).

———. 1950b. "Equilibrium Points in N-Person Games." *Proceedings of the National Academy of Sciences* 36: 48–9. Also in Kuhn (1997: 3–4).

Nozick, R. 1969. "Newcomb's Problem and Two Principles of Choice." In *Essays in Honor of C. G. Hempel*, N. Rescher, ed., pp. 114–46. Dordrecht: Reidel.

———. 1993. *The Nature of Rationality*. Princeton, N.J.: Princeton University Press.

Osborne, M., and A. Rubinstein. 1994. *A Course in Game Theory*. Cambridge, Mass.: MIT Press.

Pearce, D. 1984. "Rationalizable Strategic Behavior and the Problem of Perfection." *Econometrica* 52: 1029–50.

Plantinga, A. 1993a. *Warrant and Proper Function*. New York: Oxford University Press.

———. 1993b. *Warrant: The Current Debate*. New York: Oxford University Press.

Plato. 1973. *The Republic of Plato*. F. Cornford, trans. New York: Oxford University Press.

Pollock, J. 1984. "How Do You Maximize Expectation Value?" *Noûs* 17: 409–21.

———. 1986. *Contemporary Theories of Knowledge*. Totowa, N.J.: Rowman & Littlefield.

Pratt, J., H. Raiffa, and R. Schlaifer. 1995. *Introduction to Statistical Decision Theory*. Cambridge, Mass.: MIT Press.

Priest, G. 2002. "Rational Dilemmas." *Analysis* 62: 11–16.

Rabinowicz, W. 1985. "Ratificationism without Ratification." *Theory and Decision* 19: 171–200.

———. 1988. "Ratifiability and Stability." In *Decision, Probability, and Utility*, P. Gärdenfors and N. Sahlin, eds., pp. 406–25. Cambridge: Cambridge Unversity Press.

———. 1989. "Stable and Retrievable Options." *Philosophy of Science* 56: 624–41.

———. 1995. "To Have One's Cake and Eat It, Too: Sequential Choice and Expected-Utility Violations." *Journal of Philosophy* 92: 586–620.

———. 1998. "Grappling with the Centipede: Defence of Backward Induction for BI-Terminating Games." *Economics and Philosophy* 14: 95–126.

Racine, J. 1986. *Phaedra*. R. Wilbur, trans. San Diego: Harcourt Brace Jovanovich.

Raiffa, H. 1968. *Decision Analysis: Introductory Lectures on Choices under Uncertainty*. Reading, Mass.: Addison-Wesley.

Ramsey, F. 1931. *The Foundations of Mathematics*. R. Braithwaite, ed. New York: Harcourt.

———. 1990. "Weight or the Value of Knowledge." *British Journal for the Philosophy of Science* 41: 1–4.

Rapoport, A., and D. Budescu. 1992. "Generation of Random Series in Two-Person Strictly Competitive Games." *Journal of Experimental Psychology: General* 121: 352–63.

Rawling, P. 1997. "Expected Utility, Ordering, and Context Freedom." *Economics and Philosophy* 13: 79–86.

Rawls, J. 1971. *A Theory of Justice*. Cambridge, Mass.: Harvard University Press.

Regan, D. 1980. *Utilitarianism and Co-operation*. Oxford: Oxford University Press.

Resnik, M. 1987. *Choices*. Minneapolis: University of Minnesota Press.

Richardson, H. 1997. *Practical Reasoning about Final Ends*. Cambridge: Cambridge University Press.

Richter, R. 1984. "Rationality Revisited." *Australasian Journal of Philosophy* 62: 392–403.

———. 1986. "Further Comments on Decision Instability." *Australasian Journal of Philosophy* 64: 345–49.

Riker, W., and P. Ordeshook. 1973. *An Introduction to Positive Political Theory*. Englewood Cliffs, N.J.: Prentice-Hall.

Robinson, A. 1966. *Non-Standard Analysis*. Amsterdam: North Holland.

Rubinstein, A. 1998. *Modeling Bounded Rationality*. Cambridge, Mass.: MIT Press.

Russell, B. 1938. *Principles of Mathematics*. 2nd ed. New York: Norton.

Sahlin, N. 1994. "On Higher Order Beliefs." In *Philosophy of Probability*, J. Dubucs, ed., pp. 13–34. Boston: Kluwer.

Savage, L. 1972. *The Foundations of Statistics*. 2nd ed. New York: Dover.

Schick, F. 1997. *Making Choices*. Cambridge: Cambridge University Press.

Schmidtz, D. 1992. "Rationality within Reason." *Journal of Philosophy* 89: 445–66.

Selten, R. 1975. "Reexamination of the Perfectness Concept of Equilibrium in Extensive Games." *International Journal of Game Theory* 4: 25–55. Also in Kuhn (1997: 317–54).

Sen, A. 1970. *Collective Choice and Social Welfare*. San Francisco: Holden-Day.

———. 1977. "Rational Fools." *Philosophy and Public Affairs* 6: 317–44.

———. 2002. *Rationality and Freedom*. Cambridge, Mass.: Harvard University Press.

Sensat, J. 1998. "Game Theory and Rational Decision." *Erkenntnis* 47: 379–410.

Shin, H. 1991. "Two Notions of Ratifiability and Equilibrium in Games." In *Foundations of Decision Theory*, M. Bacharach and S. Hurley, eds., pp. 242–62. Oxford: Blackwell.

Simon, H. 1955. "A Behavioral Model of Rational Choice." *Quarterly Journal of Economics* 69: 99–118.

———. 1959. "Theories of Decision Making in Economics and Behavioral Science." *American Economic Review* 49: 253–83.

———. 1982. *Models of Bounded Rationality*. 2 vols. Cambridge, Mass.: MIT Press.

Skyrms, B. 1980a. *Causal Necessity*. New Haven, Conn.: Yale University Press.

———. 1980b. "Higher Order Degrees of Belief." In *Prospects for Pragmatism*, D. Mellor, ed., pp. 109–37. Cambridge: Cambridge University Press.

———. 1982. "Causal Decision Theory." *Journal of Philosophy* 79: 695–711.

———. 1984. *Pragmatism and Empiricism*. New Haven, Conn.: Yale University Press.

———. 1989. "Correlated Equilibrium and the Dynamics of Rational Deliberation." *Erkenntnis* 31: 347–64.

———. 1990a. *The Dynamics of Rational Deliberation*. Cambridge, Mass.: Harvard University Press.

———. 1990b. "Ratifiability and the Logic of Decision." In *The Philosophy of the Human Sciences*, P. French, T. Uehling, and H. Wettstein, eds. *Midwest Studies in Philosophy*, vol. 15, pp. 44–56. Notre Dame, Ind.: University of Notre Dame Press.

———. 1991. "Inductive Deliberation, Admissible Acts, and Perfect Equilibrium." In *Foundations of Decision Theory*, M. Bacharach and S. Hurley, eds., pp. 220–41. Oxford: Blackwell.

———. 1995. "Strict Coherence, Sigma Coherence and the Metaphysics of Quantity." *Philosophical Studies* 77: 39–55.

———. 1996. *Evolution of the Social Contract*. Cambridge: Cambridge University Press.

Slote, M. 1989. *Beyond Optimizing*. Cambridge, Mass.: Harvard University Press.

Smith, H. 1991. "Deciding How to Decide: Is There a Regress Problem?" In *Foundations of Decision Theory*, M. Bacharach and S. Hurley, eds., pp. 194–219. Oxford: Blackwell.

Sobel, J. H. 1976. "Utilitarianism and Past and Future Mistakes." *Noûs* 10: 195–219.

———. 1989. "Partition-Theorems for Causal Decision Theories." *Philosophy of Science* 56: 70–93.

———. 1990. "Maximization, Stability of Decision, and Actions in Accordance with Reason." *Philosophy of Science* 57: 60–77.

———. 1994. *Taking Chances: Essays on Rational Choice*. Cambridge: Cambridge University Press.

———. 1996. "Pascalian Wagers." *Synthese* 108: 11–61.

———. 1997. "Cyclical Preferences and World Bayesianism." *Philosophy of Science* 64: 42–73.

———. 1998. *Puzzles for the Will: Fatalism, Newcomb and Samarra, Determinism and Omniscience*. Toronto: University of Toronto Press.

———. 2000. "Backward Inductions without Tears?" Manuscript available at http://www.utsc.utoronto.ca/~sobel/CENTIPED.PDF.

———. 2001. "Money Pumps." *Philosophy of Science* 68: 242–57.

Sorensen, R. 1987. "Anti-Expertise, Instability, and Rational Choice." *Australasian Journal of Philosophy* 65: 301–15.

Stalnaker, R. 1981a. "A Defense of Conditional Excluded Middle." In *Ifs*, W. Harper, R. Stalnaker, and G. Pearce, eds., pp. 87–104. Dordrecht: Reidel.

———. 1981b. "A Theory of Conditionals." In *Ifs*, W. Harper, R. Stalnaker, and G. Pearce, eds., pp. 41–55. Dordrecht: Reidel.

Stocker, M. 1990. *Plural and Conflicting Values*. Oxford: Oxford University Press.

———. 1997. "Abstract and Concrete Value: Plurality, Conflict, and Maximization." In *Incommensurability, Incomparability, and Practical Reason*, R. Chang, ed., pp. 196–214. Cambridge, Mass.: Harvard University Press.

Strotz, R. 1956. "Myopia and Inconsistency in Dynamic Utility Maximization." *Review of Economic Studies* 23: 165–80.

Suppes, P. 1984. *Probabilistic Metaphysics*. Oxford: Blackwell.

Vallentyne, P. 1991. "The Problem of Unauthorized Welfare." *Noûs* 25: 295–321.

———. 2000. "Standard Decision Theory Corrected." *Synthese* 122: 261–90.

Vallentyne, P., and S. Kagan. 1997. "Infinite Value and Finitely Additive Value Theory." *Journal of Philosophy* 94: 5–26.

Vanderschraaf, P. 2001. *Learning and Coordination: Inductive Deliberation, Equilibrium, and Convention*. New York: Routledge.

van Fraassen, B. 1984. "Belief and the Will." *Journal of Philosophy* 81: 235–56.

Velleman, D. 1997. "Deciding How to Decide." In *Ethics and Practical Reason*, G. Cullity and B. Gaut, eds., pp. 29–52. Oxford: Oxford University Press.

Vickers, J. 1995. "Value and Probability in Theories of Preference." *Pacific Philosophical Quarterly* 76: 168–82.

von Neumann, J., and O. Morgenstern. 1947. *Theory of Games and Economic Behavior*. 2nd ed. Princeton, N.J.: Princeton University Press.

Wagner, C. 1999. "Misadventures in Conditional Expectation: The Two-Envelope Problem." *Erkenntnis* 51: 233–41.

Wald, A. 1950. *Statistical Decision Functions*. New York: Wiley.

Weirich, P. 1977. *Probability and Utility for Decision Theory*. PhD diss., UCLA. Ann Arbor, Mich.: University Microfilms.

———. 1980. "Conditional Utility and Its Place in Decision Theory." *Journal of Philosophy* 77: 702–15.

———. 1981. "A Bias of Rationality." *Australasian Journal of Philosophy* 59: 31–37.

———. 1982. "Decisions When Desires Are Uncertain." In *Reason and Decision*, M. Bradie and K. Sayre, eds., pp. 69–75. Bowling Green, Ohio: Bowling Green State University.

————. 1983a. "Conditional Probabilities and Probabilities Given Knowledge of a Condition." *Philosophy of Science* 50: 82–95.

————. 1983b. "A Decision Maker's Options." *Philosophical Studies* 44: 175–86.

————. 1985a. "Decision Instability." *Australasian Journal of Philosophy* 63: 465–72.

————. 1985b. "Probabilities of Conditionals in Decision Theory." *Pacific Philosophical Quarterly* 65: 59–73.

————. 1986a. "Expected Utility and Risk." *British Journal for the Philosophy of Science* 37: 419–42.

————. 1986b. "A Naturalistic Approach to Rational Deliberation." In *Naturalism and Rationality*, N. Garver and P. Hare, eds., pp. 177–88. Buffalo, N.Y.: Prometheus Books.

————. 1988. "Hierarchical Maximization of Two Kinds of Expected Utility." *Philosophy of Science* 55: 560–82.

————. 1994a. "Adam Morton on Dilemmas." *Dialogue* 33: 95–100.

————. 1994b. "The Hypothesis of Nash Equilibrium and Its Bayesian Justification." In *Logic and Philosophy of Science in Uppsala*, D. Prawitz and D. Westerståhl, eds., pp. 245–64. Dordrecht: Kluwer.

————. 1998. *Equilibrium and Rationality: Game Theory Revised by Decision Rules.* Cambridge: Cambridge University Press.

————. 1999. "Self-Supporting Strategies and Equilibria in Games." *American Philosophical Quarterly* 36: 323–36.

————. 2001a. *Decision Space: Multidimensional Utility Analysis.* Cambridge: Cambridge University Press.

————. 2001b. "Risk's Place in Decision Rules." *Synthese* 126: 427–41.

Williamson, T. 2000. *Knowledge and Its Limits.* Oxford: Oxford University Press.

Winter, S. 1964. "Economic 'Natural Selection' and the Theory of the Firm." *Yale Economic Essays* 4: 225–72.

Zimmerman, M. 1996. *The Concept of Moral Obligation.* Cambridge: Cambridge University Press.

————. 2001. *The Nature of Intrinsic Value.* Lanham, Md.: Rowman & Littlefield.

Index

act, 16–18, 194
consequences of, 195–96
evaluation of, 18–20
individuation of, 222 n. 2
outcome of, 18, 196, 205–7
utility of, 25–26, 243 n. 16
world of, 18, 196, 205
act, types
basic, 17, 194
composite, 194
extended and momentary, 17–18, 25, 194–98
mental, 18
specific, 194
strategic, 27, 195
action problem, 16–17, 26
reduction to decision problem, 198
adaptive thinking, 9
agents
errant, 47
fallible, 47
ideal, 21
perfect, 22
rational and ideal, 45–47, 103
Allais, M., 224 n. 18
Allais's Paradox, 228 n. 24
Anand, P., 227 n. 19
Anderson, E., 7
anticipation
of changes in basic goals, 146
of changes in information, 146–48

and second-order information, 147–48
Aristotle, 105
Armendt, B., 209
assumptions. *See also* idealization; restrictions
ad hoc, 35–36
unrealistic combinations of, 138, 186–87
attention-focusing processes, 139–41
Audi, R., 226 n. 7
Aumann, R., 166, 177, 224–25 n. 19, 236 n. 7, 240–41 n. 13

Bacharach, M., 13, 225 n. 7, 240 n. 11
backward induction, 57
Bandyopadhyay, P., 227 n. 18
Bayesianism, world, 29
Beebee, H., 210–12
behaviorism, 8, 20, 222 n. 5
Behn, R., 71
Berka, K., 225–26 n. 2
Bernheim, B. D., 239 n. 6
betting quotients, 224 n. 17
Bicchieri, C., 57, 239 n. 8
Binmore, K., 8, 166, 199, 221 n. 3, 228 n. 24, 241 n. 17
Blackburn, S., 223 n. 9
Brandenburger, A., 166, 177
Brandt, R., 226 n. 12, 243 n. 6
Bratman, M., 6, 135, 194, 226 n. 5, 233 n. 8
Broome, J., 64, 199, 227 n. 19, 232 n. 5
Budescu, D., 239 n. 5